Regaining Global Stability After the Financial Crisis

Bruno Sergi
Harvard University, USA

Filip Fidanoski
University of New South Wales, Australia

Magdalena Ziolo
University of Szczecin, Poland

Vladimir Naumovski
University American College Skopje, Macedonia

A volume in the Advances in Finance, Accounting, and Economics (AFAE) Book Series

IGI Global
DISSEMINATOR OF KNOWLEDGE

Published in the United States of America by
IGI Global
Business Science Reference (an imprint of IGI Global)
701 E. Chocolate Avenue
Hershey PA, USA 17033
Tel: 717-533-8845
Fax: 717-533-8661
E-mail: cust@igi-global.com
Web site: http://www.igi-global.com

Library of Congress Cataloging-in-Publication Data

Names: Sergi, Bruno S., editor. | Fidanoski, Filip, 1984- editor. | Ziolo, Magdalena, 1976- editor.
Title: Regaining global stability after the financial crisis / Bruno S. Sergi, Filip Fidanoski, Magdalena Ziolo, and Vladimir Naumovski, editors.
Description: Hershey : Business Science Reference, [2018]
Identifiers: LCCN 2017027623| ISBN 9781522540267 (hardcover) | ISBN 9781522540274 (ebook)
Subjects: LCSH: Economic stabilization--Developing countries. | Economic policy--Developing countries. | Financial institutions--Government policy--Developing countries. | Financial crises--Developing countries--Prevention.
Classification: LCC HB3732 .R44 2018 | DDC 338.5/43--dc23 LC record available at https://lccn.loc.gov/2017027623

This book is published in the IGI Global book series Advances in Finance, Accounting, and Economics (AFAE) (ISSN: 2327-5677; eISSN: 2327-5685)

British Cataloguing in Publication Data
A Cataloguing in Publication record for this book is available from the British Library.

Advances in Finance, Accounting, and Economics (AFAE) Book Series

ISSN:2327-5677
EISSN:2327-5685

Editor-in-Chief: Ahmed Driouchi, Al Akhawayn University, Morocco

MISSION

In our changing economic and business environment, it is important to consider the financial changes occurring internationally as well as within individual organizations and business environments. Understanding these changes as well as the factors that influence them is crucial in preparing for our financial future and ensuring economic sustainability and growth.

The **Advances in Finance, Accounting, and Economics (AFAE)** book series aims to publish comprehensive and informative titles in all areas of economics and economic theory, finance, and accounting to assist in advancing the available knowledge and providing for further research development in these dynamic fields.

COVERAGE

- Labor Economics
- Entrepreneurship in Accounting and Finance
- Statistical Analysis
- Public Finance
- Health Economics
- Theoretical Issues in Economics, Finance, and Accounting
- International Trade
- Economics Geography
- Finance and Accounting in SMEs
- Evidence-Based Studies

IGI Global is currently accepting manuscripts for publication within this series. To submit a proposal for a volume in this series, please contact our Acquisition Editors at Acquisitions@igi-global.com or visit: http://www.igi-global.com/publish/.

The Advances in Finance, Accounting, and Economics (AFAE) Book Series (ISSN 2327-5677) is published by IGI Global, 701 E. Chocolate Avenue, Hershey, PA 17033-1240, USA, www.igi-global.com. This series is composed of titles available for purchase individually; each title is edited to be contextually exclusive from any other title within the series. For pricing and ordering information please visit http://www.igi-global.com/book-series/advances-finance-accounting-economics/73685. Postmaster: Send all address changes to above address.

Titles in this Series

For a list of additional titles in this series, please visit:
https://www.igi-global.com/book-series/advances-finance-accounting-economics/73685

Regulation and Structure in Economic Virtualization Emerging Research and Opportunities
Denis Ushakov (Suan Sunandha Rajabhat University, Thailand)
Business Science Reference • ©2018 • 238pp • H/C (ISBN: 9781522549666) • US $145.00

Accountancy and the Changing Landscape of Integrated Reporting
Ioana Dragu (Babes-Bolyai University, Romania)
Business Science Reference • ©2018 • 303pp • H/C (ISBN: 9781522536222) • US $195.00

Foreign Direct Investments (FDIs) and Opportunities for Developing Economies in the ...
Venkataramanaiah Malepati (University of Gondar, Ethiopia) and C. Mangala Gowri (University of Gondar, Ethiopia)
Business Science Reference • ©2018 • 280pp • H/C (ISBN: 9781522530268) • US $215.00

Economic Growth in Latin America and the Impact of the Global Financial Crisis
Mauricio Garita (Universidad del Valle de Guatemala, Guatemala) and Celso Fernando Cerezo Bregni (Universidad del Valle de Guatemala, Guatemala)
Business Science Reference • ©2018 • 193pp • H/C (ISBN: 9781522549819) • US $180.00

Uncertainties and Risk Assessment in Trade Relations
Marianne Ojo (George Mason University, USA)
Business Science Reference • ©2018 • 385pp • H/C (ISBN: 9781522541318) • US $225.00

Economic Reforms for Global Competitiveness
Denis Ushakov (International College Suan Sunandha Rajabhat University, Thailand & Russian Academy of National Economy and Public Administration–South, Russia)
Business Science Reference • ©2018 • 363pp • H/C (ISBN: 9781522538561) • US $235.00

For an entire list of titles in this series, please visit:
https://www.igi-global.com/book-series/advances-finance-accounting-economics/73685

IGI Global
DISSEMINATOR OF KNOWLEDGE

701 East Chocolate Avenue, Hershey, PA 17033, USA
Tel: 717-533-8845 x100 • Fax: 717-533-8661
E-Mail: cust@igi-global.com • www.igi-global.com

Table of Contents

Detailed Table of Contents

Business transformation projects and enterprise architecture projects for enterprises' business and their financial strategic planning process are essential to prepare the enterprise to integrate the local and the global economies in a sustainable and iterative way. The needed strategy for the integration of financial-engineering-related risk and legal controls is fundamental for its long-term vision and business longevity. Probably because of the ongoing financial uncertainty, these finance-related risks and legal standards are not mature and are even chaotic, so these facts can damage the business transformation project or an enterprise architecture project, and they may disable the traditional business environments to be a part and to compete with the networked global economy.

A business transformation project or an innovative enterprise architecture project is needed for the enterprise's business and financial strategic planning process and to prepare this business enterprise to integrate into the globally interconnected economy in a whole and robust manner. The integration of financial engineering and information technologies is fundamental, where the latter is the gluing element that makes this fine-grained environment run efficiently. Today, these finance-related technology standards and fields are ready and can be applied as automated block-chains to enable the traditional business environments as a part of the networked global economy. An important factor in frequent business transformation projects' changes and financial reengineering iterations are the roles of the business transformation manager, project managers, finance analysts, the business environment's technological maturity, and enterprise architect(s) who should be supported by the optimal business transformation framework.

To include a business transformation project or an enterprise architecture project in the enterprise's business and financial strategic planning process and to prepare this enterprise to integrate the local and the global economy in a sustainable way, the integration of financial-engineering-related risk and legal controls is necessary and is even fundamental. These finance-related risk and legal standards are not mature and are chaotic, so these facts can damage the business transformation project or an enterprise architecture project and that may disable the traditional business environments to be a part of the networked global economy.

Financial integration is an inseparable part of economic integration. It affects capital movement and economic development. Certain studies have shown that financial integration is beneficial to the economy. However, integration may be slowed down by occurrence of a crisis. Over the past 10 years, several crises have been underway. They have affected both economic development and financial integration. The aim of the chapter is to present theoretically the relation between financial integration, crisis, and economic development. An overview of EU and SEE financial integration and economic development is given. Development and integration of both regions have been slowed down due to the global and EU crisis, but there has been an improvement over the past few years. The fact is that SEE countries do not have a very developed financial integration but they meet certain prerequisites to reach a higher level of integration.

Financing of sustainable development is a sophisticated and long-term process determined by a number of economic and non-economic factors. Financial instruments, private and public nature, exist that can be a source of financing of sustainable development. The choice of finance sources and instruments has an impact on the stability of economic systems and the efficiency of public expenditure with respect to sustainable development goals. The choice of financial instruments for financing development impact on financial stability and results in outcomes performed. The goal of the chapter is to examine relationships between financial stability reflected by public debt to gross domestic product (GDP) and sustainable development described by variables represented by three pillars of sustainable development: economic, social, and environmental. The role of environmentally related tax revenue has been identified as crucial for financing sustainable development goals.

This chapter aims to contribute to the debate on which kinds of governance and institutions are needed to ensure stability and growth in the Eurozone. Despite the economic recovery, the Eurozone does not have effective institutions to ensure stability in the face of a new economic crisis (without forgetting legitimacy, transparency, and the ability to meet the expectations of greater prosperity for Euro-area citizens). This chapter supports the view of a deep rethinking of the European monetary union (EMU) with a different governance and institutions. The new governance should imply a renewed political agreement among member states in both the Eurozone and the European Union (EU). This political agreement must lead to a reconsideration of the Maastricht parameters, a different approach of European institutions, and a change of the EU treaty. This chapter also discusses the role of institutions in balancing European interests with those of member states to provide a consistent approach to stability and growth.

Section 3
Risk Management in Crisis Era

The chapter examines the importance of fiscal fundamentals for sovereign risk spread in the period of 1995-2015, and its goal is to test whether stronger fiscal discipline reduces sovereign risk premiums. The empirical evidence is based on unbalanced annual panel data of 15 EU countries (its time span is divided into a pre-crisis and a post-crisis period). The study applies the generalized method of moments. Evidence shows that before the financial crisis, investors generally ignored bond risk factors in individual countries, but that the spreads sharply diverged starting from the year 2008. The results confirm a statistically significant impact of fiscal fundamentals on government bond yield spread. The improvement of the governments' fiscal position reduces sovereign yield spread. In a post-crisis period, findings report the raising of the importance of fiscal variables for spread, and GDP growth became a major determinant of government bond yield spreads, followed by the budget balance and debt development.

This chapter is devoted to the dynamic risk management of the investment portfolio using future contracts. The number of futures for each portfolio asset, which is determined by portfolio effectiveness and acceptability of risk at each step, serves as a control parameter. The authors define effective portfolios as the ones of the minimum variance with the expected return greater than or equal to the specified value. Risk is measured by the probability of losing a certain part of the portfolio value. Effective adaptive strategies of portfolio risk management are proposed and their comparative analysis is carried out on a concrete example. In order to determine risk management strategies, the authors implement simple methods of volatility forecasting and correlation of relative changes of price data based on exponential moving average.

This chapter first examines what caused the need to regain global stability after the financial crisis. The author provides a brief refresher of how the market crash in 2008, and subsequent Great Recession, was initially fueled while honing in on the allocation of "the fuel" coupled with the repeals of bicentennial-long legislation and the associated dangers of these economic policy changes. Notations from Nobel laureates and interagency economists from the IMF and World Bank aid in identifying the consequences of these policy decisions while simultaneously illustrating the enhanced risk within a variety of markets. Next, the author discusses the current state and relative stability of the financial markets, economic policy, and the risks associated therein. Lastly, this chapter provides recommendations for the future of monetary and fiscal policy, globalization, and what the government (and Wall Street) must consider should they seek to attain long-term financial stability from an international perspective. Monetary and fiscal policy decisions implemented and in-progress by the Federal Reserve are fastidiously examined throughout this chapter.

This chapter provides an evaluation of the influence of the most significant external and internal factors on international capital flows in the form of direct and portfolio investments for 24 developing countries during the period 1990–2015. The authors have adopted the partial adjustment model and the feasible generalized least squares estimator for panel data. Results show that the determinants of capital flow for foreign direct and portfolio investments differ. The impact of political risks on cross-border capital flows has been identified.

The purpose of this chapter is to empirically test the informational efficiency and to examine the presence of the calendar effects in 10 South Eastern European (SEE) stock markets' daily returns during the period 2007–2014. The authors use variance ratio test for exploration of random walk hypothesis. Regarding the calendar effects, the authors focus on the day-of-the-week effect, the half-month effect, and the turn-of-the-month effect. The existence of each calendar effect is analyzed by applying regression models with dummy variables for the effects in the mean returns and GARCH (1,1) models with dummy variables for the effects in the volatility of returns. The results indicate that the day-of-the-week effects in both mean and volatility are present in nine SEE stock markets. Contrary, the half-month effect in mean returns is present only in one, while half-month effect in volatility is present in five SEE stock markets. The turn-of-the- month effect in mean returns is present in six, while the turn-of-the-month effect in volatility is present in all 10 SEE stock markets.

This chapter represents an attempt to analyze the role of shocks (impulses) in business cycles in the world economy in connection with the global financial crises of the late 2000s. The theoretical explanation of the origin of any economic shock (external impulse), of economic systems' reaction to it, as well as of the way the global shocks spread its influence all over the world suggests that the analytical predictions of E. Slutsky and R. Frish can be correct. The results provide some evidence for the hypothesis that the cyclical model of development of any economic system means its adjustment to new conditions caused by external impulses (shocks). To reinforce the findings, some results associated with other theoretical investigations and analytical researches are presented.

The aim of this chapter is to examine the relationship between globalisation and the size of the welfare state taking into account the respective composition. The efficiency hypothesis argues that globalisation leads to a reduction in the size of the welfare state since this can harm international competitiveness and drive away capital flows, while the compensation hypothesis poses that globalisation induces an increase in the welfare state in order to provide citizens with wider coverage against the risks of globalisation. This relationship is analysed for 31 OECD countries over the period 1980-2010 using data on social expenditures and the KOF Index of Globalisation and their different components. The results obtained indicate that overall there is a positive association between globalisation and the size of the welfare state, more intense for spending on housing-related benefits, active labour market programs and other social policy areas, and mostly felt through political globalisation. Globalisation loses significance for the explanation of family and unemployment benefits.

Is China's development model an alternative to the Western model? The public ownership of land is the major character of the market economy of China. China's local governments take the land under their regional control as the startup asset, playing an active role in promoting China's industrialization and urbanization. One cannot understand China's model without understanding its development logic, involving land, debt, and local government. This chapter makes an in-depth observation the role of land and the financing based on land played in the cycle of capital flow that feeds China's development. Land financing is responsible for debt accumulation on the local government level, especially the period after the financial crisis of 2008. This chapter points out the paradoxical nature of China's dual-track system of land ownership and analyzes its inherent problems in the context of China's contemporary political-economic arrangement.

Foreword

The last spectacular crisis was dated in 1929 and since 2007 the economic world has been gaining new experience in dealing with this phenomenon. The financial crisis 2007 has shown the weakness of the economic systems. At the same time the well-known Keynesian ways of fiscal stimulus and mechanism of multipliers in the contemporary economies occurred not to be sufficient for public and private finance and economic growth restoration. There are also opinions that Keynesian approach creates suitable conditions for incensement of extensive deficit and debt. In this context insolvency risk management became much more important than ever before.

In the aftermath of the economic crisis of 2007, the importance of the safety and stability of financial institutions has increased as a consequence of the numerous bailouts that many states across the globe have encountered. The banking and financial system is a unique element in the business landscape. Banks and other financial institutions play a specific role in the economy and society. The growing role and size of the financial sector has generated numerous advantages and disadvantages. The financial crisis has made it clear that the present architecture for financial security and corporate governance is very fragile. The crisis exposed the shortcomings in existing risk measurement methods for financial institutions and it has made it necessary to search for new approaches to risk assessment and management in finance, with special attention paid to banking.

The crisis of 2007 strongly affected public budgets, and as a result, many public entities were financially distressed or about to fail. At the same time, access to external financing was limited - or nonexistent - because of the condition of financial sector, especially in the banking sector. It is very important to emphasize that fiscal stability is strongly determined by the condition of the financial sector, and the safety and stability of financial institutions, while taking into account bailouts and state aid. Taking into account the steps which were taken after the crisis of 2007 governments have been in a fiscal consolidation process since 2009 to stabilise their budgets with revenue and expenditure instruments, with special emphasis on budgetary fiscal rules. The big challenge in the context of fiscal consolidation, which is based on revenue, is tax evasion and increasing the effectiveness of taxation (tax rates and tax base action). The crucial challenge is also proper pricing of public good and services, especially in the sectors where monopoly exists and where environmental costs are important, like in the case of water whose price depends on the tariffs which are usually set up by local authorities. Finally, there is the problem in the assessment of the cost of public services, which varies across governments and countries, and governments do not always know the cost of public goods or services.

The main objective of the book is to present and discuss about contemporary challenges and prospects of the business, finance and banking after post-Great Recession. Also, authors try to find an intellectual answers to the problems in functioning of the present-day financial markets and institutions, governments and finally businesses presented in order to provide a thorough, consistent and integrated approach to the concept of financial stability versus economic growth and development.

This book landmarks and discuss challenges and prospects which financial sector faces in post crisis perspective. How to reach financial stability in long run perspective? What is the role of government in stabilising and supervising the financial markets? How to keep balance between making money and being sustainable? What is the role of business and financial sector in stimulating growth and development and mitigate risk after post crisis period? These and many and many other questions are covered in the next pages.

This book presents a relevant theoretical and the latest empirical research findings on the subject of financial risk, financialisation, moral hazard, macro, micro-prudential policy and public, economic and institutional policies as well toward financial stability. Specifically, this book brings at the same place scholars with diverse background, policy makers, and early career researchers by creating an academic arena of confronting economic opinions. Furthermore, this book is dedicated to the economic analysis of public policies and financial regulations in both developing and developed countries, with comparative focus.

The primary intention of the book is to provide key insights, theoretical framework for improving policy-making in finance, banking and business scope, and to review and synthesize the knowledge on the contemporary financial crisis, risk, market, institutions and public policy towards financial stability. As a result, the book proposes innovative directions for policy making with positive impact on the broader society.

The various chapters of the book constitute a very useful and timely guide for financial stability and regulations, risk management, monetary and fiscal policy, public polices fostering business of a more structural nature that can aid developing and developed countries. The work also takes into account the sustainability issues, which are advocated and supported by the *Ideas for Action* initiative, launched by the World Bank Group and the Zicklin Center for Business Ethics Research at the Wharton School of the University of Pennsylvania. In fact, this book entails many components of the initiative. All of these questions, particularly sustainability, are not the legacy of the former generations. Stability and sustainability are very important challenges for today young people who are mostly affected by the decisions of today and who should act in a creative manner. In fact, they should find new solutions for the stability and for financing sustainable development.

All in all, the book is very comprehensive and is written in a friendly reading style. The chapters in the book are well interconnected and provide new insights in terms of stability and its impact on our lives in the contemporary times.

Djordjija Petkoski
University of Pennsylvania, USA
Philadelphia, December 5, 2017

Preface

The problem of the global stability becomes very topical issue in moments of crises and particularly in the post-crisis periods, as nowadays. The latest crisis put the question on the stability again at the top of the top in the list of priorities of economic leaders. And we are now here, in the wood of diverse theories, approaches, priorities, conclusions... What is next?

Specifically, the economic slowdown and the crisis are two categories which are strictly intertwined with the global market economy. After the subprime market had broken down, and the property bubble had spoiled over, the unbalanced budgets era in Europe and outside have started. The excessive deficits and debts are nowadays one of the significant threats to economic growth, and many states reflect how complicated the problem of the unbalanced budgets might be.

Further, the financial crisis started in the US subprime market in 2007, and it has shown the several weaknesses of financial stability procedures. In the aftermath of the economic crisis of 2007, the importance of the safety and stability of financial institutions has increased. The environment of low nominal growth and high unemployment is the primary underlying factor driving the challenges to financial stability.

Considering the steps taken after the crisis of 2007 and the fiscal consolidation process since 2009, the main questions have been: what is the role of the banks and financial institutions in today's economy? What is the role of contemporary monetary and fiscal policy and the role of central banks and government to prevent next crisis and stabilize the economy? How to design budget constraints and financial instruments to secure business, households, governments and financial institutions against insolvency and bankruptcy risk and moral hazard? What's the role of auditors and rating agencies in mitigating financial risk? What's the role of the financial market and financial institutions in overwhelming new and old social risk and financial exclusion? And not only these.

THE CHALLENGES

There is a general consensus among economists that well designed economic mechanisms and policies promote business, social and economic growth by providing a sound business, financial and economic environment. From a historical point of view, economic policies improved in a majority of developing countries in the 1990s, but the expected benefits failed to meet high expectations by policy-makers. It is not so different in the developed countries as well. In addition, a series of economic disruptions worsened economic conditions (Serven & Montiel, 2004). Any shock to the economic system is likely to be reflected in the economic life and to severely change the behavior (Bleaney, 1995). These shock are the logical and integral part of our economic mindsets. It is not mistake if we say that they give the direction to the well-known *animal spirits* in the economy.

On top of this, it is important to highlight the study of Barro and Ursúa (2017) who revealed 232 stock-market crashes and 100 depressions in the considerable period. Furthermore, some of these rare macroeconomic disasters could be used as the potential explanations for some of the notable asset-pricing puzzles (such as equity-risk premium puzzle; Mehra & Prescott, 1985; Barro & Ursúa, 2012). Easterly (2001) very remarkable stressed that crises are more likely symptoms of the growth slowdown that its cause. These developments turn out the leading question: *how to regain the global stability after the crisis*? Once upon a time, the German Minister of Finance, Karl August Fritz Schiller, famously emphasised that *stability is not everything, but without stability everything becomes nothing* (Simonovska et al., 2015). The stability is c*ondition sine qua non* for a well-functioning society, since the stability importantly affects the economic expectations and the life. These words of Schiller are also the credo of our book.

The main goal of our edited volume, *Regaining Global Stability after the Financial Crisis* is to disentangle contemporary challenges and prospects of the business, finance, and banking after post-Great Recession. Such a crisis has made it clear that the present architecture for securing financial security and corporate governance is very fragile. The crisis exposed the shortcomings in existing risk measurement methods for financial institutions, and it has made it necessary to search for innovative approaches to risk assessment and management in finance, with particular attention paid to banking. Not least, *Regaining Global Stability after the Financial Crisis* aims to find intellectual answers to the present-day financial market institutions' problems and to give a thorough, consistent, and integrated approach to the concept of financial stability versus economic growth and development.

ORGANIZATION OF THE BOOK

The book's first chapter (Antoine Trad and Damir Kalpić) points out that strategy for the integration of financial engineering related risk and legal controls is fundamental to its long-term vision and business longevity. These finance related risk and legal standards are not mature and are even chaotic so that these facts can damage the business transformation project, or an enterprise architecture project and they may disable the traditional business environments to be a part and to compete with the networked global economy.

The second chapter (Antoine Trad and Damir Kalpić) enlightens the enterprise's business and financial strategic planning process to compete in a globally interconnected economy. The integration of financial engineering and information technologies is fundamental, where the latter is the gluing element that makes this fine-grained environment run efficiently. Today finance related technology standards and fields can enable the traditional business environments being a part of the networked global economy.

The third chapter (Antoine Trad and Damir Kalpić) points out that to include a business transformation project or an enterprise architecture project in the enterprise's business and financial strategic planning process and to prepare this enterprise to integrate the local and the global economy in a sustainable way, the integration of financial engineering related risk and legal controls are necessary and is even fundamental.

The fourth chapter (Sandra Jednak and Dejan Jednak) elaborates on the relationship between financial integration, crisis, and economic development. An overview of European Union (EU) and South Eastern European (SEE) financial integration and economic development is given. Development and integration of both regions have been slowed down due to the global and EU crisis, and while SEE countries do not have a very developed financial integration they might reach a higher level of integration.

The fifth chapter (Magdalena Ziolo, Ben Ghoul, and Halil İbrahim Aydın) examines the relationship between financial stability, which is reflected by public debt to GDP and sustainable development described by three pillars of sustainable development: economic, social, and environmental. The role of environmentally-related tax revenue has been found as crucial for financing sustainable development goals. The central research hypothesis assumes that financial stability is a factor consistent with sustainable development. The research sample consists of OECD nations for the period 2006–2015. The empirical part of the study based on Vector Autoregressive Model. Their research reveals that the size of the public debt correlates with the performance of sustainable development.

The sixth chapter (Daniele Schilirò) contributes to the debate on the types of governance and institutions needed to ensure stability and growth in the Eurozone. The Eurozone does not have adequate institutions to ensure stability in the face of a new economic crisis (without forgetting legitimacy, transparency, and the ability to meet the expectations of greater prosperity for euro-area citizens). This chapter supports the view of a profound rethinking of the European Monetary Union with a different governance and institutions. The new governance should imply a renewed political agreement among member states in both the Eurozone and the EU and lead to a reconsideration of the Maastricht parameters, a different approach to European institutions, and a change of the EU Treaty.

The seventh chapter (Irena Szarowská) examines the importance of fiscal fundamentals for sovereign risk spread from 1995 to2015, and its goal is to test whether stronger fiscal discipline reduces sovereign risk premiums. Based on unbalanced annual panel data of 15 EU countries, the study applies the Generalized Method of Moments and shows that investors ignored bond risk factors before the crisis, but the spreads sharply diverged starting in 2008. The results confirm a statistically-significant impact of fiscal fundamentals on government bond yield spread. The improvement of the governments' fiscal position reduces sovereign yield spread. In a post-crisis period, findings report the raising of the importance of fiscal variables for range, and GDP growth became a major determinant of government bond yield spreads, followed by the budget balance and debt development.

The eighth chapter (Alexander Kerimov and Oleg Pavlov) is devoted to the dynamic risk management of the investment portfolio using future contracts. The number of futures for each portfolio asset, which is determined by portfolio effectiveness and acceptability of risk at each step, serves as a control parameter. The authors define effective portfolios like the ones of the minimum variance with the expected return greater than or equal to the specified value. The risk is measured by the probability of losing a particular part of the portfolio value. Effective adaptive strategies for portfolio risk management are proposed, and their comparative analysis is carried out on a concrete example.

The ninth chapter (Adam Wood) examines what caused the need to regain global stability after the financial crisis. The Author provides a brief refresher of how the market crash in 2008, and subsequent Great Recession, was initially fueled while honing in on the allocation of "the fuel" coupled with the repeals of bicentennial-long legislation and the associated dangers of these economic policy changes. Notations from Nobel Laureates, and interagency economists from the IMF and World Bank aid in finding the consequences of these policy decisions while simultaneously illustrating the enhanced risk within a variety of markets. Next, the Author discusses the current state, and relative stability, of the financial markets, economic policy, and the risks associated therein. Lastly, this chapter recommends on future monetary and fiscal policy, globalization, and what the government (and Wall Street) must consider should they seek to attain long-term financial stability from an international perspective.

Chapter 10 (Svetlana Balashova, Vladimir Matyushok, and Inna Petrenko) evaluates the influence of the most significant external and internal factors on international capital flows in the form of direct and portfolio investments for 24 developing countries during the period 1990–2015. The authors have adopted the partial adjustment model and the Feasible Generalized Least Squares estimator for panel data. Results show that the determinants of capital flow for foreign direct and portfolio investments differ and an impact of political risks on cross-border capital flows has been identified.

The eleventh chapter (Vladimir Filipovski and Dragan Tevdovski) tests the informational efficiency and examines the presence of the calendar effects in ten SEE stock markets daily returns during the period 2007–2014. The Authors use variance ratio test for exploration of random walk hypothesis. Regarding the calendar effects, the authors focus on the day-of-the-week effect, the half-month effect and the turn-of-the-month effect. The existence of each calendar effect is analyzed by applying regression models with dummy variables for the effects in the mean returns and GARCH (1,1) models with dummy variables for the effects of the volatility of returns. The results show that the day-of-the-week effects in both mean and volatility are present in nine SEE stock markets. Contrary, the half-month impact on mean returns is present only in one, while half-month effect in volatility is present in five SEE stock markets. The turn-of-the-month effect in mean returns is present in six, while the turn-of-the-month effect in volatility is present in all ten SEE stock markets.

The twelfth chapter (Andrey Pilipenko and Zoya Pilipenko) is on the determination of the economic activity' sphere where it should be generated impulse capable of changing macroeconomic dynamics. It would be possible to identify the macroeconomic cycle' beginning as the economic integrities' reaction on shock influences of external impulse.

The thirteenth chapter (Irina Araújo and Marta Simões) examines the relationship between globalization and the size of the welfare state. The efficiency hypothesis argues that globalization leads to a reduction in the size of the welfare state since this can harm international competitiveness, while the compensation hypothesis poses that globalization induces an increase in the welfare state to provide citizens with wider coverage against the risks of globalization. It has been found a positive association between globalization and the size of the welfare state for 31 OECD countries, which is more intense for spending on housing-related benefits, active labor market programs, and other social policy areas.

The fourteenth chapter (Waiching Li) aims to make an in-depth observation the role of land and its related financing played in the cycle of capital flow. Land financing is responsible for local government debt accumulation, but it is essential to drive economic expansion, especially the period after the recent financial crisis. This chapter will point out the paradoxical nature of China's dual-track system of land ownership, and analyze its inherent problems, in the context of China's contemporary political-economic arrangement.

The last chapter (Filip Fidanoski, Bruno S. Sergi, Kiril Simeonovski, Vladimir Naumovski, and Igor Sazdovski) studies the effects of foreign capital penetration and bank performance in the Republic of Macedonia for the 2004-2012 period. Authors develop a specific theoretical model of foreign bank and foreign capital entry, accompanied with an econometricl model in which they use the return on average assets (ROAA), the net-interest margin (NIM) and the overhead ratio as dependent variables, and the foreign capital factors combined with other control variables on the side of independent variables. Importantly, the results from the panel regression analysis posit a positive effect on the return on average assets (ROAA) and negative implications on the net-interest margin (NIM) and the overhead ratio.

REFERENCES

Barro, R. J., & Ursúa, J. F. (2012). Rare macroeconomic disasters. *Annual Review of Economics*, *4*(1), 83–109. doi:10.1146/annurev-economics-080511-110932

Barro, R. J., & Ursúa, J. F. (2017). Stock-market crashes and depressions. *Research in Economics*, *71*(3), 384–398. doi:10.1016/j.rie.2017.04.001

Bleaney, M. F. (1996). Macroeconomic stability, investment and growth in developing countries. *Journal of Development Economics*, *48*(2), 461–477. doi:10.1016/0304-3878(95)00049-6

Easterly, W. (2001). The lost decades: Developing countries' stagnation in spite of policy reform 1980–1998. *Journal of Economic Growth*, *6*(2), 135–157. doi:10.1023/A:1011378507540

Mehra, R., & Prescott, E. C. (1985). The equity premium: A puzzle. *Journal of Monetary Economics*, *15*(2), 145–161. doi:10.1016/0304-3932(85)90061-3

Serven, L., & Montiel, P. (2004). Macroeconomic stability: The more the better? In R. Zagha & G.T. Nankan (Eds.), Economic growth in the 1990s: Learning from a decade of reforms (pp. 95-120). Washington, DC: World Bank Group.

Simonovska, I., Choudhry, M., Pesakovic, G., Fidanoski, F., & Simeonovski, K. (2015). Financial (in)stability in selected countries: What did we learn from the crises? In *International Conference on Economic recovery in the post-crisis period*. Cyril and Methodius University in Skopje.

Section 1

Crisis vs. Business Transformation

Chapter 1
The Business Transformation and Enterprise Architecture Framework:
The Financial Engineering Global Strategy

Antoine Trad
IBISTM, France

Damir Kalpić
University of Zagreb, Croatia

ABSTRACT

Business transformation projects and enterprise architecture projects for enterprises' business and their financial strategic planning process are essential to prepare the enterprise to integrate the local and the global economies in a sustainable and iterative way. The needed strategy for the integration of financial-engineering-related risk and legal controls is fundamental for its long-term vision and business longevity. Probably because of the ongoing financial uncertainty, these finance-related risks and legal standards are not mature and are even chaotic, so these facts can damage the business transformation project or an enterprise architecture project, and they may disable the traditional business environments to be a part and to compete with the networked global economy.

DOI: 10.4018/978-1-5225-4026-7.ch001

INTRODUCTION

Business transformation projects and enterprise architecture projects for enterprise's business and their financial strategic planning process are essential to prepare the enterprise to integrate the local and the global economies in a sustainable and iterative way. The needed strategy for the integration of financial engineering related risk and legal controls is fundamental for its long-term vision and business longevity. Actually, and probably because of the ongoing financial uncertainty, these finance related risk and legal standards are not mature and are even chaotic, so these facts can damage the business transformation project or an enterprise architecture project and they may disable the traditional business environments to be a part and to compete with the networked global economy (Trad & Kalpić, 2014a).

An important factor in frequent business transformation projects' changes and underlying iterations are the roles of the business transformation manager, finance strategist and enterprise architect(s) who should be supported by the optimal business transformation framework that in turn should include a global strategy model for such environments. This strategy model should be also capable of supporting the business environment's financial engineering risk management, legal control and integration in a complex block-chain globalized environment (Grewal-Carr & Marshall, 2016). To achieve this financial engineering risk and legal integration based strategy, critical success areas and critical success factors must be used to evaluate project pitfalls, risk, audit, assert, govern, automate, trace, monitor and control of the business transformation project's financial budget (IFRS, 2017). The business transformation project or an enterprise's architecture project Critical Success Factors (CSF) can be configured to measure the influence of the complexities in managing asynchronous financial flows of its local and international financial environments (Peterson, 2011). Transformed business environments' strategy model must have built-in automated block-chain controls as support, capable of recognizing fraud, black swan effects (Trad & Kalpić, 2016a; Taleb, 2007), bad investments, business transformation project budget slips, loss of (e)transactions, illegal activities and tax evasions (Trad & Kalpić, 2015a; Trad & Kalpić, 2015b).

BACKGROUND

The Business Transformation Manager's (BTM) role is of crucial importance for the implementation phase of the complex Business Transformation Projects (BTP) and also enterprise architecture projects; where the BTM or enterprise architect's decisions can be made in a just-in-time manner by using outputs from the business environment's existing tracing, monitoring and logging systems; to assess risk and legally assert, govern or control the BTP's various resources and components. Unfortunately, a huge set of automated factors can influence such an undertaking, like: 1) the influence of accounting in business transformation projects; and 2) the holistic financial (e)law control mechanisms for such projects are non-existent and are complex to implement.

A global financial subsystem's modelling approach is optimal for such control mechanisms' integration in the business environment (Daellenbach & McNickle, 2005). The Financial Engineering Risk Strategy (FERS) is based on the (re)use of microartefacts. In this research, the focus is on the FERS or financial controlling module (Trad & Kalpić, 2016a), as shown in Figure 1 where it interacts with the external world via an implemented real world framework. The BTP's global research topic's and final research question is: "Which business transformation manager characteristics and which type of support should be assured in the implementation phase of a business transformation project?" The targeted business domain is any business environment that uses: 1) internet and engineering technologies; and 2) frequent transformation iterations. For this phase of research the sub-question is: "What is the impact of the financial engineering risk strategy on (e)enterprise architecture and business transformation projects?". The current research framework will be referred to as *Environment*, as shown in Figure 2 and this research article is strongly bonded to two other articles on financial risk management:

Figure 1. The finance mechanisms interaction with business transformation project's framework

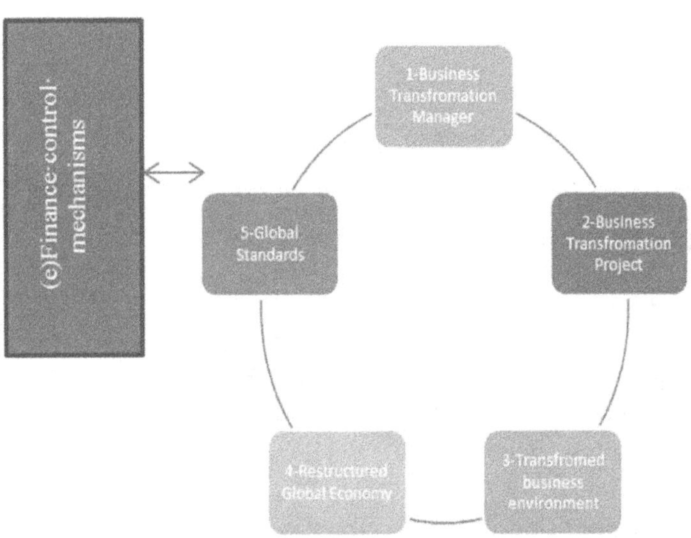

Figure 2. The business transformation project's framework

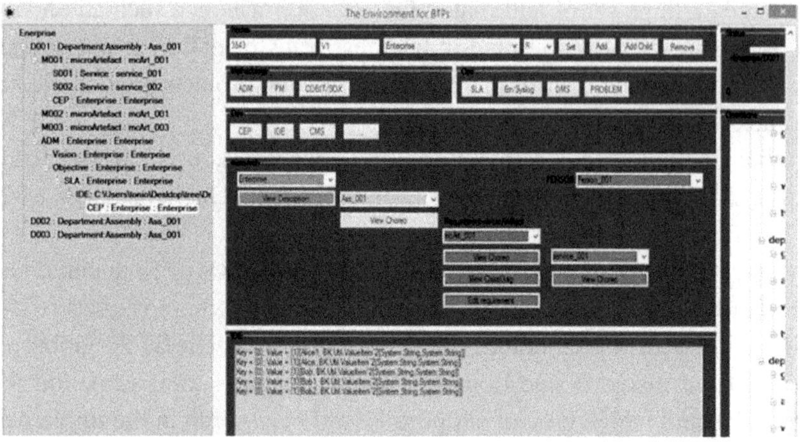

- The Business Transformation and Enterprise Architecture Framework - The Financial Engineering (e)Risk Management and (e)Law Integration (Trad, Kalpić, 2017a).
- The Business Transformation and Enterprise Architecture Framework - The Financial Engineering Technology Concept (Trad, Kalpić, 2017b).

These interrelated three articles form a whole to solve this phase's research question on global strategy that has been made credible and proved by selected set of literature and a proof of concept.

Figure 3. The goal of the strategy is to reduce the intermediaries

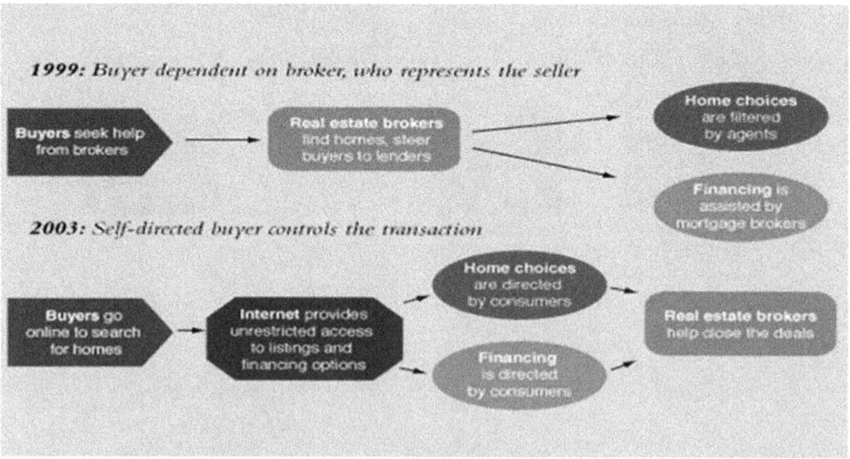

MAIN FOCUS OF THE CHAPTER

Today practically all business companies have standardized their governance, control and monitoring architecture; comparing to less than 10%; this proves that the FERS is a strategic approach for all BTPs and financial engineering subprojects (Kowall, & Fletcher, 2013). The BTM should be a member of the company's strategy team and s/he (in further text: he) should closely work with the company's risks and legal teams, where he can bring in an effective view to changes in financial engineering risk and legal regulations, control and governance integration issues (Trad, 2017); that stimulates the reduction of the number of intermediaries, as shown in Figure 3. The actual models use the following financial intermediaries: 1) banks; 2) insurance companies; 3) mutual funds; 4) finance institutions; and 5) financial service providers (Shahrokhi, 2008). Business engineering combines management sciences, business administration, law and economics with information technologies and engineering (Wikipedia, 2015; Universität St. Gallen, 2015).

DEFINING THE GLOBAL STRATEGY BASIS

An important part of existing business models provide financial services over the web. BTPs can help banks and financial institutions reshape their business programmes, like during the 2008 financial crisis, where the strategy focus was on geographical reach, redefining global initiatives and reorganizing the trade services and prioritizing a customer-centric approach. Citibank restructured its activity centres and redefined its global strategy to assist customers in solving financial problems. Citibank's BTP was very quick and the landscape for treasury and trade services was deeply modified to stand up again after the financial crisis. Multi-functional banking is a form of block-chaining, based on web technologies that enabled low cost and efficient financial operations. Citibank was the first financial institution to finalize a BTP and that had a significant impact on the business domain models that in turn are based on sets of factors (Farhoomand & Lentini, 2008).

Factors Based Strategy

Main strategy factors that influence the financial aspects of BTPs and enterprise architecture projects are (Shahrokhi, 2008; Kyte, 2010):

- The ability to protect and enhance the business environment`s ability for innovation.
- To offer added value for the business environment`s end clients.

- Following the competitors' status and activities.
- The capacity to implement customized financial services.
- To insure technology feasibility.
- To embrace globalization.
- To implement regulations for financial exchanges.
- To promote entrepreneurship.
- All the previous listed factors can support a global competitive business environment and the needed reservoir of highly technical skills to confront competition and to predict dangers.

Dangers for the Business Transformation's Strategy

Dangers that can affect the business transformation strategy (Shahrokhi, 2008):

- BTP's complexity can lead to significant financial losses.
- The BTP is a major paradigm shift and there would be a need to adopt a new and different way of working.
- The business and finance environments complete policy issues should be verified and transformed.
- Important business and finance environments are often reluctant to execute radical BTPs.
- Business and finance environments in most cases are resistant and reject major organizational and technological changes.
- Legal pitfalls.

Finance Engineering and Law Relationship

The vast majority of surveyed enterprises expressed the importance of developing a valid financial plan and a related legal framework; where they faced the various types of legal problems (European commission, 2004). FERS defines block-chain automation as a major CSF for FERS. The identification of possible financial problems is of general nature and very difficult to localize and interpret. Almost half of the encountered financial problems are due to a huge volume of financial transactions. Transaction management should become the enterprise's strategic objective and it should be treated in its vision that is based on avoiding locked-in situations (Trad & Kalpić, 2016a).

Locked-In Situations

Locked-In

A situation where an investor is unwilling or unable to exit a position because of the regulations, taxes or penalties associated with doing so. This may be an investment vehicle, such as a retirement plan, which cannot be accessed until a specified retirement date (Investopedia, 2017a; Investopedia, 2017b).

Financial Locked-In

When building the financial structure of the future transformed business environment, the BTP team and enterprise architects must be cautious of eventual financial locked-in situation(s). Even though some countries like Switzerland offer attractive financial and tax package(s), that country applies a coordinated legal and financial locked-in trap; it is sealed and represents an unwritten concept that can at any moment sweep out the financial resources from a business environment. This locked-in Swiss model combines: 1) specific mentality; é) the power of Swiss law; 3) Too Big to Fail banks; 4) Banking secrecy; 5) Ultraliberal economy; 6) Rejection of local and global standards; 7) isolationism; and 6) a finance supportive political environment. The banks and other Swiss financial institutions are under no supervision what so ever. That indirectly makes this country the financial industry's super protector that sets up fortifications against any possible intrusion; even when these institutions are executing massive irregular and illegal activities. The authors refer to this phenomenon as an instance of the Black Swan phenomena or simply the Swiss Black Swan, which business environments should try to avoid. It is probably wiser to pay more taxes and social services then to face such phenomena and traps (International Monetary Fund, 2009; Taleb, 2007).

Technological Locked-In

The implication of technologies in the actual financial domain is immense and it influences its productivity, growth and monetary policy (Panetta, 2016). It is a technology-driven domain and because the hyper evolution depends on technology, the financial institution can be driven in a locked-in situation (Balling, Lierman & Mullineux, 2003).

Anti-Locked-In Strategy

FERS requires a holistic approach that must be supported by a global business environment who should avoid locked-in situations by applying standards and not to adopt a unique tool, like the all-in-one tool (SAP, 2015). Such tools request frequent commercial product upgrades that adds to complexity of the implementation and maintenance phases. Tool's some of the needed features are delayed or never finished, what can provoke failure to deliver fundamental BTP modules. These all-in-one tools vary significantly from the defined open standards; and if a change is to be done to the (e)system's reintegration, it is often incurring very high costs and BTP risks (Sourcemaking, 2015).

Currency Usage Strategy

The business environment must choose a unique currency to be used in its financial transactions. In the last few years we have seen a convergence of the major industrial currencies as shown in Figures 4, 5 and 6. This fact shows clearly the will to adapt to an incoming electronic and unique currency (XE, 2017).

The Finance Engineering Strategy Basis Critical Success Factors

This section's (CSA: FinanceEngineeringStrategyBasis) set of filtered CSFs and their weightings are shown in Table 1.

Figure 4. The United States dollar and Swiss franc ratio
XE, 2017.

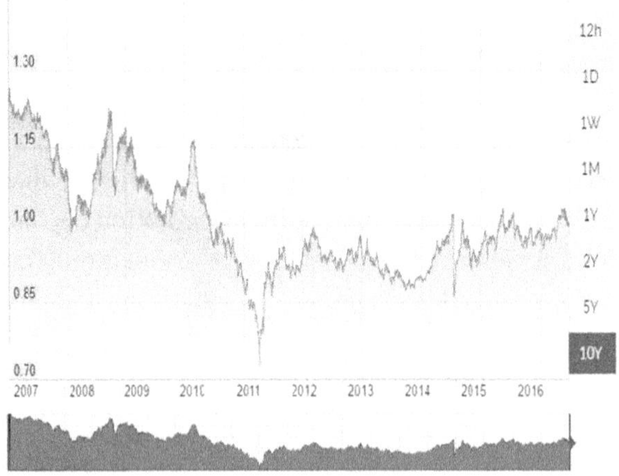

Figure 5. The United States dollar and Great Britain pound ratio
XE, 2017.

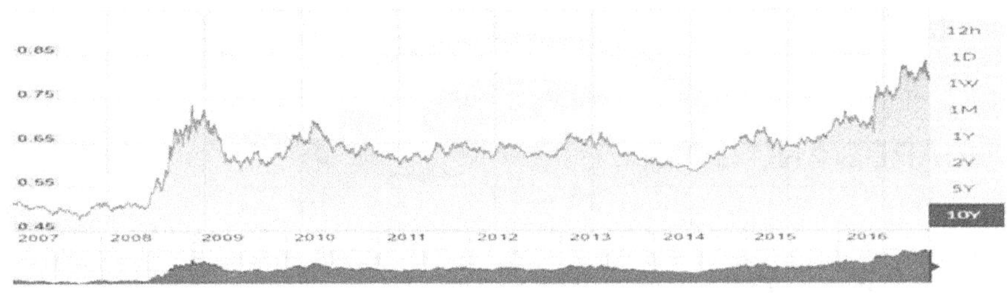

Figure 6. The United States dollar and European Union's euro ratio
XE, 2017.

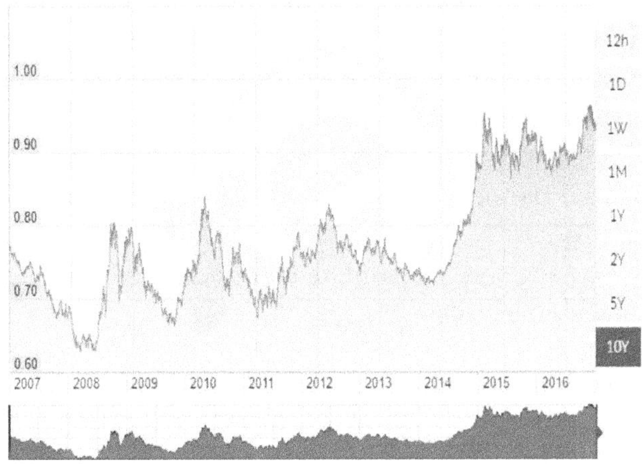

Table 1. The finance engineering strategy and application critical success factors

Critical Success Factors	KPIs	Weightings
CSF_EngineeringStrategyBasis _DefiningGlobalStrategy	Stable	From 1 to 10. **10 Selected**
CSF_EngineeringStrategyBasis_FactorsConditions	Set&Ready	From 1 to 10. **07 Selected**
CSF_EngineeringStrategyBasis_Dangers	Controlled	From 1 to 10. **10 Selected**
CSF_EngineeringStrategyBasis_EngineeringStatus	Ongoing	From 1 to 10. **04 Selected**
CSF_EngineeringStrategyBasis_ImpelementedModules	AnalysisPhase	From 1 to 10. **09 Selected**
CSF_EngineeringStrategyBasis_(e)lawLinks	Automated	From 1 to 10. **05 Selected**
CSF_EngineeringStrategyBasis_SwissBlackSwan	Active	From 1 to 10. **08 Selected**
CSF_EngineeringStrategyBasis_CurrencyUsage	EUR	From 1 to 10. **06 Selected**

The Modules Chained Link to Architecture and Infrastructure

Such an *Environment* and its strategy need specific standards and concepts.

STANDARDS AND CONCEPTS

Nowadays there are many standards and this section presents the most important ones and how they help integrate BTPs.

Financial Products Markup Language

Financial products Markup Language (FpML) is the industry-standard protocol for complex financial products. It is based on XML (eXtensible Markup Language), the standard meta-language for describing data shared between applications (XML, 2003). BTP's integration benefits by:

- Gluing financial partners' messages with a format readable by people and information systems.
- Supporting exchange between different business applications.
- Reducing processing costs.

Financial Information Exchange Markup Language

Financial Information eXchange Markup Language (FIXML) protocol is an electronic communications protocol initiated in 1992 for international real-time exchange of information related to the securities transactions and markets (XML, 2003).

Research Information Exchange Markup Language

Research Information Exchange Markup Language (RIXML) is the standard tagging language for securities research founded by asset management and sell side firms (XML, 2003). BTP's integration benefits are (Service Architecture, 2017):

- Increased efficiency for distribution of messages.
- Enabled transmission of new content types.

Extensible Business Reporting Language

eXtensible Business Reporting Language (XBRL) is an open international standard for digital business reporting, that is managed by a global non-profit consortium, XBRL International. XBRL is used globally, in many countries. A vast number of XBRL documents are created and managed every month; these documents replace the previous paper-based reports to become more manageable, effective and precise (XBRL, 2017).

The Document Standards Critical Success Factors

This section's (CSA: Standards) set of filtered CSFs and their weightings are shown in Table 2.

The Modules Chained Link to Engineering Integration

Such an *Environment* and its applied strategy need a specific strategy integration concept.

STRATEGY'S INTEGRATION

The industry needs a multimodal finance model that minimizes the dependencies between various business partners; where finance connections are established between the consumer and the end business environment with minimal risks (Jin & Zhu, 2011). An important CSF that can be integrated in the FERS is the financial cost ratio before and after the BTP completion. To calculate costs related to finance operations, there is the need to add-up the total cost of providing financial services and to divide it by the total number of successfully executed financial transactions. BTPs' finances' outcomes should be controlled in real-time and routine financial reports must be reported to the BTM and to the business enterprise's executive management. (e)finance impacts on BTPs depend on security violations (Fu & Mittnight, 2015; Xiaohong, 2011).

Table 2. The standards factors and indicators

Critical Success Factors	KPIs	Weightings
CSF_DocumentStandards_Selection	Exists	From 1 to 10. **05 Selected**
CSF_DocumentStandards_Integration	Done	From 1 to 10. **05 Selected**

Security Violations

Business environment's functions and financial transactions are orthogonal to enterprise security requirements, where the business and financial environment functions and financial transactions define the responsibility for enterprise's financial results. Management of the enterprise's financial interests, resources, governance, support, usage and reporting of security access activity, should be managed by the BTP's team or by enterprise architect(s) (Gartner, 2013). In exceptional security breaches, like the case of denial of request for access rights to vital financial and business resources, the BTM must delegate the design of the solution to the enterprise security team. Thus, the business environment's structure is an important factor that has an implication on legal control, financial auditing, governing, control, access management and monitoring of financial security. The (e)finance's security concept uses the following standards: 1) the policy framework (Oracle, 2015a); 2) business messaging is needed for domain-specific assertion languages; it defines assertions for declaring reliable-messaging policy; and 3) timestamps-based finance collaboration and processing (Oracle, 2015b; OASIS, 2009).

Timestamps Regulation

The regulation of the financial security requirements needs qualified time-stamps to build robust certification techniques. It is a fact that innovation's evolution leads to the integration of avant-garde messaging technologies that use a high level of finances' security, based on time-stamps. When a signature is not used, then the BTP team must prototype and develop qualified trust financial services to support the conformity and assessment of finance services. These trusted services should support an adequate level of financial security to comply with the rules like the ones of the European Union's regulations (European Union, 2014).

Timestamp Servers

The BTP proposes the use of timestamp servers that work using the concept of taking a hash of a block of items to be timestamped and to expose widely the hash container to all the BTP's microartefacts, as shown in Figure 7. The timestamp factor proves that the financial transaction existed at a precise time sequence. The proposed timestamp concept includes the link to the previous timestamp in its hash pointing block that forms a chain, where each timestamp reinforces the previous ones. The timestamp chains can be used to verify and replay transactions and in their legal enforcement (Nakamoto, 2008).

Figure 7. The timestamp server tree setup

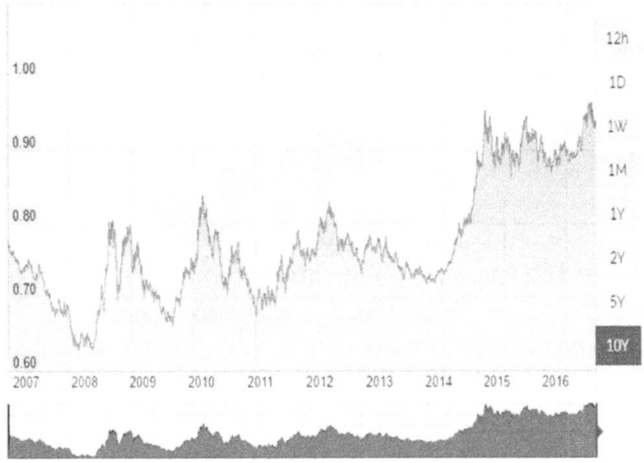

Legal Foundation

Looking from the financial engineering aspects, uniform bodies promulgate transaction acts on the global level and propagate these acts to legal enforcement in financial engineering fields. Many countries and regions have adopted financial standards to support fields like for example transactions and digital signature's legislation.

The Applied Finance Engineering Integration's Setup Critical Success Factors

This section's (CSA: AppliedStrategyIntegration) set of filtered CSFs and their weightings are shown in Table 3.

Table 3. The document standards factors and indicators

Critical Success Factors	KPIs	Weightings
CSF_AppliedStrategyIntegration_FinancesSecuritySupport	Integrated	From 1 to 10. **10 Selected**
CSF_AppliedStrategyIntegration_TimestampsRegulation	Automated	From 1 to 10. **08 Selected**
CSF_AppliedStrategyIntegration_TimestampsServers	Setup	From 1 to 10. **08 Selected**
CSF_AppliedStrategyIntegration_FinanceLaw	Automated	From 1 to 10. **07 Selected**

The Modules Chained Link to Legal Integration

Such an *Environment* setup and its applied strategy need a specific valuation concept.

VALUATION

Business valuation is a process and a related set of procedures that can be applied to estimate the value of a business environment, as shown in Figure 8. This is a complex undertaking to evaluate a business value that has to be precisely estimated and is based on the value of concrete business valuation's assumptions (ValuAdder, 2017).

Valuation's Assumptions

It is not easy to establish the real value of a business environment because business valuation understands many different factors and depends also on the managers' views. Business environments' stakeholders look at the business connection to the macro business community services. An external investor looks at the business value based on the historic perceived income. Another factor that plays an important role are the economic conditions that can be affected by how clients, partners and employees estimate that value. For example, at crisis times business buyers/sellers are active and the resultant increased competition implies higher business transaction values. The condition of a business environment's transaction affects directly its business value (ValuAdder, 2017).

Figure 8. Business valuation segments

Transactions and Business Value

Business value is in fact the expected transaction price at a selling operation where the real price is hard to estimate and it depends on institution that evaluates the business value (Investopedia, 2016). It depends whether the business environment's buyer wants the business right away because it is vital for his business goals; compared to a buyer who is interested to buy at the lowest price possible. The business environment's selling price depends also on negotiating capacities of the partners. To prepare such an operation, it is recommended to adopt the right valuation approach.

Valuation Approaches

There are three fundamental valuation approaches that can measure the business environment's value (ValuAdder, 2017):

- Asset Approach.
- Market Approach.
- Income Approach.

The Asset Approach

Asset approach figures the business environment as a set of well-defined assets and liabilities that can be used as financial building blocks to build the financial picture of the business value. The asset approach is based on the economic principle of substitution that queries the cost to create a business that would produce the exact same financial benefits for its stakeholders. A straight forward way is to determine the money value of these assets and liabilities.

Market Approach

The market approach as it sounds depends on the market place to determine the business value. In this case, the financial principle is based on the comparison of actual business environment with the one to be acquired. The gap's value must be estimated. In other words, the market approach is to evaluate the business environment in a monetary value that will be exchanged in a financial transaction.

Income Approach

The income approach looks at the core purpose for running the targeted business environment and the way it makes money. In this case, the financial principle to be met is how much money would it bring to stakeholders. The income valuation approach implies risk, since the business environment's value must be evaluated, then the expected income and related risks must be determined at this exact moment.

Valuation of a Business by Valuating Its Cash Flows

The discounting method projects the business environment's income stream over a future period of time of a few years. Then the discount rate which reflects the risk of receiving this income on time is estimated. The business value is evaluated at the end of the projection period; this is the terminal business value.

Unbundled Business Environments

BTPs play an important role in many business environments' unbundling processes. BTPs constitute the basis for a flexible, dynamic, global and sustainable unbundling process of business environments; the challenges that can be encountered are:

- The control of the financial system and the diversification of financial tools.
- That the banking environment does not stop the BTP to access financing.
- Awareness of complementary financing means, including equity financing and other.
- Tax barrier reduction.
- Corruption.
- Integration of logging systems.

The Valuation's Critical Success Factors

This section's (CSA: Valuation) set of filtered CSFs and their weightings are shown in Table 4.

Table 4. The business valuation factors and indicators

Critical Success Factors	KPIs	Weightings
CSF_Valuation_Assumptions	Established	From 1 to 10. **06 Selected**
CSF_Valuation_Approaches	Income	From 1 to 10. **02 Selected**
CSF_Valuation_CashFlows	Controlled	From 1 to 10. **10 Selected**
CSF_Valuation_InitialFactors	NotUsed	From 1 to 10. **01 Selected**
CSF_Valuation_UnbundlingProcess	Activated	From 1 to 10. **10 Selected**

The Modules Chained Link to Legal Integration

Such an *Environment* and its strategy need a specific proof of concept.

SOLUTION AND RECOMMENDATIONS

In this research phase and article, the main issue is how to define the optimal strategy. The resources discovered in the literature review phase and the *Environment's* proof of concept proved the feasibility of this research's phase and defined a related set of recommendations that are sorted by their importance:

- This phase's proof of concept: It proved the research project's feasibility by implementing the defined factors concept.
- The BTM must deploy a microartefact based strategy and an anti-locked-in approach: The FERS component must be designed by the BTP team and its implementation must be set as the company's strategic goal.
- The BTP team skills should encompass knowledge of: 1) Financial engineering and the needed logging, monitoring and assertion architectures; 2) automated real-time business environments; and 4) governance integration.
- To design and implement an adequate FERS component: For business transformation project there is a need to implement a decision system that can be easily integrated with any framework or tool (Gray, 1997).
- Decision and governance logs: To manage BTPs, the team must implement a governance logs management mechanism for the support of the financial engineering environment.
- Legal intelligence, decision making module and critical success factors: The decision-making module uses the BTP's logging system's database.
- Integrating other frameworks: Operations library and other standard frameworks can be integrated in the BTP through the use of critical success factors.
- Implement a global financial subsystem's approach for the control of financial transactions via the use of microartefacts.
- The International Institute for Analytics recommends: 1) To embrace enterprise decision making and artificial intelligence; 2) to clearly define BTM and enterprise architects' executives roles; 3) to build proof of concepts to decrease costs and to balance between prototyping and final deployment; and 4) to setup an in-house BTP and enterprise architecture framework (Laskowski, 2017).

- Implement Critical Success Areas (CSA) that is a category of Critical Success Factors (CSF) strategy where in turn a CSF is a set of Key Performance Indicators (KPI), one KPI corresponds to a single requirement.
- Application of the antifragility concept can help in having a holistic and broad guide to non-predictive decision making operations under uncertainty.
- Proactively try to avoid Black Swan phenomena.
- The business environment must choose a currency strategy to be used in its financial transactions.

The *Environment's* global strategy managerial recommendations and a real-world proof of concept, round up the FERS component's characteristics for business transformation projects.

FUTURE RESEARCH DIRECTIONS

The *Environment* future research will focus on a neural network based decision making module, which use a dynamic concept.

CONCLUSION

The FERS holistic integration is an important factor for the financial engineering environment's evolution and stability. Many industries have been implementing FERS like local solutions to respond to probable risk and legal problems and challenges in production. This research phase is part of a series of publications related to defining the strategy for financial environments. This research is based on mixed action research model; where critical success factors and areas are used to help BTPs to decrease the chances of failure. The most important managerial recommendation that was generated by the previous research phases was that the business transformation manager must be an architect of adaptive business system (Farhoomand, 2004).

ACKNOWLEDGMENT

In a work as large as this research project, technical, typographical, grammatical, or other kinds of errors are bound to be present. Ultimately, all mistakes are the authors' responsibility. Nevertheless, the authors encourage feedback from readers identifying errors in addition to comments on the work in general. It was our great pleasure to prepare this work. Now our greater hopes are for readers to receive some small measure of that pleasure.

REFERENCES

Balling, M., Lierman, F., & Mullineux, A. (2003). *Technology and Finance: Challenges for Financial Markets, Business Strategies and Policy Makers*. Routledge.

Daellenbach, H., McNickle, D., & Dye, Sh. (2012). *Management Science. Decision-making through systems thinking* (2nd ed.). Plagrave Macmillian.

European Union. (2014). *Regulation (EU) No 910/2014 of the European Par lament and of the Council - on electronic identification and trust services for electronic transactions in the internal market and repealing Directive*. 1999/93/EC The European Parlament and of the Council – Regulation. Retrieved March 2017, from http://eur-lex.europa.eu/legal-content/EN/TXT/?uri=uriserv:OJ.L_.2014.257.01.0073.01.ENG

Farhoomand, A. (2004). *Managing (e)business transformation*. Palgrave Macmillan. doi:10.1007/978-1-137-08380-7

Farhoomand, A., & Lentini, D. (2008). *e-Business Transformation in the Banking Industry: The Case of Citibank*. Retrieved January 2017, from http://www.acrc.hku.hk/case/case_showdetails.asp?ct=newly&c=944&cp=1949&pt=1

Fu, Z., & Mittnight, E. (2015). *Critical Success Factors for Continually Monitoring, Evaluating and Assessing Management of Enterprise IT*. ISACA. Retrieved August 2016, from http://www.isaca.org/COBIT/focus/Pages/critical-success-factors-for-continually-monitoring-evaluating-and-assessing-management-of-enterprise-it.aspx

Gartner. (2013). *Scenario Toolkit: Using EA to Support Business Transformation*. Gartner Inc.

Gray, P. (1997). *Artificial legal intelligence*. Dartmouth Publishing Co.

Grewal-Carr, V., & Marshall, S. (2016). *Block-chain Enigma*. London, UK: Paradox. Opportunity. Deloitte LLP.

IFRS. (2017). *IFRS Standards*. Retrieved April 2017, from http://www.ifrs.org/Pages/default.aspx. IFRS.

International Monetary Fund. (2009). Switzerland: Financial Sector Assessment Program - Detailed Assessment of Observance of Financial Sector Standards and Codes. International Monetary Fund.

Investopedia. (2016). *Business Valuation*. Retrieved April 2017, from http://www.investopedia.com/terms/b/business-valuation.asp. Investopedia.

Investopedia. (2017a). *What is 'Financial Engineering*. Retrieved April 2017, from http://www.investopedia.com/terms/f/financialengineering.asp. Investopedia.

Investopedia. (2017b). *Locked In*. Retrieved April 2017, from http://www.investopedia.com/terms/l/locked_in.asp. Investopedia.

Jin, K., & Zhu, J. (2011). *MET: Multi-party E-Commerce Transaction Model*. Privacy, Security, Risk and Trust (PASSAT). 2011 IEEE Third International Conference on Social Computing (SocialCom), 2011 IEEE Third International Conference, Boston, MA.

Kowall, J., & Fletcher, C. (2013). Modernize Your Monitoring Strategy by Combining Unified Monitoring and Log Analytics Tools. Gartner.

Kyte, A. (2010). Nine Critical Success Factors for Business Value Through Application Overhaul. Gartner Inc.

Laskowski, N. (2017). *Five analytics priorities for 2017*. Retrieved March 2017, from http://searchcio.techtarget.com/news/450410871/Five-analytics-priorities-for-2017

Nakamoto, S. (2008). *Bitcoin: A Peer-to-Peer Electronic Cash System*. Retrieved from www.bitcoin.org

OASIS. (2009). *OASIS Web Services Reliable Messaging (WS-ReliableMessaging) Version 1.2. OASIS Standard*. Retrieved January 2017, from http://docs.oasis-open.org/ws-rx/wsrm/200702/wsrm-1.2-spec-os.html

Oracle. (2015a). *Using WS-Policy in ALSB Proxy and Business Services*. Oracle. Retrieved March 2017, from http://docs.oracle.com/cd/E11036_01/alsb30/security/ws_policy.html

Oracle. (2015b). *About Web Services Policy*. Oracle. Retrieved August 2016, from http://docs.oracle.com/cd/E11036_01/alsb30/security/ws_policy.html

Panetta, K. (2016). *3 Trends Appear in the Gartner Hype Cycle for Emerging Technologies, 2016. Are block-chain, smart machines, IoT and other emerging technologies on their way up or down the Hype Cycle?* Retrieved March 2017, from http://www.gartner.com/smarterwithgartner/3-trends-appear-in-the-gartner-hype-cycle-for-emerging-technologies-2016/

Peterson, S. (2011). *Why it Worked: Critical Success Factors of a Financial Reform Project in Africa*. Faculty Research Working Paper Series. Harvard Kennedy School.

SAP. (2015). *ALM103: Implementation Tools: SAP Business All-in-One and Rapid Deployment Solutions*. SAP.

Service Architecture. (2017). *Service Architecture*. Retrieved February 2017, from http://www.service-architecture.com/articles/xml/rixml.html

Shahrokhi, M. (2008). *E-finance: Status, Innovations, Resources and Future Challenges. Managerial Finance,* 34, 365–398.

Sourcemaking. (2015). *AntiPatterns: The Survival Guide-Vendor lock in*. Retrieved March 2017, from https://sourcemaking.com/antipatterns/vendor-lock-in

Taleb, N. (2007). *The Black Swan-The Impact of the Highly Improbable*. Random House, Inc.

Trad, A. (2017). *The Transformation Framework's Resources Library*. IBISTM.

Trad, A., & Kalpić, D. (2014a). *The Selection and Training Framework (STF) for Managers in Business Innovation and Transformation Projects - Integrating the restructuring process of the global economy*. Cambridge, UK: IMRA.

Trad, A., & Kalpić, D. (2015a). *The Business Engineering Transformation Framework for (e)commerce Architecture-Modelling Projects. In Encyclopedia of E-Commerce Development, Implementation, and Management*. IGI-Global.

Trad, A., & Kalpić, D. (2015b). *The Business Engineering Transformation Framework for (e)commerce Control and Monitoring Pattern. In Encyclopedia of E-Commerce Development, Implementation, and Management*. IGI-Global.

Trad, A., & Kalpić, D. (2016a). *The Business Transformation Framework and its Financial engineering Law support for (e)transactions*. IGI-Global.

Trad, A., & Kalpić, D. (2017a). The Business Transformation and Enterprise Architecture Framework-The Financial Engineering (e)Risk Management and (e) Law Integration. IGI-Global. (under review)

Trad, A., & Kalpić, D. (2017b). The Business Transformation and Enterprise Architecture Framework- The Financial Engineering Technology Concept. IGI-Global. (under review)

Universität St. Gallen. (2015). *EMBA in Financial engineering*. Retrieved April 2017, from http://www.es.unisg.ch/de/programme/emba/embe.php

ValuAdder. (2017). *Business Valuation: The Three Approaches*. Retrieved April 2017, from http://www.valuadder.com/valuationguide/business-valuation-three-approaches.html

Wikipedia. (2015). *Master of Financial engineering*. Retrieved from https://en.wikipedia.org/wiki/Master_of_Business_Engineering

XBRL. (2017). *XBRL, the business reporting standard*. Retrieved from https://www.xbrl.org/

XE. (2017). *Currecy exchange*. Retrieved April 2017, from http://www.xe.com/currencycharts/?from=USD&to=EUR&view=10Y

Xiaohong, Ch. (2011). *Research on E-Commerce Transaction Cost-Benefit Characteristics and Evaluation Approaches*. Management and Service Science (MASS), *2011 International Conference*, Wuhan, China.

XML. (2003). *XML Standards for Financial Services*. Retrieved January 2017, from http://www.xml.com/pub/a/2003/03/26/financial.html

KEY TERMS AND DEFINITIONS

Business Engineering: The development and implementation of business solutions using business models to business processes and organizational structure.

CSFs: Can be used to manage the statuses and gaps in various project plans and gives the projects the capacity to proactively and automatically recognize erroneous building blocks and to just-in-time reschedule the project plan(s).

Enterprise Architecture: A known defined practice for driving enterprise analysis, design, planning, and implementation, using a holistic approach with the use of a system's strategy.

Environment: This research's framework.

Manager: Business transformation manager.

Project: Business transformation project.

Strategy: A high-level plan to reach one or more objectives under defined constraints.

Chapter 2
The Business Transformation and Enterprise Architecture Framework:
The Financial Engineering Technology Concept

Antoine Trad
IBISTM, France

Damir Kalpić
University of Zagreb, Croatia

ABSTRACT

A business transformation project or an innovative enterprise architecture project is needed for the enterprise's business and financial strategic planning process and to prepare this business enterprise to integrate into the globally interconnected economy in a whole and robust manner. The integration of financial engineering and information technologies is fundamental, where the latter is the gluing element that makes this fine-grained environment run efficiently. Today, these finance-related technology standards and fields are ready and can be applied as automated block-chains to enable the traditional business environments as a part of the networked global economy. An important factor in frequent business transformation projects' changes and financial reengineering iterations are the roles of the business transformation manager, project managers, finance analysts, the business environment's technological maturity, and enterprise architect(s) who should be supported by the optimal business transformation framework.

DOI: 10.4018/978-1-5225-4026-7.ch002

INTRODUCTION

A business transformation project or an innovative enterprise architecture project in needed for the enterprise's business and financial strategic planning process and to prepare this business enterprise to integrate into the globally interconnected economy in a whole and robust manner. The integration of financial engineering and information technologies is fundamental, where the latter is the gluing element that makes this fine-grained environment run efficiently. Today these finance related technology standards and fields are ready and can be applied as automated block-chains to enable the traditional business environments being a part of the networked global economy (Trad & Kalpić, 2014a).

An important factor in frequent business transformation projects' changes and financial reengineering iterations are the roles of the business transformation manager, project managers, finance analysts, the business environment's technological maturity and enterprise architect(s) who should be supported by the optimal business transformation framework and technology platform that should include holistic financial technology enablers and modellers. Technology enablers are designed in four categories of architectures as shown in Figure 1.

These technology enablers or architecture categories should also be capable of supporting the business environment's financial engineering cloud and distributed integration in a complex block-chain globalized business environment. To achieve this financial engineering technology integration, critical success areas, key performance indicators and critical success factors must be defined and used to evaluate possible technology pitfalls and risk. For a business transformation project there must be provided the audit, assert, govern, automate, trace, monitor and control of its financial status. The mentioned pitfalls depend on how the business environment's technology platform is built and on the relations between the business and: 1) data; 2) application; and 3) technology, as shown in Figure 2.

Figure 1. The four categories of architectures that can be applied

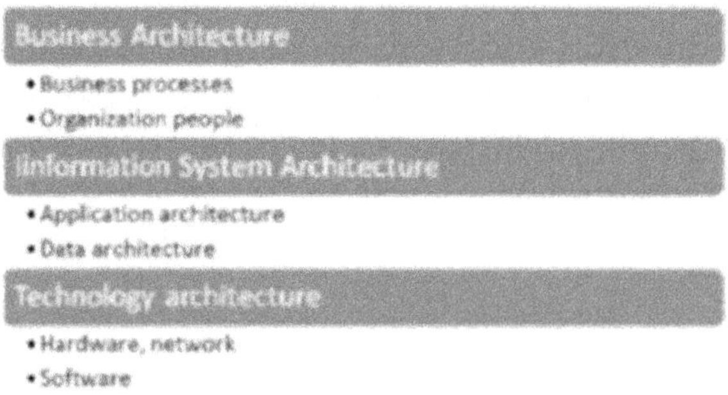

Figure 2. Traditional business architecture
The Open Group, 2014a.

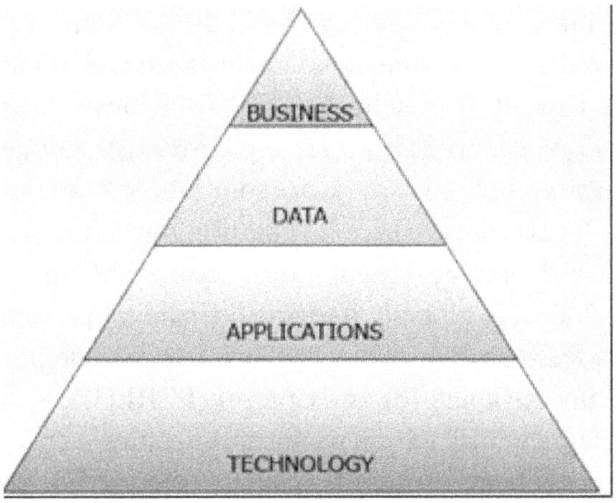

The business transformation project or/and enterprise's architecture project critical success factors can be configured to manage the complexities in handling of asynchronous financial flows in (e)business local and international financial environments. Transformed business environments need built-in automated block-chain controls that are capable of recognizing fraud, dysfunction, intentional black swan effects (Taleb, 2007; International Monetary Fund, 2009), bad investments, business transformation project budget slips, loss of (e)transactions, illegal activities and tax evasions (Trad & Kalpić, 2015a; Trad & Kalpić, 2015b). The Business Transformation Manager's (BTM) profile is of utter importance for the technical implementation phase of the complex Business Transformation Projects (BTP) and also for its skeletal enterprise architecture activities; where the BTM or enterprise architect's creatively robust design decisions are done in real-time by using outputs from the available business and financial environment's monitoring and logging subsystems (Gartner, 2013). Many factors can influence the finance engineering process, like: 1) the influence of automation of accounting in business transformation projects; 2) the automation of the business environment's block-chain(s); 3) level of resistance; 4) the holistic financial control mechanisms; and 3) level of technology maturity and background conditions.

BACKGROUND

Constant, in the sense of real-time and politically realistic business valuation is a process that incorporates a set of automated standardized procedures that can be applied to evaluate the real value of the targeted financial environment (IFRS, 2017). This valuation process is a very complex process that depends on the applied technology and its integration's stability (Kyte, 2010). Stability is supposed to be based on standardized and fully integrated governance and monitoring subsystems (ValuAdder, 2017; Kowall & Fletcher, 2013). To achieve these goals, the BTM should be a member of the company's strategic management and planning team; and s/he (in further text: he) must work or more precisely manage the company's financial risks and legal teams, where he can bring an effective view on changes in financial finance risk and legal regulations, control and governance integration issues (Shahrokhi, 2008). A globally integrated financial information subsystem's approach is optimal for such control mechanisms like the integration and use of the Financial Engineering Risk and (e)Law Control (FERLC) component via the use of finance microartefacts. FERLC draws its architecture, concept and framework implementation from the services based Financial Information and Communication Technology Systems (FICTS) built years ago and was reengineered due to the hyper evolution in information technologies and business organization. FERLC promotes (e)financial engineering driven business environments that use references to various technology fields, which are combined by using different types of methodologies and service oriented technologies; where the most common basic technology framework are the transaction's management mechanisms as a part of the block-chain automation process (Trad & Kalpić, 2017b).

MAIN FOCUS OF THE CHAPTER

The FERLC technology component is a part of the Financial management module (Fm); Fm is also a part of the Selection management, Architecture-modelling, Control-monitoring, Decision-making, Training management, Project management, and Finance management Framework (SmAmCmDmTmPmFmF, for simplification in further text the term *Environment* will be used), that is the major support for of BTP's activities; in fact the proposed very modest framework is a leader in this market (Trad, 2017a; Trad, 2017b). This research article is strongly bonded to two other articles and together they create a research whole on financial risk and technology management. These articles are:

- The Business Transformation and Enterprise Architecture Framework-The Financial Engineering The Financial Engineering Global Strategy (Trad & Kalpić, 2017a).

- The Business Transformation and Enterprise Architecture Framework-The Financial Engineering (e)Risk Management and (e)Law Integration (Trad & Kalpić, 2017b).

The *Environment* and its FERLC technology component need a specific engineering and technology integration concept, based on agile business methodologies and atomic services, which in turn are based on an anti-fragile concept [referenca na Taleba]. Building such an integration concept needs a large set of skills that includes knowledge in legal topics, as shown in Figure 3.

APPLIED FINANCE ENGINEERING AND TECHNOLOGY INTEGRATION

The industry needs a multimodal finance engineering model that minimizes the dependencies between various business partners using interoperable finance microartefacts; where finance connections and previewed operations are established between the ultimate client and the targeted business environment, using highly available and resilient technology under minimal financial risks and with adequate legal awareness (Jin & Zhu, 2011).

Finance Legal and Governance Integration

The evolution of financial and business engineering forces various industries to implement FERLC-like mechanisms into their business environments and transformation frameworks (Gray, 1997). Such frameworks must incorporate finances legal collaboration with: 1) local; 2) international; 3) national; 4) electronic and web

Figure 3. The Open Group's skills' framework
The Open Group, 2015a.

IT Architect Roles	Architecture Board Member	Architecture Sponsor	IT Architecture Manager	IT Architecture Technology	IT Architecture Data	IT Architecture Application	IT Architecture Business	Program or Project Manager	IT Designer
Legal Environment									
Contract Law	2	2	2	2	2	2	2	3	1
Data Protection Laws	3	3	4	3	3	3	3	2	2
Procurement Law	3	2	2	2	2	2	2	4	1
Fraud	3	3	3	3	3	3	3	3	1
Commercial Law	3	3	2	2	2	2	3	3	1

environments; 4) regional laws; and 5) governance frameworks and rules (ISACA, 2015). In addition to local, international and national laws, there are legal frameworks, conventions, treaties and directives to be integrated into the transformed business environment that should be supported by a specific architecture and infrastructure (Trad & Kalpić, 2017b).

FINANCE ARCHITECTURE AND INFRASTRUCTURE

Global or holistic business agility is achieved by combining various methodologies that promote business and technological agility to be used on various levels of the BTP to unbundle the existing business environment and glue its renovated parts using dynamic technology financial microartefacts. Using a bottom-up approach, the BTM and his team can design the optimal business agility concept that can handle various types of financial engineering risk models to be used in the unbundling process (Farhoomand, 2004).

The Unbundling Process

Antifragility based unbundling process is a lot more than just a simple robustness gain factor, because monolithic robust business systems might not be resistant to sudden hard problems and tribulations. The antifragile unbundling of a financial system makes it ready to be easily changed and monitored. This feature makes the whole structure of business systems flexible and changeable where many of its finance processes can be frequently modified during a complex BTP, like for example: the process of continuous financial system evolution, innovating technologies, expanding financial industries, economic success, corporate survival, legal systems etc. Antifragility as a basic unbundling structure innovation and process defines the limits between the BTP's human factor or team and the final transformed financial system. An antifragility concept can help in having a holistic and broad guide to non-predictive decision making operations under uncertainty due to various factors like: 1) business; 3) technological complexity; and 3) politics; etc. A BTP should be adapted to handle complex BTP situations in which there are complex problems, randomness, unpredictability, opacity, or incomplete understanding of problems to be solved. It is easier to find out if a problem is of fragile nature than to predict the occurrence of a specific problem that cannot be solved. Fragile finance system problems can be measured and weighted; while risk is not easily measurable. This explains the difficulty of estimating the risks of a consequential and rare problem that could be fatal to the BTP and hence to the business environment. The *Environment* must evaluate the finance related risks using its decision module and tractable events; and it cannot only pretend to have the capability of forecasting events that could cause major BTP problems. This current research cluster proposes an efficient approach to: 1) unbundling prediction; 2) proactive risk management integration; and 3) financial flow control and management; that are the basic structures of a holistic and agile business and organizational engineering approach (Taleb, 2012).

A Holistic Agile View

The BTP team must achieve an agile holistic view on the BTP management and enterprise architecture where the projected agility is integrated in the enterprise's architecture development method by various agile project management methods on various levels: 1) technical, finance and business engineering; 2) global management; 3) coordinated change management; and 4) production management, as shown in Figure 4 (APMG international 2011; The Open Group 2014b).

FERLC composes the core of (e)enterprise's financial governance for transformation, (re)engineering, project management and production management (ITGI, 2007; Tan, Carter & Toleman, 2009), where the FERLC is integrated into the *Environment* and is based on critical success factors and existing financial engineering standards, using existing business environment resources with granularities to be refined (XBRL 2017; ISDA 2017).

Financial Engineering Service's Granularity

BTP's architecture is based on business and finance services which use choreography scenarios. The use of such services depends on their granularity. These services are

Figure 4. A view on different agile methodologies
APMG international 2011.

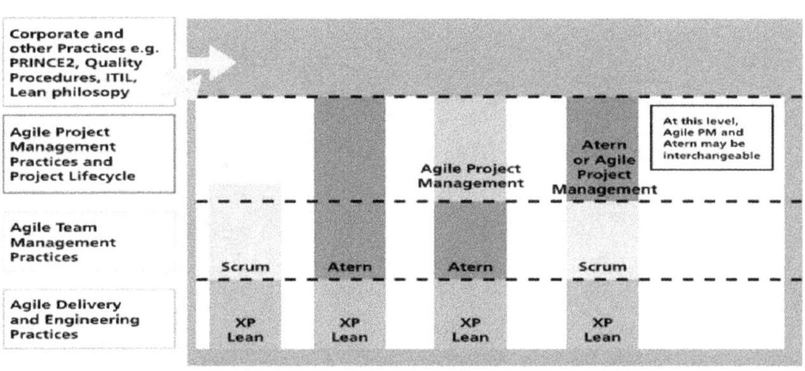

to be used in BTP's business, financial and technical microartefacts and have to be classified in categories; where their life cycle is a critical issue.

Financial Service's Life Cycle

Each financial service's life cycle should conform to the transformed enterprise architecture's vision and it is modelled as an independent microartefact value chain and is managed as an independent life-cycle of the future BTP based on a service oriented architecture (Khoshafian, 2014).

Financial Engineering Services Architecture

The specialized business services or financial services oriented architecture that is managed by the FERLC module interfaces various other BTP components by using the one-to-one mapping concept as shown is Figure 5.

Figure 5. The Environment's interaction using the one-to-one mapping system

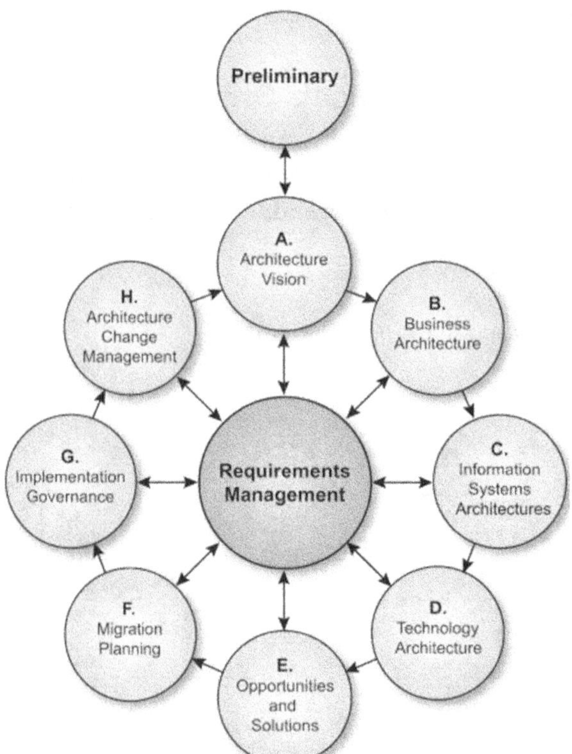

This concept: 1) helps in achieving the assertion of the business environment's internal and global financial engineering model concept; 2) sets up synchronized real-time monitoring and integration actions; 3) decouples financial data management, as shown in Figure 6; and 4) provides financial (e)transactions tracing and logging (Kabzeva, Niemann, Müller & Steinmetz, 2010).

The proposed atomic approach to financial services' management supports a well-managed unbundling process for a monolithic business environment that promotes the splitting of the old system into classified sets of business and financial services (Olson, 2008). The outcome of the unbundling process is a registry of state-full atomic finance services that can be asserted, controlled and monitored in real-time. To manage the agile and autonomic BTP's complexity in its implementation phase, an adequate assertion concept must be integrated in the architecture (OASIS, 2009). Such a FERLC concept is enabled by the development of an iterative model that can map all the BTPs financial microartefacts in a traced one-to-one manner by applying The Open Group's Architecture Framework's (TOGAF) architecture development method to assist in the establishment of the one-to-one mapping concept (Trad & Kalpić, 2015a; The Open Group, 2014b).

Architecture Development Method Integration

The Architecture Development Method's (ADM) integration in a BTP controls and automates financial activities, throughout all the iterations of ADM's phases; as shown in Figure 7.

Figure 6. The Environment's data interaction diagram

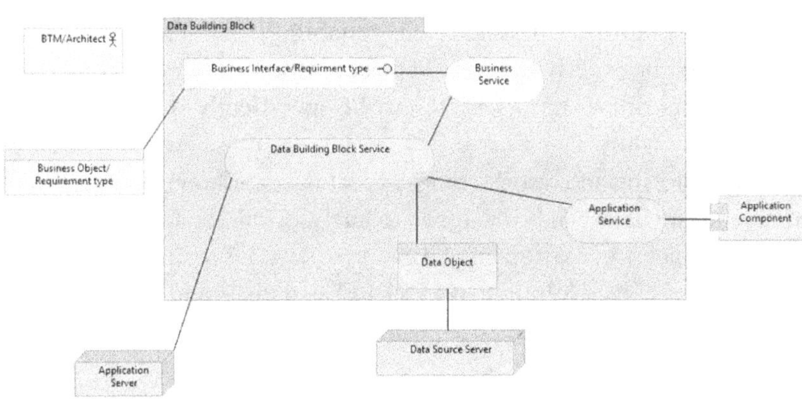

Figure 7. The architecture development method's interaction with the Finance management module

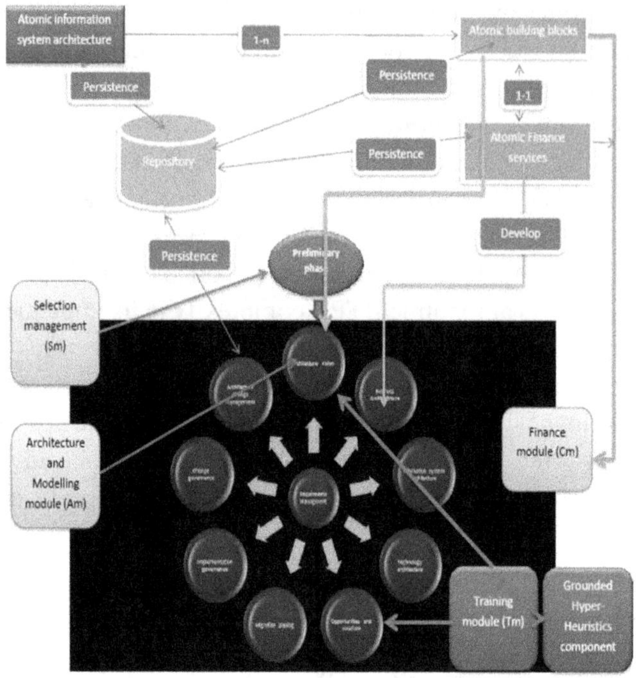

A Unified Control and Logging Subsystem

Generalized web and information technology platforms are no more dedicated to a single specific financial and/or business environment and may offer costs reduction and improve the platforms performance, reliability, maintenance and business security; where all these activities should be controlled and monitored in real-time. A Unified Logging Subsystem (ULS) must be specifically designed to support a FERLC module as shown in Figure 8. Log servers exist and they are powerful logging and monitoring subsystems that support business environments to present, sort, and tune logs. ULSs can be designed to analyse, collect and store FERLC data from various finance microartefacts. ULSs provide BTP teams with views on the data related to the BTPs evolution and FERLC's statuses and the central decision making logging system (Nagios, 2015; Cummins, 2010).

Figure 8. The Environment's components logging into a central storage

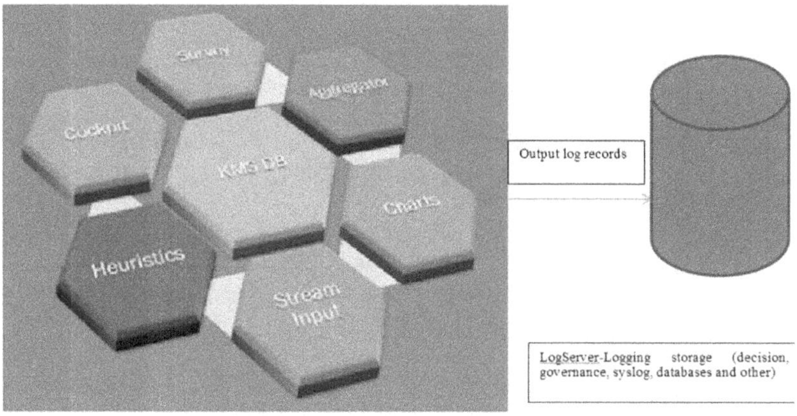

Decision Trace Store and Logs

The FERLC's decision making system's log has an important role, where these logs are based on various subsystems' inputs that are in fact outputs from various validation processes. Possible expected information returns are: 1) financial process' mechanisms feedback; 2) information technology components feedbacks; 3) fraud feedbacks; 4) financial previsions; and 5) BTP and/or enterprise architecture capability feedbacks. The FERLC is linked to the *Environment's* critical success factors pool and if the factors' constraints are to be violated, the FERLC module generates a log message to inform about the encountered violation status and type. Depending on the level of the warning, the FERLC can demand the BTP's finance team's support for domain specific finance topics. If the support team signals a problem to be solved, then the neural networks based decision making system is activated to propose a possible solution.

Neural Networks Oriented System

The *Environment's* Decision making (Dm) module is conceptually based on a mixed method, combining Action Research (AR), tree heuristics and directed quantitative analysis. The authors believe that qualitative and quantitative methods can be united in a single method. AR is applied in education research and this fact supports the BTP's capability to build finance and business intelligence microartefacts in a continuous learning process. This process inspects and learns from configurable intelligent microartefacts that are found in the decision system. The decision system

Figure 9. The neural network implementation environment that supports business and financial engineering

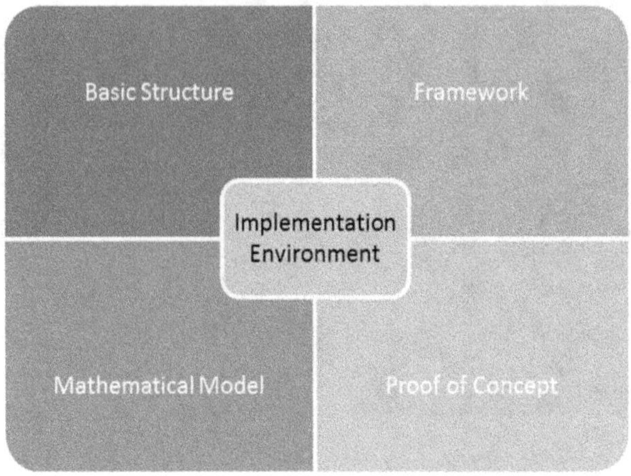

is generic and can be applied to any business domain and is easily adaptable; where its basic neural networks algorithm is based on: 1) Neural Networks and Enterprise Architecture's (NNEA) concept; and 2) Agnostic Implementation Environment (AIE). This NNEA is based on a reasoning concept that is basically a qualitative research method that manages and qualifies CSFs sets, actions and final solutions for the BTPs support (Trad & Kalpić, 2017c; Peterson) and a second step, if needed, applies a precise quantitative analysis. The FERLC's underlined model supports the BTPs in integrating microartefact scenarios that are in fact a set of interactive atomic service actions. AIE manages atomic services, what makes them more advanced and more flexible than the rigid and monolithic micro services proposal (Trad & Kalpić, 2017a). These components are all parts of the decision-making module and they all support the transformation process by building specialized finance microartefacts, where financial microartefacts are instances of building blocks.

The Financial Microartefact

The finance microartefact concept is implemented by using an iterative implementation model in which it can be mapped to all the BTPs microartefacts in a sequential one-to-one mapping concept. Such a FERLC finance microartefact is an instance of a finance building block that can interact with other BTPs microartefacts in a traced and synchronized manner. In the same time to apply TOGAF's architecture development method to assist it in the grouping of the needed services as shown in Figure 10 (Trad & Kalpić, 2015a; The Open Group, 2014b). The BTP can adopt

Figure 10. The finance microartefact design view

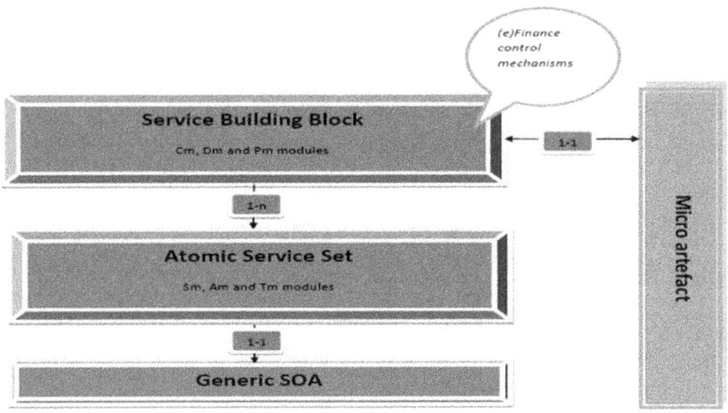

a finance management strategy by mimicking neural networks, to gain immense computational capabilities and to overcome the traditional silo-like computer science approach that is very dominant in the financial domain.

Decision and Risk Management System

Residual risks should be managed by existing governance frameworks where the verification and final acceptance of residual risks has to be managed by a specialized interface. If residual risks are to be accepted by the BTM, then the corresponding solution set of actions must be launched. These actions have to be cautiously monitored to ensure that the concerned business environment would not be exposed to unknown excessive risks that can cause failure. The risk identification process and actions' assessment designs are maintained by the governance processes and are maintained by the TOGAF's phase G that is responsible for implementation governance process that adjusts the business view. Risk monitoring must be implemented in all the BTP finance microartefacts and in the implementation governance so that the business environment can identify critical risks that are to be managed and which might need many iterations to be mitigated (The Open Group, 2011a).

The Finance Architecture and Infrastructure Critical Success Factors

This section's (CSA: FinanceArchitectureInfrastructure) set of filtered CSFs and their weightings are presented in Table 1.

Table 1. The finance architecture and infrastructure factors and indicators

Critical Success Factors	KPIs	Weightings
CSF_FinanceArchitectureInfrastructure_ HolisiticAgileView	ManagementView	From 1 to 10. **10 Selected**
CSF_FinanceArchitectureInfrastructure_RoleOfStandards	Mandatory	From 1 to 10. **05 Selected**
CSF_FinanceArchitectureInfrastructure_ServicesArchitecture	SOA	From 1 to 10. **07 Selected**
CSF_FinanceArchitectureInfrastructure_ADM	TOGAF	From 1 to 10. **04 Selected**
CSF_FinanceArchitectureInfrastructure_LoggingSystem	SYSLOG	From 1 to 10. **09 Selected**
CSF_FinanceArchitectureInfr	AR	From 1 to 10. **09 Selected**
CSF_FinanceArchitectureInfrastructure_MicroartefactDesign	DDD	From 1 to 10. **09 Selected**

The Modules Chained Link to Architecture and Infrastructure

The described *Environment* and its Fm need a specific finance engineering application that is based on various strategies and application concepts.

FINANCE BLOCK-CHAIN

A Radical Business Transformation Process

A block-chain, as shown in Figure 11, is a term that is used for a technology that permits business partners, who don't know each other, to commit trustful financial operations and to share the logging records of all financial (e)transactions, in a transparent manner. This sharing of logging records is virtual and is distributed to all users on the internet who use their computers to execute (e)transactions and this fact obsoletes the need for adding a third party to manage block-chains' interaction. These block-chains intermediaries are abundant and cause various types of problems and a loss of resources like money. Besides the Bitcoin block-chain, there are many block-chains supporters that have emerged in the recent decade. But none of these block-chains supporters has advanced like the Bitcoin block-chain, even if they propose services, like better performing (e)transactions, bigger data storages, alternate synchronization protocols and more robust business, hence financial functionalities. The Bitcoin block-chain protocol and the underlined internet support are the modern block-chain infrastructure that is a financial transfer platform. Besides these facts, a fundamental goal is to secure: 1) contracts; 2) physical and digital property; 3)

Figure 11. The Bitcoin block-chain
Grewal-Carr & Marshall, 2016.

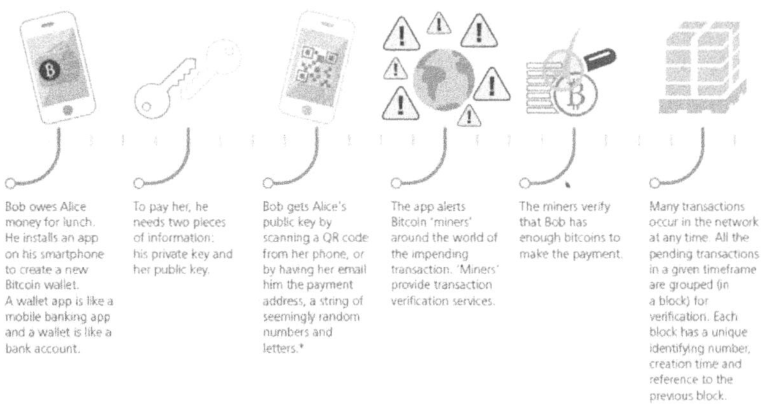

equities; 4) bonds; and many other types of financial operations. Automated decision making systems and applications are being created to support such block-chains like the Bitcoin protocol (Grewal-Carr & Marshall, 2016).

Bitcoin Block-Chain

It is an actual peer-to-peer (e)cash system that allows web based financial (e) transactions, including parties from different financial institutions. (e)Signatures secure such (e)transactions and they provide an important part to the final block-chain solution, where the main benefits can be lost if a trusted third party is needed. The solution to the supplementary costs problem is to use an automated peer-to-peer communication. The communication timestamps (e)transactions by hashing them into an ongoing block-chain of the hash-based subsystem, that creates logging records, which cannot be modified. The communication infrastructure requires minimal supplementary resources. Financial messages are broadcasted asynchronously, and communication nodes can join or leave dynamically, keeping the proof-of-work sequence on what has been executed. (e)Commerce relies practically only on financial institutions that support (e)payments. The transformed business system should work for all (e)transactions, but unfortunately there are inherent weaknesses of the basic infrastructure in all business environments. It is not possible to achieve hundred percent security of non-reversible (e)transactions, because financial institutions cannot function without mediating conflicts (Nakamoto, 2008).

Block-Chain (E)Transaction

The (e)coin is a sequence of digital (e)signatures where each coin owner transfers his (e)coin to the next node by electronically signing a hash and linking it to the previous (e)transaction and the public key of the next coin owner and adding them to the end of the (e)coin. The recipient node can verify the (e)signatures to verify the sequence of ownership. The problem lies in the recipient's inability to check whether some of the coin owners has used the coin multiple times. A BTP solution is to implement a trusted unique authority that checks each single (e)transaction for single usage. After the execution of a (e)transaction, the (e)coin must be transferred to the central authority and let it issue a new coin. Only the (e)coins that have been issued by the recipient are trusted to be used once. The difficulty that is related to the solution is that the management of the whole (e)money system is in the hands of the company that owns the central authority. The BTP must implement a control that insures that the recipient knows if the previous coin owners have joined previous (e) transactions. For that goal the previous (e)transaction is the point of reference and future activities are ignored. The unique method to control (e)transactions is to have them all centrally controlled. In the central authority control model that manages all (e)transactions, it can deduce which one was first received. To apply such a control mechanism without a trusted third party, is that (e)transactions must be publicly visible, and the transformed business environment must offer to participants the possibility to agree on a unique logging record subsystem that respects the order of reception, using timestamps servers and filters. The recipients need proof of the (e) transaction's execution and the synchronization of active node, as shown in Figure 12 (Nakamoto, 2008; Dai, 1998).

Bitcoin Block-Chain Status

A robust peer-to-peer protocol of (e)cash allows (e)payments to be executed from any node of the block-chain. The Gartner Hype Cycle provides a diagram of the (e) money maturity and adoption, and it shows how it is becoming relevant to solve real business problems. This Hype Cycle indicates that in 5 to 10 years the block-chain will reach global adoption, as shown in Figure 13.

The Bitcoin is further ahead of other block-chain technologies and the existing programmable economy group of companies. The block-chain neared the peak of the Gartner hype cycle for emerging technologies in the year 2016. Having the capacity to persist multiple concurrent (e)transactions in one unique ledger, that can be accessed by all trusted parties and is managed by a distributed network, this fact permits the block-chain to have an important transformational impact on business environments. The Bitcoin is emerging as the block-chain main actor and the block-

Figure 12. The (e)transaction execution sequence
Grewal-Carr & Marshall, 2016.

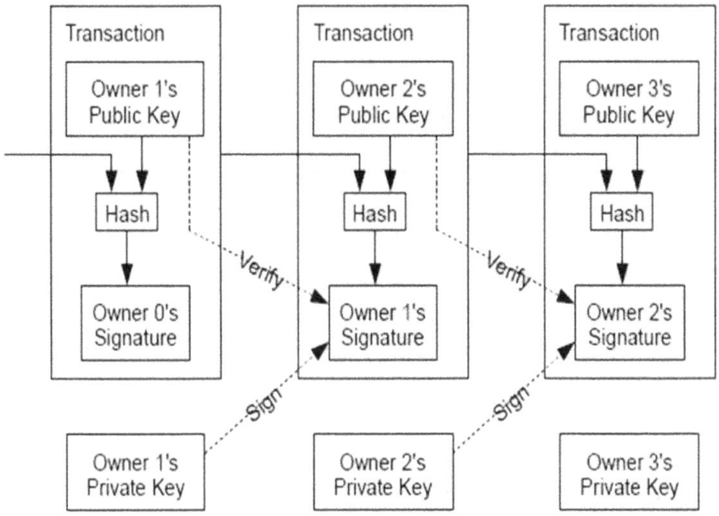

Figure 13. The hype cycle shows that in 5 to 10 years the block-chain will reach global adoption
Panetta, 2016.

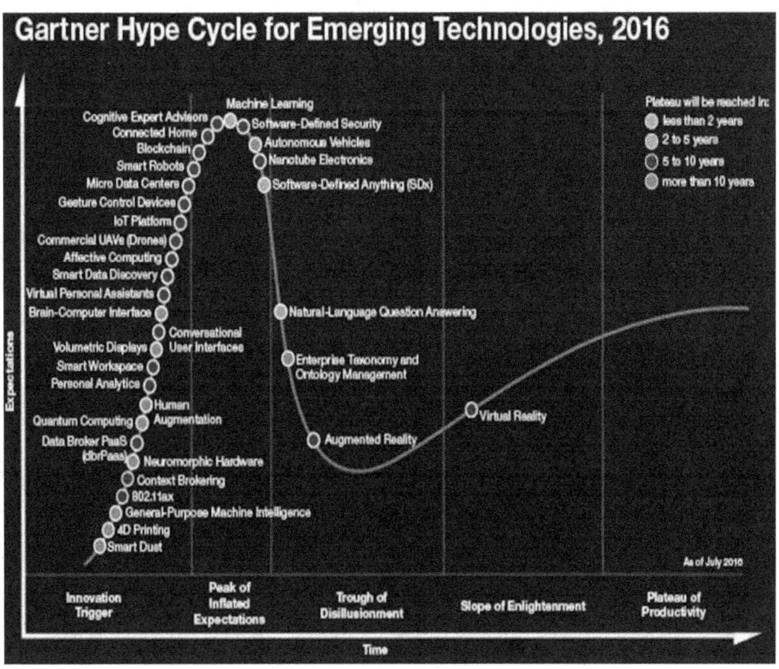

**For a more accurate representation see the electronic version.*

chain phenomena has evolved to include many other actors. Actually block-chain technologies are advancing because they give the hope that they could transform the actual financial domain operating models into dynamic and agile models. It is also a technology enabler that could revolutionise the underlying financial platforms. "Enterprise architects who are focused on technology innovation must evaluate these high-level trends and the featured technologies, as well as their potential impact value and risk for their businesses," said Mike Walker, research director at Gartner (Panetta, 2016).

The Finance Block-Chain's Setup Critical Success Factors

This section's (CSA: FinanceBlock-chain) set of filtered CSFs and their weightings are presented in Table 2.

SOLUTIONS AND RECOMMENDATIONS

The FERLC component's holistic integration is an important factor for the financial engineering environment's evolution and stability but this depends on the business environments technological maturity. Many industries have been implementing FERLC like local solutions to respond to probable risk and legal problems and challenges in production; and faced major technology challenges that jeopardised their BTPs.

FUTURE RESEARCH DIRECTIONS

The *Environment* future research will focus on a neural network based decision making module, which use a dynamic concept.

Table 2. The finance and legal integration factors and indicators

Critical Success Factors	KPIs	Weightings
CSF_FinanceBlock-chain_RadicalBusinessTransformation	Possible	From 1 to 10. **04 Selected**
CSF_FinanceBlock-chain_BitcoinBlock-chain	Mature	From 1 to 10. **03 Selected**
CSF_FinanceBlock-chain_Block-chainTransaction	Errors	From 1 to 10. **03 Selected**
CSF_FinanceBlock-chain_Bitcoin_Block-chainStatus	Automated	From 1 to 10. **02 Selected**

CONCLUSION

This research phase is part of a series of publications related to the business transformation projects and architectures and is based on mixed action research model; where critical success factors and areas are offered to help BTP architects to decrease the chances of failure. In this chapter the main focus was on the applied technology. Using and integrating technology is a key factor for the success of complex financial systems.

ACKNOWLEDGMENT

In a work as large as this research project, technical, typographical, grammatical, or other kinds of errors are bound to be present. Ultimately, all mistakes are the authors' responsibility. Nevertheless, the authors encourage feedback from readers identifying errors in addition to comments on the work in general. It was our great pleasure to prepare this work. Now our greater hopes are for readers to receive some small measure of that pleasure.

REFERENCES

APMG International. (2011). *Agile Project Management White Paper*. APMG International.

Cummins, F. (2010). Building the Agile Enterprise-with SOA, business process model and MBM. Morgan Kaufmann Publications.

Farhoomand, A. (2004). *Managing (e)business transformation*. Palgrave Macmillan. doi:10.1007/978-1-137-08380-7

Gartner. (2013). *Scenario Toolkit: Using EA to Support Business Transformation*. Gartner Inc.

Gray, P. (1997). *Artificial legal intelligence*. Dartmouth Publishing Co.

Grewal-Carr, V., & Marshall, S. (2016). *Block-chain Enigma. Paradox. Opportunity*. London, UK: Deloitte LLP.

IFRS. (2017). *IFRS Standards*. Retrieved April 2017, from http://www.ifrs.org/Pages/default.aspx. IFRS.

International Monetary Fund. (2009). Switzerland: Financial Sector Assessment Program - Detailed Assessment of Observance of Financial Sector Standards and Codes. International Monetary Fund.

ISACA. (2015). *IT Control Objectives for Sarbanes-Oxley Using COBIT 5* (3rd ed.). ISACA.

ISDA. (2017). *FpML*. Retrieved April 2017, from https://www2.isda.org/functional-areas/technology-infrastructure/fpml/

ITGI. (2007). *COBIT 4.1- Framework Control Objectives Management Guidelines Maturity Models*. IT Governance Institute.

Jin, K., & Zhu, J. (2011). *MET: Multi-party E-Commerce Transaction Model. Privacy, Security, Risk and Trust (PASSAT)*. 2011 IEEE Third International Conference on Social Computing (SocialCom), 2011 IEEE Third International Conference, Boston, MA.

Jin, K., & Zhu, J. (2011). *MET: Multi-party E-Commerce Transaction Model*. IEEE Third International Conference on Social Computing (SocialCom), 2011 IEEE Third International Conference, Boston, MA.

Kabzeva, A., Niemann, M., Müller, P., & Steinmetz, P. (2010). Applying TOGAF to Define and Govern a Service-oriented Architecture in a Large-scale "research & development" (R&D). *Proceedings of the Sixteenth Americas Conference on Information Systems*.

Khoshafian, D. (2014). *Intelligent BPM the next wave for customer-centric business applications*. Pegasystems Inc.

Kowall, J., & Fletcher, C. (2013). Modernize Your Monitoring Strategy by Combining Unified Monitoring and Log Analytics Tools. Gartner.

Kyte, A. (2010). Nine Critical Success Factors for Business Value -Through Application Overhaul. Gartner Inc.

Nagois log server. (2015). *Unified logging system. Nag*ios. Retrieved April 2017, from https://exchange.nagios.org/directory/Addons/Log-File-Management/Nagios-Log-Server/details

Nakamoto, S. (2008). *Bitcoin: A Peer-to-Peer Electronic Cash System*. Retrieved from www.bitcoin.org

OASIS. (2009). *OASIS Web Services Reliable Messaging (WS-ReliableMessaging) Version 1.2*. OASIS Standard. Retrieved January 2017, from http://docs.oasis-open.org/ws-rx/wsrm/200702/wsrm-1.2-spec-os.html

Olson, L. (2008). *Synchronize UDDI registries with WebSphere Service Registry and Repository for better SOA governance*. IBM.

Panetta, K. (2016). *3 Trends Appear in the Gartner Hype Cycle for Emerging Technologies, 2016. Are block-chain, smart machines, IoT and other emerging technologies on their way up or down the Hype Cycle?* Retrieved March 2017, from http://www.gartner.com/smarterwithgartner/3-trends-appear-in-the-gartner-hype-cycle-for-emerging-technologies-2016/

Peterson, S. (2011). *Why it Worked: Critical Success Factors of a Financial Reform Project in Africa*. Faculty Research Working Paper Series. Harvard Kennedy School.

Shahrokhi, M. (2008). E-finance: Status, Innovations, Resources and Future Challenges. *Managerial Finance*, *34*(6), 365–398. doi:10.1108/03074350810872787

Taleb, N. (2007). *The Black Swan-The Impact of the Highly Improbable*. Random House, Inc.

Taleb, N. (2012). *Antifragile: Things that gain from disorder*. Library of Congress Cataloguing-in-Publication Data.

Tan, W., Carter, A., & Toleman, M. (2009). *Implementing information technology services management: A case study focusing on critical success factors*. Toowoomba, Australia: Univ. of Southern Queensland.

The Open Group. (2011a). *Risk and monitoring (2014). Risk Monitoring and Governance (Phase G)*. Retrieved March 2017, from http://pubs.opengroup.org/architecture/togaf9-doc/arch/chap31.html#tag_31_07

The Open Group. (2011b). *Gap Analysis*. Retrieved March 2017, from http://pubs.opengroup.org/architecture/togaf9-doc/arch/chap27.html

The Open Group. (2014a). *The Open Group's Architecture Framework-Building blocks-Module 13*. Retrieved March 2017, from www.open-group.com/togaf

The Open Group. (2014b). *The Open Group's Architecture Framework*. Retrieved March 2017, from www.open-group.com/togaf

The Open Group. (2015a). *Architecture Skills Framework*. The Open Group. Retrieved April 2017, from http://pubs.opengroup.org/architecture/togaf8-doc/arch/chap30.html

Trad, A. (2017a). *Using Google analytics to determine the leading business transformation framework that are based on enterprise architecture*. IBISTM.

Trad, A. (2017b). *The Transformation Framework's Resources Library*. IBISTM.

Trad, A., & Kalpić, D. (2015a). *The Business Engineering Transformation Framework for (e)commerce Architecture-Modelling Projects. In Encyclopedia of E-Commerce Development, Implementation, and Management*. IGI-Global.

Trad, A., & Kalpić, D. (2015b). *The Business Engineering Transformation Framework for (e)commerce Control and Monitoring Pattern. In Encyclopedia of E-Commerce Development, Implementation, and Management*. IGI-Global.

Trad, A., & Kalpić, D. (2017a). The Business Transformation and Enterprise Architecture Framework-The Financial Engineering Global Strategy. IGI-Global. (under review)

Trad, A., & Kalpić, D. (2017b). The Business Transformation and Enterprise Architecture Framework-The The Financial Engineering (e)Risk Management and (e)Law Integration. IGI-Global. (under review)

Trad, A. & Kalpić, D. (2017c). *A Neural Networks Portable and Agnostic Implementation Environment for Business Transformation Projects-The Agnostic Implementation Environment.* Submitted article.

Trad, A., & Kalpić, D. (2014a). The Selection and Training Framework (STF) for Managers in Business Innovation and Transformation Projects - Integrating the restructuring process of the global economy. IMRA.

ValuAdder. (2017). *Business Valuation: The Three Approaches*. Retrieved March 2017, from http://www.valuadder.com/valuationguide/business-valuation-three-approaches.html

XBRL. (2017). *XBRL, the business reporting standard*. Retrieved January 2017, from https://www.xbrl.org

ADDITIONAL READING

Farhoomand, A. (2004). *Managing Business Engineering transformation*. Palgrave Macmillan.

KEY TERMS AND THEIR DEFINITIONS

Business Engineering: The development and implementation of business solutions using business models to business processes and organizational structure.

CSFs: Can be used to manage the statuses and gaps in various project plans and gives the projects the capacity to proactively and automatically recognize erroneous building blocks and to just-in-time reschedule the project plan(s).

Environment: This research's framework.

Manager: Business transformation manager.

Project: Business transformation project.

Chapter 3
The Business Transformation and Enterprise Architecture Framework:
The Financial Engineering E-Risk Management and E-Law Integration

Antoine Trad
IBISTM, France

Damir Kalpić
University of Zagreb, Croatia

ABSTRACT

To include a business transformation project or an enterprise architecture project in the enterprise's business and financial strategic planning process and to prepare this enterprise to integrate the local and the global economy in a sustainable way, the integration of financial-engineering-related risk and legal controls is necessary and is even fundamental. These finance-related risk and legal standards are not mature and are chaotic, so these facts can damage the business transformation project or an enterprise architecture project and that may disable the traditional business environments to be a part of the networked global economy.

DOI: 10.4018/978-1-5225-4026-7.ch003

INTRODUCTION

To include a business transformation project or an enterprise architecture project in the enterprise's business and financial strategic planning process and to prepare this enterprise to integrate the local and the global economy in a sustainable way, the integration of financial engineering related risk and legal controls is necessary and is even fundamental. Actually, these finance related risk and legal standards are not mature and are chaotic, so these facts can damage the business transformation project or an enterprise architecture project and that may disable the traditional business environments to be a part of the networked global economy (Trad & Kalpić, 2014a). An important factor in frequent business transformation projects' changes and iterations are the roles of the business transformation manager, finance analysts and enterprise architect(s) who should be supported by the optimal business transformation framework that should include holistic financial control mechanisms. These holistic mechanisms should be also capable of supporting the business environment's financial engineering risk management, legal control and integration in a complex block-chain globalized environment. To achieve this financial engineering risk and legal integration, critical success areas and critical success factors must be used to evaluate legal pitfalls, risk, audit, assert, govern, automate, trace, monitor and control of the business transformation project's financial budget. The business transformation project or an enterprise's architecture project critical success factors can be configured to manage the complexities in managing asynchronous financial flows of (e)business local and international financial environments. Transformed business environments have to have built-in automated block-chain controls capable of recognizing fraud, black swan effects (Taleb, 2007), bad investments, business transformation project budget slips, loss of (e)transactions, illegal activities and tax evasions (Trad & Kalpić, 2015a; Trad & Kalpić, 2015b).

The Business Transformation Project's (BTM) role is of crucial importance for the implementation phase of the complex Business Transformation Projects (BTP) and also enterprise architecture projects; where the BTM or enterprise architect's decisions can be made in a just-in-time manner by using outputs from the business environment's existing tracing, monitoring and logging systems; to asses risk and legally assert, govern or control the BTP's various resources and components. Unfortunately, a huge set of automated factors can influence such an undertaking, like: 1) the influence of accounting in business transformation projects; and 2) the holistic financial (e)law control mechanisms for such projects are non-existent and are complex to implement.

Figure 1. The (e)finance mechanisms interaction with business transformation project's framework

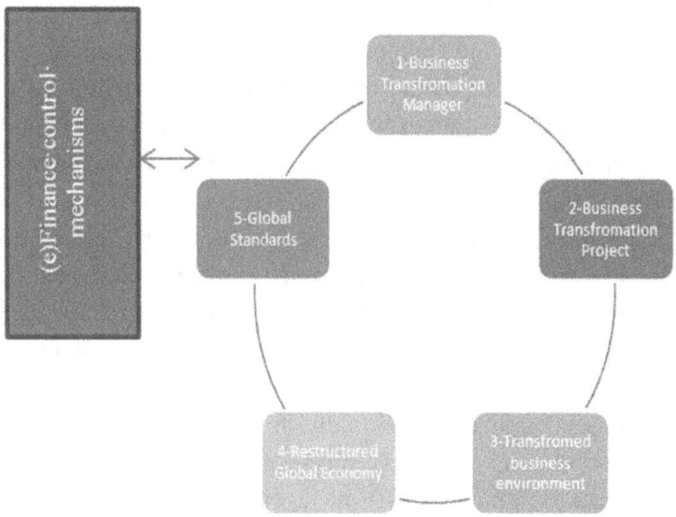

A global financial subsystem's approach is optimal for such control mechanisms like the integration and use of the Financial Engineering Risk and (e)Law Control (FERLC) component via the use of microartefacts (Daellenbach & McNickle, 2005). In this research the focus is on FERLC module that is a part of this research project's finance module (Trad & Kalpić, 2016a), as shown in Figure 1 where it interacts with the external world via an implemented framework.

The BTM has to handle the complex and chaotic technical implementation phase of the BTP and define its enterprise architecture structure comprising actions that can cause high failure rates and important budget losses (CapGemini, 2009). Therefore the implementations of web technologies resources in BTPs require specific (e)financial engineering architecture strategy and implementation knowledge (Investopedia, 2017a). A financial engineering training curriculum must combine finance, management sciences, risk management, enterprise architecture, maths, statistics, traditional inefficient business administration, law, economics, technology, finance and business engineering. Such a curriculum is in fact a specialized business, finance engineering and technology programme that should be enforced with business administration topics (Wikipedia, 2015; Universität St. Gallen, 2015). For this specific goal the Institute of Business and Information Systems' Transformation Management (IBISTM) has developed: 1) a real world framework; 2) business education curriculum; 3) specialized training programmes; and 4) various certification programmes, to support BTMs and hence BTPs (Trad, 2017a; Trad, 2017b).

BACKGROUND

The Research and Development Project

The BTPs' oriented research and development project is based on the main fact that only about 12% of business companies successfully terminate business transformation projects and have the capacity to finally outperform any concurrent organization (Tidd & Bessant, 2009; Tidd, 2006). BTP's research is a very complex study that takes many years and demands a large effort, because it is a huge subject and requests a study from various angles of perspective (Trad & Kalpić, 2015c), where a BTP specialized transformation framework is essential for the BTP's financial engineering topics and its main goal is to propose a set of finance specific managerial recommendations to enforce FERLCs' requirements (Trad, 2017a; Trad, 2017b). Such a BTP framework would help to avoid financial traps and business conflicts that can cause very high costs (Ford, 2007). This research article is strongly bonded to two other articles and they create a whole on financial risk management:

- The Business Transformation and Enterprise Architecture Framework-The Financial Engineering Technology Concept (Trad, Kalpić, 2017a).
- The Business Transformation and Enterprise Architecture Framework-The Financial Engineering Technology Concept (Trad, Kalpić, 2017b).

These interrelated three articles form a whole to solve this phase's research question and they are this question is proved by a unique set of literature and a proof of concept.

(e)Business Transformation

Managing (e)business transformation is the journey from an archaic monolithic enterprise to an internetworked enterprise where information technologies are the main structure and they link business clients, suppliers, partners and employees to create economic value. The transformation privileges the integration of internet technologies throughout the business environment's value chain and that is essential to manage client relationships. Such a transformation binds business, finance and economic principles within the context of a networked business environment; and that enhance the business environments decision making capacities (Farhoomand, Lynne, Markus, Gable, Khan, 2004). The International Institute for Analytics recommends: 1) to embrace enterprise decision making and artificial intelligence; 2) to clearly define BTM and enterprise architects' executives roles; 3) to build a proof of concepts to decrease costs and to balance between prototyping and final deployment; and 4) to setup an in-house BTP and enterprise architecture framework that includes a global strategy for financial requirements in business transformation projects (Laskowski, 2017).

Defining the Global Strategy

(e)Business is a business engineering field that combines management sciences, business administration, (e)law and economics with information technologies and engineering (Wikipedia, 2015; Universität St. Gallen, 2015). An important part of (e)business provides financial services or (e)finance over the web. Today many business companies have standardized their governance, control and monitoring architecture; comparing this to less than 10% in 2014; this proves that the FERLC's integration is a strategic goal for BTPs and financial engineering projects (Kowall, & Fletcher, 2013; Shahrokhi, 2008: BTP can help banks and financial institutions reshape their e-business program, like during the 2008 financial crisis, where the strategy focus was on geographical reach, redefining global initiatives and reorganizing the trade services and prioritizing a customer-centric approach. Citibank restructured its activity centres and redefined its global strategy to assist customers in solving financial problems. Citibank's BTP was very quick and the landscape for treasury and trade services was deeply modified to stand up again after the financial crisis. Multi-functional-banking which is a form of block-chaining based on web technologies enabled low cost and efficient financial operations. Citibank was the first financial institution to finalize a BTP and that had a significant impact on the banking business model for (e) finance engineering integration (Farhoomand & Lentini, 2008; Trad & Kalpić, 2017b).

Applied (e)Finance Engineering Integration

The industry needs a multimode (e)finance model that minimizes the dependencies between various business partners; where (e)finance connections are established between the consumer and the end business environment with minimal risks (Jin & Zhu, 2011). An important CSF that can be integrated in the BTP is the cost of (e) finance ratio before and after the BTP completion. To calculate costs related to (e) finance operations there is the need to add-up the total cost of providing financial services and to divide it by the total number of successfully executed financial (e) transactions (Government Service Design, 2015). BTPs' (e)finances' outcomes have to be controlled in real-time and routine financial reports must be reported to the BTM and to the business enterprise's executive management (Fu & Mittnight, 2015; Xiaohong, 2011). (e)finance impact's on BTPs depends on security violations and the degree of needed automation. Knowing that integration means an (e)finance block–chain integration which is in most cases a radical transformation process (Trad, Kalpić, 2017b).

(e)Finance Block-Chain-A Radical Business Transformation Process

A block-chain, is a term that is used for an applied technology that it supports business partners, who don't know each other and want to commit trustful financial operations and to share the logging records of all financial (e)transactions, in a transparent manner. This sharing of logging records is virtual and is distributed to all users on the internet who use their work stations to execute (e)transactions and this fact obsoletes the need for adding a third party to manage block-chains. These block-chains intermediaries are many and cause various types of problems and loss of money. Besides the Bitcoin block-chain there are many block-chains supporters that have emerged in the recent decade. But none of these block-chains supporters have advanced like the Bitcoin block-chain, even if they propose services, like better performing (e)transactions, bigger data storages, alternate synchronization protocols and more robust business, hence financial functionalities and these are this article's main focus (Trad & Kalpić, 2017a).

MAIN FOCUS OF THE ARTICLE

Financial residual risks have to be evaluated by existing governance frameworks where the BTP's monitoring of financial residual risks is an essential undertaking. In the case that financial residual risks have been accepted by the BTM and his team, then the needed actions are launched to insure a solution. The applied actions have to be carefully monitored to ensure that the concerned business environment would not face excessive risks that can cause the BTP's failure. The risk identification process and actions' assessment designs are maintained by the governance processes and are maintained by The Open Group's Architecture Framework's (TOGAF) phase G that is responsible for the implementation of governance processes that adjust the business view. Financial risk monitoring must be implemented in all of the BTP microartefacts and the implementation of financial governance must be able to identify critical risks and evaluate the business competiveness (The Open Group, 2011a; Trad & Kalpić, 2017a). Business valuation is a process and a related set of procedures that can be applied to estimate the value of a business environment, this is a complex undertaking to evaluate a business value that has to be precisely estimated and is based on the value of concrete business valuation's assumptions that can be configured with a transformation framework (ValuAdder, 2017; Trad & Kalpić, 2017a).

FRAMEWORK SETUP

FERLC draws its architecture, concept and framework implementation from the services based Financial Information and Communication Technology Systems (FICTS) built years ago and was reengineered because of the hyper evolution in web technologies and business organization (Trad, 2007). FERLC promotes (e) financial engineering driven business environments that use reference to various types of financial activities that are conducted by using different types of avant-garde technologies, electronic media and services oriented technologies; where the most common form is the business that makes its transactions and revenue via the web, using block-chain automation (e-business, 2014). The FERLC can be applied to many BTPs and general financial engineering fields; and this component is the main focus of this research phase. The FERLC component is a part of the Financial management module (Fm); Fm is also a part of the Selection management, Architecture-modelling, Control-monitoring, Decision-making, Training management, Project management, and Finance management Framework, as shown in Figure 2 (SmAmCmDmTmPmFmF, for simplification in further text the term *Environment* will be used), that is the major support for of BTP's activities; in fact the proposed very modest framework is a leader in this market (Trad, 2017a; Trad, 2017b).

In 2015, we could simply talk of plain financial engineering, because many engineering artefacts like service oriented architecture, business process choreography have merged with financial engineering fields; therefore there is a need for financial engineering risk and legal robustness that are supported by the *Environment*'s Fm module, which covers all the financial engineering domain aspects.

The BTP's global research topic's and final research question (hypothesis #1-1) is: "Which business transformation manager characteristics and which type of support should be assured in the implementation phase of a business transformation project?" The targeted business domain is any business environment that uses: 1) internet and engineering technologies; and 2) frequent transformation iterations. For this phase of research the sub-question (hypothesis #7-1) is: "What is the impact of the financial engineering risk management and legal support on (e)enterprise architecture and business transformation projects?". The *Environment* or the SmAmCmDmTmPmFmF acronym is composed of the following modules (Trad, 2015a; Trad, 2015b):

- "Sm" for the selection management of the BTM (based on the set of hypotheses #1-x).
- "Am" for the architecture and modelling strategy that can be applied by the BTM (based on the set of hypotheses #2-x).
- "Cm" for the control and monitoring strategy that can be applied by the BTM (based on the set of hypotheses #3-x).
- "Dm" for the decision making strategy that can be applied by the BTM (based on the set of hypotheses #4-x).
- "Tm" for the training management of the BTM (based on the set of hypotheses #5-x).
- "Pm" for the project management strategy that can be applied by the BTM (based on the set of hypotheses #6-x).
- "Fm" for the Financial management's support to the BTPs (based on the set of hypotheses #7-x).

The Environment

In this research phase the authors are targeting the FERLC component's integration that is a part of the Financial management (Fm) module and analysing its influence on BTPs. Actually there is a lack of awareness of financial engineering integration that can hinder the financial status of business environments. This barrier for a successful BTP's finalization has to be handled and in this article the authors use industrial experiences made and lessons learned from surveying many enterprises. The literature review's outcome was that business enterprises are insufficiently informed about the effects of financial engineering risk and legal mechanisms that

Figure 2. The Environment case tool

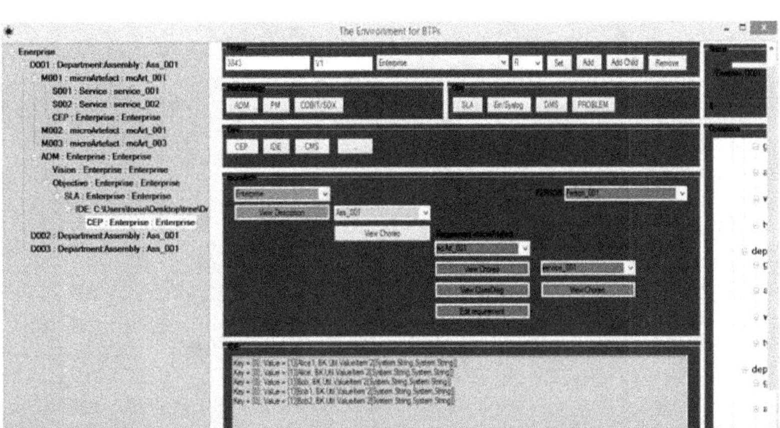

can be integrated in their enterprise architecture. An important number of these enterprises (45.8%) have brought up this fact and it seems that the problem lies in the current possibilities to integrate financial engineering's related controls. This integration can be considered to be a global legal barrier and a BTP major issue where the arising financial risk and legal problems can impact all the partners of the (e)finances' execution process (Merriam-Webster, 2015).

Critical Success Areas and Factors

Critical Success Area (CSA) is a category of Critical Success Factors (CSF) where in turn a CSF is a set of Key Performance Indicators (KPIs), where a KPI corresponds to a single requirement, as shown in Figure 3. CSFs for a BTP or business environment are a limited number of business sub-areas in which values are satisfactory if ensuring successful competitive business performance. CSFs reflect performance areas that map to strategic goals and defined financial constraints. The BTP must

Figure 3. The factors and indicators' relationships

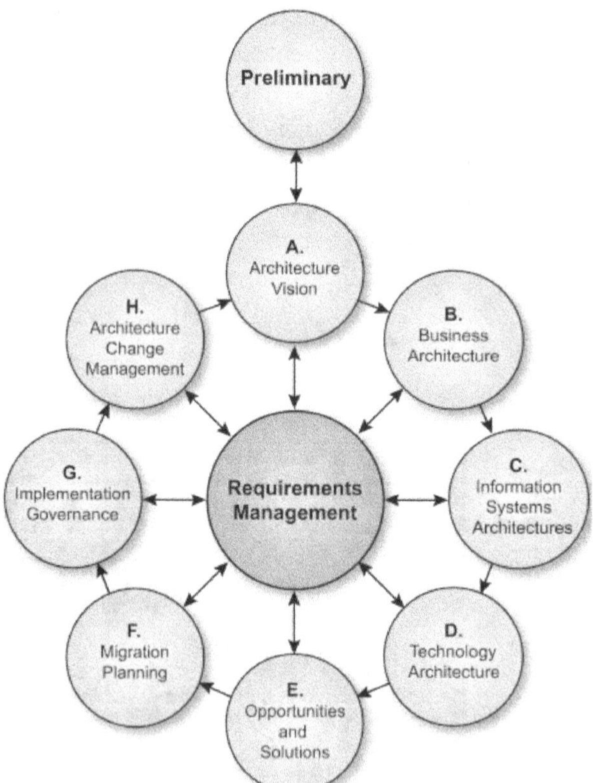

select the right CSFs in order to survive and to prepare for competition. For that goal the BTP must find the Critical Success Areas (CSAs) that require constant and special care in real-time; added to that it needs important attention from the business environment's executive management. According to Rockart, who published in the Harvard Business Review: "Critical success factors for any business are the limited number of areas in which results, if they meet business goals, will ensure successful competitive performance for the organization". Therefore, CSFs reflect performance areas that must meet strategic goals and defined financial constraints; if the target business environment wants to have a sane business future. Measurements are used to evaluate performance in each CSA, where CSFs can be internal and/or external; like for example: 1) budget gap analysis is an internal CSF; and 2) percent of market share is an external CSF. The *Environment* method to select the CSA category and the corresponding CSFs is to audit the enterprise architecture vision and strategic planning process. Once the initial set of CSFs has been identified, then the BTP has to use the decision making module to verify the CSFs and to give them the right weightings. The BTP team has to identify the initial set of CSFs to be used for the performance measurement system. Hence CSFs are the most important mapping/relation between strategic planning, enterprise architecture vision and decision making system's performance measurement systems; and an example of possible operational CSAs, CSFs and KPIs can be (Peterson, 2011; Evans, 2017):

- **Customer Service CSA:** CSFs: 1) Price; 2) Delivery; 3) Support; and 4) Satisfaction; CSF KPIs I) Price; and II) number of deliveries; etc.
- **Internal Operations CAS:** CSFs: 1) Efficiency; 2) Costs; 3) Production; and 4) Inventories. CSF KPIs I) Cycle times; II) inventory turnovers; and III) targets met etc.
- **Innovation CSA. CSFs:** 1) develop products; 2; e) marketing; 3) avant-garde technologies; and 4) research and development ;...) CSF KPI's: I) Number of new products; II) number of patents; III) new technologies adopted; and IV) system improvements implemented, etc.
- **Financial CSA:** CSFs: 1) Profitability; 2) Growth; and 3) Value. CSF KPI's: I) Return on equity; II) growth rate compared to industry growth rate; and III) levels of operating cash flow, etc.

The Framework's Setup Critical Success Factors

This section's (CSA: FrameworkSetup) set of filtered CSFs and their weightings are shown in Table 1.

Table 1. The framework setup factors and indicators

Critical Success Factors	KPIs	Weightings
CSF_FrameworkSetup_AllModulesExist.	NoFilter	From 1 to 10. **10 Selected**
CSF_FrameworkSetup_CSFManagementComponentExists.	CSA Private	From 1 to 10. **10 Selected**
CSF_FrameworkSetup_IntegratedDevelopmentEnvironments.	MS VS 2013	From 1 to 10. **07 Selected**
CSF_FrameworkSetup_BTPTeamHaveTheSkills4Framework.	Engineers&Above	From 1 to 10. **08 Selected**
CSF_FrameworkSetup_Operations.	CustomerService	From 1 to 10. **08 Selected**

The Modules Chained Link to Legal Integration

The *Environment* and its Fm module need a legal integration concept that is based on agile business methodologies and atomic services based on an anti-fragile concept.

(e)FINANCE AND LEGAL INTEGRATION

The evolution of financial and business engineering forces various industries to implement FERLC like mechanisms into their business transformation frameworks. Such frameworks must incorporate (e)finances legal collaboration with: 1) international; 2) national; 3) electronic; and 4) local-regional laws, governance frameworks and rules. Added to international and national laws there are legal frameworks, conventions, treaties and directives to be integrated to support the transformed business environment as shown in Figure 4.

The United Nations Commission on International Trade Law

The hyper evolution of web technologies in finance has enabled the stakeholders to embrace regulations for (e)finances operations (Wright, 1991). The flagrant rise in the volume of (e)finances operations has imposed new rules to this complex issue. The ever increasing numbers of (e)finances in international, national and local financial and trade operations are stored by means of standardized financial messages interchange using web technologies. (e)finance replaces the archaic traditional finance transactions exchanges and replaces the monolithic systems' based exchanges to enhance productivity and to enable real-time FERLC supervision (Chissick & Kelman, 2000).

The United Nations Commission pushes to establish an International Trade Law (UNCITRAL), which is a basic model for (e)law related domains. This (e)law framework is downwards compatible with all national and regional legal systems. The

Figure 4. Financial transaction automation and regulation
OASIS, 2009.

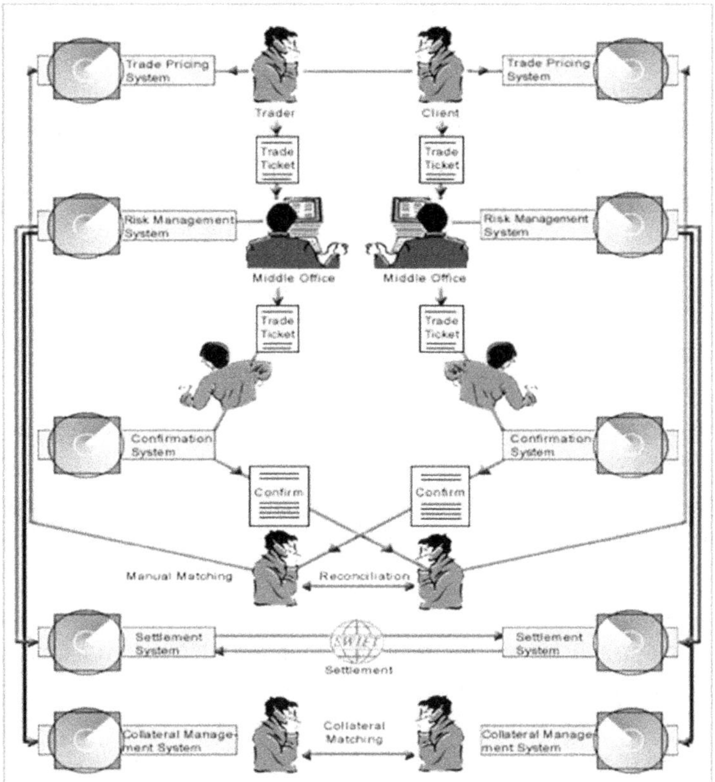

BTMs should be aware of various (e)law frameworks which regulate cross-border (e)finance and (e)commerce collaboration, that is a crucial undertaking for global BTPs. The future BTP should accommodate all future legal issues and challenges in the future business environment. Based on this feature, the FERLC integration must be tuneable, flexible, feasible and portable; this can be achieved by linking a specific (e)law act with a specific CSF or KPI. The *Environment* offers a tuneable FERLC to wrap the existing national legal corpus and to be synchronized with the international legal frameworks that manage the borderless nature of (e)finances (United Nations, 2004).

The European Union's (e)Commerce Directive

The European commission offers a legislation that can be implemented to govern (e)finance collaboration, and that is an important support for the FERLC. European commission's member states have implemented and enforced Financial engineering related national practices (European commission, 2015a). The integration of the FERLC module is done with the use of the standardized financial and legal environments of The Open Group's Architecture Framework (The Open Group, 2015a). This financial and legal environments support financial data protection laws, contract and transaction laws, procurement law, fraud law and many other legislation domains. The BTP team and enterprise architects must design a finance microartefact pattern that binds:

- The initial financial requirement, with
- The applied financial or business process model, with
- The (e)finance building blocks and services, with
- The service level agreement, with
- A well-defined and automated set of (e)law articles and regulations to be respected by the financial service, with
- The possible set of legal and business risks, which are represented by a critical success factor.

The BTM and his team must have the needed set of skills to design a financial microartefact pattern that integrates various finance and legislation topics to be used by the *Environment's* Decision management (Dm) subsystem.

Decision System Integration and Risk Management

The Dm subsystem is a generic subsystem that delivers a set of possible solutions to encountered problems or queries. It is generic because it can assist the BTP in solving various types of problems, such as possible financial and legal pitfalls. The Dm can be also represented as an implementation of a heuristics tree model; such a model is optimal because of the empirical nature of the problems to be solved (Trad & Kalpić, 2014c).

The Finance and Legal Integration's Setup Critical Success Factors

This section's (CSA: FinanceLegalIntegration) set of filtered CSFs and their weightings are shown in Table 2.

The Module's Chained Link to the Proof of Concept

Such an *Environment* and its Fm subsystem need to be proved by a proof of concept.

Table 2. Finance and legal integration factors and indicators

Critical Success Factors	KPIs	Weightings
CSF_FinanceLegalIntegration_DecisionSystemRiskMng	Integrated	From 1 to 10. **10 Selected**
CSF_ FinanceLegalIntegration _InternationalRegulations	Automated	From 1 to 10. **04 Selected**
CSF_ FinanceLegalIntegration _EuropeanRegulations	Automated	From 1 to 10. **06 Selected**

PROOF OF CONCEPT

The proof of concept was built using the *Environment* that has been built using the Microsoft Visual Studio .NET development environment; the proof of concept is based on the CSFs' indicators binding to a requirement, where the FERLC was prototyped using Sparxsystem's Enterprise Architect environment. FERLC uses atomic services that make calls to the FERLC microartefacts. The reasoning model represents the relations between the (e)finance's requirement, microartefacts or building block and the ADM. Where:

- The proof of concept uses all the *Environment's* modules and more specifically, the decision making module.
- The BTM, the BTP team members and the (e)enterprise's risk and legal team, link the KPIs to the targeted requirements in a one-to-one manner.
- Risk and legal constraints relate to specific (e)finances' building blocks. This linking is done through the use of critical factors to specific legal acts to be asserted.
- The (e)finances' model contains exception classes which check the legal constraints and if one or more of these constraints are violated, the (e)finance is paused and warning messages are stored in the (e)system's log-server. The warnings are escalated to the support team.
- The financial engineering component scans the log-server for possible violations and if found, they are automatically reported to corresponding enterprise's department.

Critical Success Areas, Factors, and Indicators Setup

The initial values have been presented in this article in Tables 1 and 2. Critical success factors' indicators bind requirements to various legal acts, frameworks, standards, rules and service agreements; they can be selected from the *Environment's* widget, as shown in Figure 5.

Figure 5. Factors and indicators selection

As shown in Figure 6, the factors and indicators are stored in an XML file where the link CSA, CSF, KPI and requirements is presented.

The Risk and Legal Requirement Link to Problem Solving

In Figure 6 the REQ_ID refers to a special section of the requirements XML document that contains also the needed information on actions and constraints to solve the problem, as shown in Figure 7.

Solution Providing

The decision making system delivers that the environment must define a setup phase if the budget permits, otherwise just ignore this phase.

Figure 6. Factors and indicators file

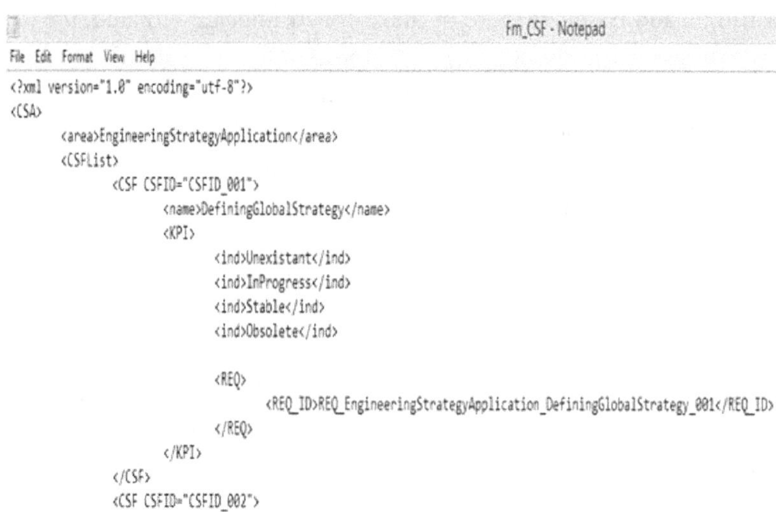


```
<?xml version="1.0" encoding="utf-8"?>
<CSA>
        <area>EngineeringStrategyApplication</area>
        <CSFList>
                <CSF CSFID="CSFID_001">
                        <name>DefiningGlobalStrategy</name>
                        <KPI>
                                <ind>Unexistant</ind>
                                <ind>InProgress</ind>
                                <ind>Stable</ind>
                                <ind>Obsolete</ind>

                                <REQ>
                                        <REQ_ID>REQ_EngineeringStrategyApplication_DefiningGlobalStrategy_001</REQ_ID>
                                </REQ>
                        </KPI>
                </CSF>
                <CSF CSFID="CSFID_002">
```

Figure 7. Requirements and actions mapping

```
<REQS>
      <Set>EngineeringStrategyApplication</Set>
      <REQ  ID="DefiningGlobalStrategy_001">
            <name>DefiningGlobalStrategy</name>
            <Problems>
                  <Problem>Unexistant</Problem>
                        <Action>Setup</Action>
                        <Action>Ignore</Action>
                        <Action>Audit</Action>

            </Problems>
      </REQ>
```

CONCLUSION

The FERLC component's holistic integration is an important factor for the financial engineering environment's evolution and stability. Many industries have been implementing FERLC like local solutions to respond to probable risk and legal problems and challenges in production. This research phase is part of a series of publications related to the business transformation projects and architectures. This research is based on mixed action research model; where critical success factors and areas are offered to help BTP architects to decrease the chances of failure. The *Environment's* FERLC offers managerial recommendations and a real-world proof of concept that rounds up the FERLC component's characteristics for business transformation projects.

ACKNOWLEDGMENT

In a work as large as this research project, technical, typographical, grammatical, or other kinds of errors are bound to be present. Ultimately, all mistakes are the authors' responsibility. Nevertheless, the authors encourage feedback from readers identifying errors in addition to comments on the work in general. It was our great pleasure to prepare this work. Now our greater hopes are for readers to receive some small measure of that pleasure.

REFERENCES

Capgemini. (2009). *Business transformation: From crisis response to radical changes that will create tomorrow's business.* A Capgemini Consulting Survey.

Chissick, M., & Kelman, A. (2000). *Electronic commerce: law and practice* (2nd ed.). London: Sweet & Maxwell.

Daellenbach, H., McNickle, D., & Dye, S. (2012). *Management Science. Decision-making through systems thinking* (2nd ed.). Plagrave Macmillian.

E-Business. (2014). Retrieved from http://dictionary.reference.com/browse/e-business.dictionary.com

European Commission. (2015a). *e-Business legal aspects*. European Commission. Retrieved from http://ec.europa.eu/enterprise/sectors/ict/documents/e-business/index_en.htm

Evans, M. (2017). Critical Success Factors Defined. *Exinfm*. Retrieved from http://www.exinfm.com/board/critical_success_factors.htm

Farhoomand, A. (2004). *Managing (e)business transformation*. Palgrave Macmillan. doi:10.1007/978-1-137-08380-7

Farhoomand, A., & Lentini, D. (2008). *e-Business Transformation in the Banking Industry: The Case of Citibank*. Retrieved from http://www.acrc.hku.hk/case/case_showdetails.asp?ct=newly&c=944&cp=1949&pt=1

Farhoomand, A., Lynne, M., Markus, M., Gable, G., & Khan, H. (2004). *Managing (e) business Transformation: A global Perspective*. Palgrave Macmillan. doi:10.1007/978-1-137-08380-7

Ford, J. (2007). *How Much Is Conflict Costing You?* John Ford and Associates. Retrieved from www.johnford.com

Fu, Z., & Mittnight, E. (2015). *Critical Success Factors for Continually Monitoring, Evaluating and Assessing Management of Enterprise IT*. ISACA. Retrieved from http://www.isaca.org/COBIT/focus/Pages/critical-success-factors-for-continually-monitoring-evaluating-and-assessing-management-of-enterprise-it.aspx

Investopedia. (2017a). *What is 'Financial Engineering'*. Retrieved from http://www.investopedia.com/terms/f/financialengineering.asp

Jin, K., & Zhu, J. (2011). *MET: Multi-party E-Commerce Transaction Model*. Privacy, Security, Risk and Trust (PASSAT) and 2011 IEEE Third International Conference on Social Computing (SocialCom), 2011 IEEE Third International Conference, Boston, MA.

Kowall, J., & Fletcher, C. (2013). Modernize Your Monitoring Strategy by Combining Unified Monitoring and Log Analytics Tools. Gartner.

Laskowski, N. (2017). *Five analytics priorities for 2017*. Retrieved from http://searchcio.techtarget.com/news/450410871/Five-analytics-priorities-for-2017

Merriam-Webster. (2015). *Transaction*. Merriam-Webster an Encyclopædia Britannica Company Dictionary.

OASIS. (2009). *OASIS Web Services Reliable Messaging (WS-ReliableMessaging) Version 1.2*. OASIS Standard. Retrieved from http://docs.oasis-open.org/ws-rx/wsrm/200702/wsrm-1.2-spec-os.html

Peterson, S. (2011). *Why it Worked: Critical Success Factors of a Financial Reform Project in Africa*. Faculty Research Working Paper Series. Harvard Kennedy School.

Service Architecture. (2017). Retrieved from http://www.service-architecture.com/articles/xml/rixml.html

Shahrokhi, M. (2008). *E-finance: Status, Innovations, Resources and Future Challenges. Managerial Finance,* 34, 365–398.

Taleb, N. (2007). *The Black Swan-The Impact of the Highly Improbable*. Random House, Inc.

The Open Group. (2015a). *Architecture Skills Framework*. The Open Group. Retrieved from http://pubs.opengroup.org/architecture/togaf8-doc/arch/chap30.html

Tidd, J. (2006). *From Knowledge Management to Strategic Competence* (2nd ed.). London, UK: Imperial College. doi:10.1142/p439

Tidd, J., & Bessant, J. (2009). *Managing Innovation, Integrating Technological, Market and Organizational Change* (4th ed.). Wiley.

Trad, A. (2007). *Financial Information and Communication Technology Systems (FICTS). University of applied sciences*. Zurich, Switzerland: HWZ.

Trad, A. (2017a). *Using Google analytics to determine the leading business transformation framework that are based on enterprise architecture*. IBISTM.

Trad, A. (2017b). The Transformation Framework's Resources Library. IBISTM.

Trad, A., & Kalpić, D. (2014a). *The Selection and Training Framework (STF) for Managers in Business Innovation and Transformation Projects - Integrating the restructuring process of the global economy*. Cambridge, UK: IMRA.

Trad, A., & Kalpić, D. (2014c). *The Selection and Training Framework (STF) for Managers in Business Innovation and Transformation Projects - The profile of an Architect of adaptive business systems*. IMRA.

Trad, A., & Kalpić, D. (2015a). *The Business Engineering Transformation Framework for (e)commerce Architecture-Modelling Projects. In Encyclopedia of E-Commerce Development, Implementation, and Management*. IGI-Global.

Trad, A., & Kalpić, D. (2015b). *The Business Engineering Transformation Framework for (e)commerce Control and Monitoring Pattern. In Encyclopedia of E-Commerce Development, Implementation, and Management*. IGI-Global.

Trad, A., & Kalpić, D. (2015c). *The Business Transformation Framework for Managers in Business Innovation Transformation Projects-An educational financial engineering and transformation module*. Academic Press.

Trad, A., & Kalpić, D. (2016a). *The Business Transformation Framework and its Financial engineering Law support for (e)transactions*. IGI-Global.

Trad, A., & Kalpić, D. (2017a). The Business Transformation and Enterprise Architecture Framework-The Financial Engineering Technology Concept. IGI-Global. (under review)

Trad, A., & Kalpić, D. (2017b). The Business Transformation and Enterprise Architecture Framework-The Financial Engineering Global Strategy. IGI-Global. (under review)

United Nations. (2004). *Harmonized development of legal and regulatory systems for e-commerce in Asia and the Pacific: Current challenges and capacity-building needs*. New York: UN.

Universität St. Gallen. (2015). *EMBA in Financial engineering*. Retrieved from http://www.es.unisg.ch/de/programme/emba/embe.php

Wikipedia. (2015). *Master of Financial engineering*. Retrieved from https://en.wikipedia.org/wiki/Master_of_Business_Engineering

Wright, B. (1991). *Review of "The Law of Electronic Commerce EDI, Fax, and E-mail: Technology, Proof, and Liability"*. Little, Brown and Company.

Xiaohong, C. (2011). *Research on E-Commerce Transaction Cost-Benefit Characteristics and Evaluation Approaches.* Management and Service Science (MASS), *2011 International Conference*, Wuhan, China.

ADDITIONAL READING

Farhoomand, A. (2004). *Managing Business Engineering transformation*. Palgrave Macmillan.

KEY TERMS AND DEFINITIONS

Business Engineering: The development and implementation of business solutions using business models to business processes and organizational structure.

CSFs: Can be used to manage the statuses and gaps in various project plans and gives the projects the capacity to proactively and automatically recognize erroneous building blocks and to just-in-time reschedule the project plan(s).

Environment: This research's framework.

Manager: Business transformation manager.

Project: Business transformation project.

Section 2

Finance:
Stability and Crisis

Chapter 4
Financial Integration:
Crisis and Economic Development

Sandra Jednak
University of Belgrade, Serbia

Dejan Jednak
Belgrade City Markets, Serbia

ABSTRACT

Financial integration is an inseparable part of economic integration. It affects capital movement and economic development. Certain studies have shown that financial integration is beneficial to the economy. However, integration may be slowed down by occurrence of a crisis. Over the past 10 years, several crises have been underway. They have affected both economic development and financial integration. The aim of the chapter is to present theoretically the relation between financial integration, crisis, and economic development. An overview of EU and SEE financial integration and economic development is given. Development and integration of both regions have been slowed down due to the global and EU crisis, but there has been an improvement over the past few years. The fact is that SEE countries do not have a very developed financial integration but they meet certain prerequisites to reach a higher level of integration.

DOI: 10.4018/978-1-5225-4026-7.ch004

INTRODUCTION

Financial integration has become necessary due to globalisation. Various economic or political integrations lead to financial integration. Today, integration is the most common issue because of the advantages it brings to an economy. Integration of financial institutions and capital on regional basis provides liberalisation of capital movements. Such liberalisation provides funding and inflow of capital in the developing countries. International capital, particularly foreign direct investments (FDI), is the primary source of economic growth and development financing of countries in transition (Prasad et al., 2007; Globerman et al., 2006, Damijan et al., 2013; Parezanin et al., 2017). High interest rate and profit that attracts foreign capital, on one hand, and loans from abroad, on the other, provide capital for funding economic development. Moreover, financial integration influences the exchange rate, consumption, competitiveness and other economic performances that also push up economic development. Even if financial integration exists and provides benefits for an economy, crises and imbalances can cause decrease in inflows of capital. Prior to the global crisis, liquidity was high. However, during and after the crisis liquidity decreased and risk aversion rose. The availability of foreign borrowing dropped. Consequently, economic growth and development were slowed down in developing countries.

The aim of this chapter is mostly a theoretical analysis of relationships between financial integration, crisis and economic development. Financial integration in the EU and South-Eastern European (SEE) countries will be reviewed, with a particular emphasis on Serbia.

The structure of the chapter is as follows: after Introduction, there is Background section that presents a theoretical framework of financial integration and various types of crises. The global economic crisis and the EU crisis, along with the policies and solutions for overcoming the crises are overviewed. The Main Focus section of the chapter provides the analysis of EU and SEES financial integration, development and crisis. The following sections provide solutions and recommendations, as well as future research. The last section provides concluding marks.

BACKGROUND

Financial Integration

Economic integration has an integral part of the global world. Due to changes, the integration has brought different benefits to economies, regions and markets. The benefits are: efficiency, competition, production and trade increase, better quality of products, mobility of inputs, coordination and coherence of policies, a rise in productivity, income and growth, a decrease in deficit of current account and fiscal budget. Economic integration is followed by financial integration, which is obtained when financial markets, institutions and infrastructure are integrated, the law of one price existence, when all the participants have the access to a single market under the same conditions, regulations, prices, etc. According to Agenor (2003), potential benefits of financial integrations are: consumption smoothing, domestic investment and growth, better macroeconomic discipline and enhanced banking system efficiency and financial stability. However, there are potential costs: concentration and possible misallocation of capital flows, volatility and procyclicality of capital flows, jeopardising macroeconomic stability and risks of entry by foreign banks. Even so, the main advantages of financial integration are: better allocation of resources, risks diversification, providing more opportunities for investments, achieving economic growth, and obtaining financial and economic development.

Financial Integration, Capital Flows, and Development

Financial systems and markets of the countries that are going towards total economic integration have shifted their structure. In order to reach a complete integration, these economies have implemented various levels of integrations, including financial integration. Such countries are the EU countries and developing countries that are implementing economic reforms and transition. European financial integration refers to the integration of financial system and markets by capital liberalisation and coherent monetary policy. In order to allow free movement of capital, it was necessary to open the economy, to integrate into the regional/ single market, to remove national boundaries and barriers and to create a better quality of financial institutions.

Financial integration may influence the movement of capital and drivers of economic growth and development (Oprea, 2016; Ferreira, 2010). The movements of capital have been directed from developed to developing countries, and inflows of capital are of great importance for the developing countries. The states with high productivity growth have received more net capital inflows (Gourinchas & Jeanne, 2013). Therefore, financial integration is the most important for the countries with a lack of capital. Return to capital, a volume of net capital flows and a current account balance determine capital flows (Alfaro et al., 2010). Macroeconomic conditions, structure and policy are also essential in the movement of capital (Chen & Quang, 2014). Aizenman et al. (2013) have found a relationship between FDI and growth. Still, the relationship between growth and capital flows depends on "the type of flows, economic structure, and global growth patterns". Osada & Saito (2010) claim that the effects of financial integration on economic growth are different and depend on the type of external assets and liabilities, and development of financial integration in a particular country. In order to attract foreign capital, countries rely on financial and trade liberalisation and integration. Financial openness and liberalisation are usually associated with capital flows and economic growth (Bekaer et al., 2005, Edison et al., 2002, Obstfeld, 2009; Ekinci et al., 2009, Aizenman et al., 2013) in a way that liberalisation of capital markets provides inflows of foreign capital. According to a different economic theory of growth, there are two options for growth. First, the neoclassic model of growth shows that capital increases economic growth, but technology is needed to be added in order to multiply that rise. Second, the endogenous growth theory is based on human capital i.e. knowledge. If financial markets are integrated, then human capital will be created, and economic growth will be achieved. Furthermore, financial integration influences competition, financial markets and institutions (Edwards, 2001). Financial openness provides development of the banking sector, the stock market and financial institutions (Bekaert et al., 2009). Lower cost of capital and efficiency of financial institutions and the financial system are developed, which influences the changes in economic structure and development. Foreign direct investments improve factor productivity which is more important than investment growth to achieve economic growth. The increase in sources of capital and convergences (Gourinchas & Jeanne, 2006) due to financial integration leads to inflows of foreign direct investments that provide economic growth. However, Gourinchas & Jeanne (2006) have found that although financial integration provides a significant inflow of capital in developing countries, it may not obtain economic growth because of imperfect capital mobility. The capital markets do not allocate capital across the economy as is given in economic theory. Besides, capital flows could impact current account. Sarisoy-Guerin (2003) found that inflows do cause current account imbalance in developing countries. This situation will lead to lower economic performances, like decrease in economic growth, employment, income and increase in deficit of both current account and fiscal budget. Parasad et al. (2007) have also found a negative correlation between inflows of capital and economic growth. They have found that there exists a positive correlation between current account balances and growth among nonindustrial countries. This can be explained by the fact that these countries reduced reliance on foreign capital as a factor of higher growth. There are limited absorptive capacities for foreign capital due to weak financial markets or to overvalued capital inflows.

There is a high volume of capital flows, but also risks associated with them (Jednak & Jednak, 2013). Risks are: exchange rate, macroeconomic conditions, monetary and financial stability, etc. Hoxha et al. (2007) revised the previous finding, which implied that welfare gains from financial integration are not so significant. They found that "estimates suggest that the welfare gains of integration are 8.6 times larger than previously estimated". According to Kose et al. (2009), developing countries can benefit from financial globalisation, but there is not enough evidence that financial globalisation leads to developing country growth crises. Kose et al. (2009a) show that "indirect effects of financial globalisation on development of financial sector, institutions, governance and macroeconomic stability are more important than any direct effect on progress by capital accumulation or portfolio diversification".

There is a relation between financial integration and capital flows, but also between capital flows and both economic development and crisis. At the beginning of the 1990's, the movements of capital increased. Capital flows in the short run influence higher liquidity, while capital flows in the long run have impact on economic development, alleviate external shocks and balance consumption. There are different types of capital flows, but foreign direct investments (FDI) are the dominant ones. Globalisation, integration, economic reforms and transition have made FDI a primary source of funding due to: 1) the law and/or regulatory framework which was appropriate for foreign investors in many countries; 2) enabling higher and free access to global financial markets; 3) mergers & acquisitions boom in the world (mostly through privatisation) in emerging and transition economies; 4) the reduction of capital flows due to the crisis in Asia, Russia and the global crisis (Servén, 2011). FDI have had a positive impact on the development of countries in transition and emerging economies (Damijan et al., 2013; Parezanin et al., 2017). However, the crises in these countries are associated with a sudden stop in capital movements. During expansions, foreigners invest more in other countries and domestic investors abroad, while during the crises, total gross flows collapse. Financial turbulence (crisis) is associated with the reduction of gross flows. Both domestic and foreign investors significantly reduce their flows (Broner et al., 2012). Foreign investors do not invest, and domestic investors withdraw their money. That leads to a reduction in capital flows, production and consumption shrinking, and national currency depreciation. Additionally, unlike gross flows, net flows serve to finance current account deficit. If there is a surplus of net flows, foreign exchange reserves increase. Emerging economies and some developing countries have large foreign exchange reserves, and they use it for maintaining the exchange rate (for example, China). When suddenly the flows stop, the Central Bank does not have enough foreign exchange reserves to defend the domestic currency, and the domestic currency depresses. Financial integration enables capital flows that lead to the growth, low deficits and other positive economic performances, while sudden stops in capital inflows can result in crisis and imbalances in the economy.

Financial Integration and Economic Crisis

There are many benefits of financial integration, but indirectly it can influence a crisis. A crisis can slow down economic activity and cause different problems in the economy. Some countries have a lack of capital and both inflows and outflows of capital influence the exchange rate. Fluctuation of the exchange rate has an impact on price, competitiveness and consumption. Furthermore, the crisis could lead to a reduced capitalisation, fall of banking activities, decline in transactions, rise of risks, decrease of returns, increase in public debt, shrinking of the economic and business activities and drop in GDP. The economic crisis has negative impact on the economic growth and prosperity.

The crisis could occur in different markets and can be the result of a) severe structural changes, b) the government's rejection and inability, c) inadequate and poor management/governance and d) incompatibility of control mechanisms. Prior to the Global Economic Crisis (2007-2008) the most common crises were regional, short-term and rapid fitting crises. Their duration was from one to three years (Reinhart & Rogoff, 2008). Boom or bubble usually leads to a crisis. The economic boom is the period of growth in production, productivity, sales, wages and salaries, demand but also inflation (e.g. IT boom). Boom usually turns to bust (Claessens & Kose, 2013). Boom and bust go together and a steady increase in several economic indicators is followed by strong and rapid contraction and fall. A bubble of real estate is connected with house prices that mark an incredible growth. House prices increase more than inflation, and when the balloon breaks down, house prices fall and cause a collapse in the real estate market, most often followed by a recession in the field. A global crisis begins by banking / financial crisis which leads to recession and finally the expansion of the budget deficit (public debt). A combination of external shocks, volatile macroeconomic policies, microeconomic rigidities, and undeveloped institutions result in instability (Loayza et al., 2007). Different countries have had varieties of crises – sovereign default, financial crises, exchange rate crashes, and inflation explosions.

Sovereign default is external and internal debt crisis (defaults) that begins with a stop or a failure on repayment of government's debt obligations to the creditors. Argentina is the country that was hit by this type of crisis. The problem after default of debt payment is having difficulties with borrowing new loans from both foreign and domestic lenders. Not only Argentina underwent a debt crisis, but Europe as well. Several European countries were faced with the collapse of financial institutions, high public debt and the rapid growth in bond yields. The crisis was both banking and sovereign debt crisis (Constâncio, 2014). Then the financial crisis pushed the EU in recessions, raising the EU countries' deficits and debt levels. By 2010, the EU countries met debt problems (Broner et al., 2014). It began with the collapse of the island banking system in 2008. During 2009 it spread across a few countries - in Ireland by real estate boom, then in Greece due to indebtedness and high consumption and Portugal because of indebtedness and high unemployment. It became even stronger in 2012 when Spain had a real estate boom. The debt had consequences in high debts of households and a large deficit of current account. Current account deficit was the result of increasing domestic demands, the rise of wages and salaries and a decrease in the risk of the exchange rate. Moreover, the crisis was worsened due to high unemployment and low budget returns. This debt crisis led to a crisis of confidence in the European economy. Credit rating was falling, and the IMF intervention and help were necessary. However, the EU provided some proposals for solving the crisis: establishing a European Fiscal Union and European Monetary Fund, withdrawing debts and issue of European bonds.

Financial/banking crisis can cause a global economic crisis. According to Summers (2000), devaluations can presage international financial crisis. There are two situations that initiate this kind of crisis: 1) run on the bank for withdrawing money from bank accounts or 2) close, merge and bailout of financial institutions. Financial crisis affects asset prices, saving deposits and investment decision. Low asset prices, withdrawals of saving and reduction in investments influence a slowdown of economic activities that can cause a recession. They emerge suddenly, and there is a connection with political, economic and social issues. After such events (i.e. crises), bank credibility is inevitably ruined, so there is a need for regaining confidence, financial institutions restructuring and asset management.

Exchange rate crashes or currency crises have been accompanied by a balance of payment deficit and doubt if there are enough foreign exchange reserves for maintaining national exchange rate. The research so far has been focused on the exchange rate depreciation. According to Frankel and Rose (1996), the basic threshold is 25% annual depreciation. Besides that, foreign exchange reserves and key policy rate should be observed. Roots of this crisis lie in fixed exchange rate, globalisation and movement of capital, too many loans, moral hazard and boom of real estate and banking crises. Moreover, Frankel and Rose (1996) say that "crashes tend to occur if the output growth is weak, the growth of domestic credit is high, and the foreign interest rates are high. Besides, a low ratio of FDI to debt is associated with a high likelihood of a crash." Maintaining a fixed exchange rate requires a reduction in foreign exchange reserves, an increase in the fiscal deficit and public debt, which can cause a collapse of the fixed exchange rate and devaluation of the domestic currency. Currency devaluation will trigger the withdrawal of foreign capital. The only possibility to keep foreign capital in the country is the interest rates increase. However, this is not feasible for a long time. Also, the government could print money for the bank bailout. In the end, the devaluation causes hyperinflation leading to a recession. The solution is to find an optimal monetary policy (Burnside et al., 2007).

Inflation explosions last for many years. Economies eliminate debt through high inflation. One of the ways for funding growth in transition countries has been inflationary financing. The high rate of inflation, i.e. hyperinflation was suffered by the East European countries in transition. The inflation threshold of 40% per annum is considered as the beginning of a crisis (Hungary, Yugoslavia, etc.). Inflation over 10% is considered dangerous. Therefore, countries tend to run an appropriate economic policy that holds inflation rate at a low single number rate and increase financial integration, because it could reduce inflation rate.

Long term financial openness may lead to bank and currency crises. In financially liberalised economies, systemic risk taking is encouraged and increases investments that rise growth, but also influence the incidence of crises (Ranciere et al., 2008). However, the financial openness does not significantly impact the crisis occurrence. The gain of financial liberalisation exceeds the output loss from the crisis (Bekaer et al., 2005). Alfaro et al. (2010) say there is a negative correlation between capital flows and growth due to the role of sovereign-to-sovereign borrowing (debt or aid). Integration may lead to different crises, and crises also have feedback on the further financial integration. Lane and Milesi-Ferretti (2017) analyse the effects of the global economic and other crises on the international financial integration. The results are as follows: 1) weaker capital flows from and to advanced economies, 2) emerging economies have lower external assets and liabilities than advanced economies, 3) FDI still dominates investments due to multinational companies and 4) rise in the foreign holding of debt securities issued by emerging economies. Financial crisis diminishes financial flows and financial integration in the EU. Development of EU financial integration has been slowed down. The impacts were different based on the segments of integration, i.e. money, equity, bond and banking markets. Both European and emerging economies have experienced consequences of global crisis at macroeconomic and financial levels and performances.

MAIN FOCUS OF THE CHAPTER

EU and SEE Countries Development and Financial Integration

European Financial Integration

Economic efficiency means high productivity and economic growth rates, while economic stability means price stability in the national economy. Improvements and progress of financial system contribute to better performance and activities of the national economy. This is all essential for financial integration and financial development. Financial integration influences financial development. Further financial development creates conditions for obtaining economic development. At the regional level, financial integration depends on trade liberalisation and openness, income per capita and market capitalization of financial assets. Trade liberalisation provides capital and right movements and increases competitiveness and export.

According to Vithessonthi & Kumarasinghe (2016), trade integration does not have a positive effect on stock market integration, while financial development does. Comparing financial and economic integration, financial integration should be reflected in discount rates, and economic integration in capitalised growth opportunities. These two integrations are complementary and have mutual benefits. The real sector which is developed through the economic integration depends on the capital obtained on the capital market. If this market integrates into other regional markets it could bring down the interest rate and better allocation of capital. In that way, financial integration influences not only financial development, but economic development, as well.

European economies have gone through the various integrations. European economic integration has been followed by financial integration. In the EU, financial integration is a part of all integration processes due to established economic and monetary union. In order to run and govern Euro zone efficiently, European Central Bank needs a single monetary policy, financial and monetary stability, and efficient payment system. If that is obtained, financial integration brings economic benefits for achieving sustainable and non-inflationary growth. Financial integration is the integration of money, banking, bond and equity markets. Only money market is completely integrated and stable, while other markets are still on the path of full integrations (Guiso et al., 2004).

A single financial market has been created in the EU, but the integration processes are uneven in some of its segments. Integration of the wholesale European financial markets (securities trading) is higher than that of the retail financial markets (mortgages, household loans, small and medium-sized enterprises). Wholesale financial markets are more liquid, with more rational capital allocation and integrated infrastructure. Differences in the financial integration are different interest rates on loans in certain countries and limitations between retail activities (Boškoska, 2007). Over the years, the volume of all bonds issued surpasses the volume of US bonds issued in Europe. Euro area is a large market. According to European Central Bank (2017) euro area has a mixed development. Money market integration is stable, while banking, bond and equity markets are diverse. In 2016, two financial policies were developed to improve further integration: The Banking Union and the Capital Market Union. For a complete banking union, risk reduction and risk sharing is an important issue. The two leading composite indicators are established for measuring the improvement of financial integrations: price-based and quantity-based indexes. They take into account and measure money, bond, equity and banking markets. The scale is from 0 to 1, where 1 is total integration. Figure 1 shows financial integration indicators for the period from 1995 till 2014. The most important events, like introducing the euro, the crises and announcement of Banking and Capital Market

Union are also shown in Figure 1. It can be seen that the crises had adverse effects on the financial integration.

After different crises, financial markets were reintegrated. In 2016, the price-based index of integration was volatile, while quantity-based index flattened out. This is the result of counterbalancing effects within and across different markets. It is influenced by various economic performances across countries, fluctuating global risk aversion and political uncertainty (European Central Bank, 2017). Besides, EU monetary policy supported financial integration. Even cross-border lending decreased and the slowdown in financial integration lead to a drop in output in Europe. Since the global financial crisis, Chakraborty et al., (2016) estimate that financial frictions have increased around 50% post-crisis and further financial integration would increase the output. The estimation is that financial integration will continue improvement. Most studies have had a focus on the pre-crisis period from 1990 to 2007. This period covers the beginning of expansion of both financial and economic integrations. The EU created a single market, and some of the countries introduced the euro. Bekaert et al. (2017) analysed the effect of EU membership and a common currency (euro), i.e. Euro area, on the economic and financial integration. They examined discount rates and growth opportunities. The results are as follows: before the 2007 crisis, equity market integration was rather the result of the adoption of the Euro, than EU membership. Furthermore, joining the EU decreased discount rate (financial integration) and expected growth across countries (economic integration). The EU has suffered several sovereign debt and banking crises, and the most recent was Brexit (The United Kingdom has left the EU). After the crisis, the main findings are that EU membership increases integration, while adoption the euro does not. They have also found that over the past few years, integration benefits due to EU membership have decreased, while segmentation between Euro area countries has

Figure 1. Financial integration indicator (FINTEC)
Source: European Central Bank, www.ecb.europa.eu.

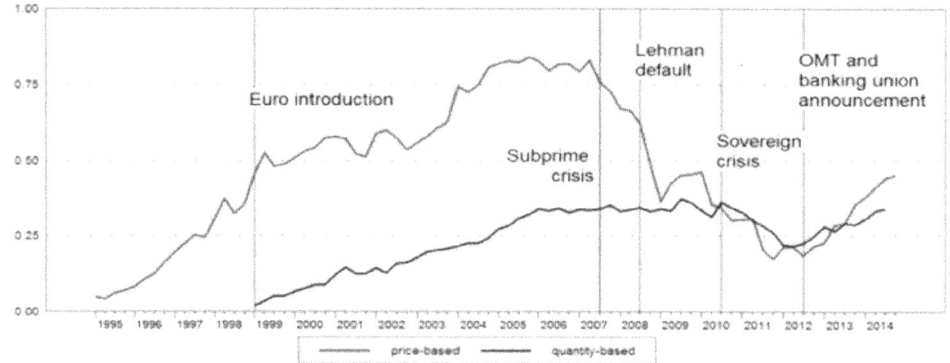

slightly increased. Kılınç et al., (2017) show that banking and stock market converge across the EU by controlling the quality of institutions and a range of macroeconomic variables. They claim that the EU financial integration has been a success and the integration should be accelerated.

South-East European Countries Development and Financial Integration

Developing countries have many economic issues. South-East European countries have carried out economic reform and transformed their economies from command to market economies. One of the sources for financing the economic growth and development has been foreign capital - foreign direct investments or loans. These countries have encountered a lack of capital, and financial instability (Jednak et al., 2017). Moreover, they have been affected by the global economic crisis, as well as the EU crisis. In order to overcome the existing problems, governments borrow loans. Budget deficit and public debt are the effects of borrowing. Governments have faced several own crises. High public debt has become one of the threats for the debt crisis. Besides, unemployment has increased. However, inflation is not an issue any more, as it used to be during the beginning of the transition. Low-level foreign capital, borrowing and macroeconomic policies that promote saving over consumption, have slowed economy and decreased economic growth rate. Countries have attempted to find a solution to restore financial and macroeconomic stability. IMF and the World Bank have proposed measures (savings) to establish stability and achieve economic progress.

Financial integration obtains capital due to high global liquidity. SEE countries could take loans at affordable interest rates. Prior to the global crisis, capital inflows (loans) in those countries increased. However, global imbalances started with the global crisis. The world financial crisis reduced liquidity and increased risk aversion. The availability of foreign capital decreased, and the interest rates rose. The weak inflows of foreign capital slowed down economic growth. Besides, EU trade partners' demand for SEE export dropped (Kadiu, 2015). Many countries ran both current account and fiscal deficit. Furthermore, the financial crisis was reflected on the public finances crisis and turned into a crisis of the real sector with a fall in economic activity and GDP. That raised the issue of funding the economic development in SEE countries. For Serbia, which is one of the SEE countries, the most significant effect of financial integration is a large financial capital inflow that has influenced economic growth and increased the standard of living. Economic growth has been achieved due to increased consumption, demand and investments. However, competitiveness has been reduced due to domestic currency appreciation because of capital inflows, and currency depreciation due to the decrease in capital inflows. Furthermore, the lower competitiveness is the consequence of: higher costs rise than increase of productivity, restrictive monetary policy, large public debt and current account deficit (Atanasijevic & Cupic, 2012). For these reasons, the economic growth strategy has been changed and oriented towards domestic sources of finance, while financial integration has been carried out in order to harmonise institutions and regulations with the EU.

The EU financial integration development is the prerequisite for the development of SEE countries and Serbian financial market. The SEE financial markets, especially stock markets, are not mature markets when compared to European financial market (Ganic & Mamuti, 2016; Horvath& Petrovski, 2013; Kenourgios & Samitas, 2011). They also lack a substantial market depth (regarding listed companies and capitalisation) and have a short active presence as compared to mature EU markets (Syriopoulos, 2011). During the period of transition and privatisation (2000-2006), the volume of the trade, i.e. turnover of these markets increases, as well as the price. Even so, markets stay small in terms of capitalisation, turnover and liquidity as compared to the EU (Kenourgios & Samitas, 2011). According to Bonetto et al. (2009), domestic credit and market capitalisation have an important role in the catching-up process increase in the speed of convergence to EU financial and economic integration. SEE financial markets have a different degree of the development due to the process of association to the EU. Some SEE countries are members of the EU (Romania, Bulgaria and Croatia), some are candidate countries (Albania, Montenegro, Serbia, and Macedonia), and there are other potential candidates (Bosnia and Herzegovina). Due to this fact, Bulgaria, Romania and Croatia have more developed financial markets and financial integration as compared to other SEE countries.

To obtain higher EU financial integration, there is a need to fulfill EU convergence criteria, monetary stability, low inflation, the stable exchange rate of constant economic progress. It is also important that monetary policy should be coherent with the EU monetary policy in order to get prepared for becoming an EU member and a member of the Euro area. Serbian financial market development corresponds to the development of the EU financial integration, i.e. Serbian financial market has shown high correlation with the evolution of the EU financial market. However, this market has insufficient domestic accumulation, and a lack of adequate regulatory framework that would mitigate negative external shocks. SEE and Serbian financial market development depends very much on the EU financial market (Radosavljevic, 2013). Comparing general government gross debt % of GDP and government debt securities issues % of GDP, SEE countries have a high fiscal deficit and a high share of debt securities issues. In almost half the countries, debt securities issue accounts for more than 80% of the total public debt.

Banking market covers about 90% of financial markets. Other financial markets are not developed enough to fulfill financial integration. The banking sector is dominant in SEE countries. The first reforms that have been carried out were in the banking sector. Over the time, banking market improved. It was developing till 2009, when it started to stagnate. In SEE banking sector, foreign banks have high market shares and dominant role in financial activities (Tornjanski et al., 2017). This brings advantages for further SEE financial integration. Competition is intense, so domestic banks need to be more efficient, better organised, innovative and profitable. Foreign banks have more advanced risk management than domestic banks. Therefore, foreign banks try to make efficient selection of credits and loans and avoid uncertain and risky projects. Diversification contributes to financial stability, as it reduces the chances of the local financial crisis. Furthermore, depositors have lost confidence in domestic banks, so foreign banks hold most of the deposits. It provides the stabilisation of credit flows and reduces the depositors' tendency towards the withdrawal of deposits and bankruptcy cannot be triggered. Foreign banks can obtain capital from abroad (Jednak & Jednak, 2013; Lukic, 2014). Banking market and stock market are crucial for obtaining economic growth. If companies use external sources for funding their business, then a well-developed financial market is necessary.

Financial integration provides development of national markets and better conditions, i.e. availability of capital, lower interest cost, etc. Some researchers have analysed the relation between integration and other economic performances. For example, Tang (2016) analyses the effects of European financial integration on the East European countries' exports. The results of the study indicate that the stock market and bank development rather have negative than positive effect on exports. SEE financial integration is not well-developed. Some markets are developed, mostly banking market, while other markets and institutions have reached a certain degree of integration. In order to become members of the EU and make economic progress, these countries should continue developing financial integration.

SOLUTIONS AND RECOMMENDATIONS

Countries usually follow global movements toward economic and financial integration. Economic integration has its stages: free trade area, customs union, common market, economic and monetary union, and complete integration. Each of the stages has a positive influence on economic development. Reducing and elimination of trade barriers and tariffs bring about a higher volume of trade among countries. Moreover, a single currency increases trade and stability. Trade affects structural adjustments, economic restructuring, competition and the rise in production, output, employment, export and economic growth. Various countries have a mixed economic integration development. Along with economic integration, financial integration has a significant role in economic development. High level of financial integration development affects both capital flows rise and economic growth. Financial development and financial integration have contributed to economic growth in the European Union (de Guevara Radoselovics & Villarroya, 2010). The integration also has a role in the transmission of monetary policy in the euro area, provides financial stability, stable payment system and completing the EU single market (European Central Bank, 2017). Furthermore, capital flow changes due to the rate of return. SEE countries open their economies and financial markets and provide a high rate of return. Financial development and integration allow access to credits and mitigate macroeconomic volatility that attracts foreign capital, FDI (Berglöf et al., 2009). In these countries, during the 1990s and 2000s foreign direct investments had growth and were the drivers of economic growth and development. Notwithstanding positive effects, due to global economic crisis and EU crisis, capital inflows have dropped, and economic activities and development have slowed down. SEE have not developed financial markets and system as EU has. Financial integration enables competition, expands markets, increases efficiency of financial systems and reduces costs. It also provides risk sharing, consumption smoothing, investments due to external assets and liabilities (especially FDI and debt inflows), macroeconomic discipline, banking system efficiency and financial stability (Agenor, 2003). All this can mitigate the effects of economic crises. To gain all these benefits, SEE countries should carry out both economic and financial integrations, which is challenging because many reforms could be obtained by foreign banks and financial capital and institutions. However, certain obligations have to be implemented and fulfilled as requirements to become a part of the EU.

FUTURE RESEARCH DIRECTIONS

Regional and national crises and global imbalances will always exist throughout the world. However, the aim of each economy is economic development. This goal will be obtained by carrying out economic policies and integrations. Each integration has both benefits and costs. However, benefits should overcome costs. According to this, further research work might have a few directions: 1) analysing the relation between financial integration and economic development, 2) development of financial integration in a particular region, like the EU or the emerging Asia, 3) what impact a particular crisis has on the financial system and economic development, and 4) empirical analysis of the role of financial integration in economic development of the Southeast European countries or a particular SEE country.

CONCLUSION

Financial integration i.e. developed financial markets and institutions can contribute to economic growth, but can cause financial crises, as well. International financial integration can deliver different outcomes across countries, which depend on their development and pre- or post-crisis or expansion period (Lane, 2013). Financial integration brings benefits for an economy like gaining more capital flows, integrating financial market, risks diversification, efficient allocation of financial resources, identification and financing profitable and harmless investments. Capital is important for SEE countries because they suffer from low accumulation of domestic capital. Financial integration is an issue that should be done in order to obtain foreign capital and integrate into the EU and global markets. Foreign capital will push up progress in their economy, but due to a sudden stop or occurrence of crises, it may also put the economy in recession. Financial integration is well developed in the EU. However, during the global economic crisis and the EU crisis, financial integration process was slowed down. EU integration has recently recovered and reintegrated. The crisis has hit SEE countries, as well. SEE were left without foreign capital, with large fiscal and current account deficit and public debt. These countries have focused on domestic funds in order to get better economic performances. Their obligation is to fulfill the EU convergence criteria in order to become the EU members and members of European monetary union. Coherent monetary policy, finance and monetary stability are prerequisites for financial and economic development. Countries of this region have developing economies, and they are quite vulnerable to external shocks. To mitigate external impacts and crises, they should integrate better and remove restrictions and barriers for capital flows. They should continue to integrate economic and financial markets and institutions.

REFERENCES

Agénor, P. R. (2003). Benefits and costs of international financial integration: Theory and facts. *World Economy*, *26*(8), 1089–1118. doi:10.1111/1467-9701.00564

Aizenman, J., Jinjarak, Y., & Park, D. (2013). Capital flows and economic growth in the era of financial integration and crisis, 1990–2010. *Open Economies Review*, *24*(3), 371–396. doi:10.100711079-012-9247-3

Alfaro, L., Kalemli-Ozcan, S., & Volosovych, V. (2010). *International capital allocation, sovereign borrowing, and growth.* Boston: Harvard Business School Working Paper.

Atanasijevic, J. & Cupic, V. (2012). *Finansijska integracija, privredni rast I drugi izazovi*. Makroekonomske analize i trendovi - MAT. Br.209

Bekaert, G., Harvey, C. R., & Lundblad, C. (2005). Does financial liberalization spur growth? *Journal of Financial Economics*, *77*(1), 3–55. doi:10.1016/j.jfineco.2004.05.007

Bekaert, G., Harvey, C. R., & Lundblad, C. (2011). Financial openness and productivity. *World Development*, *39*(1), 1–19. doi:10.1016/j.worlddev.2010.06.016

Bekaert, G., Harvey, C. R., Lundblad, C. T., & Siegel, S. (2017). *Economic and Financial Integration in Europe*. Academic Press.

Berglöf, E., Korniyenko, Y., Zettelmeyer, J., & Plekhanov, A. (2009). Understanding the crisis in emerging. *Europe*.

Bonetto, F., Redžepagić, S., & Tykhonenko, A. (2009). *Balkan countries: catching up and their integration in the European financial system*. Academic Press.

Boškoska, M. (2007). *Integracija evropskih finansijskih tržišta*. Conference paper.

Broner, F., Didier, T., Erce, A., & Schmukler, S. L. (2013). Gross capital flows: Dynamics and crises. *Journal of Monetary Economics*, *60*(1), 113–133. doi:10.1016/j.jmoneco.2012.12.004

Broner, F., Erce, A., Martin, A., & Ventura, J. (2014). Sovereign debt markets in turbulent times: Creditor discrimination and crowding-out effects. *Journal of Monetary Economics*, *61*, 114–142. doi:10.1016/j.jmoneco.2013.11.009

Burnside, C., Eichenbaum, M., & Rebelo, S. (2007). *Currency crisis models*. Retrieved from http://www.kellogg.northwestern.edu/faculty/rebelo/htm/currency%20crisis%20models%20Ed.pdf

Chakraborty, I., Hai, R., Holter, H. A., & Stepanchuk, S. (2016). *The Real Effects of Financial (Dis) integration: A Spatial Equilibrium Analysis of Europe*. Academic Press.

Chen, J., & Quang, T. (2014). The impact of international financial integration on economic growth: New evidence on threshold effects. *Economic Modelling*, *42*, 475–489. doi:10.1016/j.econmod.2014.06.011

Claessens, S., & Kose, M. M. A. (2013). Financial crises explanations, types, and implications (No. 13-28). International Monetary Fund.

Constâncio, V. (2014). The European crisis and the role of the financial system. *Journal of Macroeconomics*, *39*, 250–259. doi:10.1016/j.jmacro.2013.08.009

Damijan, J. P., Rojec, M., Majcen, B., & Knell, M. (2013). Impact of firm heterogeneity on direct and spillover effects of FDI: Micro-evidence from ten transition countries. *Journal of Comparative Economics*, *41*(3), 895–922. doi:10.1016/j.jce.2012.12.001

de Guevara Radoselovics, J. F., & Villarroya, J. M. (2010). *Financial Crisis, Financial Integration and Economic Growth*. Fundacion BBVA.

Edison, H. J., Levine, R., Ricci, L., & Sløk, T. (2002). International financial integration and economic growth. *Journal of International Money and Finance*, *21*(6), 749–776. doi:10.1016/S0261-5606(02)00021-9

Edwards, S. (2001). *Capital mobility and economic performance: are emerging economies different?* (No. w8076). National Bureau of Economic Research.

Ekinci, M. F., Kalemli-Özcan, Ş., & Sørensen, B. E. (2009, January). Financial integration within EU countries: The role of institutions, confidence and trust. In *NBER International Seminar on Macroeconomics 2007* (pp. 325-391). University of Chicago Press.

European Central Bank. (2017). *Financial integration in Europe*. Retrieved from https://www.ecb.europa.eu/pub/pdf/other/ecb.financialintegrationineurope201705.en.pdf

Ferreira, C. (2010). European Financial Integration and Economic Growth. *JMFS*, 26.

Frankel, J. A., & Rose, A. K. (1996). Currency crashes in emerging markets: An empirical treatment. *Journal of International Economics*, *41*(3), 351–366. doi:10.1016/S0022-1996(96)01441-9

Ganic, M., & Mamuti, A. (2016). Developments, Trends And Features Of Financial Integration In The Western Balkan Region-Crosscountry Comparisons. *International Journal of Management Economics & Business*, *12*, 1.

Globerman, S., Shapiro, D., & Tang, Y. (2006). Foreign direct investment in emerging and transition European countries. In *Emerging European financial markets: Independence and integration post-enlargement* (pp. 431–459). Emerald Group Publishing Limited. doi:10.1016/S1569-3767(05)06017-6

Gourinchas, P. O., & Jeanne, O. (2006). The elusive gains from international financial integration. *The Review of Economic Studies*, *73*(3), 715–741. doi:10.1111/j.1467-937X.2006.00393.x

Gourinchas, P. O., & Jeanne, O. (2013). Capital flows to developing countries: The allocation puzzle. *The Review of Economic Studies*.

Guiso, L., Jappelli, T., Padula, M., & Pagano, M. (2004). Financial market integration and economic growth in the EU. *Economic Policy*, *19*(40), 524–577. doi:10.1111/j.1468-0327.2004.00131.x

Horvath, R., & Petrovski, D. (2013). International stock market integration: Central and South Eastern Europe compared. *Economic Systems*, *37*(1), 81–91. doi:10.1016/j.ecosys.2012.07.004

Hoxha, I., Kalemli-Ozcan, S., & Vollrath, D. (2013). How big are the gains from international financial integration? *Journal of Development Economics*, *103*, 90–98. doi:10.1016/j.jdeveco.2013.02.003

Jednak, D., & Jednak, J. (2013). Operational Risk Management in Financial Institutions. *Management*, (66).

Jednak, S., Kragulj, D., & Bulajic, M. (2017). A comparative analysis of development in Southeast European countries. *Technological and Economic Development of Economy*, 1–18. doi:10.3846/20294913.2016.1212438

Kadiu, F. (2015). Economic Overview and Financial Instability in Balkans. *Procedia Economics and Finance*, *26*, 1141–1145. doi:10.1016/S2212-5671(15)00943-0

Kenourgios, D., & Samitas, A. (2011). Equity market integration in emerging Balkan markets. *Research in International Business and Finance*, *25*(3), 296–307. doi:10.1016/j.ribaf.2011.02.004

Kılınç, D., Seven, Ü., & Yetkiner, H. (2017). *Financial development convergence: New evidence for the EU*. Central Bank Review.

Kose, M. A., Prasad, E., Rogoff, K., & Wei, S. J. (2009). Financial globalisation: A reappraisal. *IMF Staff Papers*, *56*(1), 8–62. doi:10.1057/imfsp.2008.36

Kose, M. A., Prasad, E., Rogoff, K., & Wei, S. J. (2009a). Finansijska globalizacija: Ponovna procena. *Panoeconomicus*, *56*(2), 143–197. doi:10.2298/PAN0902143K

Lane, P. R. (2013). Financial globalisation and the crisis. *Open Economies Review*, *24*(3), 555–580. doi:10.100711079-012-9266-0

Lane, P. R., & Milesi-Ferretti, G. M. M. (2017). *International financial integration in the aftermath of the global financial crisis*. IMF Working Paper No. 17/115.

Loayza, N. V., Ranciere, R., Servén, L., & Ventura, J. (2007). Macroeconomic volatility and welfare in developing countries: An introduction. *The World Bank Economic Review*, *21*(3), 343–357. doi:10.1093/wber/lhm017

Lukic, V. (2014). *Financial Integration- Theoretical and Empirical Analysis.* Doctoral Dissertation.

Obstfeld, M. (2009). International finance and growth in developing countries: What have we learned? *IMF Staff Papers, 56*(1), 63–111. doi:10.1057/imfsp.2008.32

Oprea, O. R. (2016). European Financial Integration and Economic Growth. *Journal of Public Administration. Finance and Law., 10*, 173–181.

Osada, M., & Saito, M. (2010). *Financial integration and economic growth: An empirical analysis using international panel data from 1974-2007.* Research and Statistics Department, Bank of Japan.

Parežanin, M., Jednak, S., & Kragulj, D. (2016). The Impact of FDI on the Economic Growth of Serbia. *Management: Journal of Sustainable Business and Management Solutions in Emerging Economies, 21*(78), 25–32.

Prasad, E. S., Rajan, R. G., & Subramanian, A. (2007). *Foreign capital and economic growth (No. w13619).* National Bureau of Economic Research. doi:10.3386/w13619

Radosavljevic, R. (2013). *Financial integration of the European Union and its impacts on the financial market of Serbia.* Doctoral Dissertation.

Ranciere, R., Tornell, A., & Westermann, F. (2008). Systemic crises and growth. *The Quarterly Journal of Economics, 123*(1), 359–406. doi:10.1162/qjec.2008.123.1.359

Reinhart, C. M., & Rogoff, K. S. (2008). *This time is different: A panoramic view of eight centuries of financial crises (No. w13882).* National Bureau of Economic Research. doi:10.3386/w13882

Sarisoy-Guerin, S. (2003). *The relationship between capital flows and current account: volatility and causality* (Unpublished Manuscript). Dublin: Trinity College.

Servén, L. (2011). *Financial globalisation and financial crisis. Teaching notes.* CEMFI.

Summers, L. H. (2000). International financial crises: Causes, prevention, and cures. *The American Economic Review, 90*(2), 1–16. doi:10.1257/aer.90.2.1 PMID:18459243

Syriopoulos, T. (2011). Financial integration and portfolio investments to emerging Balkan equity markets. *Journal of Multinational Financial Management, 21*(1), 40–54. doi:10.1016/j.mulfin.2010.12.006

Tang, D. (2016). Has the Financial Integration affected the European Union (EU) trade with the New Member Countries from Central and Eastern Europe (CEEC) during 1994–2013? *Journal of Economic Asymmetries*, *13*, 8–20. doi:10.1016/j.jeca.2015.10.004

Tornjanski, V., Knežević, S., & Delibašić, B. (2017). A CRM Performance Measurement in Banking Using Integrated BSC and Customized ANP-BOCR Approach. *Management: Journal of Sustainable Business and Management Solutions in Emerging Economies*, *22*(1), 71–85.

Vithessonthi, C., & Kumarasinghe, S. (2016). Financial development, international trade integration, and stock market integration: Evidence from Asia. *Journal of Multinational Financial Management*, *35*, 79–92. doi:10.1016/j.mulfin.2016.03.001

KEY TERMS AND DEFINITIONS

Capital Flows: Inflows and outflows influence economic activity and stability.

Capital Movements: International capital flows could be foreign direct investments, portfolio/security investments, loans, and aids.

Economic Crisis: Economic crisis in a situation when the economy has a slowdown of economic activities due to financial/bank crisis, inflation, currency crashes, or sovereign debt.

Economic Growth: Economic growth is a rise in output (i.e., GDP rise).

Economic Integration: The integration of economies to the single area through the reduction and elimination trade barriers and coordination of economic policies.

Economic Progress: The progress of national economy to raise output, wellbeing, living standard, and quality of life. It is a multidimensional, coherent, and slow process.

EU Financial Integration: European financial integration is integration of money, equity, bond, and banking markets. EU financial integration is run in order to establish economic and monetary union and Euro area.

Eurozone Crisis: The European debt crisis (European sovereign debt crisis) in 2009 began with a debt default in Greece, Portugal, Spain, Ireland, and Italy.

Financial Development: Financial development is the development of institutions, markets, and instruments of financial sector.

Financial Markets: The markets where securities (equities, bonds, currencies, and financial derivatives) are traded.

FINTEC: The composite indicator of financial integration in Europe (i.e., Euro area that covers money, bond, equity, and banking markets and presents the overall development of financial integration). It is the price-based and the quantity-based financial integration composites.

Foreign Direct Investment: Foreign direct investment is investment from an investor from one country to another country (abroad) in order to become the owner of business abroad and make a profit.

SEE Countries: South-East European countries are countries in transition and in the process to become members of the EU. The countries are in the region of South-East Europe and include Albania, Bosnia and Herzegovina, Bulgaria, Croatia, Macedonia, Moldova, Montenegro, Romania, and Serbia.

Chapter 5
Financial Stability vs. Sustainable Development and Its Financing

Magdalena Ziolo
University of Szczecin, Poland

Marwa Ben Ghoul Ben Ghoul
Anadolu University, Turkey

Halil İbrahim Aydın
Batman University, Turkey

ABSTRACT

Financing of sustainable development is a sophisticated and long-term process determined by a number of economic and non-economic factors. Financial instruments, private and public nature, exist that can be a source of financing of sustainable development. The choice of finance sources and instruments has an impact on the stability of economic systems and the efficiency of public expenditure with respect to sustainable development goals. The choice of financial instruments for financing development impact on financial stability and results in outcomes performed. The goal of the chapter is to examine relationships between financial stability reflected by public debt to gross domestic product (GDP) and sustainable development described by variables represented by three pillars of sustainable development: economic, social, and environmental. The role of environmentally related tax revenue has been identified as crucial for financing sustainable development goals.

DOI: 10.4018/978-1-5225-4026-7.ch005

INTRODUCTION

Financing of sustainable development is a sophisticated and long-term process determined by a number of economic and non-economic factors. Financial instruments, private and public nature, exist that can be a source of financing of sustainable development. The choice of finance sources and instruments has an impact on the stability of economic systems and the efficiency of public expenditure with respect to on sustainable development goals. The choice of financial instruments for financing development impact on financial stability and results in outcomes performed.

Sustainability is a crucial issue in distressed, socio-economic environments. A welfare state crisis and the regulations failure which were revealed after 2008 highlight a need to search for new ways and solutions for stabilizing of national economies and creating conditions for sustainable economic development. Social and financial exclusion, increasing income disparities, inefficient redistribution system, and negative economic externalities (including environment protection problems) are some of the challenges facing states and local governments.

Sustainable development, when seen from an economic point of view has been widely described in literature. Despite numerous publications and papers on the subject, it remains under recognized with a definitional standpoint, of the impact on the economy and stakeholders. The diagnosis applies in particular to the issue of financing of sustainable development.

Research on sustainable development and its financing are desirable as a means to counteract the impact of negative externalities on the economy, society and the environment, and to provide comparable dynamics of development (but the growth as well) to its beneficiaries. It is worth noting the special role of sustainable development in tackling wider and socially harmful phenomena, namely the exclusion and increase of inequality.

Theoretical and empirical dimensions of sustainable development as a phenomenon of the research are important. Specifically, the volume of public and private funds allocated to the funding, the scale of the expected impact on the economy and society and the strategic dimension of the concept of being reflected in the public to public policy are each critical considerations requiring empirical study. Each highlights that the issue requires in-depth research and an analysis for identification reasons, conditions and efficiency of its financing.

The legitimacy of research on the financing of sustainable development is determined by the provision of funding is a prerequisite for the implementation of the concept. Financing and effective management of funds has an impact on the realization of the principles of sustainable development. Such determines the efficiency of sustainable development in itself, as it displays the efficiency and effectiveness of spending of funds for the purpose.

Sustainable development has a role in tackling the phenomena of increasing inequality (Gini). Theoretical and empirical dimensions of sustainable development as a phenomenon of the research, the volume of public and private funds allocated to the funding, the scale of the expected impact on the economy and society and the strategic dimension of the concept of being reflected in the public to public policy, which makes the issue in need of in-depth research and, an analysis of identification reasons, conditions and efficiency of its financing.

Sustainable development, if placed in an economic category, requires attention, but seeing the cognitive category from the perspective of the discipline of finance, the latter is unsatisfactory, and a number of research questions remain unanswered. In contrast, the rank problem, its strategic dimension and the amount of financial resources allocated and disbursed for the purposes of focusing around sustainable development, identification of financial phenomena accompanying the category is seen as a priority.

The goal of the chapter is to diagnose the relationship between financial sustainability and sustainable development outcomes. The main research hypothesis assumes that financial stability is a precondition for the sustainable development and its financing.

The chapter is divided into six sections. Section one is introduction. I section two theoretical background of sustainability has been presented and discussed based on related work review. Section three relates to linkages between financial sustainability and financing of sustainable development. Section four describes the research methodology and variables. In section five research results has been presented. The last section, section six, sums up the main considerations and results of the research.

A THEORETICAL FRAMEWORK FOR SUSTAINABLE DEVELOPMENT AND ITS IMPACT ON CONVENTIONAL FINANCE

The first, although indirect, references to the idea of "*sustainability*" occurred several hundred years ago. They involved, descriptions and discussion of the problem of overexploitation of natural goods. In the seventeenth century, Hans Carl von Carlowitz, in the study *Sylvicultura Oeconomica*, described the concept of "*sustainability*" broadly and the scholar remains accredited as one of the founders of the term (Grober, 2007). Von Carlowitz was responsible for administering one of the Saxon silver mines for 40 years, learning at that time the dependence of mining on natural resources.

In 1714, von Carlowitz published a monograph summarizing his professional experience in which he concluded how the care and maintenance of silver should be conducted to ensure long-term and "*sustainable*" output. In the further period, references to the idea of sustainable development can be found. The classical theorists of economics, such as Adam Smith, argued that capitalist systems to function properly in the long run must be based on honesty and consistency, otherwise they will be destroyed (1776).

The concept of sustainable development has evolved largely since the Conference of United Nations ('UN') that took place in 1972 in Stockholm (UNCHE, 1972) then the global agenda in1987 was declared by World Commission on Environment and Development ('WCED') (1987)[1]. The definition of sustainable development was first formally presented in the Brundtland Report and Agenda 21.

Within the framework, the international reputation and esteem institution, the UN, has implemented its own definition of sustainable development. By specifying the category as: "*a process aimed at satisfying the development aspirations of the present generation in a way that enables the same aspirations to succeed generations*". Agenda 21 issued the notion of "*eco development*" not only related to the natural environment but also with the ethical legal and social system as one of the main objectives needed for implementation by individual national authorities (WCED, 1987).

Since that time the term sustainable development has received much attention in a number of spheres and attracting people from a number of disciplines (Enders and Remig, 2015). In sum sustainable development can be considered as agenda for change requiring involvement of people over the word. the assumption is included in Johannesburg Declaration on Sustainable Development which was adopted at the World Summit on Sustainable Development ('WSSD') (2002, p. 1) that states collective responsibility to advance and strengthen three pillars of sustainable development, namely economic, social and environmental (Sudana, 2015, p. 159).

Sustainable development as a concept covers a number of aspects such as: government policy, business strategy and business models, financial matters (green taxes, green financial products) even lifestyle decisions such as green consumerism. Especially, sustainable development is a well-established concept in the field of environmental economics (Soppe, 2004). There are a number of aspects of sustainable development, including sustainable economy, sustainable growth or sustainable finance and banking or more general sustainable finance. Soppe (2004) has pointed out that there is one key point to understanding sustainable development as a whole, the basic concept of sustainable development, to exist between current and future generations.

In a nut shell, sustainable development is a notion that strives to strike a balance between social, economic and environmental issues and is a key requirement for quality of living for future generations. The balance is particularly important in terms of the economics of inequality (Piketty, 2015) with particular emphasis on growing income disparities, aging populations, social problems, capitalist crises and unprecedented environmental challenges that will become millstones (Ziolo et al., 2016).

The extent of the aforementioned problems creates costs and consequences that have a negative impact on sustainable development. Problems need to be solved as they have a strong impact on quality of life, economic performance and fundamental social rights and values such as freedom, equality, justice and justice. The requires strong involvement of government, society and companies, especially that there are evidence that sustainability does pay off (Epstein and Roy, 2001; Jeucken, 2001).

The results of research and analysis show that enterprises that implemented principles of corporate social responsibility ('CSR') are characterized by having lower cost of capital (Ghoul et al. 2014). When it comes to interpreting the results, Environmental, Social, Governance ('ESG') risk is difficult to manage, requiring more managers and skills than managers in other risk categories and implies better financial results issued by enterprises running business in ESG risk-sensitive sectors (Fullwiler, 2015, p. 5).

ESG risk influences the stability and liquidity of financial institutions such as banks, as banks take responsibility for consequences of financial distress and insolvency risk of debtors. Dirty companies, namely those financial penalties debtors should pay for non-compliance with the regulations and taking actions harmful to the environment. Another financial consequence for banks is the probability of a loss of market value of legal security for the repayment of their loans as a result of environmental pollution.

Contaminated land / property are difficult to sell at market price, and as a legal security for the repayment of such real estate will not be for banks as full-value creditors. Banking and financial institutions should redefine the importance, and approach, to operational risk in their business including ESG risk.

Debt, socially responsible investments and capital investments are starting to encourage companies to consider social, environmental, and corporate and climate issues in their financial statements, policies, disclosures, credit assessments, and lending guidelines.

A helpful guide to best practices for financial institutions dealing with the environment is the Equator Principles and the UN Principles on Responsible Investment. Equator Principles is a set of socially and environmentally responsible practices that are voluntarily accepted over 63 of the world's largest financial institutions (Wilhelm, 2013; Ziolo et al. 2016).

Yet, there are no reliable and unified standards for measuring and evaluating sustainability risks and returns-compared to financial risks and returns. A theory of conventional finance needs to be developed and incorporate the socio-ecologically specified nature of finance towards new paradigm sustainable finance (Fullwiler, 2015, p. 18; Ziolo et al., 2016).

The concept of sustainable finance has received attention in recent decades. The general approach to sustainable finance is to encompass the economic, environmental, and social sustainability of finance (Wilson, 2010).

In contrast, sustainable finance can be considered as a creation of institutional arrangements in the financial system that can contribute to the sustainable development of the economy (see more in Pisano, Martinuzzi and Bruckner, 2012). In the context, sustainable finance would include financial instruments, institutions and markets that take into account issues such as the environmental and social responsibility of those who seek funding. Sustainability and accountability in finance and investment require ethics. Ethics does not mean ethical investments but awareness of social connections due to business financing (Haigh, 2012).

Ethical, or green, financial instruments include provisions relating to the purposes that financial funds receive as a result of their issue and may be used for compensated financial operations. Ethical, or socially responsible, financial institutions would have their investment policy objectives including sustainability funding providers such as: environmental protection, social responsibility and high standards of governance.

They would also take into account environmental, social and administrative risks in the process of designing risk management processes. Socially responsible financial markets have created market structures that enable environmental / social / management companies to achieve lower financial costs through higher standards of transparency and commitment to sustainability (Ziolo et al., 2016).

The literature on the subject confirms the role of social and environmental aspects (determining ESG risk threat) in finance will increase and impact on the economic results of public and private entities. Also such factors as will increase the significance (Bank Truck Manual):

- Intensifying interactions between climate change and biodiversity and new technologies that will shape a new approach to investment, risk and return;
- High ESG ratings, which will significantly determine the cost of capital, and in particular the low cost of debt financing, which may constitute significant competition and threat to municipal bond financing;
- ESG risk weighted assets classes will be reclassified (assets not exposed to environmental risk due to changes in the environment may increase exposure to the risk), which will allow the formation of new strategies for diversification and risk management of transactions.

Taking into account the mentioned considerations, ESG risk is significant from the perspective of evaluation and functioning of banking and financial institutions. It refers to such risks as environmental risk and reputation risk.

The contemporary financial sphere is influenced by a number of factors that determine the need to implement innovative financing solutions. In the context, sustainable finance would include financial instruments, institutions and markets which would take into consideration the issues such as environmental and social responsibility of entities that seek to get finance.

Sustainability and responsibility in finance requires an ethic approach. The ethical financial instruments would properly involve provisions related to the purposes which financial funds provided by their issuance and may be used for advanced financial operations (Ziolo et al, 2016).

Contemporary financial markets still have limited adaptation to the requirements of sustainable growth and development. The low level is demonstrated by problems of: internalization of external costs, measurement and risk measurement in the activities of banking and financial institutions, lack of a comprehensive approach to balanced financial reporting, and dominant short-termism in financial decisions.

Expectations towards the role of the financial sphere are changing. The adjustment process to the sustainable finance paradigm is long-lasting and requires compromises. Key to its efficient execution is an understanding of the need for change by market participants and the cooperation between the public, private and third sectors since each of the sectors has a significant impact on the success and dissemination of the rules and principles of sustainable finance.

THE IMPACT OF FINANCIAL STABILITY ON FINANCING SUSTAINABLE DEVELOPMENT

One of the most important problems that developing countries face in the development process is the problem of financing development.

Capitalism is talking about structural crises that can't be overcome in some way, and the unsustainable development of the anti-governmental neoliberal thesis, poverty, unemployment and misery that grows, destabilizing the destruction of the environment, no longer in development but in sustainable development (Partant, 2002, p. 17). The notion of sustainable development is not just sufficient for economic growth, but rather a fair and equitable distribution of wealth between countries, regions and income groups, while also protecting environmental values (Source, 2011, p. 56). There is no doubt that economic stability is important for achieving a sustainable development. Stability is at the forefront of this point, and it is evident that financial stability is indispensable for development.

The word meaning of stability is explained in the form of continuity and determination in the same decision and form. Economic stability is defined as the absence of fluctuations such as a decrease in general economic activity and excessive increase. Two things are important in terms of stability. The first is price stability and the second is the level of full employment. In summary, stability; and that the developments in the economy continue at the expected and desired level (Karabacak, 2000, p. 50).

The phenomenon of economic instability is a problem faced by undeveloped and developing countries, and it is important to analyze the sources of economic instability thoroughly so that these countries can complete their economic development adventure (Karagöz and Ergin, 2010, p. 170).

The financial stability phenomenon, however, is confronted by some developments in recent years, not only by the supervisory authorities but also by policy makers as a topic that is discussed at the top of the day. The mentioned developments are the high growth in the volume of financial transactions, the increasing complexity of financial instruments, and the high cost of crises in the national financial system (Crockett, p. 1997).

The concept of financial stability, the existence of liquid assets in economies and the capital movements macroeconomic through financial markets have gained importance with the results (Tüzün ve Kahyaoğlu, 2015, p. 26).

In the narrowest definition of the concept of financial stability, stability, the functioning of the financial system and with the financial crises where payment systems are prevented from functioning, is considered as a situation that is not encountered. Such crises, since the monetary policy has given way to the transfer mechanism, it is also very important in terms of central banks (Doğan ve Tunalı, 2011, p. 57-58). The differences between price stability and financial stability are presented in Table 1.

Table 1. Differences between price stability and financial stability

Category	Price Stability	Financial Stability
Measurement and Definition	Yes, subject to technical queries	Hardly, except by its absence
Instrument for control	Yes, subject to lags	Limited, and difficult to adjust
Accountable	Yes	Hardly
Forecasting Structure	Central tendency of distribution	Tails of distribution
Forecasting Procedure	Standard Forecasts	Simulations or Stress Tests
Administrative Procedure	Simple	Difficult

Source: Aspachs, O., C. Goodhart, Segoviano M., Tsomocos D., Zicchino L. (2006). Searching for a Metric for Financial Stability. LSE Financial Markets Group Special Paper Series. 167, p.1-38.

Financial stability is an important step for economic stability. There will be no ambiguity and reluctance in maintaining an economy, savings owners and investors' activities in which financial stability is established and maintained. In the case of financial instability, there is a rapid increase in the real output deficit, excessive volatility in the value of financial assets and variables, and sudden decreases, resulting in the possibility of banking, money crisis and systematic crisis (Darıca, 2012, p. 3). The economic downturn that is the subject of the problem is a problem at the point of sustainability of development.

In order to establish financial stability in a country, three important conditions must be set. These conditions are the fact that important institutional intermediaries act actively and prudently, the transparency and transparency of the markets in which they trade, and finally, the infrastructure of financial transactions is robust and understandable (Delice, 2007). At this point, it is stated that a solid financial system is very important for financial stability.

Inflation-free financing, physical equilibrium and monetary equilibrium are important for meeting the financing needs of economic development. In this context, financial stability appears to be a significant influence on sustainable development.

Funding sources for development are divided into domestic financing sources and external financing sources. External financing resources are classified as foreign private capital, foreign debts, grants and external aid (Şen et al., 2011, p. 4), while internal financing resources are classified as tax and capital markets, domestic borrowing, voluntary individual and institutional savings, and inflationary financing.

Developing countries lacking an advanced, advanced money market and facing inadequate internal resources are at odds as main vehicle tax policies for the mobilization of public resources. Taxation is the most important source of financing of economic development due to both the direct contributions it makes and the indirect effects it creates in terms of control and incentives (Demircan, 2003, p. 100). Capital market importance for financial stability (CBRT, 2015, p. 6), which is defined in a wide range of cases from when the core functions of the finance market are fulfilled to when there are no financial crises.

The general approach to sustainable financing includes the economic, environmental and social sustainability of financing. Since finance and the economy are strictly and consistently solid, sustainable finance can be a vehicle for securing and supporting the framing process for sustainable development and sustainable growth; On the other hand, it may be one of the sources of distress in a particular economy. The phenomenon of financing is the best proof that finance and the financial system can be dangerous to the economy and society without effective control (Ziolo et al., 2016, 198).

In addition to price stability for sustained growth and sustainable employment growth, the existence of a stable financial environment and a healthy banking system is described as the key to the economy. For the efficient use of resources in the economy, the financial system must fulfill its intermediary function effectively. A well-functioning financial sector supports the more efficient operation of the fund flow to the economy and more resources for research and development work (CBT, 2006, p. 1).

METHODOLOGY AND DATA SET

Data and Variables

This section presents the data used in the analysis. The study sample is composed of 29 countries[2]. The frequency is yearly from 2005 to 2015. The variables are available in OECD website[3]. In the research, the variables are classified into three groups: economic, social and environmental.

The economic group includes Green tax revenues and Total central government debt % of GDP. The variable Total central government debt % of GDP is used as a proxy for economic development and we will use it as the dependent variable in the model (Y).

An overview regarding the variables used is summarized in Table 2.

Table 2. Definition of variables[4]

Group	Variable	Description	Notation
Economic	Total central government debt(Y) Environmentally related tax revenue	Debt % of GDP Max 60% of GDP Tax revenue, % of GDP	GDP TAX
Social	Income distribution and poverty, Gini Age-sex standardized rate	It ranges between 0 in the case of perfect equality and 1 in the case of perfect inequality per 100 000 population	POV HEALTH
Environmental	Environmental protection expenditure and revenues Land use Greenhouse gas emissions	Millions national currency Square kilometers Tones of CO2 equivalent, Thousands	EXP LAND GAS

Sources: OECD Data and Eurostat.

All variables mentioned above are described in details in OECD data set[5]. Total central government debt (%GDP) is limited to central government debt issuance and excludes therefore state and local government debt and social security funds. It is an indicator of an economy's health and a key factor for the sustainability of government finance. "Debt" is commonly defined as a specific subset of liabilities identified according to the types of financial instruments included or excluded.

Environmentally related taxes are an important instrument for governments to shape relative prices of goods and services. The characteristics of such taxes included in the database (e.g. revenue, tax base, tax rates, exemptions, etc.) are used to construct the environmentally related tax revenues with a breakdown by environmental domain.

The Gini coefficient is based on the comparison of cumulative proportions of the population against cumulative proportions of income they receive. Income is defined as household disposable income in a particular year. It consists of earnings, self-employment and capital income and public cash transfers; income taxes and social security contributions paid by households are deducted.

The age-standardised death rates are necessary for comparing the level of mortality across countries and over time since they take into account the differences in age structure of the populations.

Environmental protection (EP) is defined as all activities directly aimed at the prevention, reduction and elimination of pollution or any other degradation of the environment. The dataset provides information on all purposeful activities directly aimed at the prevention, reduction and elimination of pollution or any other degradation of the environment resulting from production or consumption processes.

Land resources are one of the four components of the natural environment: water, air, land and living resources. The data set gives information concerning land use state and changes (e.g. agricultural land, forest land).

The Green gas emission dataset presents trends in man-made emissions of major greenhouse gases and emissions by gas.

The variables have been selected based on the UN Commission on Sustainable Development (UNCSD), the European Commission (EC) and the OECD approach which have compiled a list of indicators for tracking sustainable development regarding three pillars / dimensions of sustainability. The sustainable development indicators proposed by OECD countries, however, shows great diversity under each of the three categories and themes proposed by the UNCSD (OECD, 2002).

Empirical Research and Results

In this section, we first provide summary statistics and investigate the relationship between the variables. Then, we will present the results of the VAR model.

The statistical analysis is carried out in the context of Vector Autoregressive Model ('VAR'). The VAR model is especially useful for describing the dynamic behavior of economic and financial time series and for forecasting.

VAR models have the advantage over traditional large-scale macroeconometric models in that the results are not hidden by a large and complicated structure (the "black box"). The results are easily interpreted and available using VAR. Sims (1980) argued that VARs provide a more systematic approach to imposing restrictions and could lead one to capture empirical regularities which remain hidden to standard procedures.

The results from policy exercises on large scale macreconometric models are hard to compare and recreate, and can easily be amended by their users with judgmental ex-post decisions. Finally, the lack of consensus about the appropriate structural model to use has led a number of economists instead to favour the use of a VAR model to examine the effects of different policies (Bjørnland, 2000).

The VAR is often perceived as an alternative to the simultaneous equation method. It is a systems regression model in that there is more than one dependent variable. In the most basic bivariate example, where there are just two variables, then each of their current values will depend on combinations of the previous values of variables and error terms.

$$y_t = \alpha_0 + \alpha_1 x_{t-1} + \beta_1 y_{t-1} \ldots\ldots + \alpha_k x_{t-k} + \beta_k y_{t-k} + u_t$$
$$x_t = \chi_0 + \chi_1 x_{t-1} + \delta_1 y_{t-1} \ldots\ldots + \chi_k x_{t-k} + \delta_k y_{t-k} + v_t$$

The number of lags included in the VAR depends on either the data (i.e. monthly data would require 12 lags) or the minimization of the Akaike or Schwarz-Bayesian criteria (maximizing in some text books depending on how the criteria is set up). In addition, it is assumed that the error term is not serially correlated. The system can be expanded to include any number of variables and is used extensively in the finance literature.

VAR models have a number of advantages over univariate time series models, for instance there is no need to specify which variables are exogenous and which endogenous, variables are by definition endogenous. (However it is possible to specify a purely exogenous variable as a regressor, in the case there would be no equation in which it was a dependent variable). In addition, the issue of model identification does not occur when using a VAR. Providing there are no contemporaneous terms acting as regressors, OLS can be used to estimate each equation individually, as the regressors are lagged so treated as pre-determined. In addition VARs are often highly efficient at forecasting compared to traditional models.

A limitation of the VAR approach is that it has to be estimated to low order systems. Effects of omitted variables will be in the residuals. The may lead to major distortions in the impulse responses, making them of little use for structural interpretations (see e.g. Hendry 1995), although the system may still be useful for predictions (see e.g. Hendry and Doornik 1997, and the references stated there). Further, measurement errors or misspecifications of the model will also induce unexplained information left in the disturbance terms, making interpretations of the impulse responses even more difficult (Bjørnland, 2000) (Hendry D., 1995).

The first figure shows the %debt GDP by country and year. We note fluctuations for the level of % debt GDP for the most of the countries with the presence of dramatically falls for some countries as Portugal in 2011 and significantly for Hungary in 2012 and Germany in 2014.

The highest level of public debt (%GDP) has been noted for PIIGS country group (Figure 2).

Studying the correlation between the variables, by using the Pearson-coefficients, fails to show any strong correlations between the variables except between land use and green gas emissions. Before the VAR estimation, we tested the series for unit roots using the augmented Dickey-Fuller (ADF) and KPSS tests[6]. The % debt GDP and the other series except income poverty and green tax revenues are not stationary[7].

Running the Granger causality[8] between the variables did not demonstrate any causality between the series. The order of the VAR model is selected according to the AIC criterion.

Figure 1. Public debt in OECD countries (%GDP)
Source: Own elaborations OECD data set.

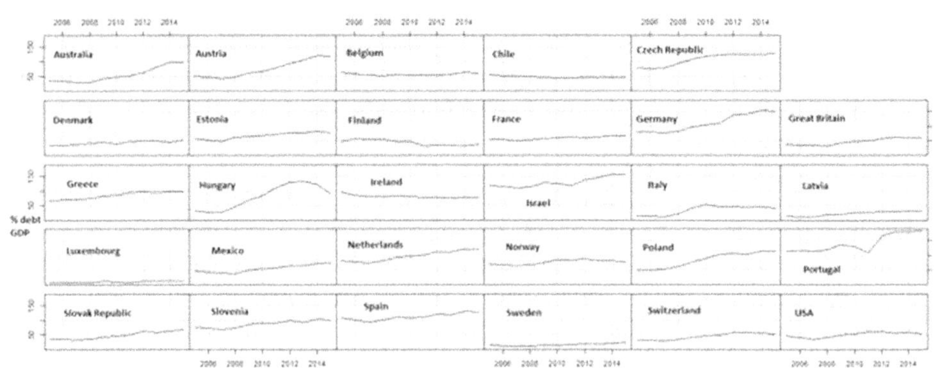

Figure 2. Public debt in OECD countries (%GDP): Comparative approach
Source: Own elaborations OECD data set.

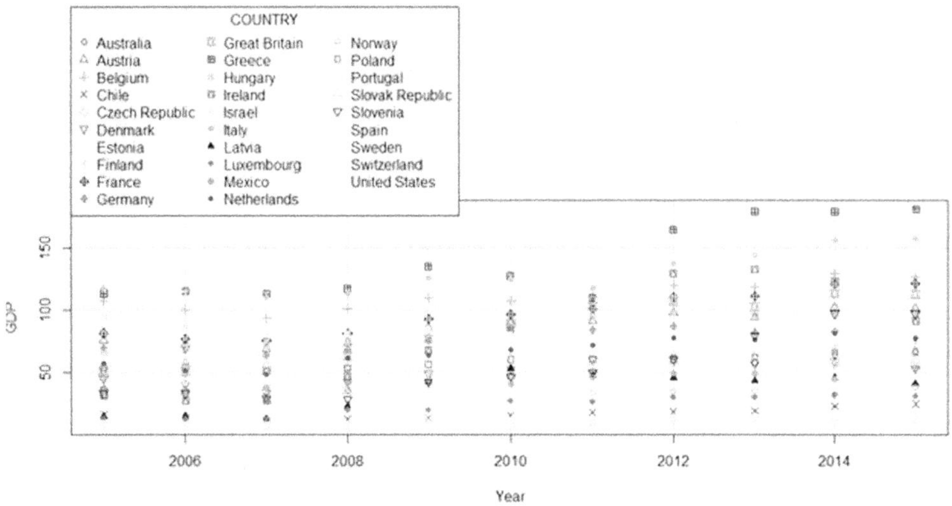

To examine the relationships between the GDP and the rest of variables, a model VAR[9] was estimated by using the lagged %debt GDP (Table 3).

Following the Table 3, we note that most coefficients are not nulls. However, the most significant ones which are significant at the level of 5% are environmentally related tax revenue, health care and land use. The Income distribution and poverty

Table 3. Estimation of VAR model

	Coefficient	Std. Error	t-Statistic	Prob.
GDP(-1)*	-0.560478	0.127351	-4.401062	0.0001
GDP(-2)	-0.140539	0.104120	-1.349782	0.1855
C	-8.154504	3.074894	-2.651963	0.0118
Environmentally related tax revenue *	-25.34447	5.407684	-4.686752	0.0000
Health care*	19.61035	2.994899	6.547917	0.0000
Income distribution and poverty (Gini)	-42.14329	65.48868	-0.643520	0.5240
Land use*	-0.000111	4.96E-05	-2.242329	0.0312
Green gas emissions	0.000109	7.20E-05	1.514227	0.1387
Environment protection expenditures and revenues	-0.003123	0.002461	-1.269039	0.2126

Note: Signs * and** denote statistical significance at the level of 5%.

has a high negative coefficient but was not significant in the model. In addition, Environment expenditures and revenues has negative coefficient but non-significant. The Environmentally related tax revenue and the land use have negative coefficients.

Environmentally related tax revenue has negative coefficient, explanation may be an effect of fiscal consolidation after the crisis 2008+. The effects of fiscal consolidation are different, and determined by many factors. The kind of fiscal consolidation[10] also matters according to its final effect. Alberto Alesina, Silvia Ardagna and Roberto Perotti emphasized that the output effect of fiscal consolidation based on expenditure is much more sustainable than if it were based on revenue. One of the crucial outcomes of fiscal consolidation should be debt reduction, as austerity programs are designed for dealing with excessive debt. Fiscal consolidation based on revenue (taxes) may result in effect described by Laffer Curve. Excessive debt needs financing so governments increase tax rates but higher tax rates could not translate into higher total tax revenue.

Contemporary land use is related to a variety of determinants not easy to observe comprehensively at the global and domestic level, among them: international capital flows, the informal economy, land use policy, and generalized transport costs. In high income countries, rates of urban land expansion are slower and increasingly related to GDP growth[11]. Negative coefficient in Land use case shows that population growth contributes more to urban expansion than land expansion. Additionally, spatial policy is also a crucial factor as increasing land use not always means higher taxes revenue and higher financial stability.

There are many theories that assumes and search the relationship between income inequality and fiscal stability, anyway based on economic literature review one significant proof of the existence of such a relationship has not been empirically tested up and proofed. There are three kind of interactions that are described based on research results. The first approach assumes that income inequality impacts on public finance only when left oriented governments rules the country and benefits from deficit financed redistribution. Second inequality occurs when the governments face political instability that deteriorates fiscal performance. The third the relations occurs when the government is supported by poor voters and deficit and fiscal unsustainability comes as a result of it[12].

The link between life expectation and public expenditures for health care is diagnosed, in sum the societies live longer as health expenditure increases. The health expenditure increases and affects public spending and public finance balance. The mortality and life long expectancy does matter and impact on financial sustainability.

CONCLUSION

The study aims to search relationship between financial stability and sustainable development and its financing. The main assumption of the research carried out was that the financial stability is a precondition for sustainable development and its financing. The countries with excessive deficit and debt (financially unstable) meet problems with balancing their budget and in case of European Union member states meet excessive deficit procedure and debt reduction requirements (austerity programs).

It is usually harmful for development process that slow down or stop and become unbalanced due to lack of public sources of financing and debt financing as well (financial distress impacted on credit worthiness and rating) and finally cut out the access to commercial financing (provided by financial sector entities). After closing restructuring process and public budget balancing, it is difficult to catch up developed countries and achieve sustainability, as it is a long term process that requires long term financing and thus good financial standing.

Taking the assumption into account the first step of the analysis was to diagnose the level of public debt (%) for every single OECD country in the period 2006-2015. The debt level (%GDP) is one of the leading measure of financial stability as it reflects the debt financing of unbalanced budget. Due to the crisis 2008 the fluctuations of debt level among OECD countries were since 2008 significant. Before and after crisis the over debt group (over 60% of GDP) was the PIIGS countries but not only (example Belgium and so on.).

The variables selected as representatives for three pillars of sustainable development were correlated with debt level. The research confirmed that there is significant relationship among financial stability and sustainable development and it is financing.

The relationship has been probed for every of three pillars of sustainable development: economic (Green tax revenues), social (Health care) and environmental (Environment protection expenditures and revenues). From an economic pillar perspective, the research result is especially significant, as it also confirmed that green taxes matter for financing of sustainable development. The Environmentally related tax revenue and the land use have negative coefficients.

The research has limitations. The most crucial is data set and missing variables, and finally missing observation that need to be estimated based on historical data or no variables that can be compared such as deficit level (%GDP). Future work will extend the number of observations and include more variable in the empirical research section.

REFERENCES

Alesina & Perotti. (1997). Fiscal adjustments in OECD countries: Composition and macroeconomic effects. *International Monetary Fund Staff Papers*, *44*, 210–248.

Ardagna, S. (2004). Fiscal stabilizations: When do they work and why. *European Economic Review*, *48*(5), 1047–1074.

Aspachs, O., Goodhart, C., Segoviano, M., Tsomocos, D., & Zicchino, L. (2006). Searching for a Metric for Financial Stability. *LSE Financial Markets Group Special Paper Series.*, *167*, 1–38.

BankTrack Manual. (n.d.). *The do's and don'ts of sustainable banking*. Academic Press.

Bordon, I., & Schmitz, B. (2015). *Financial Stability as a Precondition for the Financing of Sustainable Development in Emerging and Developing Countries. Briefing Paper no 23*. German Development Institute.

Crockett, A. (1997). *Why is Financial Stability a Goal of Public Policy?* Retrieved from https://www.kansascityfed.org/publicat/sympos/1997/pdf/s97crock.pdf

Darıcı, B. (2012). Finansal İstikrar ve Finansal İstikrara Yönelik Kamusal Sorumluluk Çerçevesinde Para Politikası: Türkiye Analizi. *Bankacılar*, 34-66.

Delice, G. (2007). *Uluslararası Finansal Kuruluşlar ve Finansal İstikrar Sorunu. 1. Basım*. Ankara: Nobel Yayın Dağıtım.

Demircan, E. S. (2003). *Vergilendirmenin Ekonomik Büyüme ve Kalkınmaya Etkisi, Erciyes Üniversitesi İktisadi ve İdari Bilimler Fakültesi Dergisi, Sayı.21*. Temmuz-Aralık.

Doğan, S., & Tunalı, Ç. B. (2011). Küreselleşme Sürecinde Finansal İstikrar-Para Politikası İlişkisi: Türkiye için Bir Değerlendirme (2001 Krizi Sonrası). *İktisat Fakültesi Mecmuası*, *61*, 51–81.

Enders, J. C., & Remig, M. (2015). Theories of sustainable development: An introduction. In J.C. Enders & M. Remig (Eds.), Theories of sustainable development (pp. 1-5). Routledge.

Epstein, M. J., & Roy, M.-J. (2001). Sustainability in action: Identifying and measuring the key performance drivers. *Long Range Planning*, *34*(5), 585–604. doi:10.1016/S0024-6301(01)00084-X

Fullwiler, S. T. (2015). *Sustainable Finance. Building a More General Theory of Finance*. Working Paper No. 106.

Ghoul, S., Guedhami, O., Kwok, H., & Mishra, K. (2014). *Corporate Environmental Responsibility and the Cost of Capital—International Evidence*. KAIST College of Business Working Paper Series, No. 2014-008.

Grober, U. (2007). *Deep roots: A conceptual history of' "sustainable development" (Nachhaltigkeit)*. WZB Discussion Paper, No. P 2007-002.

Haigh, M. (2012). Publishing and defining sustainable finance and investment. *Journal of Sustainable Finance & Investment*, *2*(2), 88–94.

Hüseyin, Saruç, & Keskin. (2011). Kalkınmanın Finansmanı. In Kalkınma Ekonomisi: Seçme Konular. Baskı: Ekin Yayınevi.

Jeucken, M. (2001). *Sustainable finance and banking: The financial sector and the future of the planet*. London: Earthscan Publications Ltd.

Karabıçak, M. (2000). Türkiye'de Ekonomik İstikrarsızlığın Tarihsel Gelişim Süreci. *Süleyman Demirel Üniversitesi İktisadi ve İdari Bilimler Fakültesi, 5*(2), 49-65.

Karagöz, K., & Ergün, S. (2010). Türkiye'de Ekonomik İstikrarsızlığın Kaynakları: Ekonometrik Bir Değerlendirme. *Süleyman Demirel Üniversitesi İktisadi ve idari Bilimler Fakültesi Dergisi, 15*(2), 169-185.

Kaynak, M. (2011). Kalkınma İktisadı. Ankara: Gazi Kitabevi.

Larch, M. (2010). Fiscal performance and income inequality: Are unequal societies more deficit – prone? Some cross country evidence. *Economic Papers, 414*. http://ec.europa.eu/economy_finance/publications/economic_paper/2010/pdf/ecp414_en.pdf

OECD. (2002). *Overview of Sustainable Development Indicators Used by National and International Agencies*. Paris: OECD.

Partant, F. (2002). Kalkınmanın Sonu "Bir Alternatif mi Doğuyor?". *Türkiye ve Orta-Doğu Forumu Vakfı, Özgür Üniversite Kitaplığı, 35*, 2.

Piketty, T. (2015). The economics of inequality. Cambridge, MA: The Belknap Press of Harvard University Press. doi:10.4159/9780674915565

Pisano, U., Martinuzzi, A., & Bruckner, B. (2012). *The financial sector and sustainable development: Logics, principles and actors*. European Sustainable Development Network, Quarterly Report No. 27.

Smith, A. (2008). *The wealth of nations. Radford.* Wilder Publications. (Original work published 1776)

Soppe, A. (2004). Sustainable corporate finance. *Journal of Business Ethics*, *53*(1-2), 213–224. doi:10.1023/B:BUSI.0000039410.18373.12

Sudana, I. P. (2015). *Sustainable development and reconceptualization of financial statements. In Procedia – Social and Behavioral Sciences 2011* (pp. 157–162). Elsevier.

TCMB. (2006). *Finansal İstikrar ve Merkez Bankaları, Bülten, Sayı.3, Eylül, Ankara.* Retrieved from http://www.tcmb.gov.tr/wps/wcm/connect/94348b7d-dc4d-4e99-a7a5-6950b9b4faf9/bulten-turkce3.pdf?MOD=AJPERES&CACHEID=94348b7d-dc4d-4e99-a7a5-6950b9b4faf9

TCMB. (2015). *Finansal İstikrar*. Ankara: Türkiye'de Finansal İstikrar Gelişmeleri, Türkiye Cumhuriyet Merkez Bankası.

Tüzün, O., & Kahyaoğlu, H. (2015). Makro İhtiyati Para Politikası Amacı Olarak Finansal İstikrar: Türkiye Üzerine Bir Uygulama. Finans Politik ve Ekonomik Yorumlar Dergisi, *52(603)*, 25–45.

UNCHE. (1972). *Declaration of United Nations Conference on the Human Environment* (No. A/Conf.48/5). Stockholm: UNCHE.

WCED. (1987). *Report of the World Commision on Environment and Development: "Our common future" (No.A/42/427)*. World Commision on Environment and Development.

Wilhelm, K. (2013). *Return on sustainability: How business can increase profitability and address climate change in an uncertain economy*. FT Press.

Wilson, C. (2010). Why should sustainable finance be given priority? Lessons from pollution and biodiversity degradation. *Accounting Research Journal*, *23*(3), 267–280. doi:10.1108/10309611011092592

WSSD. (2002). *Report of the Word Summit on Sustainable Development* (No. A/Conf.199/20). New York: United Nations.

Ziolo, M., Fidanoski, F., Simeonovski, K., Filipovski, V., & Jovanovska, K. (2016). *Sustainable Finance Role in Creating Conditions for Sustainable Economic Growth and Development*. Springer International Publishing.

ENDNOTES

1 Also known as Bruntland Report.

2 Australia, Austria, Belgium, Chile, Czech Republic, Denmark, Estonia, Finland, France, Germany, Great Britain,Greece,Hungary,Ireland,Israel,Italy,Latvia,L uxembourg,Mexico,Netherlands,Norway,Poland,Portugal,Slovak Republic, Slovenia, Spain, Sweden, Switzerland, United States.

3 http://stats.oecd.org(access: 15.08.2017)

4 We should note that we have some missing observations.

5 Description of variables based on OECD data set.

6 To confirm the test results obtained from the ADF and PP tests, *Kwiatkowski Phillips, Schmidt and Shin's* test (1992) (*KPSS*) is suggested to eliminate a possible low power against stationary near unit root processes which occurs in the *ADF* and PP tests.

7 The results are not reported but are available upon request.

8 According to Ajmi et al. (2014), the traditional approach for testing Granger causality compares the prediction errors obtained by a model that relates Y to past and current values of X and Y. The approach is naturally attractive as the test is simply asked to determine whether the coefficients of the regression model, associated with past and current values of X, are significant. The bivariate Granger (1969) framework investigates the linear Granger causality between two processes X and Y, and involves estimating a p- order linear vector autoregressive model, VAR(p).

9 The order of the VAR model is selected according to the AIC criterion.

10 Fiscal consolidation based on expenditures or revenue based fiscal consolidation.

11 See more: Seto, K. C., Fragkias, M., Güneralp, B., & Reilly, M. K. (2011). *A Meta-Analysis of Global Urban Land Expansion.* PLoS ONE, 6(8), e23777. http://doi.org/10.1371/journal.pone.0023777

12 More: M. Larch, Fiscal performance and income inequality: Are unequal societies more deficit – prone ? Some cross country evidence. Economic Papers 414, June 2010, http://ec.europa.eu/economy_finance/publications/economic_paper/2010/pdf/ecp414_en.pdf [access: 12.09.2017]

Chapter 6
Governance and Institutions for Stability and Growth in the Eurozone

Daniele Schiliro
University of Messina, Italy

ABSTRACT

This chapter aims to contribute to the debate on which kinds of governance and institutions are needed to ensure stability and growth in the Eurozone. Despite the economic recovery, the Eurozone does not have effective institutions to ensure stability in the face of a new economic crisis (without forgetting legitimacy, transparency, and the ability to meet the expectations of greater prosperity for Euro-area citizens). This chapter supports the view of a deep rethinking of the European monetary union (EMU) with a different governance and institutions. The new governance should imply a renewed political agreement among member states in both the Eurozone and the European Union (EU). This political agreement must lead to a reconsideration of the Maastricht parameters, a different approach of European institutions, and a change of the EU treaty. This chapter also discusses the role of institutions in balancing European interests with those of member states to provide a consistent approach to stability and growth.

DOI: 10.4018/978-1-5225-4026-7.ch006

INTRODUCTION

Financial fragility has been the main cause of difficulties in the world economy, particularly in the Eurozone since 2008. In fact, growth and unemployment in the Eurozone have significantly suffered since the global financial crisis. Along with the financial crisis of 2008, member states of the EMU experienced a debt crisis in 2010 that caused national-level instability. It was both a private and public debt crisis with huge imbalances (Baldwin & Giavazzi, 2015). As showed by De Grauwe (2010), during the emergence of the global financial crisis (2007-2008), the private debt of households and financial institutions increased in an unsustainable way. Bank liabilities increased their debt from less than 200% to more than 250% of gross domestic product (GDP).

However, the crisis showed that EMU's institutional architecture was flawed. In the last few years, economic conditions in the countries of the Eurozone have improved due to *ad hoc* crisis management measures, governance changes, and attempts to implement long-term reforms. Today, EMU has gained strength, but it cannot guarantee stability and growth in difficult times (European Commission, 2017b). The Eurozone does not have adequate governance or institutions in terms of economic convergence between Eurozone members. In addition, Eurozone institutions cannot ensure stability in the face of a new economic crisis (without forgetting transparency, legitimacy, and the ability to meet the expectations of greater prosperity for euro-area citizens). The following questions remain:

- Which kind of governance is more suitable for the Eurozone?
- How can stability in the Eurozone be achieved and maintained without a negative impact on growth?
- How can European institutions sustain legitimacy and accountability?

A sustainable currency union requires a governance that guarantees stability and security, coordination and growth of economic policies, and transparent and legitimate institutions. Today, the European Commission, as well as European institutions, are more aware of the needs of a sustainable currency union. However, translating awareness into operative and effective decisions and policies is problematic.

This chapter contributes to the debate on which kinds of governance and institutions are required to ensure stability and growth in the Eurozone. It supports a deep rethinking of EMU with a change to governance and institutions. The new governance should imply a renewed political agreement between the Eurozone member states, but also within the EU. This political agreement must lead to a reconsideration of the Maastricht parameters, a different approach by European institutions, and a change of the EU Treaty. This chapter will also discuss institutions' roles in balancing European and member states' interests to provide a consistent approach to stability and growth.

Next, the chapter provides an overview of the EMU governance. Then, it examines open issues in the governance and reviews which kinds of governance are needed for survival of the Eurozone. The chapter ends with a conclusion section.

GOVERNANCE OF THE EMU

The EMU has been an incomplete system because it is a monetary union without fiscal union (Eichengreen & von Hagen, 1996) even if it has some degree of centralization of the budgetary policy of several member states (Commission of the European Communities, 1977). Furthermore, the Eurozone does not meet requirements for an optimal currency area. In fact, it lacks the fiscal capacity and labour mobility advocated by the optimum currency area theory (Bayoumi & Eichengreen, 1993). In addition, its member states have not conveyed sufficiently.[1]

The EMU has a single currency. However, it is without a state (Padoa-Schioppa, 2004). There is a basic contradiction between a single supranational currency and the continuation of the nation-state-based economic policies. This contradiction has been a key factor of the European debt crisis. Since the inception of the EMU, there has neither been consensus nor political will on the balance of additional integration necessary to the appropriate functioning of the system. A challenge to this balance relies in the structural differences between the economies of the member states. This resulted in labour costs, productivity, and inflation divergences, which brought about divergences in price- and cost-competitiveness.

Another major challenge lies in balancing the trade-off between independence (in the areas of fiscal and financial policy) and coordination within a monetary union. When the Eurozone crisis began in 2010, the EMU governance system was devoid of market-sharing mechanisms and fiscal stabilization mechanisms (Alcidi & Gros, 2015).

The EMU governance[2] is built on a rules-based system with sanctions for non-compliance. However, many member countries have shown an unwillingness or inability to implement rules, namely those who advocated for strict compliance with rules like Germany and France. Since 1999, member states inconsistently applied rules to budgetary policies. A recent study of the International Monetary Fund (IMF) (Eyraud, Poghosyan & Gaspar, 2017) confirmed that EU countries were running excessive deficits and distorted budgets as they complied poorly with financial rules in the single currency area. Due to the crisis, European authorities and member states agreed to reform the governance of the EMU. Thus, the introduction of the European Semester (November 2010) as the main pillar of the new governance framework was established. This emphasized economic policy coordination and macroeconomic surveillance in the EU without changing the principle of the rules-based approach.

Apart from the European Semester, other adopted measures aimed to enhance integration and stability. Sovereign debt resolution mechanisms and bailing out facilities within the Eurozone became operational. These included the European Financial Stability Facility (EFSF) in June 2010 and the European Stability Mechanism (ESM) in October 2012. The implementation of the six-pack[3] (European Commission, 2011, December 12) and two-pack (May 2013) legislation included rules to deal with shocks and policy coordination. In January 2013, the Treaty on Stability, Coordination, and Governance in the EMU (or the Fiscal Compact[4]) reinforced the financial stability of the Eurozone through a stricter coordination of the national budget policies. This included the definition of benchmarks for structural deficit and debt-to-GDP ratio, as well as a judicial enforcement mechanism for noncompliance with such benchmarks. If followed by member states, these stability-based rules would produce convergence toward export-oriented growth and competitiveness.

The introduction of the banking union was an important step in building an integrated financial framework to safeguard financial stability and minimize the cost of bank failures. The single supervisory mechanism (SSM) and single resolution mechanism (SRM) were agreed to in 2013 and 2014. This involved the supervision and resolution of banks at national Eurozone levels. The surveillance role was given to the European Central Bank (ECB) to overcome the doom loop determined by the sovereign debt crisis. The establishment of a European deposit insurance scheme (EDIS) remained missing in the completion of the banking union. Véron (2015) underlined that a European deposit insurance with a credible backstop was an essential element of the banking union. However, it has not occurred because of a country's fear (e.g., Germany) of becoming a perennial net contributor to a deposit guarantee.[5]

Another missing element in the governance framework of the banking union is the fiscal backstop because crises affecting banks are commonly macroeconomic and general in nature. A European-level centralized fiscal backstop to finance deposit insurance and bank resolution is needed for fund credibility (Obstfeld, 2013; Schoenmaker, 2015). However, this financial focus indicates a shift in favour of the view that a single currency and financial stability are incompatible with national supervision given the interdependence of sovereigns with their banks (Pisani-Ferry, 2012). To ensure financial stability, the European Commission has established new regulations for financial systems concerning capital requirements, hedge and equity funds, and some derivatives. Regarding fiscal policy, in accordance with the Five President's Report in Completing Europe's Economic and Monetary Union (June 2015), on October 25, 2015 the European Commission established the European Fiscal Board (EFB) to implement an integrated framework for sound fiscal policies. This independent institution is tasked with coordinating the network of national fiscal councils and finding an equilibrium between compliance with tax rules in each country of the Eurozone and the results of overall fiscal policy. Finally, the ECB expanded its role of implementing unconventional monetary policies, first with the Outright Market Transactions (OMT) program in 2012 and later, in January 2015, with quantitative easing. This reinforced the tendency to supranationalism.[6]

Governance change has been slow and laborious. Political decisions were often taken only when the situation became critical.

The EMU's rules-based system suffers from several limitations. First, rules suffer from low anticipatory power. To deal with emerging risks, it is necessary to be able to quickly or automatically employ significant instruments rather than have inflexible rules (Zuleeg, 2015). A second limitation concerns the selection of appropriate rules or targets adapted to both the European economic environment and country-specific conditions. Rules and uniform policies do not fit both the European and national levels. Furthermore, cross-country spill over effects exist. Yet, their size and timing depend on economic conditions. Stringent rules may lead to suboptimal outcomes (Alcidi & Gros, 2015). Another point is that the rules are often asymmetrical. For instance, they focus on current account deficits rather than surplus, which is considered a demonstration of economic efficiency (Gros & Busse, 2013). Consequently, the correction of the evolution of internal demand of surplus countries is problematic. The rules-based system is complicated by the need to interpret rules. This leads to disagreements because the decision-making process reflects a series of compromises between EU institutions, member states, and nongovernmental interests. The body of laws and rules, as well as the available instruments, are too complex to be understood and implemented by policy-makers. Furthermore, there is the perennial question of enforcement mechanisms (Zuleeg, 2015).[7] The European Commission is the major institution in charge of enforcing the rules.[8] Lastly, in its present form, the rules-based governance framework lacks a democratic feedback mechanism through which voters effectively influence the decision-making process in Brussels (Alcidi, Giovannini, & Piedrafita, 2014).

The goal of building a European federation through evolution from the economic union to a political union has failed. The systemic problems of the Eurozone require a far-reaching degree of political union to sustain the monetary union (De Grauwe, 1992; Kaldor, 1978). The treaties of the EU and the Eurozone aim at additional integration—to a more federal, political, and fiscal union—but the current situation does not meet this goal.

The EU and the Eurozone suffer the distortion represented by the primacy of economics over politics. This is due to the existence of an economic sovereignty in the absence of a political sovereignty. Ordo-liberalism became dominant in the design of the euro, which is an ideology that has become part of the Treaty of Lisbon. While the European states' constitutional laws are often equipped with a welfare system to respond to the idea of a social market economy and the EU Treaty contains principles regarding a social market economy,[9] such institutional and political systems are under attack. The main reasons are troubles with public budgets and financial markets.[10] Thus, the conflict between the economic sovereignty of the regulators and the policy of the member states leads to the emergence of a debate amongst the reasons for stability and those of growth.

OPEN ISSUES IN THE EMU GOVERNANCE

The Eurozone crisis has brought about a fundamental shift in the EU's existing legal and institutional structures. The decision-making process combines highly centralized supranational intervention (especially monetary policy by the ECB and, to a lesser extent, budgetary policy by the European Commission) with intergovernmental control of key political decisions.[11] However, the intergovernmental method has not been able to guarantee an effective decision-making process or legitimacy to the EMU. Governments have demanded more of Europe, but not at the cost of national decision-making (Hertie School of Governance, 2015).

It follows that the economic crisis in Europe has also caused an institutional crisis, which put member countries in a bind. On the one hand, they cannot go back from the integration process. On the other hand, it is difficult to proceed with workable and effective solutions. As the crisis deepened, there has been a tendency toward nationalism, which is opposite to favourable feelings of the EU and the EMU.

In addition, the European Council, which serves the intergovernmental approach, lacks democratic legitimacy. In fact, the community method (the co-decision model of policymaking) has been overcome by a new intergovernmentalism, in which intergovernmental actors have become more active in exercising leadership (Schmidt, 2016). Big member states are exercising power outside of the formal institutions.[12] Therefore, it is necessary to act on the deficit of representation that characterize European institutions, the mechanism for the approval of laws, and, more generally, the governance (as well as the political and legal accountability lacking in the Eurozone economic governance).

The issue of fiscal union, which is important to complete the banking union, is an emblematic case. A fiscal union would empower European authorities to raise taxes. The statement, "no taxation without representation," requires equal representation for all citizens. Yet, this is a main flaw of the EU system.

Sixty years after the signing of the founding Treaty of the European Community,[13] several significant successes underpinned peace on the continent as it created a single market and single currency. Yet, the EU project faces serious political problems and economic difficulties. The evident flaws in the Euro crisis must still be fixed. Political, economic, and legal issues surrounding the functioning of the EMU remain open. At the same time, prolonged economic pain caused dissatisfaction and distrust toward the EU and its institutions, particularly the Eurozone. Populist and anti-European parties are attacking the EU's existence. The most dramatic result of the anti-EU movement is Brexit. The main political victim is the union. As Van Rompuy (2017, p. 10), former president of the European Council, maintained:

[The European Union] project is now no longer irreversible. The idea of the Founding Fathers was precisely to create irreversible economic bonds so that war would be precluded. Trade at the service of peace. Interdependence was the aim.

A typical response from Brussels regarding challenges has simply been to muddle through. This latter response favored the status quo. However, problems are not properly addressed by muddling through; the crisis remains latent. Recently, the European Commission released the *White Paper on the Future of Europe* (2017a). This paper presented five scenarios regarding the potential state of the EU by 2025 depending on choices of the member states and European institutions. The possibilities covered by the five scenarios ranged from the status quo to a change of scope and priorities to a partial or collective leap forward (European Commission, 2017a). The third scenario stated that "those who want more and more" allowed the willing member states from the EU to achieve more together in specific areas. As a result, both the Eurozone member states and other EU countries deepened their cooperation on budgetary arrangements and worked on taxation[14] and social matters.

This latter scenario embraces the idea of a multispeed Europe, which means that core members (particularly the Eurozone member states) should be able to pursue common policies and integration in areas like fiscal and welfare policy, to implement a proper banking union and a common debt instrument through sharing institutions, and collaborate in the area of defence. This group of countries should accept, for instance, the Eurogroup finance minister and the Eurozone treasury. Other EU members belong to a group that is unable to accept the sacrifice of sovereignty to join the euro. Instead, they accept the single market. However, they are united by a common set of institutions, including the council, the commission, and the European parliament, as well as interactions among member state representatives in those institutions. The Eurozone is already differentiated and strongly divided in economic policy preferences between Northern and Southern member countries. Therefore, it is preferable to reject additional uniformity. Integration should focus on compatibility and the united in diversity vision of the Draft Constitutional Treaty of the European Convention of 2003 (Hertie School of Governance, 2015). Moreover, the balance between solidarity and conditionality should be more transparent, predictable, and legitimate.

Integration and crisis management instruments must be implemented through a renewed constitutional condition to regain legitimacy. In fact, any process involving the centralization of powers and resources to a greater level of integration requires a higher degree of political union. It is necessary to provide democratic legitimacy and accountability because these kinds of proposals imply a profound transfer of sovereignty from member states to European institutions. In addition, these reforms will require new institutions and changes to the mandates of existing institutions. It follows that new actors (e.g., the European parliament) must be involved.[15] However, to achieve a more radical but necessary reform, member states should find an agreement toward a new treaty. Although it is an unfeasible goal to reach immediately, treaty change is ultimately the only realistic path to greater legitimacy and symmetric union. For instance, changes in the treaties are required for institutional issues, including the independence of the ECB, its role as a lender of last resort, fiscal austerity, and being a part of the EU Treaty.[16] According to Schmidt (2016), intergovernmental decision-making causes the council to suffer from the unanimity rule in several areas. This rule involves the treaties, which makes it difficult to forge consensus and alter existing treaties. The unanimity rule implies that lowest-common-denominator agreements are most likely where the issues are most challenging. In supranational decision making, the commission and the ECB are hemmed in by suboptimal treaties and rules agreed upon by the council. This creates insufficient flexibility or discretion to take steps to effectively implement the policies. While the EU-level institutions have strengthened in the new governance framework, the national-level government has weakened, which creates a conflict between the EU institutions and national states on fundamental issues (i.e., money, borders, and security). This creates a problem of democracy and legitimacy. As Schmidt observed, "National democracies … have increasingly become the domain of 'politics without policy,' whereas the EU level appears as 'policy without politics'" (Schmidt, 2016, p. 9). However, the European democracy consists of policies determined at the EU level, which are generally in an apolitical or technocratic manner. In the meantime, politics remain national.

Any further reform of the EMU governance must consider EU-level impacts on national democracy. This required new ways of thinking to decentralize and/or deconcentrate power and responsibility to the national level for the sake of national democracy and legitimacy (Schmidt, 2016).

GOVERNANCE FOR SURVIVAL OF THE EUROZONE

The European Commission (2017b, p. 16) acknowledges that:

The overall governance has improved but remains sub-optimal to allow the euro area to perform as well as it could, to be as responsive as it should be to changing economic circumstances and economic shocks, and to win over the mistrust of some parts of the population.

Thus, the Eurozone must simultaneously pursue growth, monetary and financial stability, and reform. The previous analysis revealed that a new governance design of the Eurozone requires a deep rethinking of EMU and the management of single currency. The Eurozone does not need, however, a centralized governance characterized by restrictive rules and sanction-triggering numbers. In particular, constraining fiscal policy limits the one avenue available to countries to cushion against asymmetric shocks. Fiscal policy can do more to support internal demand of member countries (Posen et al., 2014; Schilirò, 2017).

The rules based approach that governs the EMU has manifested its limits. Therefore, the question is whether this approach is the best route to coordinate the Eurozone economies. It is clear that strengthening the Eurozone via rules is too complex and ineffective. Analysis of the Eurozone governance suggests that its extensive and complex set of rules and procedures needs greater transparency and simplification. In addition, the Eurozone should coordinate macroeconomic governance while decentralizing microeconomic governance to the benefit of the member states. In addition, supranationalism is necessary to guarantee the overall functioning of the system and to avoid the tendency to excessive fragmentation.

A major proposal consists of reconsidering the Maastricht parameters. Should the debt criterion be set to 60% of GDP without adjusting it to a value closer to the value that emerged after the exceptional crisis that hit the Eurozone (Schilirò, 2017)?[17] Why maintain the same parameter for all the Eurozone countries? Another suggestion (Schmidt, 2016) is to make macroeconomic governance by the ECB more flexible by using the Maastricht criteria as guidelines for variable yearly targets. This would depend upon the Eurozone's employment, as well as inflation prospects. It would clearly extend the mandate of the ECB. Regarding the completion of the banking union, the ECB should continue to become a normal central bank and take the lender role as a last resort (Eichengreen & Wyplosz, 2016). In addition, ESM should directly recapitalize the banks (Schoenmaker, 2015). The deposit insurance function should be exercised at the Eurozone level. Financial stability will be improved by the implication that the fiscal backstop related to these functions is no longer at the national level.

Another important element that can contribute to overall resilience of the financial sector is the capital markets union (CMU), as stressed by the European Commission's *Reflection Paper* (2017b). CMU could augment economic risk sharing, set the right conditions for a more dynamic development of risk capital for high-growth firms, and improve choice and returns for savers (Véron & Wolff, 2015). This significant change is ongoing with some difficulties due to a system of regulated services that, in turn, imply institutions with a different regulatory enforcement and an adequate infrastructure of system-wide surveillance.

Moreover, an oriented-growth policy must be founded on a program of investments. The Juncker plan to mobilize €630 billion of extra investment for the EU is a significant decision in the right direction. However, more effort is needed. Such a policy must be founded on strengthening the aggregate demand rather than pursuing stability. This is the opposite of procyclical policies based on continued austerity (De Grauwe, 2013; Posen et al., 2014; Schmidt, 2015; Schilirò, 2017).

It is also important to make this a bottom-up process. This would be convenient when using the existing national institutional architecture of the European Semester in a decentralized manner. At that same time, it keeps the coordination at the EU level. This would make the Eurozone governance more democratically legitimate, especially if national parliaments were asked for consultation with the European parliament. Structural reforms are important to the effective functioning of the EMU. Given the interconnections across the Eurozone, macroeconomic coordination between member states and European institutions must be better addressed. Furthermore, the Eurogroup can play a greater role in the coordination of economic policies (national and Eurozone) as it considers transparent and accountable decisions.

Establishing the European finance minister, as proposed by President Juncker (who is a member of the commission, chair of the Eurogroup, and a minister responsible to the European parliament and national parliaments), can create confusion at the institutional level and prove to be a weak practice. In fact, it would become a tool of national governments within the commission. How can this minister be accountable to the 19 national parliaments? How can these parliaments sanction choices that they do not share? Finally, a European finance minister should manage a European budget under the control of the European parliament. Yet, this is far from a tax capacity independent of the financial transfers of member states.

It may be more important to have an effective process to coordinate monetary, financial, and structural policies in the Eurozone, as well as the institutions responsible for them. A close coordination between the ECB and other policy authorities is needed on macroprudential policies. A coordination by the Eurogroup of overall economic policies is also needed. The ESM could play an important role through its budget and capacity to intervene in support of the member states (as in the case of exceptional natural events that, within the constraints of budgets, would damage converging growth). Thus, the ESM should become the European Monetary Fund and the financial pillar of the EMU to help the real economy of the Eurozone.[18] With this view, the ESM could also issue Eurobonds.[19] The literature and the proposals on Eurobonds are numerous (e.g., von Weizsäcker & Delpla, 2010; Favero & Missale,

2012; Pâris, & Wyplosz, 2014; Quadrio Curzio, 2011; Tonveronachi, 2014). In fact, completing EMU with some forms of debt mutualization (i.e., Eurobonds) has been debated and interpreted as a sort of fiscal union. This fiscal union is necessary because a surviving monetary zone needs monetary integration coupled with a considerable degree of fiscal integration. The Eurozone case is a hybrid solution. It has a limited common budget and is without capacity for macroeconomic stabilization. Yet, it has a strong conditionality for fiscal discipline. In addition, a successful monetary zone needs political union (e.g., one of different types of federalism, Rodrigues, 2015).

While it is not easily achieved, a renewed political agreement is necessary for the EMU governance (Schilirò, 2017). Such political agreement must implement legislative change on crucial issues. One way to overcome these hurdles is through treaties involving the Eurozone (e.g., the stability and growth pact or the fiscal compact). They should become ordinary legislation amendable by simple majority through the community method (Schmidt, 2015). This would imply that such legislation would be open to amendment through political debate and compromise.

In addition, EU institutions require greater legitimacy, which means that they must be more accountable, open, and inclusive. It also needs greater citizen participation and representation. National parliaments would need to be better integrated into the policymaking process, which differs from the yearly European parliament-national parliament meetings established in the Lisbon Treaty. The European Commission (2017b) is aware of this debated issue. It proposed arrangements with European institutions and bodies involved in decisions on matters related to the Eurozone. However, more direct citizen access to European institutions is necessary to counter technocratic beliefs in the benefits of top-down hierarchy. This would make the governance more effective and legitimate. The recent proposal of direct election by the citizens of the president of the European Council is a step in this direction.

CONCLUSION

This chapter is a critical analysis of the current governance of the EMU. This contribution aimed to highlight the governance and institutions needed for the stability and growth of the Eurozone. The Eurozone has undergone fundamental changes due to the crisis. Although many European citizens are sceptical about the benefits of single currency, member states remain highly dependent on each other. The sharing of common interests should lead them to strengthen the EMU and its governance. Indeed, this strengthening process remains complex and delicate. It must balance the diverging interests of the Eurozone member states and their heterogeneous economies.

The *Reflection Paper on the Deepening of the Economic and Monetary Union* by the European Commission (2017b) discussed elements contributing to the completion of the EMU. This work underlined the importance of growth-oriented rather than stability-oriented policies. It also suggested other fundamental changes in the governance. A major issue in the present discussion regarded limitations of the rules-based system of the EMU. Another point focused on the method of decision-making processes. In fact, intergovernmentalism has become the primary mode of governance in the Eurozone. The analysis suggested a revision of this approach to governance due to its strong influences by the German ordo-liberalism ideology. At the same time, supranationalism has increased significantly. Although the role of the commission has grown considerably (for example, the European Semester), the ECB has become the most important actor in responding to crisis moments. The ECB has several responsibilities related to the banking union and the ESM. This growing supranationalism has been a necessary consequence of missing actions and indecisive nature of the governments of member states. It also reveals a need to rebalance tendencies to fragment the Eurozone.

Another relevant issue concerns the design of institutions. Their new role must guarantee transparency and legitimacy as it considers the interests of Europe and member states. The present contribution suggests a major role for the ESM, which is currently underutilized. It can do more for the convergence of growth in the Eurozone. In addition, decision making on Eurozone policies should include the European parliament.

Completion of the EMU is a necessary goal. However, it requires a rethinking of the entire system, which is only possible through a revision of the treaties. This process will take time and effort, as well as a new political agreement among the member states. This agreement will rework the look of the Eurozone while reforming its implementation. This approach to completing the EMU will make the Eurozone more resilient to future crises.

ACKNOWLEDGMENT

The author thanks Manuel Sanchis i Marco for his comments and observations. The usual disclaimer applies.

REFERENCES

Alcidi, C., Giovannini, A., & Piedrafita, S. (2014). *Enhancing the legitimacy of EMU governance (CEPS Special Reports No. 98)*. Brussels, Belgium: Centre for European Policy Studies.

Alcidi, C., & Gros, D. (2015). EMU governance and the limits of fiscal policy coordination. In A. P. Kyriacou (Ed.), *Redesigning European Monetary Union governance in light of the Eurozone crisis* (pp. 47–56). Barcelona, Spain: CIDOB, Barcelona Centre for International Affairs.

Baldwin, R., & Giavazzi, F. (Eds.). (2015). *The Eurozone crisis. A consensus view of the causes and a few possible remedies*. Retrieved from www.VoxEU.org

Bayoumi, T., & Eichengreen, B. (1993). Shocking aspects of European monetary unification. In F. Torres & F. Giavazzi (Eds.), *Adjustment and growth in the European Monetary Union* (pp. 193–229). New York, NY: Cambridge University Press. doi:10.1017/CBO9780511599231.014

Chang, M. (2016). The (ever) incomplete story of economic and monetary union. *Journal of Contemporary Economic Research*, *12*(1), 487–501.

Commission of the European Communities. (1977, April). *The MacDougall Report — Volume I. Report of the study group on the role of public finance in European integration. General report.* Brussels, Belgium: European Union. Retrieved from https://www.cvce.eu/obj/the_macdougall_report_volume_i_brussels_april_1977-en-c475e949-ed28-490b-81ae-a33ce9860d09.html

De Grauwe, P. (1992). *The economics of monetary integration*. Oxford, UK: Oxford University Press.

De Grauwe, P. (2010, May). *Fighting the wrong enemy*. VoxEU.org. Retrieved from http://voxeu.org/article/europe-s-private-versus-public-debt-problem-fighting-wrong-enemy

De Grauwe, P. (2013). The political economy of the euro. *Annual Review of Political Science*, *16*(1), 153–170. doi:10.1146/annurev-polisci-060911-085923

De Haan, J., Eijffinger, S., & Waller, S. (2005). *The European Central Bank: Credibility, transparency, and centralization*. Boston, MA: The MIT Press.

De Witte, B. (2012). Treaty games - Law as instrument and as constraint in the Euro crisis policy. In F. Allen, E. Carletti, & S. Simonelli (Eds.), *Governance for the Eurozone: integration or disintegration?* Philadelphia, PA: FIC Press - Wharton Financial Institutions Center.

Eichengreen, B., & Wyplosz, C. (2016). Minimal conditions for the survival of the euro. *Inter Economics*, *51*(1), 24–28. doi:10.100710272-016-0569-z

European Commission. (2011, December 12). *EU economic governance "six-pack" enters into force* (Press release). Retrieved from http://europa.eu/rapid/press-release_MEMO-11-898_en.htm

European Commission. (2017a). *White paper on the future of Europe*. Brussels, Belgium: European Union. Retrieved from https://ec.europa.eu/commission/sites/beta-political/files/white_paper_on_the_future_of_europe_en.pdf

European Commission. (2017b). *Reflection paper on the deepening of the economic and monetary union.* Brussels, Belgium: European Union. https://ec.europa.eu/commission/sites/beta-political/files/reflection-paper-emu_en.pdf

Eyraud, L., Gaspar, V., & Poghosyan, T. (2017). Fiscal politics in the Euro Area. *International Monetary Fund*. Retrieved from http://www.imf.org/en/Publications/WP/Issues/2017/01/30/Fiscal-Politics-in-the-Euro-Area-44601

Favero, C. A., & Missale, A. (2012). Sovereign spreads in the Euro Area: Which Prospects for a Eurobond? *Economic Policy*, *70*(70), 231–273. doi:10.1111/j.1468-0327.2012.00282.x

Gros, D., & Busse, M. (2013). The macroeconomic imbalance procedure and Germany: When is a current account surplus an 'imbalance'? *CEPS Policy Briefs*. Retrieved from https://papers.ssrn.com/sol3/papers.cfm?abstract_id=2360470

Hertie School of Governance. (2015). *The governance report 2015*. Oxford, UK: Oxford University Press.

Kaldor, N. (1978). The dynamic effects of the common market. In N. Kaldor (Ed.), *Further essays on applied economics* (pp. 187–220). London, UK: Duckworth.

Obstfeld, M. (2013). *Finance at a centre stage: Some lessons of the Euro crisis (European Economy, Economic Papers 493)*. Brussels, Belgium: European Commission. Retrieved from http://ec.europa.eu/economy_finance/publications/economic_paper/2013/pdf/ecp493_en.pdf

Padoa-Schioppa, T. (2004). *The euro and its central bank: Getting united after the union*. Cambridge, MA: MIT Press.

Pâris, P., & Wyplosz, C. (2014). *PADRE: Politically acceptable debt restructuring in the Eurozone (Geneva Reports on the World Economy Special Report 3)*. Geneva, Switzerland: International Center for Monetary and Banking Studies.

Pentecost, E. J., & Van Poek, A. (Eds.). (2001). *European monetary integration. Past, present and future*. Cheltenham, UK: Edward Elgar Publishing.

Pisani-Ferry, J. (2012). *The euro crisis and the new impossible trinity (Bruegel Policy Contribution, 2012/01)*. Brussels, Belgium: Bruegel.

Posen, A. S., Chopra, A., Ubide, A., Mauro, P., Kirkegaard, J. F., & Veron, N. (Eds.). (2014). *Rebuilding Europe's common future: Combining growth and reform in the Euro area (PIIE Briefing No. 14-5)*. Washington, DC: PIEE.

Quadrio Curzio, A. (2011). On the different types of Eurobonds. *Economics and Politics*, *28*(3), 279–293.

Rodrigues, M. J. (2015). The Eurozone crisis and the transformation of EU economic governance. In M. J. Rodrigues & E. Xiarchogiannopoulou (Eds.), *The Eurozone crisis and the transformation of EU Governance. Internal and external implications* (pp. 173–189). London, UK: Routledge.

Sanchis i Marco, M. (2014). *The economics of the monetary union and the Eurozone crisis*. New York, NY: Springer. doi:10.1007/978-3-319-00020-6

Schilirò, D. (2013). A new governance for the EMU and the economic policy framework. In M. C. Malaguti, B. Bossone, S. Cafaro, & S. Di Benedetto (Eds.), *Legitimacy and efficiency in global economic governance*. Newcastle upon Tyne, UK: Cambridge Scholar Publishing.

Schilirò, D. (2014). Changes in Eurozone governance after the crisis and the issue of growth. *International Journal of Social Science Studies*, *2*(2), 110–119. doi:10.11114/ijsss.v2i2.317

Schilirò, D. (2017). Rules, imbalances and growth in the Eurozone. In R. Mirdala & R. R. Canale (Eds.), Economic imbalances and institutional changes to the euro and the European Union (pp. 65-89). Bradford, UK: Emerald Publishing Limited. doi:10.1108/S1569-376720170000018005

Schmidt, V. (2015). Changing the policies, politics, and processes of the Eurozone in crisis: will this time be different? In D. Natali & B. Vanhercke (Eds.), Social developments in EU 2015. Brussels, Belgium: European Social Observatory (OSE) and European Trade Union Institute (ETUI).

Schmidt, V. A. (2016). *The new EU governance: New intergovernmentalism, new supranationalism, and new parliamentarism* (IAI Working Papers 16/11). Rome, Italy: IAI.

Schoenmaker, D. (2015). *Firmer foundations for a stronger European banking union* (Bruegel Working Paper 2015/13). Brussels, Belgium: Bruegel.

Tonveronachi, M. (2014). *The ECB and the single European financial market: A proposal to repair half of the flawed design (Public Policy Brief No. 137)*. Hudson, NY: Levy Economics Institute of Bard College.

Van Rompuy, H. (2017). Europe means more than just crisis. *Economics and Politics*, *34*(1), 1–10. doi:10.100740888-017-0055-5

Véron, N. (2015). *Europe's radical banking union (Bruegel Essay and Lecture Series)*. Brussels, Belgium: Bruegel.

Véron, N., & Wolff, G. B. (2015). *Capital markets union: A vision for the long term (Bruegel Policy Contribution, No. 2015/05)*. Brussels, Belgium: Bruegel.

von Hagen, J., & Eichengreen, B. (1996). Federalism, fiscal restraints, and European Monetary Union. *The American Economic Review*, *86*(2), 134–138.

von Weizsacker, J., & Delpla, J. (2010). *The blue bond proposal (Bruegel Policy Brief, N.2010/03)*. Brussels, Belgium: Bruegel.

Zuleeg, F. (2015). Can the Eurozone's economic governance combine political accountability, legitimacy and effectiveness? In A. P. Kyriacou (Ed.), *Redesigning European Monetary Union governance in light of the Eurozone crisis* (pp. 57–65). Barcelona, Spain: CIDOB, Barcelona Centre for International Affairs.

ENDNOTES

1 For an historical background of the EMU, see Pentecost and Van Poek (2001) and Schilirò (2013).

2 Also, the EU governance.

3 The six-pack is a set of legislative decisions to enhance economic governance. It introduced a surveillance procedure called the macroeconomic imbalance procedure. This was used to identify 10 indicators and indicative thresholds (Sanchis i Marco, 2014).

4 The core and novelty of the new treaty are in the introduction of the golden rule, which is: "the obligation to introduce into national law (preferably constitutional) the new budgetary limits defined in Article 3, para. 1, in particular a 'structural' deficit not exceeding 0.5% of the GDP" (De Witte, 2012, p.152).

5 The council, however, is continuing to work at a technical level on the commission proposal for the establishment of EDIS with the aim of strengthening the banking union.

7 OMT had spillover effects on fiscal policy (Schilirò, 2014).

8 Since the start of the EMU, ECB has been a supranational institution. ECB's primary objective, as in the Maastricht Treaty, is price stability. For an analysis of the institutional role and functioning of the ECB, see De Haan, Eijffinger, and Waller (2005).

10 For instance, the macroeconomic imbalances procedure has been limited to the detection and prevention phases. The number of member countries with excessive imbalances has increased in 2014-2016, without the corrective phase being activated.

11 However, is the commission considered to be a more political body than an independent institution?

12 The EU Treaty, Article 3 paragraph 3 states: "The Union… shall work for the sustainable development of Europe based on balanced economic growth and price stability, a highly competitive social market economy, aiming at full employment and social progress, and a high level of protection and improvement of the quality of the environment. It shall promote scientific and technological advance. It shall combat social exclusion and discrimination, and shall promote social justice and protection, …"

13 Public and private debt in Eurozone remains an important concern and an urgent priority for the European Commission (2017a).

14 EMU's main actors, however, include the ECB, the Ecofin Council and the European Commission (Chang, 2016). The Eurogroup is an informal body, which is set out in protocol 14 to the Lisbon Treaty and entered on December 1, 2009. It aims to ensure coordination of economic policies among the Eurozone member states.

15 The problem concerns mainly Germany, which of course remains the strongest country of the Eurozone. Therefore, its influence cannot be that significant. The question is whether its leadership does not become hegemony.

16 On March 25, 1957, six European countries signed the founding Treaty of a Community. This then became the EU.

17 For instance, through greater harmonization of tax rules and rates, thus reducing compliance costs and limiting tax evasion.

18 In the case of Eurozone governance, the European parliament became involved via the community method when it was asked to legislate on the stability rules, including the six-pack and the two-pack (Schmidt, 2016).

19 The ECB does not have the power to act as a lender of last resort since Article 123 TFEU prohibits monetary financing.

20 The suggestion of raising the level of the debt ratio does not imply that high debt countries can renounce fiscal discipline and sustainable public finances in the long run. It means that the 60% criterion is unrealistic.

21 Germany, through its minister, Schauble, proposes that the ESM becomes the EMU's budget auditor. This would subtract the role to the European Commission, which is considered a political body following a lax fiscal policy.

22 ESM currently issues bonds on a small scale.

Section 3
Risk Management in Crisis Era

Chapter 7
Importance of Fiscal Fundamentals for Sovereign Risk Spread

Irena Szarowská
Silesian University, Czech Republic

ABSTRACT

The chapter examines the importance of fiscal fundamentals for sovereign risk spread in the period of 1995-2015, and its goal is to test whether stronger fiscal discipline reduces sovereign risk premiums. The empirical evidence is based on unbalanced annual panel data of 15 EU countries (its time span is divided into a pre-crisis and a post-crisis period). The study applies the generalized method of moments. Evidence shows that before the financial crisis, investors generally ignored bond risk factors in individual countries, but that the spreads sharply diverged starting from the year 2008. The results confirm a statistically significant impact of fiscal fundamentals on government bond yield spread. The improvement of the governments' fiscal position reduces sovereign yield spread. In a post-crisis period, findings report the raising of the importance of fiscal variables for spread, and GDP growth became a major determinant of government bond yield spreads, followed by the budget balance and debt development.

DOI: 10.4018/978-1-5225-4026-7.ch007

INTRODUCTION

Generally, a government bond is issued by a national government and is denominated in the country`s own currency. The yield required by investors to loan funds to governments should reflect inflation expectations and the likelihood that the debt will be repaid. It means that that the price of government bonds should be expected to reflect, among other factors, market confidence in governments' commitment towards ensuring sustainable fiscal policies. The financial and economic crisis has been associated with heterogeneity in financial conditions, following a period of low and more homogeneous financing costs. Money markets have become impaired, especially across national borders; and government bond yields have diverged significantly. Overall, there is increased evidence that country-specific effects have become more important in driving financial conditions (European Central Bank, 2012). As Gerlach et al. (2010) remark, part of this increase can be attributed to developments in public debt and contingent liabilities related to the banking sector. Iara and Wolff (2014) argue that fiscal governance has an impact on the government yield spreads by reducing the probability of default.

The underlying causes of the government yield spreads increase begin in the accumulation of fiscal, macroeconomic, and financial imbalances in several countries prior to the crisis, driven in particular by decreasing interest rates around the start of the EMU and by inadequate national and European policy responses. When the crisis recrudesced, the unsustainable nature of these imbalances became evident. The rapid acceleration in government borrowing needs was boosted by the fiscal response to concerns about the possibility of a severe economic slump and the re-pricing of risks which caused the real imbalances to spill over into financial developments.

In the last years, differences in government bond yields have sharply increased. That is why the chapter examines the role of fiscal fundamentals for sovereign risk spread in selected European Union member states. The aim of the chapter is to test the impact of GDP growth, budget balance, debt, and the fiscal rules index on government bond yield spread and to verify whether stronger fiscal discipline reduces sovereign risk premiums.

BACKGROUND

There is no doubt that government bond prices are closely linked to real economic activity through a variety of channels, though the theory does not clearly identify the direction of the causal relationships between variables. Already, Morck et al. (1990) identified main channels through which bond prices are linked to real economic activity. Their theory is supported by the fact that managers of big corporations make their investment decisions based on the information provided by stock markets; and they also argue that equity prices reflect the present value of dividends paid in the future. Figure 1 depicts the main linkages between the economy, the banking sector, and government bond markets. Arrows indicate the channels through which deteriorating conditions in one area affect the other two areas.

The intention of the chapter is to find the main fiscal fundamentals affecting yield spreads of EU countries' government bonds. The literature has analyzed several determinants of yield spreads. This research is based on the yield spreads of bonds issued by European countries versus the German benchmark figures. Yield spreads result from several reasons. Apart from default risk, the yield spreads are influenced by liquidity risk and market sentiments toward investments in risky bonds.

A wide range of literature deals with determinants of government bond yield spreads. Szarowská (2014) summarizes the results of main studies focused on bond spreads in the EU countries. The results are rather heterogeneous – not only for different samples, but even for rather similar samples such as the Eurozone countries – which a comparison of the results from Lemmen and Goodhart (1999) with those of von Hagen et al. (2011), for example, shows. To a certain extent, these differences may result from different observation periods. Another reason could be seen in a fact that papers also differ considerably with respect to tested variables.

Figure 1. Main linkages between the economy, the banking sector, and the bond market
Source: Author's compilation.

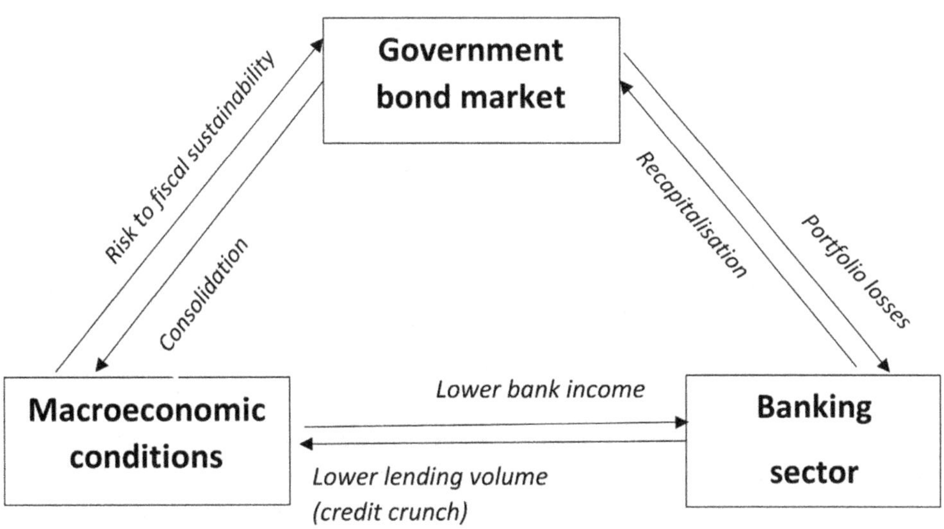

Studies on EU government bond yields fall into two categories, respectively covering the period prior to and following the global financial crisis. As Manganelli and Wolswijk (2007) notice, both groups of studies follow the literature on government bond yields; modeling the latter on three main variables:

- **International Risk:** A factor capturing the level of perceived financial risk and its unit price. Typically, this is empirically approximated using indexes either of the US stock market's implied volatility or of the spread between the yields of US corporate bonds against US treasury bills (as captured by volatility indices and/or corporate rate spreads).
- **Credit Risk:** A factor reflecting the probability of default on behalf of a borrower; approximated using indicators of past, or projections of future, fiscal performance. Existing evidence suggests that markets attach additional risks both to the loosening of observed fiscal positions and to shifts towards the loosening of fiscal policy expectations (Afonso et al., 2015).
- **Liquidity Risk:** A factor referring to the size and depth of the government bonds market and which captures the possibility of capital losses due to early liquidation or significant price reductions resulting from a small number of transactions (Favero and Missale, 2012).

Studies on European government bonds for the period preceding the global credit crunch are not unified regarding the role of each of the three variables discussed above. Before 2007, the international risk factor was an important determinant of bond yields and spreads, as suggested by studies including Codogno et al. (2003), Manganelli and Wolswijk (2007), and Favero and Missale (2012). Codogno et al. (2003) point out that the effect was stronger during periods of tightening international financial conditions and more prominent in countries with high levels of public debt.

As implied by Codogno et al (2003), Faini et al. (2006) or Manganelli and Wolswijk (2007), sovereign credit risk was priced in government bond yields. Bernoth et al. (2006) and Schuknecht et al. (2009) interpret this finding as evidence that the Stability and Growth Pact operated as a credible mechanism enforcing fiscal discipline among EMU members. This interpretation has been contested by Manganelli and Wolswijk (2007), who suggest that the penalties imposed by the markets were not sufficiently high enough to prevent unsustainable national fiscal policies, alas Greece. Similarly, Afonso et al. (2015) report that the fiscal policy events in 2002 in the EU had only small effects on government bond yield spreads; while Hallerberg and Wolff (2008) find that the effect of fiscal performance on EMU sovereign bond yields has weakened following the introduction of the euro. Bernoth et al. (2006) admit that default risk in the EMU context has been seen in the past but has been rather subdued.

The effect of liquidity risk for the period preceding the global financial crisis is questionable. Codogno et al. (2003), and Bernoth et al. (2006), as well as Pagano and von Thadden (2004), find a limited and declining liquidity effect on EMU spreads. On the other hand, Alexopoulou et al. (2010) and Manganelli and Wolswijk (2007) find that liquidity is an important determinant of yields spreads. Liquidity effects are found to be stronger during periods of tightening financial conditions and higher interest rates, during which time market participants are willing to trade lower yields for higher sovereign debt liquidity.

There is a growing focus in the literature on the crisis period. It is possible to identify two main findings. First, during the crisis period, markets have been penalizing fiscal and other macro-imbalances much more heavily than before (Afonso et al., 2015, Maltritz, 2012). Second, the observed widening in EMU spreads is largely driven by the increased global risk factor. In this period, the role of domestic banking sectors is crucial, as suggested by Gerlach et al. (2010) and Acharya et al. (2014). Global banking risk appears to have been transformed into sovereign risk through three channels:

1. Shortages in banking liquidity restricted credit to the private sector, causing economic recession and increasing fiscal imbalances.
2. Governments were obliged to recapitalize banks using public money, thereby further increasing fiscal liabilities. In relation to this, if bank bailouts are perceived to be at least partly financed through future taxation, they reduce the non-financial sector's incentives to invest—thereby hurting growth and, implicitly, expected future public revenue.
3. The announcement of a banking bailout itself lowers the price of government debt due to the anticipated dilution of newly-issued debt. With national banking sectors' having different degrees of exposure to global financial conditions, the increase in the common global risk factor causes a heterogeneous impact on national spreads. Schuknecht et al. (2010) and Afonso et al. (2012) establish the importance of the global risk factor during the crisis period and its impact on the latter through the financial/banking sector.

Although most studies are focused on the EMU, some authors also analyze Central and Eastern European (CEE) countries. Alexopoulou et al. (2010) propose an empirical assessment of the determinants of the borrowing costs of new European Union member countries. The results suggest that fundamentals still matter for market assessment of a country´s creditworthiness. In the context of heightened risk aversion, a group of countries characterized by low fiscal discipline is more exposed to domestic sources of vulnerability as well as to swings in market perceptions of sovereign risk. Ebner (2009) studies the spread between 10-year Euro-denominated

CEE government bonds and their German counterpart. While higher ECB reference rates and market volatility increase bond spreads and turn out to be their main driving factors, there is no common pattern of macroeconomic fundamentals—a fact pointing to strong heterogeneity within the CEE region. Overall, market variables are found to have been more significant than fundamentals during 1999 to 2007.

Lo Conte (2009) reviews the literature concerning the determinants of yield spreads on government bonds at the level of European and emerging markets. The value of bonds issued by emerging economies has reached high levels in the 1990's with important implications for the operation of international capital markets. This survey provides an extensive overview of the most recent explanations for the observed yield spreads on sovereign bonds. Finally, Faini et al. (2006) note that an appetite for fiscal discipline has been steadily declining among most industrial countries. In the past, fiscal profligacy would have been punished by markets with higher interest rates and, in some cases, also exchange rate depreciation. However, in post-EMU Europe, exchange rate markets no longer discipline the fiscal behavior of national governments. To limit countries' incentive to run expansionary fiscal policies, a set of rules like those embedded in the Stability and Growth Pact is needed.

Aßmann and Boysen-Hogrefe (2009) investigate determinants of government bond spreads in the Euro area during the pre-crisis and crisis periods. They conclude that default risks measured via expected debt-to-GDP ratios explain a good stake of the variation of bond spreads in the Euro area at least between 2003 and the take-off of the financial crisis. During the financial crisis, default risks – or rather, their evaluation – increased—but lost their relative importance as compared to liquidity risks.

One of the latest research studies is done by Paniagua et al. (2015), who report the importance of three groups of variables—namely, the fundamental variables of debtor economies; changes in risk-aversion; and liquidity variables. In addition, their model includes unobserved components that are estimated through the Kalman filter and which show the importance of expectations, of adding (or reducing) credibility to the future performance of the debtor´s country, and also of inducing a time-varying behavior of steady-state estimates of the parameter.

Finally, it is possible to summarize the results of the empirical studies as being rather heterogeneous; i.e., different papers report different variables as being the main drivers of spreads. This may be due to differences in the econometric models used, country samples taken, observational periods investigated, and variables considered (for details, see Szarowská 2013, 2015).

MAIN FOCUS OF THE CHAPTER

It is possible to analyze government bond yield spread using many approaches and criteria. The aim of the chapter is to test the impact of GDP growth, budget balance, debt, and the fiscal rules index on government bond yield spread and to verify whether stronger fiscal discipline reduces sovereign risk premiums. Fiscal discipline is understood as being a compliance with targets for budgetary aggregates – such as the government budget balance, debt, expenditure, or revenue developments. It should be noted that the goal of this empirical analysis is not to find the ideal model describing the behavior illustrated by the variables, but rather to analyze a nature of the relationships between sovereign risk premiums and selected fiscal fundamentals in 15 selected members of the European Union.

The study is based on unbalanced annual panel data of the EU Member States in the period from 1995 to 2015 (the newest available data are from 2015). The sample selection is limited by the availability of data. That is why the empirical examination is performed for 15 EU countries – namely, Austria (AT); Belgium (BE); Finland (FI); France (FR); Germany (DE); Greece (GR); Ireland (IE); Italy (IT); Luxembourg (LU); the Netherlands (NL); Portugal (PT); Spain (ES); Denmark (DK); Sweden (SE); and the United Kingdom (UK).

Model Specification

The empirical model uses panel data; as panel data have both cross-sectional and time series dimensions; and the application of regression models to fit econometric models are more complex than are those for simple cross-sectional datasets. Estimations are based on dynamic panel data estimators using the differenced Generalized Method of Moments (GMM) with Arellano-Bond type instruments (Arellano and Bond, 1991). The basic model is defined in equation (1):

$$spread_{it} = \alpha_i^* + \beta_1 {*}GDP_{it} + \beta_2 {*}BALANCE_{it} + \beta_3 {*}DEBT_{it} + \beta_4 {*}FRI_{it} + u_{it} \quad (1)$$

The constants are specific to the *i*-th unit (country) at time *t*—but, at the same time, are constant. β' is the vector dimension *1xK* constants and αi^* is a constant representing the effects of those variables, which are characteristic of the *i*-th observation. The government bond spread is expressed as a difference in comparison to German data, which leaves a panel dataset of 14 countries. Germany is chosen as the benchmark country, as the Bund is considered to be the benchmark bond in the respective bond market (for details, see Dunne et al., 2007). The dataset used in the analysis consists of annual data on government bond spreads (*spread*) represented by a difference between the members´ 10-year government yields and the German

Bunds' interest, a GDP growth rate (*GDP*), a budget balance listed in terms of a percentage of GDP (*BALANCE*), debt as a percentage of GDP (*DEBT*), and the fiscal rules index (*FRI*). The unit error component u_{it} represents non-significant effects of variables inherent to the *i*-team observations within a given time interval. The dataset is collected from the Eurostat database on economy and finance.

The GMM is a generic method for estimating parameters in statistical models. Verbeek (2000) writes that it is usually applied in the context of semi-parametric models where the parameter of interest is finite-dimensional, whereas the full shape of the distribution function of the data may not be known. The GMM is popular in estimating structural economic models, as it requires quite fewer conditions on model disturbances than does Maximum Likelihood. Hansen (1982) mentions another important advantage: It is easy to obtain parameter estimates that are robust to heteroscedasticity of unknown form.

Many studies point out that using a non-stationary macroeconomic variable in time series analysis causes superiority problems in regression. Thus, a unit root test should precede any empirical study employing such variables. Recent literature suggests that panel-based unit root tests have higher descriptive power than do unit root tests based on individual time series. Panel unit root tests are similar, but not identical to, unit root tests carried out on a single series (Verbeek, 2000). Used panel unit root tests confirm the stationarity of all time series on the first difference.

SOLUTIONS AND RECOMMENDATIONS

Klepsch and Wollmershäuser (2011) highlight the differentials between 10-year EMU government bond yields and German bond yields convergent with the introduction of the euro in 1999; noting that the spreads sharply diverged again at the beginning of the financial crisis in 2007. Recent studies analyzing the impact of the financial crisis on EMU government bonds have included additional variables in order to explain increasing yield spreads. Gerlach et al. (2010), for example, include a crisis dummy with a value of zero before the crisis and a value of one from the beginning of the crisis. They also use the total assets of the banking sector to find evidence of an emerging linkage between the financial sector and public budgets.

Figure 2 shows development of 10-year government bond yield listed in terms of percentage per annum (% p.a.). The two decades preceding the crisis witnessed a substantial decline in nominal interest rates and financing costs in all EU countries. Missio (2012) draws attention both to the completion of the Single Market in financial services and to the members' deeper financial integration—factors which were associated with a strong convergence in financial conditions across the EU and especially in the EMU. With the financial crisis, market uncertainty and investors' risk

Figure 2. Long-term interest rate (10-year government bond yield) in % p.a.
Source: Author's compilation, based on data from the Eurostat database.
Note: GR, PT (right-hand scale).

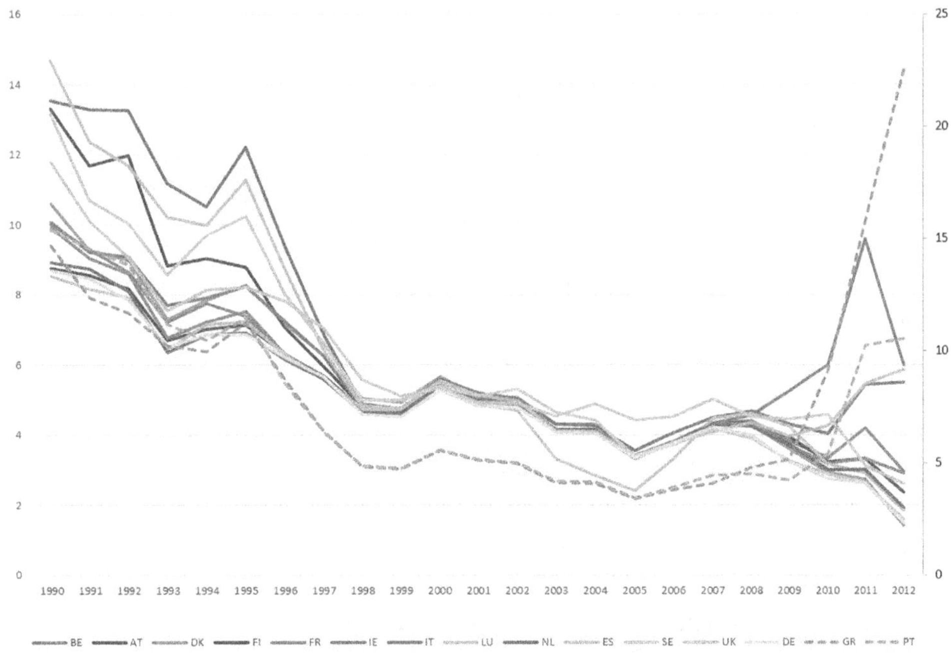

**For a more accurate representation see the electronic version.*

aversion increased. As a consequence, investors reassessed their risk, concentrating especially on the credit risk of an asset. The fiscal variables, such as debt or deficit ratios, show a positive influence on yield spreads in many studies.

Prior to the crisis, the convergence of financial conditions masked divergences in national policies and the accumulation of fiscal, macroeconomic and financial imbalances in several euro area countries. These imbalances were not adequately addressed, either at the national or at the European level. They created vulnerabilities in these countries and paved the way for the sudden return of differentiated financial conditions when risks were repriced. Imbalances related, for example, to government financial positions in some countries. Following the start of the EMU, government finances benefited from the easier access to financing that emanated from the elimination of exchange rate risk, and an under-appreciation of risk by financial market participants. Progress towards sound and sustainable public finances was limited, owing partly to a loose and, over time, a more relaxed interpretation of European budget rules. Market discipline was also weak, as reflected in very limited dispersion in interest rates on government bonds. Particularly, as a result, those governments that had experienced high interest rates before joining EMU witnessed a major relaxation of financial conditions (for details, see Szarowská, 2013).

The financial crisis that erupted in September 2008 with the default of Lehman Brothers marked a halt in the trend towards more homogenous financial conditions. The European Central Bank (2012) reported that secured and unsecured money markets became increasingly impaired, especially across national borders. Public finances deteriorated sharply on account of the crisis, against the background of persistently-high debt ratios and substantial banking sector support, especially in countries with a very large banking sector in relation to GDP. Rapidly-increasing public deficits, debt, and contingent liabilities raised questions about the sustainability of public finances in some euro area countries, as reflected in higher government bond yields (reaching a peak in 2012) and a drying up of liquidity in some markets. The government debt crisis that erupted in May 2010 was initially centered on adverse fiscal developments in Greece, but then spread to Ireland and Portugal; at a later stage, Spain and Italy also became the subject of intensified market scrutiny. The lack of confidence in governments' willingness to tackle the crisis, in combination with the lack of an effective resolution mechanism, also spread to other governments. This phenomenon is referred to as "contagion". Roaf et al. (2014) give a comprehensive and detailed overview about this development in their regional economic report.

Tackling the problems in public finance, in macroeconomics, and in banks' balance sheets is complicated because of their close linkages. During a crisis, these links may be destabilizing and potentially self-reinforcing. For instance, substantial holdings of domestic government debt in their portfolios made banks in the affected countries vulnerable to rises in government bond yields; while at the same time, the weakened financial position of domestic banks required those governments to finance additional support to the banking sector (e.g. in Ireland).

In line with public finance consolidation problems (see Figure 3, which shows general government gross debt and government deficits in terms of percentage of GDP), governments have increasingly adopted numerical fiscal rules over the last 20 years. There were 117 numerical fiscal rules in force in 2015 in comparison with the no more than 13 numerical fiscal rules in force in 1990 (OECD, 2014 and Lledó et al., 2017).

Theoretical and Expected Impact of Variables

Fiscal policy rules set numerical targets for budgetary aggregates, and they are cumulatively expressed in terms of a fiscal rules index (FRI). They pose a permanent constraint on fiscal policy which is expressed in terms of a summary indicator of fiscal outcomes, such as the government budget balance, debt, expenditure, or revenue developments. The primary objective of fiscal rules is to enhance budgetary discipline. The dataset covers all types of numerical fiscal rules (budget balance, debt, expenditure, and revenue rules) at all levels of government. Additionally,

Figure 3. Fiscal position in 2016
Source: Author's compilation, based on data from Eurostat Government finance statistics.

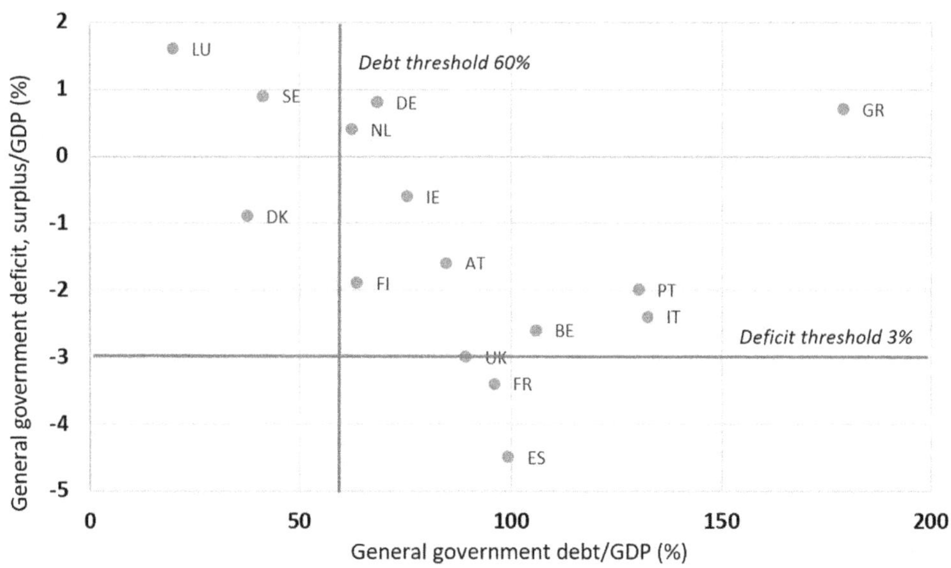

fiscal rules may further contribute to the reduction of uncertainty regarding future fiscal policy development. European Commission services have compiled a dataset on domestic fiscal rules in force since 1990 across EU countries by collecting directly this information from the EU Member States. The dataset covers all types of numerical fiscal rules (budget balance, debt, expenditure, and revenue rules) at all levels of government.

Fiscal rule index (FRI) is constructed by summing up all fiscal rule strength indices in force in the respective Member State, weighted by the coverage of general government finances of the respective rule (i.e. public expenditure of the government sub sector(s) concerned by the rule over total general government expenditure). The assigned weights are mainly determined by the fiscal strength of the rule and by its coverage. The fiscal rules database contains the time series for the 1990-2015 fiscal rule index. Most EU countries improved their fiscal discipline between 2010 and 2015, as indicated by comparing their FRI scores from each year. It is expected that the improvement of governments´ fiscal discipline and the growth of FRI reduce the sovereign bond spread.

The budget balance is the very important determinant of sovereign yield spreads which has been found to be significant in several empirical studies. The countries' budget balance plays the most prominent role (mostly in terms of deficit to GDP) in public discussion and is also named in the Maastricht Treaty as being important stability criterion that EMU countries are required to fulfill. By the theory, a negative budget balance (deficit) is supposed to lead to higher market perception of default risk and to higher yield spreads – e.g., since it points to problems in financing the government's budget by taxes, which in turn may result from a weak tax system or a weak state of the economy.

Total government debt is another important driver found to be significant in a variety of empirical studies and is also named as a stability criterion in the Maastricht Treaty. This variable reflects the hypothesis that higher indebtedness increases *ceteris paribus* (the default risk) and therefore yield spreads. This is the case because higher indebtedness means the country must spend more funds for debt servicing. For higher debt service payments, the requirements on ability and willingness to pay are higher; and thus, a default is more likely.

While the variables related to the debt situation describe the payment obligations the government has to fulfill, an additional factor is that the government's ability to meet these obligations is additionally of crucial importance for yield spreads. There are several hypotheses and variables with regards to the government's ability to meet debt service requirements. First, the overall state of the economy can be important. The most important indicator used here is the growth of GDP, which is supposed to have a negative influence on spreads. It is easier for growing economies (in comparison to stagnant economies) to assume greater debt risk (*ceteris paribus*). Earlier theoretical contributions on the sustainability of countries' debts point to the relationship between the growth rate of GDP and the growth rate of debt. From a theoretical point of view, the debt burden – even if that debt is constantly growing – is not problematic so long as the debt grows at a slower rate than the GDP does.

Inflation is also found in the literature to be a significant determinant of spreads. AS it is, inflation is not included in a dataset. This is because EMU member states face the monetary policy made by the European Central Bank; and as because other member states also deal independently with monetary policy (possibility doing so to achieve the optimal level of inflation without the support of monetary instruments is problematic and limited).

Impact of Fiscal Variables on Government Bond Yield Spread: Empirical Evidence

In order to test whether fiscal fundamentals matter for government bond yield spread. Estimated econometric models are expressed in basic form in the equation (1) cited earlier. Information criteria (Akaike criterion, Schwarz criterion, and Hannan-Quinn criterion) identified the optimal time lag as being 1 year. Splitting the time span into two periods allows for deeper analysis of structural changes as related to the impact of crises. The period was divided in two by the year 2008. Models 1 is focused on the whole period (1995; resp., 1996-2015), Model 2 on the pre-crisis period (1995;

resp., 1996-2007) and Model 3 on the post-crisis period (2008-2015). Table 1 presents the most appropriate specifications of models resulting from usage of the GMM.

For specifications of models, the Dynamic Panel Data Model Wizard is applied. The wizard aids in specifying members of the class of dynamic panel data models with fixed effects. All models include a cross-section of fixed effects (orthogonal deviations) and constant added to the instrument list. Models 2 and 3 also contain period-fixed effects as dummy variables to better capture the impact of the crisis (there are labeled in each period according to "year"). Their addition increased the statistical quality of the models. The validity of the instruments was tested using a standard Sargan test (as indicated by the J-statistic in Table 1). With regard to the number of instruments and on the 5% significance level, it is not possible to reject the hypothesis claiming that the instruments are valid. Thus estimated results are considered to be correct.

The main results concerning the effect of fiscal variables on government bond yield spread indicate that impact is stronger for a post-crisis period than a pre-crisis period. Table 1 shows that the estimated coefficients of *GDP* and *balance* are negative and statistically significant. This finding confirms that positive economic development as expressed by GDP growth as well as an increase in budget balance contribute to lower government bond yield spread. Contrary to this finding, however, it seems mixed results that increases of debt have a negative influence on government bond yield spread; as coefficients are positive, and this means increases of government bond yield spread. Coming to a conclusion about the importance of period-fixed effects is not an unambiguous process, as estimations provide mixed results regarding statistical significance. Although an increase of *FRI* expresses better fiscal discipline, results do not confirm its statistical significance and importance – although *FRI* growth reduces government bond spread in line with theoretical expectations. The reason can be seen in the fact that the price of government bonds reflects market confidence in governments' commitment towards sustainable fiscal policies and that only 44% of numerical fiscal rules reflect the development of central and general government. Moreover, *FRI* is calculated *ex-post facto*; and investors probably do not reflect its development.

The budget balance is a significant determinant of government yield spreads, and has also been found to be relevant in several empirical studies referenced above. The countries' budget balance plays the most prominent role in public discussions and is also named in the Maastricht Treaty as being an important stability criterion that EMU countries are required to fulfill. This conclusion is also reported by researchers such as, for instance,Faini et al. (2006) and/or Paniagua et al. (2015). Also Costantini et al. (2014) conclude that fiscal imbalances are the main long-run drivers of sovereign spreads. By this theory, a negative budget balance (a deficit) is supposed to lead to higher market perception of default risk and to higher yield spreads.

Table 1. Panel regression estimations (GMM)

Variable	Model 1	Model 2	Model 3
$SPREAD_{(-1)}$	0.594**	0.294**	0.311**
GDP	-0.169**	0.033**	-0.249**
BALANCE	-0.042	-0.012**	-0.129**
DEBT	0.017**	0.003**	0.018*
FRI	-0.015	-0.071**	-0.027
Period"1996"		-0.933**	
Period"1997"		-0.360**	
Period "1998"		0.0041	
Period "1999"		0.067*	
Period "2000"		-0.023	
Period "2001"		0.094*	
Period "2002"		-0.047*	
Period "2003"		-0.062	
Period "2004"		-0.037	
Period "2005"		0.014	
Period "2006"		0.007	
Period "2007"		0.070	
Period "2008"			-1.200*
Period "2009"			-1.603**
Period "2010"			-1.915**
Period "2011"			0.0549
Period "2012"			0.953*
Period "2013"			1.008
Period "2014"			-0.449
Period "2015"			-0.329
S.E. of reg.	1.024	0.342	1.599
S.D. depend. variable	1.994	0.437	2.119
Instrumental rank	173	132	44
J–statistics	148.828	105.936	37.116
Observations	289	163	112

Source: Author's calculations.

Symbols *, ** denote significance at the 5% and 1% levels; standard deviations are listed in parentheses.

Total government debt reflects the hypothesis that higher indebtedness increases *ceteris paribus* (the default risk) and therefore yield spreads. For higher debt service payments, the requirements on ability and willingness to pay are higher—and thus, a default is more presumable; and government bond yield spreads are increased.

The rising importance of fiscal variables for specifying spread, and GDP growth became a major determinant of government bond yield spreads, followed by the budget balance and debt development. It suggests that investors started to consider and valuate risks caused by the real economic imbalances to government bond yield spread.

FUTURE RESEARCH DIRECTIONS

After the financial crisis of 2007, the most important questions are:

- What is the role of contemporary monetary and fiscal policy – and, in this context, what is the role of the government – in preventing the next crisis and stabilizing the economy?
- How does one design budget constraints and financial instruments to best secure economy, business, households, governments and financial institutions?
- How does one encourage investors to regain their trust in financial markets and financial institutions?

The financial system is the primary channel through which monetary and fiscal policies affect the economy and prices. The price of government bonds should reflect, among other factors, market confidence in governments' commitment towards assuring sustainable fiscal policies.

The evidence shows that before the financial crisis, investors generally ignored bond risk factors in individual countries; but that beginning from the year 2008, the spreads sharply diverged. Findings suggest the importance of responsible fiscal policy for stabilization of the economy and government bond yield spread. The improvement of government's fiscal position reduces sovereign yield spread and the price of financial resources. In a post-crisis period, findings report that the rising importance of fiscal variables specifying spread, and GDP growth became a major determinant of government bond yield spreads, followed by the budget balance and debt development.

CONCLUSION

The aim of the chapter was to test the impact of GDP growth, budget balance, debt, and the fiscal rules index on government bond yield spread and to verify whether stronger fiscal discipline reduces sovereign risk premiums in selected European Union member states over the period from 1995 to 2015. This chapter summarizes some of principal trends in the development of government bond prices and government bond yield spread. Data show that 10-year differentials between countries´ government bond yields and German bond yields converged and that investors generally ignored bond risk factors in individual countries before the financial crisis – but that beginning from the year 2008, the spreads sharply diverged and increased.

The empirical evidence – based on the unbalanced annual panel data of 15 EU countries – confirms the statistical significance of the impact fiscal fundamentals on government bond yield spread. The study uses the Generalized Method of Moments; and the time span under analysis is divided into a pre-crisis and a post-crisis period.

In a post-crisis period, findings report that the rising significance of fiscal variables specifying spread and GDP growth became a major determinant of government bond yield spreads, followed by the budget balance and debt development. This trend is common to all models and confirms that fiscally unfavorable development can presumably lead to higher market perception of default risk; to higher yield spreads; and to the expectation that growing economies can more easily fulfill given payment obligations than stagnating economies can. The improvement of fiscal discipline – as expressed by increasing the budget balance – reduces government bond yield spreads. On the contrary, growing debt raises the possibility of state bankruptcy; and therefore, the increasing of debt has a negative effect on the price of government bonds and spread. Surprisingly, the fiscal rules index has not had a statistically-significant impact on spread.

ACKNOWLEDGMENT

This research was supported by the Ministry of Education, Youth and Sports Czech Republic within the Institutional Support for Long-term Development of a Research Organization in 2017.

REFERENCES

Acharya, V. V., Drechsler, I., & Schnabl, P. (2014). A Pyrrhic victory? Bank bailouts and sovereign credit risk. *The Journal of Finance*, *69*(6), 2689–2739. doi:10.1111/jofi.12206

Afonso, A., Arghyrou, M. G., & Kontonikas, A. (2015). *The determinants of sovereign bond yield spreads in the EMU* (Working paper). Eurosystem: European Central Bank. Retrieved from https://www.ecb.europa.eu/pub/pdf/scpwps/ecbwp1781.en.pdf

Alexopoulou, I., Bunda, I., & Ferrando, A. (2010). Determinants of Government Bond Spreads in New EU Countries. *Eastern European Economics*, *48*(5), 5–37. doi:10.2753/EEE0012-8775480502

Arellano, M., & Bond, S. (1991). Some tests of specification for panel data: Monte Carlo evidence and an application to employment equations. *The Review of Economic Studies*, *58*(2), 277–297. doi:10.2307/2297968

Aßmann, Ch., & Boysen-Hogrefe, J. (2009). *Determinants of government bond spreads in the Euro area – in good times as in bad* (Kiel Working Paper vol. 1548). Retrieved from https://www.files.ethz.ch/isn/108449/kwp-1548.pdf

Bernoth, K., von Hagen, J., & Schuknecht, L. (2012). Sovereign Risk Premiums in the European Government Bond Market. *Journal of International Money and Finance*, *31*(5), 975–995. doi:10.1016/j.jimonfin.2011.12.006

Codogno, L., Favero, C., & Missale, A. (2003). Yield spreads on EMU government bonds. *Economic Policy*, *18*(37), 503–532. doi:10.1111/1468-0327.00114_1

Costantini, M., Fragetta, M., & Melina, G. (2014). Determinants of sovereign bond yield spreads in the EMU: An optimal currency area perspective. *European Economic Review*, *70*, 337–349. doi:10.1016/j.euroecorev.2014.06.004

Dunne, P. G., Moore, M. J., & Portes, R. (2007). Benchmark Status in Fixed-Income Asset Markets. *Journal of Business Finance & Accounting*, *34*(9-10), 1615–1634.

Ebner, A. (2009). An Empirical Analysis on the Determinants of CEE Government Bond Spreads. *Emerging Markets Review*, *10*(2), 97–121. doi:10.1016/j.ememar.2009.02.001

European Central Bank. (2012). Heterogeneity in Euro Area Financial Conditions and Policy Implications. *ECB Monthly Bulletin*, *8*, 63–75.

Faini, R., Duranton, G., & Hau, H. (2006). Fiscal policy and interest rates in Europe – Discussion. *Economic Policy*, *21*(47), 443–489. doi:10.1111/j.1468-0327.2006.00163.x

Favero, C., & Missale, A. (2012). Sovereign Spreads in the Eurozone: Which Prospects for a Eurobond? *Economic Policy*, *70*(70), 231–273. doi:10.1111/j.1468-0327.2012.00282.x

Gerlach, S., Schulz, A., & Wolff, G. B. (2010). *Banking and Sovereign Risk in the Euro Area* (CEPR Discussion Paper vol. 09). Retrieved from https://www.econstor.eu/bitstream/10419/32799/1/627499228.pdf

Hallerberg, M., & Wolff, G. B. (2008). Fiscal institutions, fiscal policy and sovereign risk premia in EMU. *Public Choice*, *136*(3-4), 379–396. doi:10.100711127-008-9301-2

Iara, A., & Wolff, G. (2014). Rules and risk in the Euro area. *European Journal of Political Economy*, *34*, 222–236. doi:10.1016/j.ejpoleco.2014.02.002

Klepsch, C., & Wollmershäuser, T. (2011). Yield Spreads on EMU Government Bonds – How the Financial Crisis Has Helped Investors to Rediscover Risk. *Inter Economics*, *46*(3), 169–176. doi:10.100710272-011-0379-2

Lemmen, J., & Goodhart, C. (1999). Credit Risks and European Government Bond Markets: A Panel Data Econometric Analysis. *Eastern Economic Journal*, *25*(1), 77–107.

Lledó, V., Yoon, S., Fang, X., Mbaye, S., & Kim, Y. (2017). *Fiscal Rules at a Glance*. Washington, DC: International Monetary Fund.

Lo Conte, R. (2009). Government Bond Yield Spreads: A Survey. *Giornale degli Economisti e Annali di Economia*, *68*(3), 341–370.

Maltritz, D. (2012). Determinants of Sovereign Yield Spreads in the Eurozone: A Bayesian approach. *Journal of International Money and Finance*, *31*(3), 657–672. doi:10.1016/j.jimonfin.2011.10.010

Manganelli, S., & Wolswijk, G. (2007). *Market Discipline, Financial Integration and Fiscal Rules* (ECB Working Paper vol. 745). Retrieved from https://www.ecb.europa.eu/pub/pdf/scpwps/ecbwp745.pdf?39c651ca2ffcb63b24e84c6cbd68f7ff

Missio, S. (2012). *Government bond market integration and the EMU: Correlation based evidence* (BGPE Discussion Paper vol. 125). Retrieved from http://www.bgpe.de/texte/DP/125_Missio.pdf

Morck, R., Shleifer, S., Vishny, R. W., Shapiro, M., & Poterba, J. M. (1990). The stock market and investment: Is the market a sideshow? *Brookings Papers on Economic Activity*, *2*(2), 157–202. doi:10.2307/2534506

OECD. (2014). *OECD Sovereign Borrowing Outlook 2014*. Paris, France: OECD Publishing.

Pagano, M., & von Thadden, E. L. (2004). The European bond markets under EMU. *Oxford Review of Economic Policy*, *20*(4), 531–554. doi:10.1093/oxrep/grh031

Paniagua, J., Sapena, J., & Tamari, C. (2015). *Sovereign debt spreads in EMU: Disentangling the role of fundamentals and market perceptions*. Retrieved from: http://www.uv.es/inteco/jornadas/jornadas11/paniagua_sapena_tamarit.pdf

Roaf, J., Atoyan, R., Joshi, B., & Krogulski, K. (2014). *25 years of transition: post-communist Europe and the IMF*. Washington, DC: International Monetary Fund.

Schuknecht, L., von Hagen, J., & Wolswijk, G. (2010). *Government risk premiums in the EU revisited: The impact of the financial crisis* (ECB Working Paper vol. 1152). Retrieved from: http://www.ecb.europa.eu/pub/pdf/scpwps/ecbwp1152.pdf

Szarowská, I. (2013). Fiscal Discipline as a Driver of Sovereign Risk Spread in the European Union Countries. In *22nd IBIMA Conference on Creating Global Competitive Economies: 2020 Vision Planning & Implementation* (pp. 793-804). Rome: IBIMA.

Szarowská, I. (2014). Do Fiscal Drivers Matter for Sovereign Risk Spread in EU15? In *11th International Scientific Conference on European Financial Systems 2014* (pp. 629-637). Brno: Masaryk University.

Szarowská, I. (2015). Relationship between government bond yield spread and fiscal fundamentals in selected EU countries. In *12th International Scientific Conference on European Financial Systems 2015* (pp. 596-604). Brno: Masaryk University.

Verbeek, M. (2000). *A guide to modern econometrics*. New York: John Wiley & Sons Inc.

Von Hagen, J., Schuknecht, L., & Wolswijk, G. (2011). Government bond risk premiums in the EU revisited: The impact of the financial crisis. *European Journal of Political Economy*, *27*(1), 36–43. doi:10.1016/j.ejpoleco.2010.07.002

KEY TERMS AND DEFINITIONS

Bond Spread: The difference between a government's bond yield and German's government bond yield.

Fiscal Discipline: A compliance with targets for budgetary aggregates, such as government budget balance, debt, expenditure, or revenue developments.

Fiscal Policy Rules: A set of numerical targets for budgetary aggregates.

Fiscal Rules Index: Cumulative numerical limits on budgetary aggregates based on fiscal policy rules.

Generalized Method of Moments: A general estimation principle in statistical models. Estimators are derived from so-called moment conditions.

Government Bond: A bond issued by a national government, generally with a promise to pay periodic interest payments and to repay the face value on the maturity date.

Government Bond Yield: An amount of return an investor realizes on a government bond.

Government Debt: A debt owed by a government.

Chapter 8
Dynamic Risk Management of Investment Portfolio by Futures Contracts

Alexander K. Kerimov
RUDN University, Russia

Oleg I. Pavlov
RUDN University, Russia

ABSTRACT

This chapter is devoted to the dynamic risk management of the investment portfolio using future contracts. The number of futures for each portfolio asset, which is determined by portfolio effectiveness and acceptability of risk at each step, serves as a control parameter. The authors define effective portfolios as the ones of the minimum variance with the expected return greater than or equal to the specified value. Risk is measured by the probability of losing a certain part of the portfolio value. Effective adaptive strategies of portfolio risk management are proposed and their comparative analysis is carried out on a concrete example. In order to determine risk management strategies, the authors implement simple methods of volatility forecasting and correlation of relative changes of price data based on exponential moving average.

DOI: 10.4018/978-1-5225-4026-7.ch008

INTRODUCTION AND BACKGROUND

Risk management method of the investment portfolio that utilizes future contracts is based on a strong positive correlation between changes in the spot price and the future price for a given asset. The main issue of insurance is the estimation of the necessary number of futures contracts needed for insurance and the assessment of the effectiveness of insurance over a given period (Brown (2001); Walsh (1995); Ederington (1979); Haustalter (2000); Hull (2017); Bhargava and Brooks (2001); Petersen and Thiagarajan (2000)). The traditional method of estimating the optimal number of futures contracts involves estimation of *regression of the spot price change on changes in the futures price*. The coefficient at the futures price changes in this regression determines the necessary number of futures contracts that minimize the variance of inhomogeneous portfolios. In case of stock portfolio, one can use regression of the portfolio value on a market index.

This method has the following shortcomings. Time series of changes in the spot price and the future price are normally inhomogeneous with respect to the mean and variance. Instability of the mean leads to an inadequate forecast of the expected return. Instability of the variance (heteroscedasticity) leads to significant distortion of the hedge coefficient. Besides, the correlation coefficient between changes in the spot price and the future price varies in time. Usually, it increases significantly as expiration date approaches. Moreover, due to nonstationarity of financial time series, the traditional correlation estimation that is based on a simple averaging is often incorrect or results in problems with sample size calculation. All this makes it harder to obtain a correct estimation of the number of futures contracts that hedge a position for an asset using traditional econometric methods (see Dark (2005)).

Furthermore, the traditional approach for determining the required number of futures contracts takes into account only one parameter - variance, which characterizes price variability of a portfolio. So, such important portfolio parameters as the expected return or possible restrictions on the number of futures contracts are not taken into account. Thus, the possible additional profit through the use of derivative instruments is not taken into account

We employ stochastic control for dynamic risk-management of positions by futures contracts on the basis of effective inhomogeneous portfolios (see Kerimov (2014), Cecchetti et al. (1998)). The effective portfolios are defined as the ones of the minimum variance with the expected return greater than or equal to the specified value. In turn, we select this value in such a way that the probability of a certain level of loss is minimal or does not exceed a predefined value at each step.

The control parameters used are the number of futures for each underlying asset of portfolio. Proposed approach provides the correction of forecasts of probabilistic characteristics of an inhomogeneous portfolio as the new data is received. An essential aspect of this approach is the interpretation of financial time series as a random process, rather than a random variable. With this approach, forecasts and standard deviations of forecasts are corrected, as the new data become available (Engle (1982), Cumby et al. (1993); Kroner and Sultan (1993)). Usually, analysis and forecast of time series is a rather complicated procedure. However, the effectiveness of the dynamic risk-management is largely determined by the adequacy of forecasts and their confidence intervals. We use a fairly simple but quite satisfactory method of adaptive forecasting based on exponential moving average.

METHODOLOGY

Inhomogeneous Effective Portfolios

Consider an inhomogeneous portfolio with n assets and futures contracts for them. We use following notation: Q_{si} is the number of units of underlying asset i and k_i is the number of futures contracts for asset i ($i = 1,2,\ldots,n$) (k_i is an integer that could be positive or negative). Thus, the portfolio is determined by an integer vector

$$(Q,k),\ Q = \left(Q_{s1}, Q_{s2}, \ldots, Q_{sn}\right),\ k = \left(k_1, k_2, \ldots, k_n\right)$$

The sign of k_i determines the position of asset i according to contract: $k_i > 0$ designates a long position, $k_i < 0$ means a short one, the absolute value of k_i determines the number of open positions.

The sign and absolute value of Q_{si} have the same meaning, albeit we assume that the positions of all the underlying assets are the long ones (hence all Q_{si} are positive).

Let $S_i\left(t\right)$ and $F_i\left(t\right)$ denote the spot price and the future price of the i-th asset (in monetary terms) at time t, and q_{fi} denote the number of units of the underlying asset in futures contract number i. Then, the change in the value of the portfolio per unit time is equal to (see Hull (2017), Dark (2005), Kerimov (2014))

$$\nabla W(t) = \sum_{i=1}^{n} \nabla S_i(t) Q_{si} + \sum_{i=1}^{n} \nabla F_i(t) k_i q_{fi}$$

$\nabla W\left(t\right)$, $\nabla S_i\left(t\right)$, $\nabla F_i\left(t\right)$ are the changes in the corresponding quantities per unit time respectively. In vector notation this formula can be written as

$$\nabla W(t) = \left(\nabla S(t), Q_s\right) + \left(\nabla F(t), Q_f\right) \tag{1}$$

where $\nabla S(t), \nabla F(t), Q_f$ are vectors with components $\nabla S_i(t), \nabla F_i(t)$ and $k_i q_{fi}$ respectively. Here time is considered to be discrete and measured in days. The prices refer to the closing of the trading session and formula (1) determines portfolio win/loss over a trading session.

The probabilistic characteristics of price changes vary with time. For a given time t, prices for the next time point are considered as conditional random variables, provided that the history of prices is known up to the moment under consideration. For example, the expected value of the price change $\nabla S_i(t+1) = S_i(t+1) - S_i(t)$ of an asset at time point $t+1$ is considered under the condition that the history of prices up to time t inclusive is known. So defined conditional expected price change is interpreted as a forecast of price changes one-step ahead that is made at the current time t. Similarly, the variance of deviations of actual changes is determined under the condition that the information on prices is available up to the current moment of time (the variance forecast). As new data appear, forecast of changes and characteristics of price changes are corrected, that is, they adapt to the new data. The same remark is true for the level of correlation between the price changes of different assets - correlation (respectively, covariance) - changes over time and these changes should be adjusted as the price data is received (Nelson (1990); Engle (1982), Cumby et al. (1993)).

In the following statement, all the probabilistic characteristics in question (the expected value, variance and covariance) refer to the current time t and are treated as one-step ahead forecasts in the above sense. The current time t is fixed and not explicitly indicated.

The expected change in the value of the portfolio and the variance of its change at a given time t are determined by the equalities (Kerimov (2014))

$$M(\nabla W) = (m_s, Q_s) + (m_f, Q_f) \tag{2}$$

$$D(\nabla W) = \left(C_{ss}, Q_s, Q_s\right) + 2\left(C_{sf} Q_f, Q_s\right) + \left(C_{ff}, Q_f, Q_f\right), \tag{3}$$

where $m_s = \left(m_{s1}, m_{s2}, \ldots m_{sn}\right)$, $m_f = \left(m_{f1}, m_{f2}, \ldots m_{fn}\right)$ are the vectors of expected changes in the spot and futures prices respectively, obtained at the present moment t for the next time point, C_{ss}, C_{sf}, C_{ff} are estimates of covariance matrices

$$\{Cov(\nabla S_i, \nabla S_j)\}, \{Cov(\nabla S_i, \nabla F_j)\}, \{Cov(\nabla F_i, \nabla F_j)\}$$

of size n, also obtained at the present moment for the next time point.

The Classical Approach to Effective Hedging

The classical problem of effective hedging is based on the following problems.

Problem 1

Portfolio contains shares of companies $A_1, \ldots, A_n$ in quantities $Q = (Q_{s1}, Q_{s2}, \ldots Q_{sn})$. Find a vector $k = (k_1, k_2, \ldots, k_n)$ that contains the numbers of futures contracts for the shares in question and that minimizes the portfolio variance after the addition of these contracts.

Mathematically, this problem reduces to minimizing the variance of the portfolio with respect to the vector k. More precisely, the optimal number of futures contracts is defined as the solution of the following minimization problem

$$D(\nabla W) = (C_{ss}Q_s, Q_s) + 2(C_{sf}Q_f, Q_s) + (C_{ff}Q_f, Q_f) \to \text{min with respect } k$$

subject to the constraints: Q_s is given, $Q_f = \{k_i q_{fi}\}, k_i$ is an integer for $i = 1, 2, \ldots, n$. The solution can be found analytically (assuming that matrix C_{ff} is positive definite):

$$Q_f = -C_{ff}^{-1} C_{sf}^{*} Q_s, k_i = Q_{fi} / q_{fi}, i = 1, 2, \ldots, n. \quad (4)$$

Indeed, it follows from the representation for portfolio variance (2) that the variance gradient with respect the vector Q_f is equal to

$$grad(D(\nabla W)) = 2C_{sf}^{*} + 2C_{ff}Q_f$$

By setting it equal to the zero vector, we obtain (4) as required. Since k_i must be integers, the values found according to (3) are rounded to integers. If the changes in the prices of the underlying assets are independent, the optimal number of futures contracts for the i-th asset is given by the standard formula

$$k_i = -\frac{Q_{si} Cov\left(\nabla S_i, \nabla F_i\right)}{q_{fi} D\left(\nabla F_i\right)}, i = 1,2,\dots,n$$

There are no restrictions on the expected return and the number of contracts in Problem 1, which greatly limits the effectiveness of insurance. The expected return will be taken into account if we solve the following

Problem 2: (A Portfolio of Minimum Variance With Restrictions on the Return and the Number of Contracts)

Find the minimum of the variance

$$D(\nabla W) = \left(C_{ss} Q_s, Q_s\right) + 2\left(C_{sf} Q_f, Q_s\right) + \left(C_{ff} Q_f, Q_f\right)$$

with respect to the vector $k = \left(k_1, k_2, \dots, k_n\right)$ subject to the constraints

$$Q_f = \left\{k_i q_{fi}\right\}, k_i \le k_{gi}, k_i \text{ is an integer for } i = 1,2,\dots,n$$

$$M(\nabla W) = \left(m_s, Q_s\right) + \left(m_f, Qf\right) \ge m_g,$$

m_g and Q_s are given.

Here k_{gi} are restrictions on the number of futures contracts, m_g on the expected return of the inhomogeneous portfolio. These parameters are set depending on the situation prevailing in the market. Restrictions on the number of contracts for the i-th asset are used if an increase in the price of this asset is expected, but the probability of its fall remains.

Dynamic Portfolio Risk Management Taking Into Account The Expected Return

Risk management involves the assessment of an effective portfolio (Problem 2) before a trading session starts with a specified level of the expected return, denoted by m_g. This level is estimated by the probability of an acceptable risk, which is defined as the probability of losing a certain portion of the portfolio value. We give the exact definitions and algorithm of adaptive control.

Let t be the current time, we identify it either with the beginning of a new trading session, or with the end of the previous one. The state of the portfolio at the current time t is determined by the integer vector (Q_s, k), where the vector Q_s is given, and the vector $k = k(t)$ determines the state of the portfolio with respect to futures contracts at the current time. Our task is to determine the vector $k = k(t+1)$ at the next moment of time, that is, at the end of the new trading session. It is assumed that at the current time all the information about the spot and futures prices for the assets under consideration is known. Risk management of the position is, actually, a determination of the number of futures contracts $k = k(t+1)$ based on available current information on prices in order to reduce the risk and obtain (if possible) an additional income.

Let α be the share of the allowable level of loss from the current value of the portfolio $W(t)$; usually α is selected from the interval 0.01-0.03. For each given return level m_g, we denote by

$$\nabla W_g(t+1) = W_g(t+1) - W(t) = (\nabla S(t+1), Q_s) + (\nabla F(t+1), Q_f), \tag{5}$$

a conditional random variable equal to the return of the effective portfolio, (Q_s, k_{opt}) which is defined as the solution of Problem 2. The probability of losing $\alpha W(t)$ monetary units in the next step determines the portfolio risk $R(t, m_g)$, i.e.

$$R(t, m_g) = P\left\{\nabla W_g(t+1) < \alpha W(t)\right\} = P_t\left\{(W_g(t+1) - W(t)) / W(t) < -\alpha\right\},$$

The index t means that the conditional probability is considered, while the random variable $\nabla W_g(t+1)$ has a minimal variance among all the portfolios with an expected return of at least m_g. In what follows, it is assumed that $\nabla W_g(t+1)$ has a normal distribution or Student distribution. Clearly, the higher is the value of m_g, the higher is the risk of the corresponding effective portfolio. That is, the risk function $R(t, m_g)$ increases monotonically with respect to m_g, since the bounding set narrows as m_g increases. The minimum value of this function $R_{\min} = R_{\min}(t, \alpha)$ corresponds to the absence of a constraint on the expected portfolio return (as in Problem 1) and is easily estimated under the considered assumptions.

Below we consider one of the possible schemes of adaptive control, taking into account the probability of loss at each step.

1. At the current time t, estimate one-step ahead forecasts of the return with respect to the assets and futures contracts of the portfolio together with its variances.
2. Estimate the covariance matrices C_{ss}, C_{sf} and C_{ff} at the next moment of time $t+1$.
3. Determine the expected return m_g from the condition that the probability of loss of share α from the value of the portfolio at the current moment is not higher than the specified probability γ:

$$R(t,m_g) = P\left\{\nabla W_g(t+1) < -\alpha W(t)\right\} \leq \gamma, \tag{6}$$

where γ is a rather small number chosen by the investor. The value of γ has to be not less than $R_{\min}(t,\alpha)$, which is the minimum value of the function of risk defined above. A way to specify γ is described in the next section. The optimal number of futures contracts at step t is assumed to be k_{g0}, which is the solution of Problem 2 for the m_g, deduced from (6). Thus, positions on futures contracts are specified before each trading session (see Duffie (1989), Randelman (1993)).

MODEL

We build a model based on the above strategy. The following facts will be used. Consider an inhomogeneous portfolio with $n=1$, containing Q_s units of a certain asset (long position) and k futures contracts for this asset, while each contract contains q_f units of the underlying asset. In this case, Problem 2 can be solved analytically. Let

$$k_0 = -\left(\beta Q_s\right) / q_f, \beta = Cov\left(\nabla S, \nabla F\right) / D\left(\nabla F\right). \tag{7}$$

It can be shown that the following assertions hold.

1. If the expected return m_f is positive, that is, an increase in the futures price is expected, then the solution of Problem 2 can be represented in the form

$$k_{g0} = \max\left\{k_0, k_g\right\}, k_g = \left(m_g - m_s Q_s\right) / \left(m_f Q_f\right), \tag{8}$$

2. If the expected return m_f is negative, that is, a decline in the futures price is expected, then the solution of Problem 2 can be represented in the form

$$k_{g0} = \min\left\{k_0, k_g\right\}, k_g = \left(m_g - m_s Q_s\right) / \left(m_f Q_f\right). \tag{9}$$

In formulae (8) and (9), k_{g0} denotes the solution of Problem 2 with $n = 1$.

Adaptive risk management involves one-step ahead correction of forecasts of the expected value and the standard deviation. To estimate the predictions of the expected changes and their variances, we use a simple random process model, which takes into account the inhomogeneity of the time series in terms of both level and variance. This model is a special form of ARCH model (Engle (1982), Bollerslev (1986), Engle and Mezrich (1995)) based on exponential moving average. The exponential average of the random process $x\left(t\right)$ is defined by the formula

$$E(t) = \alpha x(t) + \alpha\beta x(t-1) + \alpha\beta^2 x(t-2) + \alpha\beta^3 x(t-3) + \ldots$$

Here α is the smoothing factor, $0 < \alpha < 1$, $\beta = 1 - \alpha$. The weights $\omega_i = \alpha\beta^i$ decrease exponentially to zero and their sum is equal to one. Thus random process $E\left(t\right)$ is an autoregression of an infinite order. In what follows, the real-valued parameter α is determined through the time window $w > 1$ by means of formula $\alpha = 2 / \left(w + 1\right)$. The exponential average of the random process $x\left(.\right)$ at time t with window w is denoted by $E\left(t; w, x\right)$.

Let $p\left(t\right)$ be the price of the asset at time t, then $r\left(t\right) = p\left(t\right) - p\left(t-1\right)$ is the change in the price of the asset. Let $x\left(t\right) = r\left(t\right) - m\left(t\right)$ (where $m\left(t\right) = M\left(r\left(t\right)\right)$) denote the deviation from the average return. In ARCH (p) models, sequence $x\left(t\right)$ evolves according to formulae (see Zumbach (2013) and Hull (2017))

$$x\left(t\right) = \sigma\left(t\right)\varepsilon\left(t\right),\ \sigma\left(t\right)^2 = a_0 + a_1 x\left(t-1\right)^2 + \ldots a_p x\left(t-p\right)^2,$$

$$a_0 > 0,\ a_1 \geq 0, \ldots a_p \geq 0,\ t = 0,1,2,\ldots,$$

where $\varepsilon\left(t\right)$ is a sequence of independent random variables having the standard normal distribution. Hence, the conditional variance at the current moment t is determined by the preceding time series values. Thus large or small values of the squares of the previous terms $x^2(t-i)$ lead to, respectively, large or small conditional variance, which explains the clustering of the time series represented by ARCH models.

The complexity of estimating parameters in ARCH models prompts to search for estimation procedures that are simpler, but at the same time do not have significant drawbacks. The following is a possible approach. Assume that the variance of the value of the time series $x(t)$ at moment t is a weighted sum of the squares of the preceding terms of the time series with nonnegative weights whose sum is equal to the unity. That is,

$$\sigma(t)^2 = \sum_{k=1}^{+\infty} \omega_k x(t-k)^2, \ \omega_k > 0, \ \sum_{k=1}^{+\infty} \omega_k = 1.$$

If $\omega_k = \alpha(1-\alpha)^{k-1}$, then the variance can be expressed as the exponential moving average $\sigma(t)^2 = EMA(t-1; w, x^2)$. Assuming that the average level of return $r(t)$ is determined by exponential smoothing, we obtain a simplified ARCH model

$$x(t) = r(t) - EMA(t; w_1, r), \ x(t) = \sigma(t)\varepsilon(t), \ \sigma(t)^2 = EMA(t-1; w_2, x^2), \quad (10)$$

where w_1, w_2 are the parameters of the model. We assume that the process $x(t)$ has the zero mean for all t, and the residuals $\varepsilon(t)$ form a white noise with the unit variance. Unlike the classical model ARCH (p), the variance $x(t)$ in model (10) is represented as an auto regression of an infinite order. The main advantage of our model is in the simplicity of estimating its parameters. At the same time, numerical experiments have shown the effectiveness of using this model in the case when changes in the volatility of time series are not too large.

Forecasts of $r(t+1)$ and standard deviations of forecasts, made at time t for the next time point, are defined as conditional expected values and standard deviations of the conditional random variable $r(t+1)$, provided that history of prices is known. It then follows that the predictions of changes and their standard deviations for model (10) are equal to

$$r_f\left(t+1\right)=EMA\left(t;w_1,r\right),\ \sigma_f\left(t+1\right)=\sqrt{EMA\left(t;w_2,x^2\right)}\,. \tag{11}$$

RESULTS AND DISCUSSION

To test the ability of our algorithm to predict price volatility, we used the daily closing prices of Gazprom shares from 06/22/16 to 09/15/16 (retrieved from Finam Holdings database on 08/31/2017). The selected model is characterized by windows $w_1=12$, $w_2=50$, which are obtained by minimization of the weighted sum

$$M\left(\varepsilon,\boldsymbol{w}\right)+10000\left(D\left(\varepsilon,\boldsymbol{w}\right)-1\right)^2$$

among all the possible values of windows $\boldsymbol{w}=\left(\boldsymbol{w}_1,\boldsymbol{w}_2\right)$. Here $M\left(\varepsilon,\boldsymbol{w}\right)$ and $D\left(\varepsilon,\boldsymbol{w}\right)$ are the sample mean and variance respectively of the residuals obtained for a given the value of $\boldsymbol{w}$. The adequacy of the considered model was confirmed by analysis of the residuals.

The dynamics of price changes of Gazprom shares and their forecasts is displayed in Figure 1. The line of predicted price changes (trend) is given by function $r_f\left(t+1\right)=EMA\left(t;w_1,r\right)$ according to (11). The dashed lines constitute the predicted upper and lower boundaries of the corridor within which the prices are supposed to change. The upper/lower bounds are determined by formulae $r_f\left(t+1\right)+2\sigma_f\left(t+1\right)$ and $r_f\left(t+1\right)-2\sigma_f\left(t+1\right)$ respectively. It can be seen that overwhelming majority of price changes (over 92%) lie within bounds, which confirms the adequacy of the model.

In order to compare different insurance schemes, we used daily data on the spot and futures prices of Gazprom shares from 07/22/16 to 09/05/16 (retrieved from Finam Holdings database on 08/31/2017). The starting position contains 10,000 Gazprom shares ($Q_s=10000$, $q_f=100$). The results are presented in Table 1 and Figure 2.

In Table 1 and Figure 2, the line DELTA-1 represents an uninsured position, that is, changes in the value of 10 000 shares relative to initial data[1] 07/22/16. According to the data, by 09/05/16 the uninsured position has a loss over 40,000 rubles with intermediate losses exceeding 60,000 rubles.

The line DELTA-2 shows changes in the value of the portfolio insured according to classical scheme (the number of contracts is determined by formula (7) as the solution of Problem 2). Such hedging method clearly is effective as it substantially

Figure 1. Dynamics of price changes and their forecasts (in rubles)
Source: Authors' calculations based on Finam Holdings database.

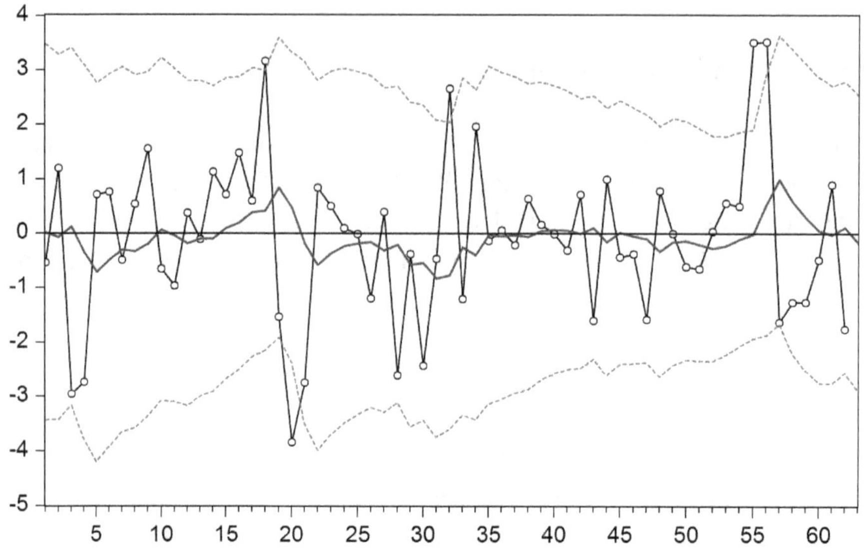

**For a more accurate representation see the electronic version.*

reduces the risk of large losses and overall volatility of portfolio value. The interim losses decreased at least threefold compared to uninsured portfolio and had not exceeded 20 000 rubles at any day. However, such dynamic insurance does not yield a significant return either, as at the end of the considered period the return reached modest 1600 rubles.

The line DELTA-3 shows changes in the value of the portfolio according to the scheme described in section Dynamic Portfolio Risk Management Taking Into Account The Expected Return. We assumed that the level of loss α is 1% and γ is equal to 0.15. The value of parameter m_g was determined as follows. At each step, the minimum risk value $R_{\min} = R_{\min}(t,\alpha)$ was established as a solution of Problem 1. If $R_{\min}$ appeared to be not larger than γ, then the optimal number of contracts was calculated as in Problem 1. If $R_{\min} > \gamma$, then the original value of $m_g = 10000$ rubles was halved. The bisection of parameter m_g was performed until inequality $R_{\min} \leq \gamma$ is obtained. As the Figure 2 attests, the dynamic control based on the expected income gives a gain of nearly 45,000 rubles in 32 days.

Table 1. Spot and futures prices of Gazprom shares (in rubles)

Date	DELTA-1	DELTA-2	DELTA -3
07/22/16	5000	4745	4745
07/25/16	6000	7786	7786
07/26/16	5900	10224	10224
07/27/16	-6000	6804	6804
07/28/16	-2000	10935	10935
07/29/16	-28000	-1652	-1652
08/01/16	-31700	756	756
08/02/16	-56000	-11748	482
08/03/16	-60600	-19848	-7618
08/04/16	-34000	-2110	10120
08/05/16	-46000	-7324	11906
08/08/16	-26300	4047	15813
08/09/16	-27600	2143	13909
08/10/16	-27000	2593	14298
08/11/16	-29100	1613	14431
08/12/16	-22700	4967	16265
08/15/16	-21000	2365	13664
08/16/16	-21100	9098	19608
08/17/16	-24200	5495	16005
08/18/16	-17000	8057	18567
08/19/16	-33000	675	11184
08/22/16	-23000	7044	15149
08/23/16	-27300	7268	18126
08/24/16	-31000	5092	17386
08/25/16	-46800	1268	28771
08/26/16	-39000	10596	39265
08/29/16	-39000	2897	31566
08/30/16	-45100	3155	43530
08/31/16	-51500	567	44402
09/01/16	-51100	-2276	40486
09/02/16	-45500	4006	47344
09/05/16	-40500	1609	44947

Figure 2. The dynamics of changes in the value of the portfolio for different methods of risk management (in rubles)
Source: Authors' calculations based on Finam Holdings database.

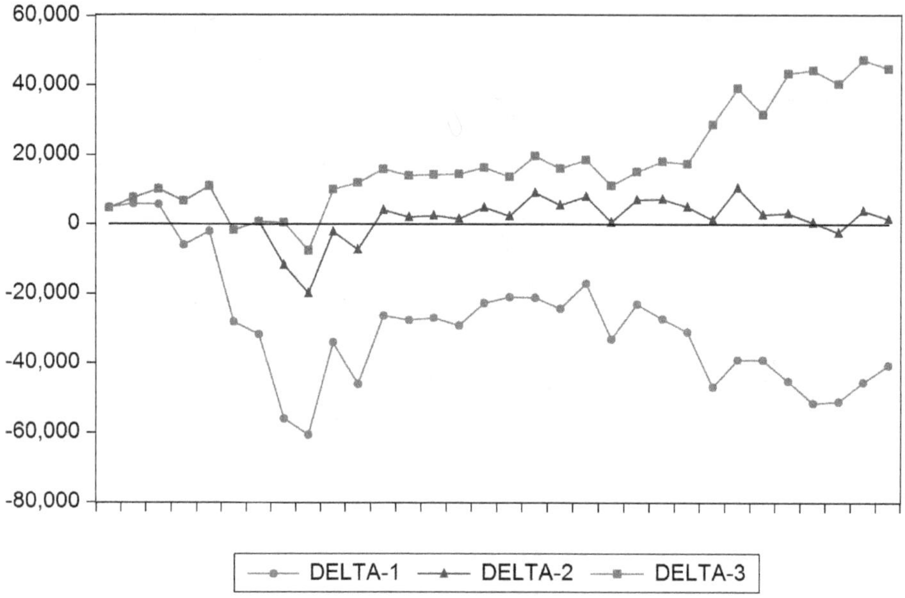

CONCLUSION

The problem of dynamic management of the risk of the investment portfolio with the use of futures contracts as control parameters is considered. A risk management strategy that takes into account the expected return is defined. A necessary ingredient in the proposed strategy is a technic of forecasting volatility of changes in price data and of determining effective inhomogeneous portfolios. The effective portfolio is defined as the one of the minimum variance subject to constraints on the expected return and the number of futures contracts. To forecast the return and its standard deviations, simple-to-implement methods based on exponential moving average are used. The effectiveness of the proposed approach is demonstrated on a concrete example of dynamic risk management of Gazprom shares.

ACKNOWLEDGMENT

This study was facilitated by International Centre for Emerging Markets Research.

REFERENCES

Bhargava, V., & Brooks, R. (2001). Hedging currency risk using futures. In Research in Finance. Emerald Group Publishing Limited.

Bollerslev, T. (1986). Generalized Autoregressive Conditional Heteroscedasticity. *Journal of Econometrics*, *36*(3), 307–327. doi:10.1016/0304-4076(86)90063-1

Brown, G. W. (2001). Managing Foreign Exchange Risk with Derivatives. *Journal of Financial Economics*, *60*(2-3), 401–448. doi:10.1016/S0304-405X(01)00049-6

Cecchetti, S. G., Cumby, R. E., & Figlewski, S. (1998). Estimation of the optimal future hedge. *The Review of Economics and Statistics*, *7*, 624–635.

Cumby, R., Figlewski, S., & Hasbrouk, J. (1993). Forecasting Volatility and Correlations with EGARCH Models. *Journal of Derivatives*, *1*(2), 51–63. doi:10.3905/jod.1993.407877

Dark, J. (2005). A Critique of Minimum Variance Hedging. *Accounting Research Journal*, *18*(1), 40–49. doi:10.1108/10309610580000674

Duffie, D. (1989). *Futures Markets*. Upper Saddle River, NJ: Prentice Hall.

Ederington, L. H. (1979). The Hedging Performance of the New Future Markets. *The Journal of Finance*, *34*(1), 157–170. doi:10.1111/j.1540-6261.1979.tb02077.x

Engle, R. F. (1982). Autoregressive Conditional Heteroscedasticity with Estimates of the Variance of United Kingdom Inflation. *Econometrica*, *50*(4), 987–1008. doi:10.2307/1912773

Engle, R. F., & Mezrich, J. (1995). Grappling with GARCH. Retrieved from https://www.finam.ru/profile/moex–akcii/gazprom/export/

Haustalter, G. D. (2000). Financing Policy, Basis Risk and Corporate Hedging. *The Journal of Finance*, *55*(1), 107–152. doi:10.1111/0022-1082.00202

Hilliard, J., & Jordan, S. (1989). Hedging Interest Rate Risk with Futures Portfolios under Full-Rank Assumptions. *Journal of Financial and Quantitative Analysis*, *24*(2), 217–240. doi:10.2307/2330773

Hull, J. (2017). *Option, Futures and Other Derivatives* (10th ed.). Pearson.

Kerimov A.K. (2014) Mean-variance future hedging for security portfolio. *Bulletin of Peoples' Friendship University of Russia. Series Economics*, (3), 109–116. (in Russian)

Kroner, K., & Sultan, J. (1993). Time-Varying Distributions and Dynamic Hedging with Foreign Currency Futures. *Journal of Financial and Quantitative Analysis, 28*(4), 535–551. doi:10.2307/2331164

Nelson, D. (1990). Conditional Heteroscedasticity and Assert Return. A New Approach. *Econometrica, 59*(2), 347–370. doi:10.2307/2938260

Petersen, M. F., & Thiagarajan, S. R. (2000). Risk Management and Hedging: With and Without Derivatives. *Financial Management, 29*(4), 5–30. doi:10.2307/3666367

Randelman, R. (1993). A Reconciliation of Potentially Conflicting Approaches to Hedging with Futures. *Advances in Futures and Options Research, 6*, 81–92.

Stulz, R. M. (1984). Optimal Hedging Policies. *Journal of Financial and Quantitative Analysis, 19*(2), 127–140. doi:10.2307/2330894

Walsh, D. (1995). Risk Management Using Derivative Securities. *Managerial Finance, 21*(1), 43–65. doi:10.1108/eb018496

Zumbach, G. (2013). *Discrete Time Series, Processes, and Applications in Finance*. Springer. doi:10.1007/978-3-642-31742-2

ENDNOTE

1 The value of the uninsured portfolio at moment t is equal to $Q_s\left(p\left(t\right)-p\left(0\right)\right)$, where $p\left(t\right)$ is the price of one share at moment t.

Chapter 9
Market Challenges, Risks, and Policy:
The Attempts to Regain Global Stability After the Financial Crisis

Adam Christopher Wood
Harvard University, USA

ABSTRACT

This chapter first examines what caused the need to regain global stability after the financial crisis. The author provides a brief refresher of how the market crash in 2008, and subsequent Great Recession, was initially fueled while honing in on the allocation of "the fuel" coupled with the repeals of bicentennial-long legislation and the associated dangers of these economic policy changes. Notations from Nobel laureates and interagency economists from the IMF and World Bank aid in identifying the consequences of these policy decisions while simultaneously illustrating the enhanced risk within a variety of markets. Next, the author discusses the current state and relative stability of the financial markets, economic policy, and the risks associated therein. Lastly, this chapter provides recommendations for the future of monetary and fiscal policy, globalization, and what the government (and Wall Street) must consider should they seek to attain long-term financial stability from an international perspective. Monetary and fiscal policy decisions implemented and in-progress by the Federal Reserve are fastidiously examined throughout this chapter.

DOI: 10.4018/978-1-5225-4026-7.ch009

INTRODUCTION

This chapter first covers what caused the Great Recession within the financial markets, economic policy, and risks associated with that policy while noting the history of economic policy and financial innovations dating back to 1980. This portion of the chapter also includes notations on the financial services industry, economic policy repeals, brief leverage analysis, and a review (concurrence) of the Financial Crisis Inquiry Commission's analysis, in that, the Financial Crisis of 2008 was, in fact, avoidable ("Financial Crisis Inquiry Report Commission", 2011). Quantitative easing will be notated, the current bull market, and what is required to achieve global financial stability in the future from the perspective of the United States.

Regaining financial stability implies that the markets have yet to achieve the coveted stability it so frequently seeks. What's fueling the markets today in 2017 is not what fueled them in the earlier 2000s or even the mid-1990s, but the rhetoric is verisimilar.

The 2016 US Presidential Election OF Donald Trump did nothing to drive U.S. market indexes to all-time highs; rather it was merely the market *expectations* predicated on a campaign promise of a $1 trillion dollar infrastructure bill, which is still sorely needed. The pulling out of the Trans-Pacific Partnership (Baker, 2017), withdraw from the Paris Climate Accord (Epstein, 2017), and threats of governments shutdowns, all while antagonizing enemies, and alienating the United States' allies has been the economic policy of incompetence of the Trump Administration. What's more important; however, is how the world arrived at this level of instability, as transitions of power are only one variable in the complex equation.

1979 THROUGH 2006: THE END OF STABILITY AND ERA OF DEREGULATION - REAGAN, CHINA, AND THE CRISIS

To begin, it's most important to understand how the actors within the financial markets, banks, and governmental agencies arrived at the prestigious addresses they reside today. Only when the historical context has been sufficiently provided can one grasp why Wall Street's economic power yields its current level of governmental control and the like. However, before investigating, analyzing, and proving that Wall Street is not the enemy in this chapter, we must review what stability is, who contributed to it before the crisis, and those who subsequently came into the monetary fold, seemingly making all that was good and stable in the international political environment evaporate little by little as if it never existed in the first place.

Merriam-Webster's Definition of Stability (Merriam-Webster, 2003):

Stability

plural stabilities

1: the quality, state, or degree of being stable: such as

A: the strength to stand or endure: firmness

B: the property of a body that causes it when disturbed from a condition of equilibrium or steady motion to develop forces or moments that restore the original condition

C: resistance to chemical change or physical disintegration

Nearly every notation within this section is a disruptive property of stability.

Paul Volcker, one of the premier American economists of this generation, helped clear the table of high inflation that plagued the US and its respective trade partners for a majority of the 1970s and early 1980s. During his tenure as Chairman of the Federal Reserve from 1979 to 1987, Volcker consistently invoked monetary policy curb inflation, at one point raising the Federal Funds Rate to over 20%[5]. Although the Federal Board of Governors and Fed Chair Volcker's monetary policy was relatively unpopular within the Reagan administration, those policies provided the US, her trade partners, and citizens with the strength to endure global shocks for nearly fifteen years even while China reinvested their manufacturing proceeds into the US Housing Market (Anand, 2017). Unfortunately, the stability that Paul Volcker brought to the Federal Reserve, and, by extension, the positive externality it yields in both monetary policy (established by the Fed) and fiscal policy (established by Congress) were simply not good enough for President Ronald Reagan's Wall Street.

Enter Alan Greenspan. If ever there were a more prominent individual susceptible to the proponents of deregulation, it was Dr. Greenspan. Dr. Greenspan served as the Chairman of the Federal Reserve from August 11, 1987 – January 31, 2006 during such time the disruptive technology, or "the fuel", mortgage-backed securities (MBS), collateralized debt obligations (CDO), and synthetic CDOs (known as S^2) and banks leveraging positions 33 to 1 in both directions (short and long) that contributed to how the Great Recession was created, modified, mutated, and absorbed by that same Fed just a few years later. The aftermath wasn't just the length and duration of unemployment lines, closing of Lehman Brothers, consolidation of the world's largest banking system, and global economic distress throughout 2009. The true dilemma was the "product" utilized to curtail the downward spiral after monetary policy had failed, quantitative easing, or QE. QE, which has present-day, and future implications for both monetary and fiscal policy, has now morphed into what amounts to $4.5 trillion dollars in toxic mortgage-backed securities cloaked in treasury bonds (Amaro, 2017).

In essence, the appointment of Alan Greenspan as Chairman of the Federal Reserve in 1987 by President Reagan ushered in a new era of the Federal Reserve and Wall Street. This era's influence, which spanned two decades, culminated with the worst financial crisis seen since the Great Depression. The Greenspan Era included; the full repeal of the Glass-Steagall Act in 1999 via the Gramm-Leach-Biley Act, which allowed investment and commercial banks to merge, the Commodity Futures Modernization Act of 2000, which deregulated the over-the-counter (OTC) derivatives market, thus allowing un-checked futures trading and leverage for said trading, and perhaps the most egregious of them all; gross incompetence relative to the reduction of interest rates as the US economy grew at an astounding pace between 2002 - 2004. Brooksley Born, who was the Chairperson of the Commodity Futures Trading Commission (CFTC), during these regulatory rollbacks, was pressured by members of government to stifle her warnings of the potential circumspect nature of exchange-traded derivatives, and was essentially forced to resign as a retaliatory measure of the very citizens she'd tried to protect.

As a result, the combination of trillions of dollars spent on multiple wars (fiscal), reduced taxes under the George W. Bush administration (fiscal), reduced interest rates by the Federal Reserve amid a thriving economy (monetary), and increased predatory lending practices to lower-income market participants further fueling an unsustainable US Housing market should have been obvious as it was to Nobel Laureates Paul Krugman, Robert J. Shiller, and Daniel Kahneman, as well as esteemed credit to the global economic community, Peter Schiff, and Raghuram Rajan. Each one of these gentlemen provided ample warning in the form of papers, television interviews, even books, years in advance of the 08' crisis, yet were met with feverish criticism and rebukes at the highest levels of government. No one wanted to wait for the music to stop.

When the smoke had cleared over four-million American homes had been foreclosed. Twenty-six million Americans were laid-off or terminated from their jobs. $20 trillion dollars in wealth, savings, and retirement accounts seemingly evaporated by March of 2009. What happened? It begged a comforting answer. An answer that could have been blame-shifted to highly-sophisticated computer systems that simply malfunctioned. Perhaps an answer that could implicate China, or Russia, or any other notation that failed in an advanced economy with a controlling stake in macro-prudential economic policy that was perhaps convenient for the government to point a stern finger. Unfortunately, these aren't the right answers and "what happened" isn't the right question - at all. The appropriate question is, was it avoidable? And the answer is an unequivocal, yes. Two equally appropriate follow-up questions are, who could have prevented it, and what can be done to regain the financial stability in the future? The answers to those key questions lay within this chapter.

The Financial Crisis of 2008 was found to be avoidable by the Financial Crisis Inquiry Report Commission (concluded in 2011). The empirical evidence supporting the Commission's analysis includes; over a decade of deregulation, special interests groups in the form of banking lobbyists pouring money to impact key legislation, which further yielded government control by the aforementioned, preferential treatment of appointees bordering on nepotism, and highly questionable cabinet appointments by the Presidents Clinton and George W. Bush. In the aggregate, the order of magnitude relative to conflicts of interest, moral hazard, and the blatant disregard of regulatory official(s) advisements was tantamount to professional negligence. For the sake of brevity, this section of the chapter shows the correlation between the deregulation of commodities markets (Gramm–Leach–Bliley Act of 1999 and Commodity Futures Modernization Act of 2000) coupled with the reduction of interest rates and the aforementioned conflicts of interest by way of cabinet appointments truly staged the storm for the worst financial crisis since the Great Depression. The key takeaway from the data presented is to distill the lessons learned from this era so as not to replicate them in the future. In short, to regain global stability to thwart another financial crisis.

What these charts indicate, during the time period of 1987 - 2008, is simply that the non-existent regulatory oversight of the SEC, CFTC, and Federal Reserve Board, among others, proved that moral hazard was not limited to those banks on Wall Street labeled "Too Big to Fail." From Dr. Larry Summers Treasury Secretary

Figure 1. US GDP Growth rate (greenspan through market bottom)

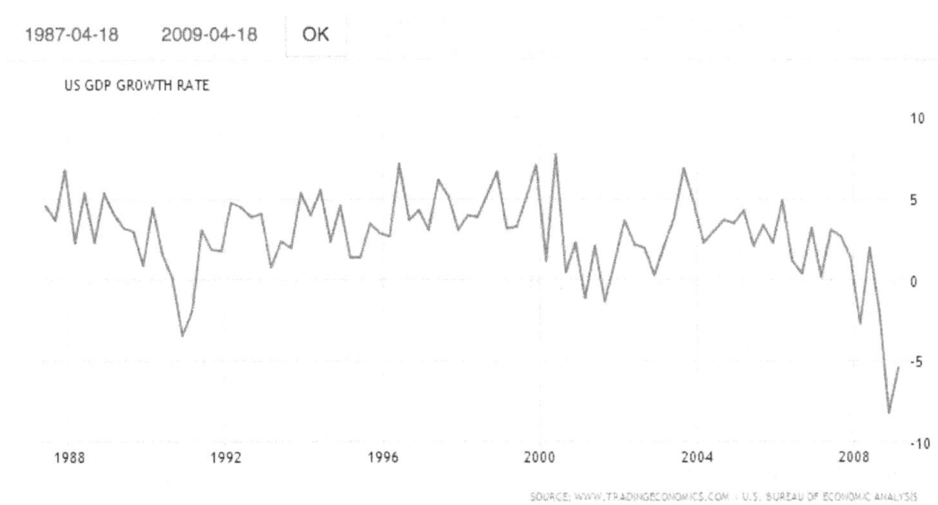

Figure 2. Federal funds interest rates (A)

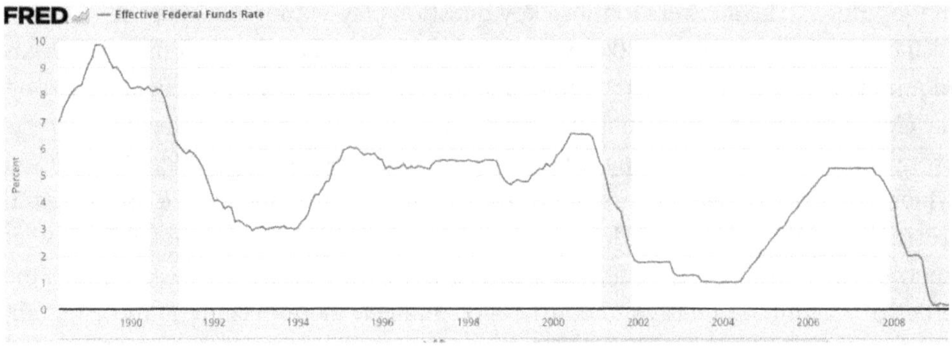

99-01', Alan Greenspan Federal Reserve Chair 1987-2006, Hank Paulson Treasury Secretary 06-09', Ben Bernake Federal Reserve Chair 06-14', Timothy Geithner Federal Reserve Bank of New York President 03'-09' and Treasury Secretary 09'-13', Arthur Levitt SEC Chair 93'-01', Glenn Hubbard Deputy Assistant Secretary (Treasury) 91'-93', and Frederic Mishkin Fed Governor 06-08' (subsequently resigned to "edit a textbook"), Martin Franklin Raines, Bill Clinton's former budget director, these gentlemen simply argued for more deregulation, or how cited that derivatives *reduced* volatility, and/or looked the other way while the markets ran, ratings agencies profits rose exponentially, interest rates fell, and home loans (most notably the subprime distribution) rose by a factor of 4 from 2002 to 2006.

Academic conflicts of interest - irrelevant. Deregulation by regulatory agencies - irrelevant. Anyone of the esteemed academics or politicians above could counter this premise by noting this was a scenario of "the collective." They could note a sound-bite for the news media that it's "A national issue, not one predicated upon a failure of government." The truly bold may even go insofar as to blame those who, "Purchased homes they couldn't afford," therefore being explicitly harsh as they blame-shift the crisis upon the unsophisticated, purchaser. Everyone was "playing the same game" they could argue, but everyone was not playing the same game. The counter-argument would recognize those who lost their retirement accounts, because of the unnecessary, and reckless deregulation. These individuals had no interest in home speculation, so why did they lose?

Throughout Greenspan's tenure the United States witnessed an unprecedented decoupling of wages and productivity, which has a direct correlation to one of today's issue, a lack of inflation. Subsequently, as the divergence in economic wealth, share of wealth, and exclusive prosperity placed the top 1% of the population in possession of over more than 40% of the total nation's wealth, whereas the bottom 80% of the population accounts for a mere 7%. To dilate these statistics, the top 1% currently

Figure 3. S&P 500

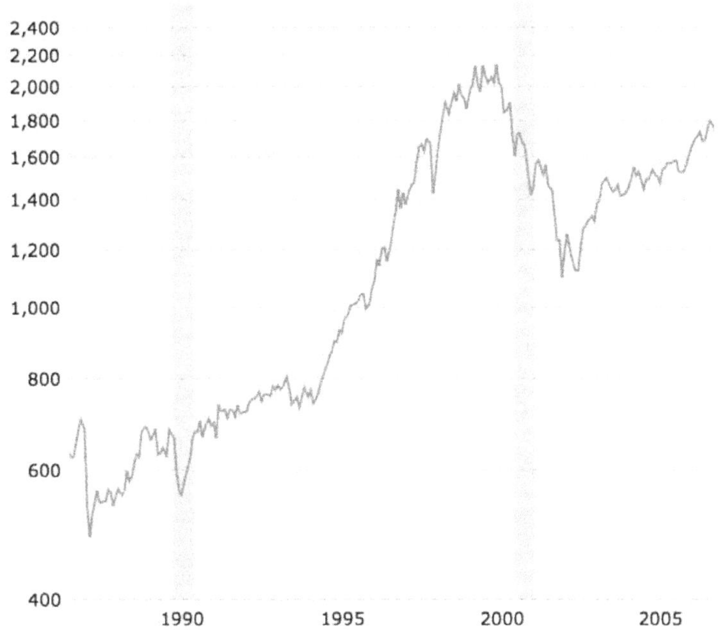

Figure 4. Rating agency profits

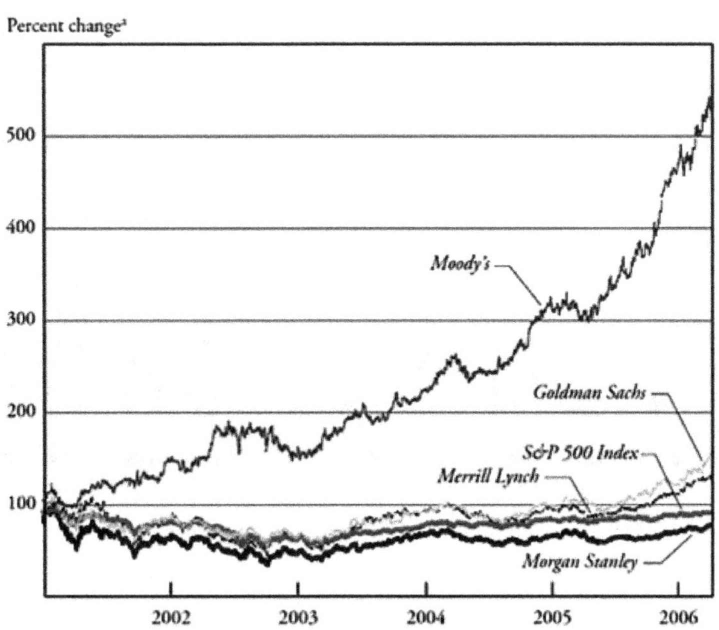

Source: http://finance.yahoo.com

Figure 5. Interest rates (B)

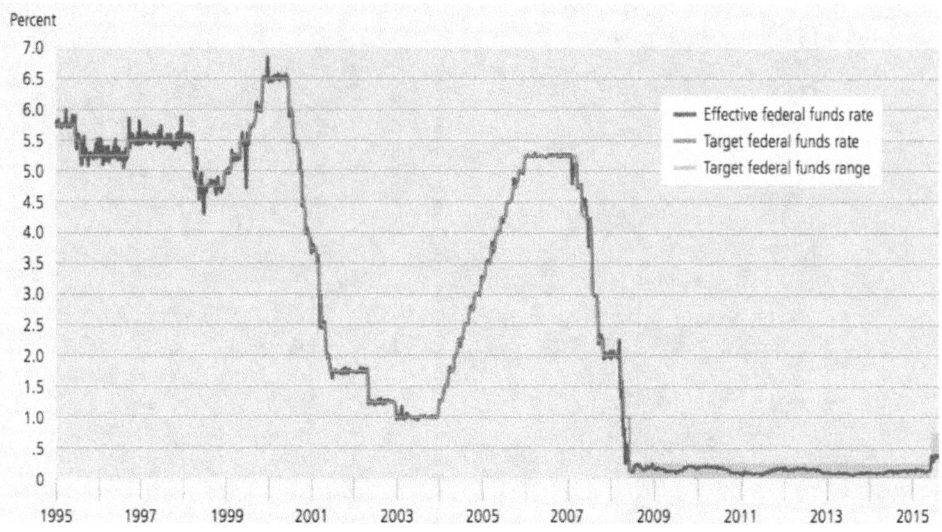

Figure 6. Subprime's exponential rise

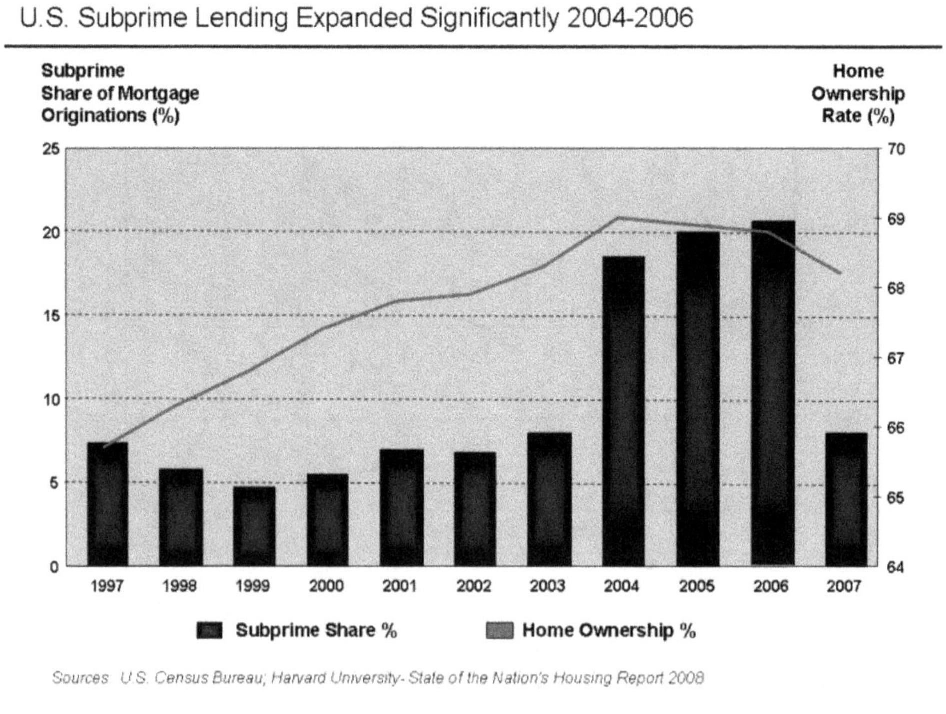

Figure 7. Case-Shiller CoreLogic composite

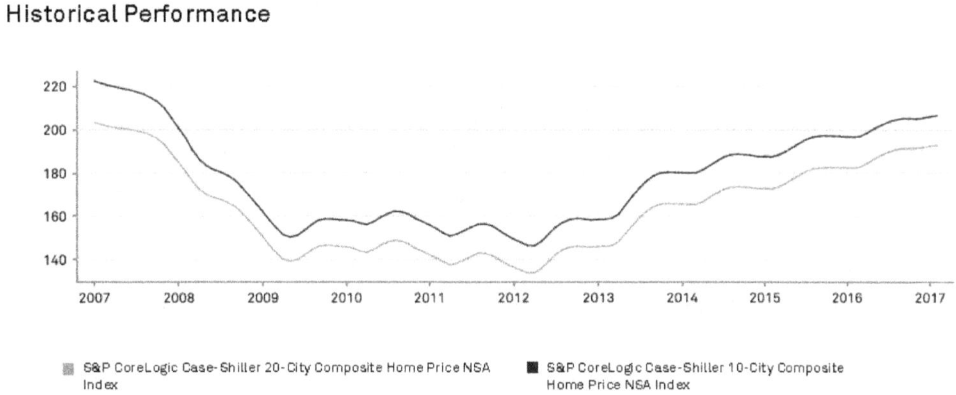

owns over 50% of the nations stocks, bonds, and equities, as well. The bottom 50% of the population own just .5% of the financial products noted[8]. These figures are unequivocally owned by the Greenspan tenure and subsequent crisis in 2008.

The summation for this portion of the chapter is a simple one. People like Brooksley Born, Raghuram Rajan, Peter Schiff, and the triumvirate of Nobel Laureates (Krugman, Shiller, Kahneman) who tried time and time again to warn those at the helm could not break onto the appropriate wavelength. The oscillations were "off." A different language was being spoken. In the end, it resulted in Main Street footing the bill, while scraping by on unemployment compensation and with less than half

Figure 8.

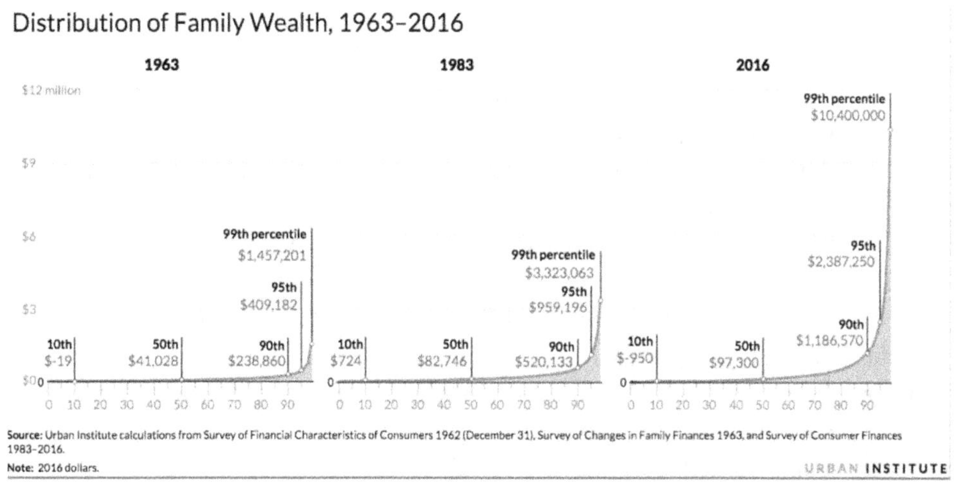

their retirement accounts remaining. Any why? When it was all avoidable, why? An epic failure of the government, not markets, not Wall Street.

2017 ISSUES, CONTROVERSIES, PROBLEMS: THE SOFT POWER SHIFT MARKET EXPECTATIONS, TPP, PARIS CLIMATE ACCORD, BELT AND ROAD, AND NORTH KOREA

There is no denying that the current state of the international political economy is rife with its share of both broad and nuanced issues, controversies, and problems. Since November 4, 2016, the exponential increase in the global indices are notably unsubstantiated, market expectations which were predicated on President Trump's campaign promise of both comprehensive tax reform coupled with a $1 trillion dollar infrastructure deal to rebuild the United States eroding highways, bridges, and water systems. To date, the S&P 500 is up 22.4%, the NASDAQ 30.9%, and the Dow Jones Industrial 27.56% with nearly nothing to support the rise outside of speculation of future economic policy amid an abysmal inflation rate of 1.7%.

In addition to the lack of economic achievement made by the current administration, the president has also withdrawn from several cornerstone deals set forth by the Obama administration that led to the rise in economic recovery and global stability. Within the first week of taking office, President Trump withdrew from the Trans-Pacific Partnership Agreement which was President Obama's trade jewel. As a result, China immediately rejoiced knowing that the remaining 11 nations locked into the multinational trade deal would assume China as their key trade partner as opposed to the United States. Despite political conjecture, the nations involved in the TPP, which include(d) Brunei Darussalam, Chile, New Zealand, Singapore, Australia, Canada, Japan, Malaysia, Mexico, Peru, the United States, and Vietnam, were all seen to receive net positive benefits either in regional stability relative to geopolitical capital and/or substantial positive externalities relative to economic impact.

According to Victor Shih, an expert on China's political economy at the University of California, San Diego, withdrawing from the T.P.P. was noted as having an adverse impact on America's image in the region."The U.S. will be seen as an unreliable partner both economically and perhaps even in the security arena," he said. "While some countries in Asia have no choice but to be close to the U.S., others may begin to look to China."

China has already sought to capitalize by making a push to complete an alternative pact, the Regional Comprehensive Economic Partnership, which aims to unite 10 members of the Association of Southeast Asian Nations with Japan, South Korea, Australia, New Zealand and India, an up and coming economic powerhouse in their own right if approached with proper analysis.

As previously noted, perhaps even more prevalent than the rebuke of the TPP was Trump's withdraw from the Paris Climate Accord and his comments during the G20 Summit, or lack thereof. The protests throughout Germany ahead of the G20 Summit came as no surprise to a majority of the world. And following the Summit, it was all but apparent that it is Germany, China, and the European Union who will attempt to grasp the reins of leadership let go by the Trump Administration. The U.S. exit from the Paris Climate Agreement virtually cemented the end of Pax Americana. The subsequent reaction from the international community teetered between disappointment and outrage. However, even before Donald Trump assumed the office of President of the United States, Chinese President Xi Jinping's directive at the World Economic Forum in January this year in Davos, Switzerland, was clear: China was ready to lead the international system if the U.S. would not.

This pronounced message denoted that Beijing was not only in a position to overtake the United States in both hard and soft power but willing to accept the responsibility should America's leadership continue on a tenuous path of diplomacy. Given the United States global dominance in national security and trade, what's peculiar is that Washington, D.C. should have been more concerned about losing their absolute advantage relative to the aforementioned global influence. And while some members of that very same bureaucracy feel that the current issues surrounding the Trump Administration are simply transitory in nature, the data is beginning to outstrip the exemplarity rhetoric.

The proliferation of China's Belt and Road project has now seen sixty countries express interest in collaborating with President Jinping on the initiative and for good reason. President Jinping's initiative is seemingly more concerned with capital investment than his Twitter feed, has entered into strategic economic cooperation with the formidable surrounding nations of India, Pakistan, Russia just to name a few. The bilateral agreements reach into the core of western Europe. Through these comprehensive agreements in finance and trade, China has the potential to achieve the coveted position of the world's number one economic power simply by executing a robust, yet sound policy - soft, not hard power as the United States clamors to pass a $700 billion dollar defense bill.

While the people of the United States who voted for the current president grow impatient for the Trump administration to produce the highly touted infrastructure plan he presumptuously ranted about for nearly eighteen months, the Intercontinental Belt and Road project has accumulated tens of billions of dollars in funding via the Silk Road Fund and the Asian Infrastructure Investment Bank (AIIB), while witnessing a myriad of support seeing over 200 private companies in energy, utilities, and high-speed-rail.

To date, the Silk Road Fund, in conjunction with the AIIB, has committed $40 billion in finance. This staggering amount of cash inflows is dedicated solely for the use of infrastructure projects

and serves as a multilateral intergovernmental institution focused on supporting its economic interlinkages while promoting transparency, openness, and sustainability, all while stimulating economic growth. And this is where it gets interesting - no economist has yet to identify the associated money multiplier. Additionally, all of this economic power will undoubtedly yield political power. Accruing first will be hard power, but that's not what's concerning. Soft power, a rare commodity for which the United States has had an absolute advantage since 1918 is what most certainly does matter.

The framework of the Silk Road Fund follows a sound policy, which could yield a positive-sum game for the public good through financing support via economic trade cooperation and connectivity. The Silk Road Fund aims to establish new infrastructure projects, develop clean and green energy development, utilize finite resources while simultaneously coupled with a forward-looking agenda.

Statistically, soft-power yields tremendous cooperation and unity throughout the international community and is quantified annually through the *Institute of Government* (Monocle), Elcano's *Global Presence Report*, and Portland's *The Soft Power 30*. And while traditional hard-power gauge's a country's influence on their military assets, GDP, and overall population, the inherent nature for which soft-power operates is much more comprehensive as it encourages joint action across nations, seeks to quantify social inclusion, human rights, and perhaps the generator of all that this globe depends on - economic growth.

Again, Donald Trump promised a $1 trillion dollar infrastructure plan dedicated to repairing and replacing the nation's weathered bridges, roads, and dilapidated buildings. The stock market rallied and continues to produce solid gains week-over-week. Main Street appears to have already priced in the benefits of a noteworthy money multiplier of $4 to $5 trillion, but for only one country - the U.S. China's Belt and Road initiative is not only economically inclusive, but it's also culturally cognizant. When it comes to economics and foreign policy, Trump isn't even close to playing the correct game.

Meanwhile, in Germany the international trade and finance community adequately synthesized, new mentions of potential tariffs on imported steel and other mass-produced products. Specifically for review purposes, trade restrictions do not benefit any nation, producing what's known as a negative-sum game, and quite often harm the very workers within the labor force they're designed to protect. Additionally, while the lower quintile suffers the most economic injustice, the divergent metric of exploitation has been apparent throughout the history of industrialized nations, whereas the CEOs, and policymakers profit from the hardships of the proletariat.

The isolationist narrative began when US President, Donald Trump, Vice President, Mike Pence, and Commerce Secretary, Wilbur Ross eschewed the majority of the assembled cabinet (22-3 opposing the trade restriction proposal) to engage in trade restriction dialogue. Notwithstanding the Trump administration's recent abysmal approval ratings, the global economy, specifically China, continues to grow at a moderate pace with a gradation tightening in most monetary policy aspects. However, what many fail to see is the correlation between the foundational elements of the United States and China's economic rise and by comparative analysis the deduction of continued growth, or pullback. The fact is that these economies began much like one another. The question is will China supersede America sooner than projected? To answer that question in the most basic of terms, historical references are once again required, and with that history, the hope to yield context will prevail.

The comparative analysis began over 150 years ago. For nearly forty (40) years, from 1865 through 1905, American business owners, such as Cornelius Vanderbilt, Andrew Carnegie, and John D. Rockefeller laid the foundation for what would translate into modern-day economic and operational processes throughout the country. These cornerstone enterprises gained substantial market share in prime areas of infrastructure, e.g., transportation, energy, and construction, even though the factories of these business magnates were highly contested due to dire working conditions and low pay.

Since 1978, China to has laid the foundation for economic expansion and investment. And much like America's foundation of forty years (40) before it became a hegemonic power following WWI, next year will mark the Asian powerhouse's fortieth year of economic improvement and market gains. But what could possibly be next? As US and Chinese GDP appears to be on a collision course for convergence (see chart below) within the next few years, any restrictions imposed by the United States could expedite the precipitous nature of the intersection.

Incidentally, if the discussion of any major movements within the scope of international trade is to register, it would be prudent to identify China's share of the international steel market, for which it has been no stranger to controversy in recent years. The surfeit of steel inundated throughout the market has prompted an all too familiar rhetoric from those simply unwilling or worse, incompetent when it comes to matters of international trade, most notably the Trump Administration. Is it possible that Jack Ma of Alibaba could step into this type of infrastructure and trade much like the titans of US capitalism during the late-nineteenth century?

The G20 Summit provided key economic indicators as it accounts for 80% of the global output in GDP. Will the Chinese steel, coal, and transportation sectors form an alliance with Germany and enter into a trade war with the United States? Will Chinese corporations begin to face scrutiny for continuing to pay skilled laborers 30% less than American factory workers were paid even in the most abdominal

Figure 9.

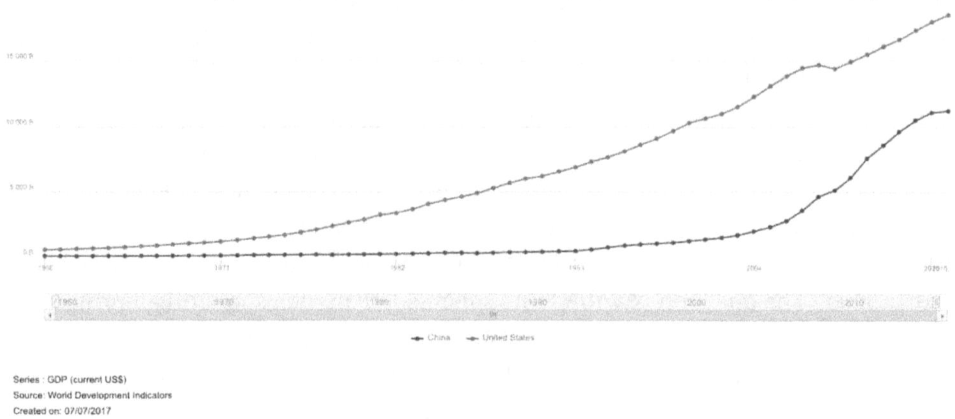

**For a more accurate representation see the electronic version.*

conditions in 1896? Or will pragmatism surface during this G20 Summit and quell the recent stir of uncertainty? Of course, we'd advocate for the latter, as it is advantageous for all nations to keep international markets free from restrictions and open for business. However, only time will tell if the robust global equities market, increasing price-to-earnings ratios, and healthy domestic and international sales can continue on their parabolic trajectory in a global trade relationship that seems to change its missive daily.

Make no mistake; traditional hard-power is still incredibly popular. For some nation's, this one included, hard-power has provided the very foundation for which most of us bear the freedom to write, research, and breathe. However, the complications marked by the corrosive tweets stoking the fires throughout the American landscape is slowly draining the soft-power capital which has accrued over the past century. Enter the future of soft-power Economics between the United States and China. Where the prospective for positive and transparent public policy, media, and, most importantly, the consideration for people of all nations to have an equal opportunity to embark on a more inclusive and convergent economic trend becomes a reality.

Lastly, this portion of the chapter would be remiss without mentioning the current notation of geopolitical tensions currently impacting the international economic landscape. North Korea is the main focus of the geopolitical tensions, although, given the recent threat by President Trump to scrap the Iranian nuclear treaty, that bears consideration in the future. North Korea; however, has been a topic of concern in the daily news for most of 2017. Thus it is there that requires a prompt solution.

Regaining global stability after the financial crisis asserts stability of many things, two of which are geopolitical stability and economic. In the scenario of North Korea, one necessitates the other. From the perspective of commerce; however, the direct implication is trade. The question; How will this impact trade domestically and internationally? First, in the event of a preemptive attack, which is not warranted, nor recommended, our trade relationship with China would grind to a halt. Simply put, the cheap exports from China to the United States would cease driving up consumer prices in the US. Additionally, the US could no longer export technology, consulting services, or energy to China. The translation on that front; a drastic hit to the nation's GDP. China has been explicit regarding the ramifications of such a move, and it is prudent to heed such a warning from the United States number one trade partner.

Conversely, working with China and the United States' allies would prove advantageous for the global community as a whole, promoting stability, while yielding a desperately needed reestablishment of inclusion and international political capital that has been lost since January 21, 2017. These are some of the final, yet key takeaways in the final portion of this chapter.

FUTURE SOLUTIONS AND RECOMMENDATIONS: EDUCATION, INFRASTRUCTURE, AND PARTNERSHIPS - ELEMENTS THAT YIELD PEACE, CONVERGENCE, AND INCLUSIVITY

Solutions for North Korea

The Commerce Department, with the understanding that proper and effective communication has first been established with the Joint Chiefs, Department of Defense, State Department, and Vice President, should first speak with the Federal Reserve (Presidents and Board Governors), as well as the respective banks on Wall Street (all major banks). This communication would establish a direct line of correspondence for the aforementioned parties in the event of an attack to thwart any attempted cyber attack on US financial institutions and US-allied. Additionally, the framework for a temporary, yet attractive energy deal should be discussed with China to aide in restoring positive relations, as well as providing assistance in their sustainable energy cycle from four (4) dirty to (2) dirty per annum. Incidentally, the attractiveness of this framework would also be productive in an Indian format. Therefore, India, the world's largest democracy, should also be approached by US diplomats to further cultivate mutually beneficial trade relationships while simultaneously aiding in the balance of threat and power within the region. Considerations in communication with the World Trade Organization (WTO), International Monetary Fund (IMF), World Bank, the Reserve Bank of India, and the Ministry in Beijing should be ongoing, not just until the crisis is resolved, but long-term. Contextually, improved trade relations have almost always yielded peace, democracy, and pro-trade alliances. North Korea should not deter, nor preclude the world and Her people from continuing to progress in health, education, and well-being.

Solutions for the Regression in the US Education System

In order to regain global stability, prior to employment, Congress must consider what qualifies individuals for the labor market in the first place - education. There are many reasons as to why the United States has regressed on the global stage of educational excellence. One of those root causes can be traced directly to the ramifications of the consolidation of locally-elected districts and their respective school boards. As was consistent in the past, the modern-day school district, an entity with a history rife with patronage and nepotism (Peterson 2011), it comes as no surprise that these gargantuan locally-elected district school boards should be abolished.

According to Peterson, a professor at the Harvard Kennedy School of Government notes, "Any state can totally abolish any school district in the state, and many schools have been abolished by the state." As a result of these abolishments, the US Education system is even more complex than in years past when all Horace Mann wanted to accomplish in his agenda was compulsory education, state-approved textbooks and teachers devoid of religious orthodoxy, and the data compilation of the state to make sure that states were following state expectations.

There are currently two key issues engulfing locally-elected district school boards which are correlated to critical demographics, e.g., quality of education based off of socioeconomic status across districts and the voters of the school boards and their tendencies, which exacerbate the already inherent inefficiencies of the districts expressed therein. The bureaucratic nature inherent in locally-elected district school boards is clearly negative, as it targets the lowest on the socioeconomic ladder, while maintaining a patronage-type structure for otherwise unqualified career board members. And, the more complex the education system becomes at the local level, the more pervasive the issues in cost, curriculum disparities, loss of efficacy, and general level of preparedness learned by the most disadvantaged student's decreases.

Those who oppose the abolishment of locally-elected school boards cite the following argument(s) in attempts to qualify their own positions within the system. "Although an elected board still hires teachers, raises revenue via local taxes, establishes a uniformed curriculum, and decides who graduates, school boards are now controlled, predominately by the principals and superintendents, which implies a misguided element objectivity." Peterson notes that it might be that a particular school district's attorney that wields similar powers as the superintendent due to his/hers intimate knowledge of education policy and law. An attorney with a keen acumen is generally viewed as a value-add; however, I respectfully disagree with this assumption as I believe that a seasoned attorney in education policy and law is more susceptible to the lobbying powers that be in our nation's Capitol. Coincidentally, the locally-elected district school board administration's being led by attorney's is not the most pressing counterargument to their unequivocal abolishment.

Another issue is that school boards are now held accountable to the states for their students' performance. Under normal circumstances, this would be a positive notation; however given the United States regression relative to global competitiveness in the Program for International Student Assessment (PISA) which measures the United States against all participating members sponsored by the Organization for Economic Cooperation and Development, as well as progress quantified overtime time as by the National Assessment of Educational Progress (NAEP). It is there that, relative to US Education policy, accountability has been statistically proven to have the propensity to be disregarded with the exception of a few states, Massachusetts being the highest performing (Peterson 2011).

There are many reasons as to why the United States has lost educational clout throughout the past forty years. For a system skilled more in the prevalence of inefficiency, ineffectiveness, and iniquitous distribution, it is not difficult to explain the divergence across states and countries. Both the history and bureaucratic nature of locally-elected school boards within antiquated school districts is one of the variables within the education equation that requires an immediate policy change. Therefore, it is my conclusion that locally-elected school boards should be abolished; however, the solutions that have, historically, caused both policy and political discourse must be considered in part with further root causes/variables, as a package to aid in the easing of a newly structured system.

Additionally, disruptive technology has often been met with stiff resistance by traditionalists with means, power, and, by extension, far-reaching influence with no desire to alter the status quo. Coincidentally, the passing of time and lessons learned from economic countertrends relative to opportunities in technology and innovation not taken, still has neither precluded, nor enlightened those influential individuals to embrace efficiency and efficacy improvements comparable to the quality of consumer products, such as the Sony transistor radio, health and wellness advances, such as amino acids and vitamins, and blended learning in education. Traditionalists, inherent in their societal norms to "stay the course" therefore pose nearly impenetrable obstacles inherent in the adoption of progressive movements to improve processes in any context, most notably concerning the integration of mainstreaming blended learning.

First, what is a disruptive technology and why is it and of itself an obstacle to blended learning? Quite directly, disruptive innovation is technology that is, initially, difficult to quantify and therefore even more so difficult to communicate the primary benefits of the product. Additionally, the product may also be priced lower as a way past the initial barrier-to-entry to gain market share as the design is perfected. The example of the high-priced RCA vacuum tube radios that sat stationary in homes across America vs. Sony's portable, pocket-sized transistor radio. Peterson articulates the fallacies within RCA executives traditionalists' mindset, as they practiced status-quo, vacuum-tube economics while the team at Sony perfected their transistor radio little by little eventually becoming the progressive product one couldn't be without much like that of the capacities of the personal computer, online education, and blended learning. The lack of knowledge as it applies to a disruptive technology such as blended learning or even a pocket radio is in and of itself an obstacle that will have to her overcome over time.

To dilate the disruptive technology argument, one of the leading obstacles hindering the widespread implementation of blended learning are career educators or traditionalists. Experts such as Stanford Professor Larry Cuban, is a quintessential proponent of conventional brick-and-mortar institution, stating that, "Our extensive focus on technology use in schools" (could threaten) "historic civic idealism and broad social purposes public schools serve in a democracy (Peterson, 2011). Additionally, using the example of a literature review, Cuban notes that self-contained classrooms, "Have the propensity to yield more direct, rapid-fire conversation and debate among the student body," (Peterson, 2011) while implying that blended learning does not contain these properties. Traditionalists; How many times have they seen how this episode ends?

Unfortunately for Professor Cuban, his argument is neither valid nor sound, as it has been proven both socially, and statistically, that the 'social interactions in most high schools do not produce "historic civic idealism" rather it has the propensity to create a status hierarchy in which athletes and cheerleaders come first, nerds last' (Peterson, 2011). In fact, Professor Cuban has conceded this much after reviewing the data supporting it. Additionally, Peterson aptly provides the case study of the Florida Virtual School (FLVS) which provides additional positive externalities seen by the program such as; student flexibility and curricula that will aid those students who either A) Have disabilities or B) Have difficulties working in a conventional classroom. Lastly, in a blended setting, teachers serve the education system as they should; As coaches encouraging students to maximize their full academic potential while cultivating confidence student-over-student, not class over class wherein many students are lost in the haze.

It's true that the microeconomic elements of disruptive technology have traditionally been disbursed to those with the highest willingness-to-pay (WTP) first. However, as modern-day economics would both quantify and substantiate this claim, the technological revolution argument wherein there can be no race to the bottom as competitors are forced to improve their product or be forced out of the marketplace is absolutely valid. Google has a superior product to Bing. When was the last time you used Bing? Amazon has single-handedly dominated Walmart,

Kroger's, and Sam's Club due to their data analytics division, Amazon Web Services (AWS) while perfecting their supply chain distribution.

In summation, the concept of blended learning is, at first, a challenging one, and with challenges there are obstacles. However, there should be no fear associated with a sound policy coupled with both global coherence and clarity relative to specific tracks, grade-levels, and equitable standards in content quality. While it is true that disruptive technology, has been prone to initially drawing the common theme of "fear of the unknown" it has proven to be widely accepted over time. Blended learning curricula are no different than the transistor radio or personal computer. Therefore, it should come as no surprise to see classrooms rife with blended learning structures in the not so distant future.

Lastly, national standards and why they should be required in the US public education system. Rigorous education standards implemented on the national scale have statistically shown to yield exponential gains in the academic progress of those countries which require their students to participate in such programs. In fact, those countries that require adherence to national education standards continuously outperform nations that operate on antiquated, state-based models. Therefore, this section advocates that the United States should have national standards established for all students in the public education system.

The principle reason as to why the United States Department of Education should implement national academic standards going into the future is quite straightforward; They are a matter of national interest. Academics in the United States have never been under federal control, and, while the US was fortunate from the 1920s through the 1970s to have a manageable population relative to the rest of the world and be the benefactor of two world wars, the model that once served both of these axiomatic truths well has become as complex as it is antiquated. Addressing the need for the US to increase its competitiveness in global education as it has a direct correlation to economic prosperity (Peterson, 2011). Additionally, it is prudent that the US advocate for required, federal Common Core Standards, as countries that operate off of a uniformed model of rigorous requirements in science, technologically, engineering, and math have statistically shown to outperform countries that do not. The US, once a world leader in education, it is not surprising that advanced, and even moderately innovative countries with uniformed standards have not only converged on US education dominance but have surpassed the lenient state-based model as they've thrived economically via the successfully implemented national requirements and is sustained by the PISA examinations. The Race-to-the-Top (RttT) initiative was promising; however, it still allows states to choose what is acceptable, and the incentives for success just aren't enough to produce a nationwide implementation. State-based oversight has failed the education system, and, as such, it's time to establish national standards.

The potential side-constraints that may preclude this thesis from being proven both attractive and feasible are also, relatively basic. The main constraints lie in procuring a collective agreement from the states as to which standards and curriculum are adopted, continuing education and training for teachers, performance-based testing to ensure standards are being adhered to via NAEP, and the level of proficiency for which students are required to meet in order to gain credentials. The political and policy discourse for which these debates have been subjected to is a significant side-constraint. However, should the appropriate progressives champion the policy, while reaching a bipartisan consensus before submitting a comprehensive proposal, it is not out of the realm of possibility that this agenda of national academic requirements become a reality.

The United States has fallen woefully behind in the considerations of global education excellence. One of the root causes of that regression is due to how and by whom for which the standards of our students are currently constructed, as well as the oversight required to ensure that those criteria are being met. Empirical data shows that economically speaking, countries who do not participate in nationally required standards as is applicable to academic curricula regress in a myriad of capacities including, standards of living, GDP, and global power. It is the utilization of this inference tied to global prosperity that the United States consider the establishment of nationally required educational criteria. For if the United States is to regain its competitive advantage in educational and global economic dominance, its most prudent course of policy action would be first to implement the uniformed requirement of national academic standards.

Solutions for US Infrastructure and Renewed Global Partnerships

Following education, infrastructure is imperative to global economics, efficiency, and prosperity.

The United States currently has an unemployment rate of 4.2%, the lowest in 17 years. However, after reviewing lagging sectors in construction and utilities, the unemployment rate elasticity has the ability to dip below the 3% mark. The current level of unemployment is a resource constraint. Therefore, in order to maximize the value of infrastructure projects and accomplish the target objective of 3% unemployment, the mitigation of this constraint by introducing job training programs prior to excavation and construction is recommended.

Additionally, as has been observable in economic data, as well as corroborated by Federal Reserve Board Governor Lael Brainard, inflation has stagnated further exacerbating the ability to raise interest rates which would be a monetary tool against market instability. In order to gain inflation, a thriving middle class (the labor supply) must first, be paid a higher wage. Second, the participation rate must also increase, especially is key demographics that have lagged in the past, such as construction and utilities. Infrastructure aids in solving these variables.

Infrastructure projects, in the short-term, provide the following benefits:

- Economic boom nationwide driving domestic consumption while generating exponential levels of tax revenue
- Cost-savings in FEW (food, energy, water) via sustainable agriculture's net-positive handprint
- Cost-savings in Supply Chain, Logistics, and Transportation
- Agricultural export improvement further stimulating the economy
- Improved relationships with trade partners via economics, health, and well-being

Long-Term Benefits

- Sustainable smart solutions to prevent environmental degradation
- Improved water conservation and potability
- Exponential Economic money multiplier
- Trillions of dollars (USD) in combined revenues, energy cost-savings, and upward mobility factors reducing national debt while "raising all boats."
- Better functioning cities, hospitals, agriculture, all while reducing oil dependency
- $40,000 Net Present Value per person (lower bound) in the American society (public and private sectors) using a 4% discount rate returns $2.70 per dollar invested.

Drilling-Down

Assuming a participation rate of 70%, the annualized return of infrastructure projects is $4 trillion dollars in net present value benefits to the American society alone.

In summation, the distribution of the benefits has inherent properties of equity. Furthermore, historical data provides the confidence that given the past success relative to field implementation and wealth of experience of US talent in the labor market, this policy recommendation isn't simply based on theory; rather its substantive feasibility is derived from the efficacy generated on past projects. Lastly, the sustainability of this project refers to the capacity of the policy to maintain its integrity and deploy core principles to stave off any risks to ROI and net benefits to the public. Generating bipartisan support in American constituencies, citizens, businesses, andCongress is absolutely imperative to solidifying the United States future.

CONCLUSION

The effort in appropriate coalitions put forth will not only build tangible assets for the United States and the world but use new, sustainable technology but also increase social inclusion and upward mobility that are the sum product of infrastructure and education yields. The inclusivity of this global endeavor will promote these axiomatic principles while growing global GDP at a sustainable, and potentially, exponential rate. Building on this premise is but one note relative to including the inherent potential to shape and improve the globe's technological hubs, financial centers, and climate shift, all while strengthening the middle class for generations, which is required to drive inflation and maintain price stability.

Robust and comprehensive outlines of new infrastructure projects, education and medical facilities, and job training are required for human progression. Developing sound policies for select hard, soft, and smart infrastructure projects, which have been specifically designed to utilize available and sustainable technology, as well as developmental considerations for implementation and integration. The creation of new infrastructure will first establish an efficient and reliable electrical grid, improving current industrial capacity and agriculture via green technology, which will simultaneously provide a positive externality to the environment and society as a whole. As public goods are concerned, the synchronicity pertaining to the implementation of green technology and new employment opportunities throughout the country will pay a respectable multiplier and dividends for decades. While these policy recommendations and their framework as specific to the United States in promoting global stability, it seeks to serve as an enduring template for other economies who wish to participate at the advisement of the corresponding research centers.

Lastly, listen to the experts, think critically, and ask questions. The following individuals are experts in their fields and breed global coherence among policymakers, market players, and other relevant actors. JP Morgan Chase's CEO Jamie Dimon, Federal Reserve Chair Dr. Janet Yellen, Federal Reserve Board Governor Dr. Lael Brainard, Christine Lagarde of the IMF, ECB President, Mario Draghi, and proven internationally renowned economists; Raghuram Rajan, Peter Schiff, Daniel Kahneman, Robert J. Shiller, Jeffrey Sachs, Clayton M. Christensen, David Tepper, and former/current Federal Reserve Governors Kevin Warsh and Jerome H. Powell are all deserving of the time to ascertain and deduce appropriate groundwork relative to the global climate and stability of markets and policy. These esteemed professionals will almost always cite terms and concepts such as, Growth of US Economy (GDP), imports/exports, 'transitory in nature' (short-lived), the Housing Market, Consumer Confidence, CPI, PPI, inflation, wage growth, and unemployment (Federal Reserve Mandates and the side constraints and limitations of the mandate), Trade Balance/

Deficit (divergence or convergence) and Prospective Growth relative to Sectors both leading and regressing, which, at the moment, the Leading Sectors are: Tech and Healthcare, whereas, there is plenty of room for vast improvement in Construction and Utilities, i.e., Infrastructure.

Technology tends to reward those who innovate or can work within advanced technological economies wherein they garner substantial advantages. This puts them into ideal positions of or access to power where they often shape rules to their benefit even though different rules could be initiated and implemented for everyone. This has been the case for the past one hundred and fifty years. The United States and Her allies changed the world. But this new rule, the global rule has the potential to provide enduring benefits every single person in every single nation.

Wall Street needs Main Street, and Main Street needs Wall Street, just as North America needs Europe, Asia, Africa, Australia, and South America. We can do this together. We can grow and learn and educate with our families with our neighbors with our countries. We can collaborate as a unified world, with a common purpose that everyone can enjoy and respect. That at the beginning of each new day truly brings with it the opportunity to have a better life for you and your family than the day before.

ACKNOWLEDGMENT

I'd like to acknowledge a few people who both supported my work and aided in my ability to remain relatively objective over the past few years. First, Patrik Eriksson of Concordance from Sweden. Had it not been for you and our trips to the literal end of the road in India, I would not possess the breadth of time and place knowledge that both renewed and propelled my sense of service to this world of ours. If it were not for you, I would not be where I am today. Additionally, to Debra Holtham to whom I owe more than I could ever quantify. Those very same trips across the globe would not have been possible without the moral support, as well as the timely care packages that kept me going throughout the years of grueling desert, tundra, and jungle travel. To Dr. Bruno Sergi, one of the premier international economists who provided me with an opportunity to engage once more in the international monetary market. Thank you for taking the time to include me in this project, as I look forward to many more years of influential and purposeful work for which we can contribute to the world. Last, but certainly not least, special thanks to John Paul Rollert of the University of Chicago. Your blueprint and mentorship have raised my diplomatic bar such that no matter what setting I find myself engaged in I think to myself, "What would John Paul do?" I too, look forward to our work in the future, helping as many people along the way as humanly possible.

To my family, my friends located on every corner of the globe, our allies, and past, present, and future acquaintances; None of these words, present or forthcoming, would have been possible without knowing all of you. We're all human, and as such, imperfection is as common as a fluke. I truly appreciate any kindness ever shown, as it's cultivated this man into someone who genuinely cares about the greater good. I sincerely appreciate every single one of you. Lastly, to those who have passed on, whether by choice or the finite call in time, knowing all of you shaped me, and there isn't a day that goes by that I don't think of you with love and appreciation for knowing you while you were here.

REFERENCES

Amaro, S. (2017). *Wealth manager warns on bond markets creating the 'biggest financial crisis of our lifetime'*. Retrieved October 12, 2017 from https://www.cnbc.com/2017/10/06/ wealth-manager-warns-on-bond-markets-creating-the-biggest-financial-crisis-of-our-life time.html

Anand, B., (2017). *Economics for Managers*. Harvard Business School, HBX CORe.

Baker, P. (2017). *Trump Abandons Trans-Pacific Partnership, Obama's Signature Trade Deal*. Retrieved June 7, 2017 from https://www.nytimes.com/2017/01/23/us/politics/tpp- trump-trade-nafta.html

Coors, C. (2011). *Credit Rating Agencies - Too Big Too Fail?* Thomson Reuters.

Dudley, W., & Hubbard, G. (2004). *How Capital Markets Enhance Economic Performance and Facilitate Job Creation*. Global Markets Institute.

Epstein, J. (2017). *Trump Threatens Government Shutdown Over Border Wall Funding*. Retrieved October 12, 2017 from https://www.bloomberg.com/news/articles/2017-08-23/trump-threatens-government-shutdown-to-secure-border-wall-funds

Federal Reserve Bank of St. Louis. (2017). *Financial Crisis - Full Timeline*. Retrieved April 10, 2017 from https://www.stlouisfed.org/financial-crisis/full-timeline

Financial Crisis Inquiry Report Commission. (2011). *The Financial Crisis Inquiry Report*. Author.

Jejunum. (2003). In *Merriam-Webster's dictionary* (11th ed.). Springfield, MA: Merriam-Webster.

McKernan, S. M., Ratcliffe, C., Steuerle, E., Quakenbush, C., & Kalish, E. (2017). *Nine Charts about Wealth Inequality in America*. Urban Institute. Retrieved October 12, 2017 from http://apps.urban.org/features/wealth-inequality-charts/

National Bureau of Economic Research. (2012). *US Business Cycles Expansions and Contractions*, Retrieved August 12, 2107 from http://www.nber.org/cycles/US_Business_Cy cle_Expansions_and_Contractions_20120423.pdf

Peterson, P. (2010). *Saving Schools: From Horace Mann to Virtual Learning*. Harvard University Press.

KEY TERMS AND DEFINITIONS

Collateralized Debt Obligation: A collateralized debt obligation (CDO) is so-called because the pooled assets—such as mortgages, bonds, and loans—are essentially debt obligations that serve as collateral for the CDO. The tranches in a CDO vary substantially in their risk profile.

Consumer Confidence: Consumer confidence is an economic indicator that measures the degree of optimism that consumers feel about the overall state of the economy and their personal financial situation.

Consumer Price Index (CPI): Program produces monthly data on changes in the prices paid by urban consumers for a representative basket of goods and services.

G20: An international forum for the governments and central bank governors from Argentina, Australia, Brazil, China, France, Germany, India, Indonesia, Italy, Japan, Mexico, Russian Federation, Saudi Arabia, South Africa, South Korea, Turkey, United Kingdom, United States, and the European Union.

Hard Power: A coercive approach to international political relations, especially one that involves the use of military power.

Macro-Prudential Policy: Macroprudential regulation is the approach to financial regulation that aims to mitigate risk to the financial system as a whole (or "systemic risk").

Mortgage-Backed Security: A mortgage-backed security (MBS) is a type of asset-backed security that is secured by a mortgage or collection of mortgages. The mortgages are sold to a group of individuals (a government agency or investment bank) that securitizes, or packages, the loans together into a security that investors can buy.

Quantitative Easing: Quantitative easing (QE), also known as large-scale assets purchases, is an expansionary monetary policy whereby a central bank buys predetermined amounts of government bonds or other financial assets in order to stimulate the economy.

Producer Price Index (PPI): Program measures the average change over time in the selling prices received by domestic producers for their output. The prices included in the PPI are from the first commercial transaction for many products and some services.

Soft Power: A concept developed by Joseph Nye of Harvard University to describe the ability to attract and co-opt rather than by coercion (hard power), using force or giving money as a means of persuasion. Soft power is the ability to shape the preferences of others through appeal and attraction. A defining feature of soft power is that it is noncoercive; the currency of soft power is culture, political values, and foreign policies.

Section 4

Market Towards Crisis Challenges

Chapter 10
Modern Trends in Capital Flows in Emerging Markets

Svetlana Balashova
RUDN University, Russia

Vladimir Matyushok
RUDN University, Russia

Inna Petrenko
RUDN University, Russia

ABSTRACT

This chapter provides an evaluation of the influence of the most significant external and internal factors on international capital flows in the form of direct and portfolio investments for 24 developing countries during the period 1990–2015. The authors have adopted the partial adjustment model and the feasible generalized least squares estimator for panel data. Results show that the determinants of capital flow for foreign direct and portfolio investments differ. The impact of political risks on cross-border capital flows has been identified.

DOI: 10.4018/978-1-5225-4026-7.ch010

INTRODUCTION

International capital flow plays a central role in the global economy, affects the macroeconomic policy, but also brings some benefits and risks for recipient countries. However, in contrast to labour and natural economic resources, historically, capital can move and accumulate quickly. In the last decades, in search of profitable areas of application, capital has rushed to developing countries, whose share in the international capital flows has grown significantly. Thus, these countries have become not only importers but also exporters of capital. Despite the fact that in absolute terms the biggest part of financial flows is concentrated in developed countries, this distribution also depends on the financial stability of emerging markets (EM) which are particularly vulnerable to market fluctuations caused by inflows or outflows of foreign capital. After the global financial crisis 2008-2009, countries with EM faced unprecedented volatility in capital inflows. Before the financial crisis, developing countries policymakers feared that excessive capital inflows could provoke an economic overheating. However, they have been concerned about a reduction in capital inflows or even its net outflows in recent years.

The main challenge for the entire developing world is to deal optimally with the challenges of economic growth in conditions of the volatility of capital flows. It is common knowledge that the influx of international capital into a country stimulates economic growth through investment financing, with which new technologies arrive and, due to the increased income, a higher level of household consumption is provided (Obstfeld, 1998; 2009). Moreover, capital inflows contribute to a better diversification of asset portfolios of developing countries. However, a surplus of capital may be accompanied by adverse macroeconomic effects, such as an intensive increase in the money supply, excessive strengthening of the national currency in real terms, and inflationary pressures.

Determinants of capital flows can be grouped into 2 categories: External and internal factors to the economy in which capital flows. External factors stimulating the influx of international capital in developing economies are: Capital surplus and its relative cheapness (lower interest rates on borrowed capital), lower gross domestic product (GDP) growth rates, higher taxes and labour, raw materials, energy costs, purchase or lease of land, and, as a result, the lower efficient use of capital, reflected in the stock indices of developed countries. Low interest rates in developed countries make investments in countries with EM more attractive. The impact of this effect is strengthened if the developing country is interested in external borrowing and low global interest rates ensure its greater solvency. Internal factors that affect capital flows include political risks, availability of economic resources (labour and natural resources) and their value, the capacity of the domestic market, higher GDP growth rates, lower taxes and labour, raw materials, energy costs, purchase or lease of land

and as a result the higher efficient use of capital, the volatility of the real exchange rate, external debt, and conditions of the investment environment.

Large external liabilities and a sharp reduction in financial flows create the risk for those developing countries, where the previously active inflow of capital was registered on the stage of recovery of the global financial cycle and when EM were more liquid (Ayala, Nedeljkovic, & Saborowski, 2015). The slowing down of capital inflows in EM and risk of capital flight is becoming an increasingly significant factor in the destabilization of the financial system and the threat of a decline in economic growth. Portfolio investments will cease to be liquid, and financing costs may rise sharply in the run-up to increase in the interest rate of U.S. Federal Reserve System (FED) in the short term, which will subsequently exert a strong pressure on exchange rates, stock quotes, and international currency reserves of developing countries. Such a scenario may aggravate the already severe economic situation with regard to the volatility of capital flows in EM. The adjustment and adaptation of emerging market economies to the new global conditions, including a reduction in the liquidity of the financial market and commodity prices, will create new challenges for monetary and fiscal policies in the medium term.

In this study, the authors have analyzed and identified the most significant external and internal factors which influence on international capital flows for 24 developing countries for the period 1990–2015. In order to assess the contribution of these factors, the authors have used the partial adjustment model and the Feasible Generalized Least Squares estimator for panel data. Partial adjustment model is a model used to assess short- and long-run influence of exogenous factors on the endogenous variable. The Feasible Generalized Least Squares estimator for panel data is used to avoid the consequences of cross-section heteroskedasticity since the model is estimated over a non-homogeneous group of developing countries. In particular, the authors have shown that the political stability in the country, quality of institutions, fundamental democratic rights and freedoms, positive investors' expectations, high rates of economic growth, and inflows of foreign direct investment FDI in previous periods have a positive impact on the inflow of foreign direct investments. Major constraints of FDI are their greater accumulated volume, a rise in the real effective exchange rate, and public debt. The increase in international reserves, political stability in the country, quality of state institutions as well as an absence of violence have a positive impact on portfolio equity investments. The real exchange rate volatility, increases of the Federal Fund rate as well as the short-term interest rates in developed countries reduce the influx of portfolio equity. The obtained outcomes are critical for government regulators, institutional and corporate investors, and training in the area of economics and finance.

BACKGROUND

Existing empirical literature traditionally groups determinants of capital movements in two categories, that is "push" and "pull" factors. The first category is typical for financial and economic indicators of donor countries, while the second one refers to the recipients of foreign capital. Baek (2006) used the panel study of country fixed effects for 9 emerging market economies and concludes that "push" factors have a greater impact on portfolio investments in developing countries in Asia and Latin America. De Vita and Khine (2008) estimated a structural vector autoregression model for 5 EM economies and suggested that EM productivity growth is more important for FDI than for portfolio flows, while the accumulated reserves are the dominant factor for portfolio inflows.

Albuquerque, Loayza, and Serven (2005) investigated the relationship between global market integration and FDI flows and concluded that global factors are more significant, while the impact of internal economic factors, such as productivity growth, trade openness, and financial market depth, were less significant.

The global crisis of 2008-2009 caused a significant decrease in the volume of foreign capital, which soon became the subject of greater academic research. The crisis shifted the focus of literature directly on gross capital inflows, which includes external assets and liabilities, as opposed to the net inflow, which reflects the financial account balance. Obstfeld (2009) saw an intensive growth of capital flow in the years before the crisis when gross flows of foreign capital exceeded the net inflow and came to the conclusion that the large external liabilities are a major symptom of financial instability in developing countries. Broner, Didier, Erce, & Schmukler, (2013) analysed the cyclical movement of gross capital inflows in 103 countries and subdivided them into low-, medium-, and high-income countries. The conclusion of this research says that during the economic downturn gross capital flows were financially more volatile than net inflows. Forbes and Warnock (2012) presented a systematic analysis of the extreme episodes of the financial flows, which the authors classified into four categories: Surges (of nonresident inflows), stops (of nonresident inflows), flight (of resident outward investment), and retrenchment (of resident outward investment). In this study, the authors found the largest mobility of foreign capital between 1980 and 2009, due to global factors, particularly the factor of global risk aversion. This result was also confirmed by Ghosh, Kim, Mahvash, and Zalduendo in 2014.

In the past few years, considerable attention was paid to the role of monetary factors of capital flows to EM, with special emphasis on the FED's quantitative easing policy. In a research on the FED's policy, Ahmed and Zlate (2013) sustained that the unconventional monetary policy of the United States did not affect the volume of financial flows; however, it turned capital flows into portfolio investments. Koepke

(2014) took a broader approach to the impact of the USA monetary policy, focusing on changes in market expectations regarding future FED interest rates, which, according to the author, are a key factor in the inflow/outflow of portfolio investment in/from EM. In this chapter, the authors have focused on capital flows in the form of FDI and portfolio investments in EM[1], not segmenting the latter on a regional basis, nor on the size of the economies, economic growth or ongoing monetary policy. The contribution of the present study is to determine the general financial and economic capital drivers, which are sufficiently universal for all countries with the EM, as well as to assess a nonfinancial group of factors determining the dynamics of capital–the group of political risk indicators. In the following, the chapter describes general characteristics of the capital flows in EM and developed countries, then, it offers a description of the data and the models. The subsequent sections provide the core results and the conclusion, respectively.

WORLD CAPITAL FLOWS OVERALL VIEW

Developing countries are one of the important elements of the modern world economy. Faster growth rates of developing countries in comparison with developed countries and the corresponding change in the structural proportions of the world economy are essential. Early in the 1990s, developing countries accounted for 22-23% of world GDP; by 2015 this share rose to 35% according to the World Bank. Since the 2000s, developing countries took the initiative from developed ones, which were dominated by economic growth in the previous century: The growth rates of the economies of the developing world in this period exceed the growth rates of developed economies (Figure 1). Growing market capacity of the developing countries, high-yielding investment were a powerful incentive for the foreign investment in these countries.

The liberalization and structural reforms in developing countries have contributed to the increase of their attractiveness for foreign investors (Kostyunina, 2005). The improvement of the macroeconomic situation of EM has led to a high growth rate of portfolio equities (Figure 2). Net capital flows for global EM were negative in 2015, which was the first time it had happened since 1988, the Institute of International Finance (IIF) said in its report. Capital outflow, together with the decline in commodity prices, led, in particular, to a suspension of the liberalization of capital transactions in China. Figure 2 presents the dynamics of portfolio investments by the group of countries. Data show that the influx of foreign capital into EM increased rapidly since the early 2000s up to 2008, while developed countries experienced a negative increase of capital during the period 2001-2002 ("dot-com" crisis), and the downward trend in capital inflows was formed prior to the global crisis 2007-2008. Following the global financial crisis, portfolio equity flows in developed countries, and EMs

Figure 1. Economic growth rates and share of world GDP of high income (HI) and low- and middle-income countries (LMY) 1990-2015[2]
Source: Authors' calculations based on WDI database.

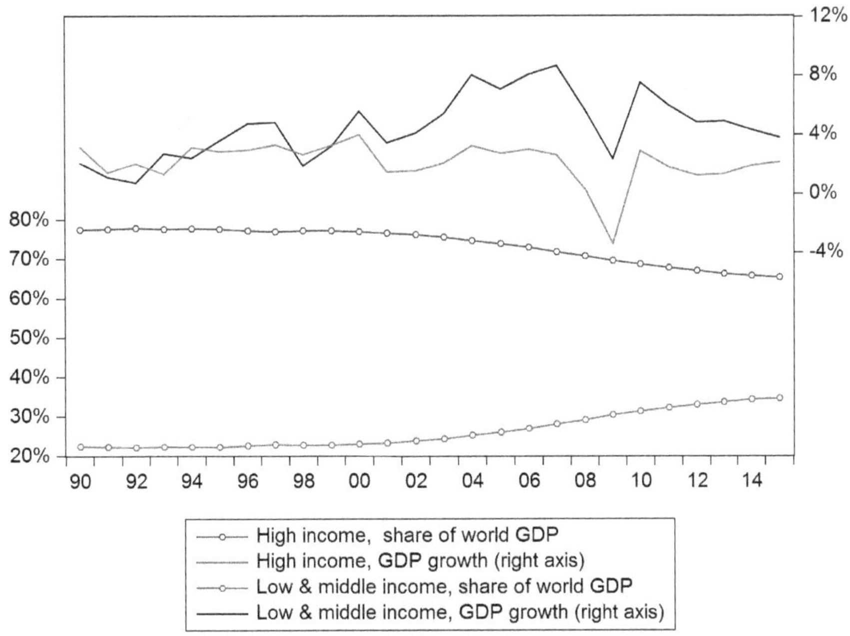

**For a more accurate representation see the electronic version.*

are highly synchronized. However, portfolio equity inflows in EM predominate the developed ones. During the period 2014-2015, asset prices of EM depreciated sharply. As this development seems to have been prompted primarily by a shift in market expectations towards the FED's policy, a decline in portfolio equity inflows in EM can be observed.

Dynamics of foreign direct investments in developed (high income) countries shows pronounced cycles associated with the crises of 2000 and 2007-2008: An intense increase in pre-crisis period and its reduction by 2001 and 2008 while emerging economies showed the active flow up to 2008 (Figure 3). The global financial crisis has led to drop in FDI inflow. However, developing countries showed rather rapid economic growth even after the crisis, outpace developed countries. This can be regarded as one of the reasons for the increase in the foreign direct investment inflow in these markets during the period under study.

Despite the growing influx of foreign investments into EM during the period under review, in general, the developed countries continue to play a dominant role in the world FDI market. Indeed, the accumulated capital since 1990 (excluding depreciation) in advanced economies is almost 3 times higher than accumulated

Figure 2. Portfolio equity and net inflows in the group of high income (left axis) and low and middle income (right axis) countries, bln US$
Source: WDI database.

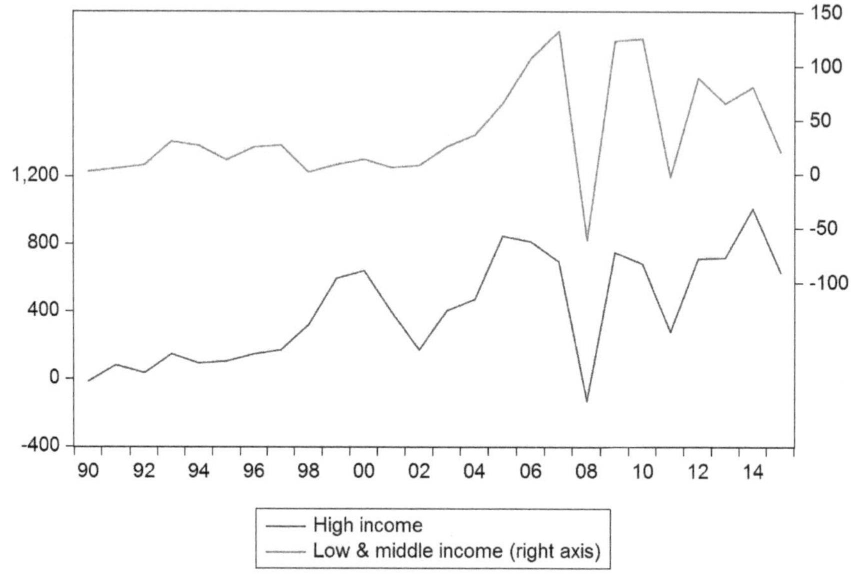

**For a more accurate representation see the electronic version.*

capital in EM countries (Figure 4). Developing countries are fighting actively for FDI, conducting the large-scale liberalization policy and regulation of the legal framework of national economies.

Noticeably, until the 2000s the capital had been leaking from developed economies to developing ones since the relative change of FDI flows occurred in an antiphase. Changes in FDI flows in developed and EM occurred quite synchronously beyond 2000 (Figure 5). It appears that this observation can be true for portfolio investments, although they are largely more volatile.

DATASET AND METHODOLOGY

Data Description

The authors studied the movement of capital flows in the form of FDI and portfolio equities in 24 EM[3] with data obtained from the World Development Indicators World Bank and International Monetary Fund (IMF) database. All indicators are annual; the examined period is from 1990 to 2015. In order to identify the parameters of the model, the following "pull" factors were used: Macroeconomic and financial

Figure 3. FDI inflow and net inflow in the group of high income (left axis) and low and middle income (right axis) countries, bln US$
Source: WDI database.

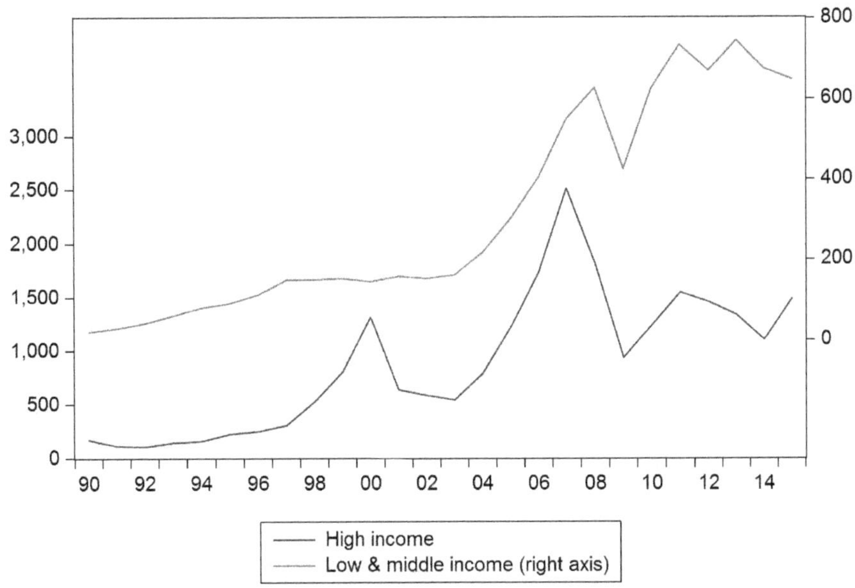

**For a more accurate representation see the electronic version.*

Figure 4. FDI cumulative inflows in high and low and middle-income countries since 1990 till 2015, bln UD$
Source: Authors' calculations based on WDI database.

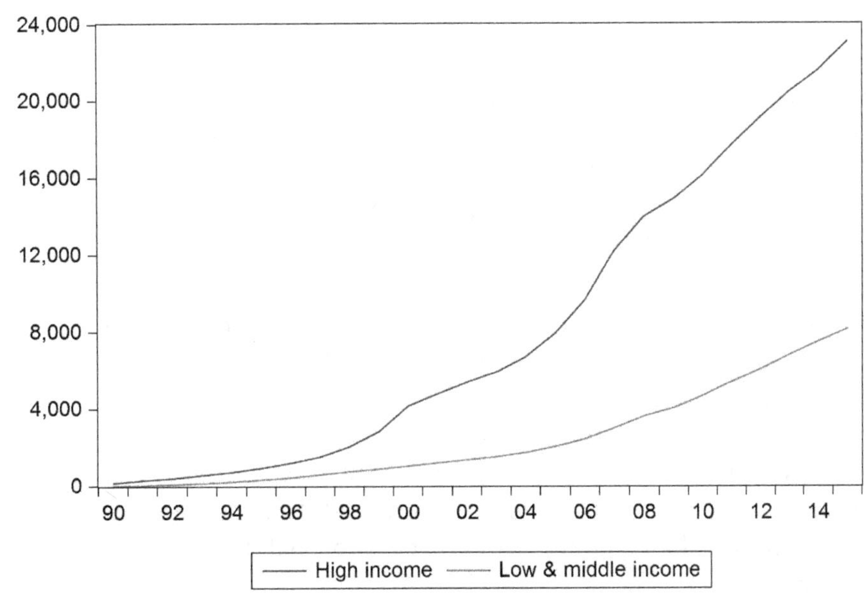

**For a more accurate representation see the electronic version.*

Figure 5. Percentage change of FDI and Portfolio Equity (PE) in high and low and middle-income countries (for positive inflows)
Source: Authors' calculations based on WDI database.

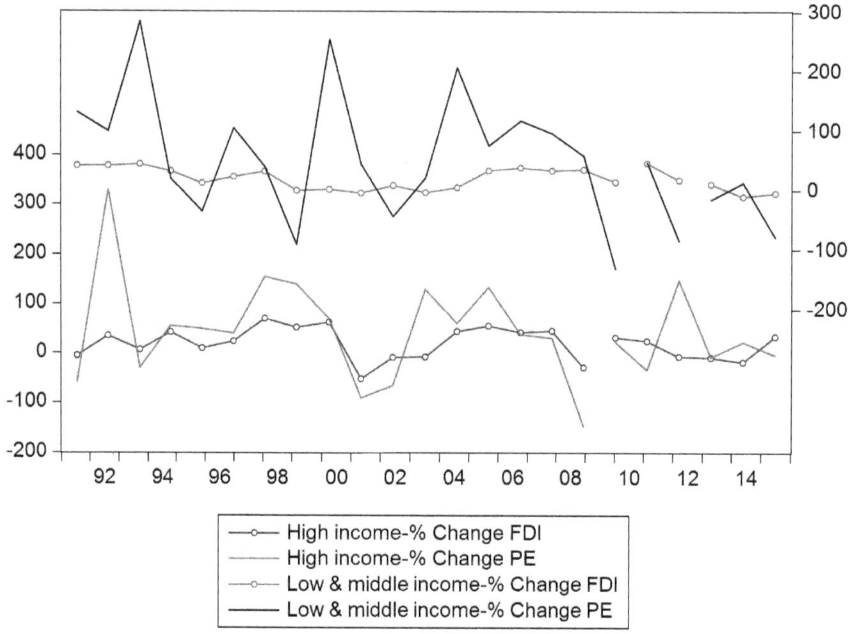

**For a more accurate representation see the electronic version.*

indicators of the recipient country (i.e., GDP growth rate, stock market index, real effective exchange rate, international reserves, and general government gross debt as a percentage of GDP) and the International Country Risk Indicator reported by The International Country Risk Guide. The International Country Risk Indicator includes a Political Risk Index, which in turn consists of 12 components measuring various dimensions of the political and business environment facing firms operating in a country. As "push" factors, the following elements are considered: the U.S. Federal Fund rate, the U.S. stock market index, the U.S. real short-term interest rate, and the weighted average GDP growth rate of developed countries. All the examined variables are presented in Table 1.

To avoid the spurious regression problem the series must be checked for the weak stationarity. A number of panel unit root tests have been developed by various authors. Amongst the most common ones are LLC (Levin, Li, Chi's, 2002) as well as Fisher-type tests ADF (The Augmented Dickey-Fuller Test; Fuller, 1996) and PP (Phillips-Perron individual unit root tests; Phillips & Perron 1988). The authors performed panel unit root tests, using individual fixed effects as regressors, automatic lag length selection based on the Schwartz criterion and the Newey-West method,

Table 1. Variables and definitions

Variable	Full Name	Description	Source	Available Observation Period
XFDI_GDP	Foreign direct investment, net inflows as a percent of GDP.	Direct investment in the reporting economy. It is the sum of equity capital, reinvestment of earnings, and other capital.	WDI World Bank.	1990-2015 no data for the Czech Republic for 1990-1992, RF for 1990-1991, Greece for 1998.
XPE_GDP	Portfolio equity, net inflows as a percentage of GDP.	Portfolio equity includes net inflows from equity securities other than those recorded as direct investment and including shares, stocks, depository receipts, and direct purchases of shares in local stock markets by foreign investors.	WDI World Bank.	1990-2015
D_GDP_GR	The difference in growth rates EM and advanced.	The GDP growth rate of a developing country–the weighted average GDP growth rate of a group of high-income countries (World Bank data).	Authors' calculation based on WDI.	1990-2015
FDI_COM	The net accumulated inflow of FDI.	The accumulated net inflow of FDI without depreciation since 1990.	Authors' calculation based on World Bank.	1990–2015
GDP_GR	GDP growth.	The real economic growth rate is a measure of the rate of change that a nation's GDP experiences from one year to another.	World Bank, WEO.	1990-2015
MSCI/MSCI_USA	MSCI Index.	Weighted index based on adjusted market capitalization. All indices are reduced to 100 as at 1994.	MSCI index database.	1994-2016, except Venezuela.
REER	Real effective exchange rate.	The real effective exchange rate is the nominal effective exchange rate (a measure of the value of a currency against a weighted average of several foreign currencies), divided by a price deflator or index of costs.	WDI World Bank.	1990-2016, except Qatar and, United Arab Emirates.
REER_VOL	Real effective exchange rate volatility.	The authors define REER_VOL in a given year as a st.dev of monthly REER for each country	Authors' calculation based on ICRG.	1990-2016, except Qatar and The United Arab Emirates.
XGVD_GROSS	General government gross debt as percent of GDP.	The indicator is defined as consolidated general government gross debt at nominal value, outstanding at the end of the year in the following categories of government liabilities: Currency and deposits, debt securities, and loans.	IMF, WEO.	1990-2016, no data for Brazil, Peru, Indonesia, Turkey, SA, and UAE till 2000, Venezuela and RF till 1998, Egypt till 2002, and Mexico and Thailand till 1996.
RES_TOT	International reserves.	International reserves, including gold, in current billions of U.S. dollars.	WDI World Bank.	1990-2014
FFR	Federal Funds rate.	The interest rate at which a depository institution lends funds maintained at the Federal Reserve to another depository institution overnight.	Federal Reserve Bank of New York.	1990-2016
RIR_USA	The real short-term interest rate the USA.	The interest rate that has been adjusted to remove the effects of inflation to reflect the real cost of funds to the borrower and the real yield to the lender or an investor. Real Interest Rate USA=Nominal Interest Rate USA-Inflation USA (expected or actual).	OECD	1990-2016

continued on following page

Table 1. Continued

Variable	Full Name	Description	Source	Available Observation Period
PRS_VA	Voice and accountability.	Military in politics, democratic accountability. Scale from 0 (the riskiest) to 1 (the least risky country) for all PRS	International Country Risk Guide (ICRG)	1996-2015
PRS_PV	Political stability and absence of violence.	Government stability, internal conflict, external conflict, ethnic tensions.		
PRS_GE	Government effectiveness.	Bureaucratic quality.		
PRS_RQ	Regulatory quality.	Investment profile.		
PRS_RL	Rule of law.	Law and order.		
PRS_CC	Control of corruption	Corruption.		
Risk	Political risk.	Dummy variable equal to 1, if $(PRS\_VA + PRS\_PV + PRS\_GE$ $+ PRS\_RQ + PRS\_RL + PRS\_CC) < 3$ and 0 otherwise.	Authors' calculation based on ICRG.	1996-2015

and Bartlett kernel for bandwidth selection. The null hypothesis for LLC is a unit root for all forms of the test; the alternative is no unit root for LLC. On the other hand, the ADF-Fisher test and the PP-Fisher test all assume that the autoregressive parameters can be heterogeneous across the cross-sections.

The results of the tests presented in Table 2 suggest that all considered series are stationary, except the series REST_TOT, which is nonstationary. Thus, the series REST_TOT is transformed into the series:

$$D\left(RES\_TOT\right)_{it} / RES\_TOT_{it-1} = \left(RES\_TOT_{it} - RES\_TOT_{it-1}\right) / RES\_TOT_{it-1}$$

which proved to be stationary.

Empirical Model

Pre-Empirical Survey

The authors consider capital flows in EM in 2 main forms: Foreign direct investment and portfolio equity, based on the methodology and statistics of the IMF and the World Bank. The following a priori assumptions have prevailed after reviewing of theoretical and empirical literature and analysis of the dynamics of capital flows.

Table 2. Unit root tests

Variables/Statistic	LLC	ADF	PP
XFDI_GDP	–6.22 (prob.=0.000)	135 (prob.=0.000)	122 (prob.=0.000)
XPE_GDP	–11.06 (prob.=0.000)	184 (prob.=0.000)	210 (prob.=0.000)
D_GDP_GR	–8.97 (prob.=0.000)	189 (prob.=0.000)	210 (prob.=0.000)
GDP_GR	–12.22 (prob.=0.000)	236 (prob.=0.000)	237 (prob.=0.000)
MSCI	–3.50 (prob.=0.000)	64 (prob.=0.000)	66 (prob.=0.000)
REER	–2.93 (prob.=0.002)	63 (prob.=0.03)	63 (prob.=0.004)
REER_VOL	–10.7 (prob.=0.000)	226 (prob.=0.000)	226 (prob.=0.000)
XGVD_GROSS	–5.50 (prob.=0.000)	74(prob.=0.009)	108 (prob.=0.000)
RES_TOT	3.43 (prob.=0.99)	18.00 (prob.=0.99)	13 (prob.=0.99)
FFR[4]	–2.67 (prob.=0.004)	—	—
RIR_USA[4]	–1.75 (prob.=0.04)	—	—

The main exporters of capital are industrialized countries (i.e., countries with high incomes, according to the terminology of the World Bank); the main motive of capital export is the higher rate of return. Therefore, the main factor determining the flow of capital to EM should be the economic growth rate of the recipient country in comparison with the similar indicator of developed countries. An essential role should be played not only by past and current values but also by investors' expectations with regard to the future state of the economy. The stock market can be an important and applicable indicator of investors' perceptions. The authors assume that the increase of the stock indices of a developing country reflects positive expectations for further economic growth and stimulates capital inflows.

Direct investments are generally associated with the exporter's interest to master new commodity markets, paving the way for the subsequent export of goods and stimulating demand from the developing country for goods and services of the donor country. A significant accumulation of foreign direct investment in the past may be an obstacle to their further increase, other things being equal.

Indicators of the financial system of the recipient country play a significant role in explaining the capital inflow in countries with EM. Having carefully studied the various theoretical and empirical aspects of the interdependence of capital flows and public debt, the authors assume that a high level of public debt can lead to a reduction in the inflow of foreign capital. The increase of public debt leads to the instability of the credit rating and growing investors' concerns that the government would announce the country defaulted on its debts. The change in government debt (increase or decrease) is a key factor in determining the credit rating for debt obligations, and sovereign risk, in turn, affects the flows of foreign capital (Bruno & Shin, 2014). International reserves are another factor for attracting the foreign capital. In the conditions of slow economic growth, accumulated reserves are often used to repay the external debt. The reduction of the foreign currency reserves in some developing countries which were registered in the year 2015 was primarily influenced by the dollar becoming more expensive in comparison to the euro and other world currencies, so the reserves are partly declining due to the revaluation of their amounts. However, in general, the authors do not expect a significant influence of this factor in capital flows in the form of FDI, by having all other variables under control. A justification to enable the real effective exchange rate is the hypothesis that the strengthening of the national currency improves the balance of the country and increases the ability to repay foreign loans by local incomes. A strong and stable local currency, in combination with a positive balance of payments, allows the credit risk of the bank to decline; investors are willing to consider the purchase of new assets, and as a result, an increase in the inflow of foreign capital occurs (Bruno & Shin, 2014). On the other hand, the weak national currency can support the competitiveness of the national economy and attract foreign capital through the relative cheapness of the purchased assets. Thus, the change in the exchange rate has a multidirectional impact on cross-border capital flows. At the same time, high volatility of the exchange rate may hamper the inflow of foreign capital, as it evidences the instability of the financial system and the economy in general and makes it difficult to make investment decisions. External financial factors "pushing" the capital from the donor countries include interest and discount rates. Low interest rates in the U.S. are the most significant exogenous factor, at least for more liquid portfolio investment flows encouraging investors to invest in developing economies in search of higher returns.

As another determinant of capital moving is a country-risk rate determined by political factors, primarily, institutional pillars: The constitutional order of the State, its legislative and judicial systems, and the effectiveness of legal norms and enforcement of decisions. Political risk is directly related not only to the institutions of law but also to the specific participants of the political process, key political figures who, in some situations, can have a far greater impact on the policies of the country than the current legal norms or ideologies of political parties and associations. Another significant indicator of political risk is the activities of the Executive Branch—the administrative apparatus of the State, including the Central Government and local authorities. Special attention must be given to the level of corruption in the country.

Thus, theoretically, the movement of capital can be described by the following model:

$$XNI_{it}^{*} = \sum_{k=1}^{K} \tilde{\beta}_k^k Z_{it}^k + \sum_{l=1}^{L} \tilde{\beta}^l Z_{it}^l + \alpha_i + \varepsilon_{it} \tag{1}$$

where XNI_{it}^{*} - expected capital flows into EM, Z^k represents the "push" capital drivers (*K*- number of "push" factors) and Z^l are "pull" capital drivers (L- number of "pull" factors); ε_{it} are the error terms for $i = 1, 2, ...M$ cross-sectional units observed for dated periods $t = 1, 2, ...T$. The α parameter represents a country-specific effect.

The authors assume that the unobserved expected capital flows can be described using a partial adjustment model:

$$XNI_{it} = (1 - \lambda)XNI_{it}^{*} + \lambda XNI_{it-1},$$

The adjustment parameter $(1 - \lambda)$ measures the speed of adjustment and lies between 0 and 1. The closer $(1 - \lambda)$ is to 1, the faster the speed of adjustment.

Thus the model (1) is written as follows:

$$XNI_{it} = \lambda XNI_{it-1} + \sum_{k=1}^{K} \beta_k^k Z_{it}^k + \sum_{l=1}^{L} \beta^l Z_{it}^l + \alpha_i(1 - \lambda) + \varepsilon_{it} \tag{2}$$

where the XNI_{it} is one of the examined dependent variables, namely $XNI_{it} = XFDI\_GDP$ denotes for the foreign direct investments inflow and $XNI_{it} = XPE\_GDP$ for the portfolio equity inflow to country i at the time t. In this model, $(1 - \lambda)$ is a speed of adjustment, and the short-and long-term effects of the "push" and "pull" factors are $[\beta]$ and $[\beta / (1 - \lambda)]$, respectively.

Another interpretation of the parameters of equation (2) is a combination of the current impact of factors and a certain inertia in the actions of foreign investors. The capital is rather directed to the already mastered markets, other things being equal., λ is a measure of this inertia, and the coefficients β^k and β^l reflect the current influence of "push" and "pull" factors. As an estimation technique to assess the model (2), the authors use a feasible GLS assuming the presence of cross-section heteroskedasticity. Cross-section heteroskedasticity allows for a different residual variance for each cross section. Residuals between different cross-sections and different periods are assumed to be 0. Thus, the authors assume that:

$$E\left(\varepsilon_{it}\varepsilon_{it}' \middle| X_i *\right) = \sigma^2_I$$

$$E\left(\varepsilon_{is}\varepsilon'_{jt}\left|X_i*\right.\right)=0$$

for all $i \neq j$, and $s \neq t$, where $X_i *$ contains all regressors and the relevant cross-section effects.

EMPIRICAL RESULTS

Foreign Direct Investment

Using the econometric framework which has been outlined previously, the authors estimated the interrelation between the potential explanatory variables and the investment flows, starting with the analysis of the foreign direct investment flows. They omitted observations for Hungary in years 2007, 2008, and 2010 as anomalous outliers (FDI was recorded about 50% of GDP in these periods). The results of the estimation by the method of panel EGLS (cross section weights) for FDI are presented in Table 3.

In the base model, the authors assume that difference in growth rates between EM and advanced economies, and GDP growth rates and FDI in the prior period are the main factors.

The results of the estimation model (Mod 1 in Table 3) let conclude that GDP growth stimulates the direct investments inflow. The more the economy is developed, the higher inflow of FDI is expected. Other things being equal, in the short term, an increase in the rate of GDP growth by 1 pp last year increases the average share of FDI in GDP by 0.02 pp. Investments are directed mainly to those EM that outstrips the developed countries regarding economic growth. The long-term impact of these factors is above the short-term since the rate of adjustment is 0.64. If an alternative interpretation of the basic model is adopted, then it is possible to conclude that an increase in the ratio of FDI/GDP by 1 pp in the previous period leads to an increase in this ratio in the current period by 0.36 pp (other things being equal). However, as Figure 5 illustrates, a sharp increase in investment causes their reduction in the subsequent period. In order to reflect this effect, the authors estimated the variation of the basic model, assuming that the parameter λ is not constant, but linearly dependent (with the opposite sign) on FDI/GDP in the previous period. Thus, the dependence of FDI/GDP on its previous values can be described by the ∩-curve. The estimation of the model under this assumption is presented in column Mod 2 of Table 3. The results show that for small FDI / GDP ratios, investments in the previous period stimulate the growth of current FDI flows, but gradually the stimulating effect is weakened when the share of FDI in GDP reaches a critical

Table 3. Determinants of FDI to emerging markets 1994-2015

Capital Flow Determinant	Mod 1	Mod 2	Mod 3	Mod D 4	Mod 5
XFDI_GDP(-1)	0.36 *** (0.04)	0.54*** (0.04)	0.27*** (0.04)	0.16*** (0.04)	0.13*** (0.04)
D_GDP_GR	0.03** (0.01)	0.02** (0.01)			
GDP_GR(-1)	0.02** (0.01)	0.02** (0.01)	0.03** (0.01)	0.02 (0.016)	-0.002 (0.002)
XFDI_GDP(-1)^2		-0.01*** (0.002)			
FDI_COM(-1)/GDP_NOM(-1)			-1.18** (0.60)	-1.46** (0.71)	-2.01** (0.80)
Log (MSCI/MSCI_USA)			0.36*** (0.08)	0.33*** (0.09)	0.35*** (0.10)
REER				-0.01** (0.005)	-0.01** (0.005)
XGVD_GROSS				-0.02*** (0.006)	-0.02*** (0.006)
RISK					-0.67*** (0.24)
Fixed effects	yes	yes	yes	yes	yes
R^2 weighted	0.64	0.67	0.78	0.80	0.84
R^2 unweighted	0.32	0.45	0.37	0.46	0.50
Observations	513	513	419	350	333

Standard errors are in parentheses. *** indicates the parameters that are significantly different from zero at 1% significance level, ** at 5%, * at 10%. Note, that FDI_COM(-1)/GDP_NOM(-1) is a TS-series. The results of estimating models when using the variance of the series from its trend as an explanatory variable do not differ significantly from those given in Table 3.

value of 20% (the inflection point of the ∩ curve, according to the estimates obtained). However, in the observed observation pool after elimination of emissions, the average FDI/GDP is 2.8%. Therefore, with further extensions of the basic model, the authors assume the parameter λ to be constant.

The next variation of the basic model is presented in column 3 (Mod 3) of Table 3. Investors' expectations of economic development are reflected by the stock market index, so the factor D_GDP_GR is replaced by the log (MSCI/MSCI_USA), where MSCI_USA is the stock market index for the USA, representing the developed market. Given the fact that foreign investors produce direct investments over several periods, i.e. the dynamics of FDI is cumulative, an additional factor—the accumulated direct investments was included into the model. FDI goes mainly to mastered markets. However, large amounts of accumulated investments can prevent FDI inflows because of the following reasons:

- Market ceases to be the "new", and high profitability is no longer expected.
- Cost of production factors between donors and recipients of capital is aligned.
- High FDI in the prior period hampers future investments inflow.

The obtained estimates confirm the hypothesis: The higher the investors' expectations for EM, the higher the FDI; a large amount of accumulated FDI hinders their further growth; at the same time, the higher the FDI of the previous period, the higher the current FDI. Next, the authors examined the influence of financial factors on FDI. They included effective exchange rate and the government debt as expecting the negative impact of these factors, controlling the other variables. The results in column 4 (Mod 4) suggest that the higher the debt is, the less direct investment flows are, i.e. an inverse interrelation exists between general government gross debt and FDI inflow. The results correspond to previous relevant studies (Bruno & Shin, 2014; Forbes & Warnock, 2012; Ghosh et al., 2014; Obstfeld, 2009). Noticeably, as Table 1 indicates, there are omissions in the data for the General government gross debt.

The growth of the effective exchange rate, according to the authors' estimates, is holding back the inflow of foreign capital in the form of FDI, all other things being equal. Indeed, *REER* can grow not only due to the strengthening of the national currency but also in the event that prices in the country in question grow faster than prices in the trading partner countries.

Examining the influence of political risk, the authors found that FDI is rather sensitive to regulatory quality and rule of law. The results show that law and order have a positive impact on FDI flows. Since different components of political risk measures, defined in Table 1, are rather intercorrelated, the authors defined a new dummy variable, which is equal to 1 for countries with less political rights in a given period. The resulting model estimation (see column 5 in Table 3) suggests that foreign investors are extremely sensitive to changes in the political situation in the country and to the present respect for fundamental democratic rights and freedoms. With the improvement of institutions' quality in the country and the decline in the level of political risk, respectively, the foreign direct investment inflow will increase.

Moreover, the inclusion of a dummy variable *RISK* to the base model practically does not change the estimation of the parameters for the quantitative variables given in Table 4 (column Mod 1); however, this changes the estimates of individual effects.

In order to compare the tightness of the relationship of each of the factors with the dependent variable, the authors turn to the standardized regression coefficients (Table 4) for Mod 5.

Table 4. Standardized coefficients of regression for the model with the inclusion of political risks

Variable	XFDI_ GDP	FDI_ COM_ GDP	GDP_ GR	Log(MSCI/ MSCI_USA)	REER	XGVD_ GROSS	RISK
Standard deviation	2.3	0.23	3.45	0.94	16.4	21.15	0.28
Standardized coefficients		−0.20	−0.004	0.14	−0.07	−0.20	−0.08

As Table 4 shows, the highest expectations of investors stimulate the flow of FDI when the stock market of a developing country demonstrates more positive dynamics than the U.S. stock market. In some periods, such dynamics were demonstrated by the markets of the Czech Republic, Hungary, Russia, Brazil, India, Egypt, Peru, Colombia, Turkey, and Mexico.

The most significant constraining factors are high public debt and accumulated net inflow of FDI.

Portfolio Equity

This subsection focuses on the study of the determinants of portfolio equity flows into EM. Following the same procedure as in the case of FDI flows, the authors estimated the model using panel EGLS (cross section weights) with Net Portfolio Equity Inflow as % of GDP as an explanatory variable. Outliers for Greece and Egypt in certain years were excluded. The variables that explained portfolio equity flows for the period 1994 to 2015 are the following: Changes in MSCI Emerging Market Index, changes and volatility of real effective exchange rate, international reserves, Federal Funds rate, real short-term interest rate USA, and indicators of a political risk. The results of the estimation are presented in Table 5.

The authors should admit that the goodness of fit of the estimation of the models for portfolio investments are rather low. However, all the variables have the expected sign and all are statistically significant at the corresponding level. The rate of adjustment of expectations to the actual values of portfolio investment is very high. The short-term and long-term marginal contribution of factors differs not too much.

The results of the estimations show that there is no direct link between GDP growth and portfolio equity flows when other drivers of portfolio inflows are considered. Thus, GDP_GR is excluded from modifications of the base model. Since portfolio equity flows are short-term, they react to the tools which change in short-term period.

The impact of changes in international reserves on the net flow of investments is estimated as highly significant in all extensions of the base model. The growth of

Table 5. Determinants of portfolio equity inflows to emerging markets 1994-2015

Variables	Mod 1 (Base Model)	Mod 2	Mod 3	Mod 4	Mod 5	Mod 6
XPE_GDP(-1)	0.11** (0.04)	0.13*** (0.04)	0.10** (0.05)	0.10** (0.04)	0.10** (0.04)	0.10** (0.04)
GDP_GR	0.03*** (0.009)					
D(MSCI)/MSCI(-1)	0.37*** (0.06)	0.35*** (0.06)	0.33*** (0.06)	0.31*** (0.06)	0.31*** (0.06)	0.23*** (0.06)
REER_VOL		–0.03** (0.01)	–0.03** (0.01)	–0.02* (0.01)	–0.02* (0.01)	–0.02* (0.01)
D(RES_TOT)/RES_TOT(-1)			0.40*** (0.12)	0.42*** (0.12)	0.43*** (0.12)	0.58*** (0.12)
RIR_USA(-1)				–0.03** (0.01)		
FFR(-1)					–0.02* (0.01)	–0.04*** (0.01)
PRS_PV						1.5*** (0.5)
Fixed effects	yes	yes	yes	yes	yes	yes
R^2 weighted	0.26	0.25	0.26	0.29	0.29	0.30
R^2 unweighted	0.23	0.23	0.22	0.23	0.23	0.26
Observations	413	409	389	389	389	375

Standard errors are in parentheses. *** indicates the parameters that are significantly different from zero at 1% significance level, ** at 5%, * at 10%.

gold and foreign exchange reserves increases the net flow of portfolio investments, all other things being equal.

The volatility of the real exchange rate and the growth of FED rate (or the associated value of the real short-term interest rate) reduce the influx of portfolio investment.

The results point up that political stability and absence of violence have a positive impact on portfolio equity flows. By force of influence, the factor *PRS_PV* exceeds all factors included in Mod 6 (it has the largest standardized coefficient of regression). As a result, foreign investors are sensitive to internal and external conflicts, and ethnic tensions inside the country. It is important to highlight that the influence of other indicators of political risk is not revealed when controlling other variables. One of the possible reasons for this findings is the use of proxy variables for political risk. Country risk metrics by ICRG are not perfect proxy variables and certainly have measurement errors. These can lead to bias in estimated coefficients and their variance.

CONCLUSION

Investment flows constitute a substantial part of the balance of payments. Consequently, it is crucial for policymakers to understand their behaviour and determinants, to be able to both evaluate the impact of policy decisions on the balance of payments and correctly forecast this. In this chapter, the authors have sampled to define the drivers of FDI and portfolio equity flows. The results are summarised in the Appendix.

This chapter is an attempt to find out the major drivers of capital flows, across a wide range of instruments, examining FDI and portfolio equity flows. The results illustrate that both "push" and "pull" factors are important determinants of capital flows. However, the results of the authors' studies revealed that "pull" factors are predominant in contrast to "push" variables in the movement of foreign capital in EM. Economic growth rates, real effective exchange rate volatility, government debt, and political risks are important "pull" factors in the movement of foreign capital in EM. Regarding the economic importance, exceeding the rate of economic growth of countries with developing markets in comparison to advanced markets and exceeding investors' expectations concerning profitability in EM over developed markets are key "push" determinants of FDI flows. In the case of portfolio equity flows, important "push" variables are FED rate along with the real short-term interest rate in developed countries. Political risk being "pull" capital driver in EM influences on investment flows: with the improving of the quality of institutions in the country and a decline in the level of political risk, respectively, the inflow of foreign investments increases.

The FDI flows are influenced by numerous factors, among which the higher the investors' expectations for EM and a significant amount of accumulated FDI considerably stand out. For more liquid and mobile portfolio investments the primary factor of capital movement is the investors' expectations concerning exceeding profitability in EM over the developed markets. Since portfolio equity flows are short-term, they react to the tools which change in a short-term such as changes and volatility of real effective exchange rate. In the year 2016, the economic growth rate of developing economies declined, and the downward trend is predicted to continue in 2017. The economic slowdown is affected by the sharp fall in commodity prices in emerging economies, the reduced foreign capital inflows, the rebalancing of the Chinese economy, the effects of the quantitative easing policy in developed countries, and economic difficulties associated with geopolitical factors. The returns of the stock markets in developing countries are not larger than the returns in developed countries. According to the results of the evaluation model for the foreseeable future, the flow of foreign investments into the EM is expected to reduce.

ACKNOWLEDGMENT

This research was supported by the Russian Foundation for Basic Research (Division of Humanities) [grant number 16-02-00375].

REFERENCES

Ahmed, S., & Zlate, A. (2013). Capital Flows to Emerging Market Economies: A Brave New World? *Journal of International Money and Finance*, *48*, 221–248. doi:10.1016/j.jimonfin.2014.05.015

Albuquerque, R., Loayza, N., & Serven, L. (2005). World Market Integration through the Lens of Foreign Direct Investors. *Journal of International Economics*, *66*(2), 267–295. doi:10.1016/j.jinteco.2004.07.002

Ayala, D., Nedeljkovic, M., & Saborowski, S. (2015). *What Slice of the Pie? The Corporate Bond Market Boom in Emerging Economies. Working Paper 15/148.* Washington, DC: International Monetary Fund. Retrieved from https://www.imf.org/external/pubs/ft/wp/2015/wp15148.pdf

Baek, I. (2006). Portfolio Investment Flows to Asia and Latin America: Pull, Push or Market Sentiment? *Journal of Asian Economics*, *17*(2), 363–373. doi:10.1016/j.asieco.2006.02.007

Broner, F., Didier, T., Erce, A., & Schmukler, S. (2013). Gross Capital Flows: Dynamics and Crises. *Journal of Monetary Economics*, *60*(1), 113–133. doi:10.1016/j.jmoneco.2012.12.004

Bruno, V., & Shin, H. S. (2014). *Cross-Border Banking and Global Liquidity. Working Paper 19038.* Cambridge, MA: National Bureau of Economic Research. Retrieved from http://www.nber.org/papers/w19038.pdf

Collyns, C., Huefner, F., Koepke, R., Bykere, A., Farnham, S., & Shaw, L. (n.d.). *Capital Flows to Emerging Markets.* Institute of International Finance Working Paper. Retrieved from file:///C:/Users/AC4/Downloads/cf_0515.pdf

De Vita, G., & Khine, S. K. (2008). Determinants of Capital Flows to Developing Countries: A Structural VAR Analysis. *Journal of Economic Studies (Glasgow, Scotland)*, *35*(4), 304–322. doi:10.1108/01443580810895608

Forbes, K. J., & Warnock, F. E. (2012). Capital flow waves: Surges, stops, flight, and retrenchment. *Journal of International Economics*, *88*(2), 235–251. doi:10.1016/j.jinteco.2012.03.006

Fuller, W. A. (1996). *Introduction to Statistical Time Series*. New York: Wiley.

Ghosh, A. R., Kim, J., Mahvash, Q., & Zalduendo, J. (2012). *Surges. Working Paper 12/22*. Washington, DC: International Monetary Fund. Retrieved from http://www.imf.org/external/pubs/ft/wp/2012/wp1222.pdf

Group, P. R. S. (2015). *International Country Risk Guide*. Retrieved from https://info.worldbank.org/governance/wgi/pdf/prs.xlsx

Koepke, R. (2014). *Fed Policy Expectations and Portfolio Flows to Emerging Markets*. Institute of International Finance Working Paper. Retrieved from https://mpra.ub.uni-muenchen.de/63519/1/MPRA_paper_63519.pdf

Kostyunina, G. M. (2005). International capital flow. In International economic relations (pp. 248-295). TK Velbi, Prospect.

Levin, A., Lin, C. F., & Chu, C. S. J. (2002). Unit root tests in panel data: Asymptotic and finite-sample properties. *Journal of Econometrics*, *108*(1), 1–24. doi:10.1016/S0304-4076(01)00098-7

Obstfeld, M. (1998). The Global Capital Market: Benefactor or Menace? *The Journal of Economic Perspectives*, *12*(4), 9–30. doi:10.1257/jep.12.4.9

Obstfeld, M. (2009). *International finance and growth in developing countries: what have we learned? Working Paper 14691*. Cambridge, MA: National Bureau of Economic Research. doi:10.3386/w14691

Phillips, P. C. B., & Perron, P. (1988). Testing for a unit root in time series regression. *Biometrika*, *75*(2), 335–346. doi:10.1093/biomet/75.2.335

World Bank. (2015). *Global economic prospects: The global economy in transition.* World Bank Group Report. Retrieved from http://documents.worldbank.org/curated/en/264521468179081631/Global-economic-prospects-June-2015-the-global-economy-in-transition

ENDNOTES

1 The authors mainly use the MSCI markets classification, which consists of following criteria: Economic development, size and liquidity, and market accessibility.

2 The World Bank eliminated the terms "developed" and "developing" economies from its data vocabulary in 2016 and classifies economies based on their Gross National Income (GNI) per capita.

3 (21 countries according to Morgan Stanley Capital International (MSCI) emerging countries index (https://www.msci.com/) plus Argentina, Korea, Venezuela).

4 The values of the series and are the same for all cross-sectional units. Therefore, ADF and PP tests are not applied.

APPENDIX

Table 6. Determinants of foreign investment flows in emerging markets: Summary

Type of Flow/Factor's Category	FDI	Portfolio Equity
"Push" factors	• Growth rates of the mature economy. • Stock market index of developed countries.	FED rate/ USA real short-term interest rate.
"Pull" factors	• GDP growth. • Real effective exchange rate. • Accumulated FDI. • Government debt. • Political risks.	• The growth rate of the domestic stock market. • The growth rate of the real effective exchange rate. • Real effective exchange rate volatility. • Political risks.

Chapter 11
Stock Market Efficiency in South Eastern Europe:
Testing Return Predictability and Calendar Effects

Vladimir Filipovski
Saints Cyril and Methodius University, Macedonia

Dragan Tevdovski
Saints Cyril and Methodius University, Macedonia

ABSTRACT

The purpose of this chapter is to empirically test the informational efficiency and to examine the presence of the calendar effects in 10 South Eastern European (SEE) stock markets' daily returns during the period 2007–2014. The authors use variance ratio test for exploration of random walk hypothesis. Regarding the calendar effects, the authors focus on the day-of-the-week effect, the half-month effect, and the turn-of-the-month effect. The existence of each calendar effect is analyzed by applying regression models with dummy variables for the effects in the mean returns and GARCH (1,1) models with dummy variables for the effects in the volatility of returns. The results indicate that the day-of-the-week effects in both mean and volatility are present in nine SEE stock markets. Contrary, the half-month effect in mean returns is present only in one, while half-month effect in volatility is present in five SEE stock markets. The turn-of-the- month effect in mean returns is present in six, while the turn-of-the-month effect in volatility is present in all 10 SEE stock markets.

DOI: 10.4018/978-1-5225-4026-7.ch011

INTRODUCTION

Theoretically, an informationally efficient stock market creates price system that allocate financial capital to most productive uses, and at the same time, such market reflects the underlying market structure in which intense competition for information competes away any above normal (economic) profits. One implication of an informationally efficient stock market is that subsequent changes in stock prices are unpredictable, so that no investor can earn above normal profits by using information content of historic prices. We present in our paper an analysis of the degree of unpredictability of returns for the stock markets of the South Eastern Europe by using the variance ratio methodology. The variance ratio methodology is based on the idea that when stock returns follow a random walk process their structure does not change through time and therefore, the variance for a t+k period is a linear, k-times multiplication of the variance for the t period. Hence, one cannot make superior return forecasts based on information from a long series of past return variability compared to one using only an immediate past return variability. As South Eastern European stock markets are generally considered as emerging and not completely developed markets, it can be argued that those markets generally deviate from an informationally efficient market, but also that the degree of such deviation may indicate differences in relative i.e. comparative (in)efficiency of individual markets in the region.

On the other hand, informational efficiency of the stock markets has been challenged by the evidence from some empirical finance studies suggesting that there can be detected some regular, and predictable, patterns of behavior of stock returns related to some specific points in time – the so-called calendar effects. There are various calendar effects. This paper focuses on three calendar effects: day of the week effect, half of the month effect and turn of the month effect. The day of the week effect presents an anomaly in that the stock returns on Mondays are systematically lower than returns on other days in the week. The half of the month effect presents an anomaly in that the stock returns during the first half of the month are on average higher than the returns for the rest of the month. The turn of the month effect presents an anomaly in that the stock returns tend to increase during the last few days and the first few days of each month. If these effects persist then it might be possible for some investors to earn above normal profits by trading on those time patterns of behavior of stock returns, and that would run contrary to the arguments of the so called Efficient Market Hypothesis (EMH), which argues that one cannot earn abnormal returns by trading on such time patterns of past returns. In this context we examine the existence of the selected calendar effects in the stock markets of South Eastern Europe, aiming at providing further evidence for assessing the degree of informational efficiency of those markets.

The rest of the paper is organized as follows. Section 2 reviews the literature. Section 3 presents employed methodology: the variance ratio test and the models for calendar effects estimation. Section 4 provides description of the data used in the analysis. The findings of the empirical analysis are presented in the Section 5. Section 6 concludes.

BACKGROUND

In its weak form, informational efficiency hypothesis in a sense of Fama (1970, 1991) and Roberts (1967) states that subsequent changes in stock price are unpredictable based on information content of historic prices, since all information contained in price history is fully and instantaneously reflected in current stock price. The unpredictability of stock prices may be thought to imply that the stock price dynamics is generated by some form of a random walk process. Smith (2012) and Dyakova and Smith (2013) examined this hypothesis using variance ratio tests within the emerging European stock markets. They found a wide variability of the degree of return predictability among those markets.

Dyakova and Smith (2013) measure return predictability for 14 SEE stock market indices using finite sample variance ratio tests. They point out to the idea of Campbell et al. (1997) that relative rather than an absolute return predictability assessment may be a more fruitful approach when analyzing stock market efficiency in general. The conclusion of their paper is that the return predictability of indices of the analyzed SEE markets varies widely, whereas the differences in the degree of predictability can be negatively related to the levels of capitalization, liquidity and institutional quality of different stock markets.

Testing return predictability for seven SEE stock exchanges for the period January 2002 – December 2012 using wavelet based methodology, Bogdanova and Ivanov (2014) find evidence for differences in the degree of predictability within the analyzed group of stock markets. For example, a non-diminishing return predictability is found for Bulgaria and Serbia, and a diminishing predictability is found for Croatia and Russia, while Turkish market seems to exhibit least predictability making it close to a weak-form efficient market.

Dragota and Tilica (2014) analyze 20 East European former communist countries, including the new EU member states as well as some SEE countries for a three-year period January 2008 – December 2010. They have tested return predictability as way to assess the informational efficiency (in its weak form) using several types of tests (unit roots tests, runs tests, variance ratio tests, filter rules tests, January effect tests).Their results indicate that, although the efficient market hypothesis cannot be rejected for some of individual stocks in different countries, the overall conclusion is that it is very doubtful that the analyzed markets can be considered as confirming to the concept of informational efficiency. Also, the authors point out to the significant heterogeneity of the test results among different countries.

We do not limit our analysis of weak form informational efficiency of the SEE stock markets only to testing return predictability, but we also extend our empirical investigation to incorporate the so-called calendar effects or calendar anomalies. We focus on three calendar effects: day of the week effect, half of the month effect and turn of the month effect. The day of the week effect presents an anomaly in that the stock returns on Mondays are systematically lower than returns on other days in the week. The half of the month effect presents an anomaly in that the stock returns during the first half of the month are on average higher than the returns for the rest of the month. The turn of the month effect presents an anomaly in that the stock returns tend to increase during the last few days and the first few days of each month.

The evidence on calendar effects has produced a discussion on its relevance in the context of the Efficient Market Hypothesis (EMH). On one hand, critics of the relevance of the calendar effects (and proponents of EMH) argue that such effects are essentially some temporary market anomalies and that once they are discovered by the academic research the market participants will trade them out of existence. Similarly, it is argued that such anomalies are mainly due to data mining or to a situation where many researchers test many hypothesis on the same data (Taylor, 2005, p. 59). However, there is a large body of literature that provide empirical evidence for calendar effects in developed stock markets, thus presenting a serious challenge to the weak form efficient market hypothesis. The most important papers are: Fama (1965), French (1980), Gibbons and Hess (1981), Rogalski (1984), Dyl and Maberly (1988), Agarwal and Tandon (1994), Rubinstein (2001), Schwert (2001), Steely (2001) and Sullivan et al. (2001). There are different explanations for the day of the week effect. Abraham and Ikenberry (1994) argue that the investors have the tendency to sell on Monday after the revision of their portfolios during the weekend. Chen and Singal (2003) shows that the investors closed the short positions (buy) on Fridays and open them again on Mondays (sell). Taylor (2008) comments that no satisfactory explanation has yet been given for the weekend effect. Similarly, academic community has not yet been able to reach consensus about the reasons for half of the month and turn of the month effects. Odgen (1990) points that they arise from the clusterization of salary payments and other liabilities, while Penman (1987) suggests to clusterization of the earnings announcement releases.

Calendar effects are becoming increasingly popular in developing stock markets research (see for example Brooks and Persand, 2001, Fountas and Segredakis 2002, Alagidede and Panagiotidis 2009, Guidi et al. 2011, Rojas and Kristjanpoller 2014). However, the calendar effects in South Eastern Europe (SEE) stock markets have been analyzed rather rarely. Georgantopoulos et al. (2011) investigates calendar anomalies in four SEE stock markets and provides evidence for the existence of three calendar effects (day of the week, turn of the month, time of the month) for Greece and Turkey in the period 2000-2008. Georgantopoulos and Tsamis (2011) shows that two calendar effects (day of the week and January effects) are present in the Macedonian stock market during the period 2002-2008. Georgantopoulos and Tsamis (2012) investigate also the calendar anomalies for Bulgaria and Greece during the period 2002–2008. They found that most of the tested calendar effects exist for Greece and the effects for Bulgaria are limited and exist only in variance. Karadzic and Backovic Vulic (2011) report absence of three calendar anomalies: the January effect, the turn-of the-month effect and the holiday effect for the Montenegrin capital market during the period 2004 - 2010. Tevdovski et al. (2012) found day of the week effect in the Bulgarian and Croatian stock market during the period 2006-2011. Oprea and Ţilică (2014), find some evidence of the day-of-the-week effect in several SEE and Central and east (CEE) emerging stock markets (Bosnia, Bulgaria, Croatia, Latvia, Serbia and Slovenia).

In these regards, the present paper examine the existence of the three calendar effects (day of the week effect, half of the month effect and turn of the month effect) in all ten SEE stock markets. Moreover, we analyze existence of each calendar effect separately in the mean and in the volatility of the leading stock market index returns. The period of observation is from 2007 to 2014, which covers the influence of the Global financial crisis. We provide an evidence for the existence of calendar effects in the SEE stock markets during the observed period.

EMPIRICAL METHODOLOGY

In this section, we present the empirical methodology: first the variance-ratio test that is used for exploration of random walk hypothesis, and second, models for estimation of three calendar effects that could be detected on daily data (the day of the week effect, the half month effect, and the turn of the month effect).

Variance Ratio Test

A consequence of informational efficiency is that stock returns should behave as random walk process. Random walk hypothesis is true if the variance of a multi-period return is the sum of single-period variances. There are several tests that empirically explore this property, while the most important is the variance-ratio test of Lo and MacKinlay (1988). The idea of the test is that if data follow random walk, the variance of q period returns should be q times the variance of 1-period returns. So, the variance ratio should approach to one:

$$VR(N) = \frac{\sigma^2(q)}{q\sigma^2(1)} = 1 \tag{1}$$

When the random walk hypothesis is false, $VR(q)$ equals $q\sigma^2(1)$ plus covariance terms between all pairs of distinct returns (Taylor, 2005). The variance ratio z-statistic:

$$z_N = \frac{\widehat{VR}(q) - 1}{\sqrt{\hat{\sigma}^2(q)}} \tag{2}$$

is asymptotically N(0,1) for appropriate choice of estimator $\hat{\sigma}^2(q)$. Lo and MacKinlay (1998) provide an estimator in the case of homoscedastic random walk hypothesis (i.i.d. null) and in the case of heteroscedastic random walk hypothesis (martingale null).

It is common to evaluate the z .statistics for several values of q, since the variance ratio restriction holds for every period $q > 1$. Chow and Denning (1993) propose test statistic that examines the maximum absolute value of set of multiple variance ratio statistics in order to control the size of the joint test. Improvement of the small sample properties of individual and joint variance ratio tests can be made by a wild bootstrap approach of Kim (2006).

Estimation of the Day of the Week Effect

We use a standard methodology to test for daily seasonality in stock market returns (See for example, French 1980, Rogalski 1984, Agrawal and Tandon 1994, and Mills and Couts 1995). It is the following regression model with dummy variables:

$$R_t = \alpha_1 + \sum_{i=2}^{5} \alpha_i D_{it} + u_t \tag{3}$$

$$h_t^2 = \alpha + \beta u_{t-1}^2 + \gamma h_{t-1}^2 + \sum_{i=2}^{5} \delta_i D_{it} \tag{4}$$

where, in the mean equation, R_t is the daily logarithmic return (in %) on a selected stock index; D_{it} .is binary dummy variable for various trading days in the week,

Tuesday, ..., Friday, respectively (i.e. $D_{2t} = 1$ if day t is Tuesday, zero otherwise, etc.) Monday represents the control category. The coefficient α_1 .indicates the mean daily return for Monday (control category), while α_2 to α_5 represents the difference between the mean daily return for Monday and the mean daily return for each of the other days in the week. The error term is noted as u_t and it is assumed to be identically and independently distributed (IID). Gujarati (2004) argue that this type of models are more general than the t test which can be used to compare the means of two groups or categories only. If there are no differences among index returns across days of the week, the coefficients α_2 to α_5 are zero. Therefore, the null hypothesis of the relevant Wald test is $\mathrm{H}_0 : \alpha_i = 0$ for $i = 2,\ldots,5$. If the null hypothesis is rejected, then stock returns should exhibit some form of the day of the week seasonality (Georgantopoulos and Tsamis, 2011).

The variance equation is an GARCH (1,1) model, where, h_t^2 is the conditional variance of u_t. It is used for estimation of the day of the week effect in volatility. If there is no day of the week effect in volatility, the parameters δ_2 to δ_5 are zeros, so the null hypothesis is $\mathrm{H}_0 : \delta_i = 0$ for $i = 2,\ldots,5$.

Estimation of the Half Month Effect

We use model originally proposed by Lakonishok and Smidt (1988) for estimation of the half month effect. The mean and variance equations are:

$$R_t = \alpha_0 + \alpha_1 H_{1t} + u_t \tag{5}$$

$$h_t^2 = \alpha + \beta u_{t-1}^2 + \gamma h_{t-1}^2 + \delta H_{1t} \tag{6}$$

where, H_{1t} is binary dummy variable, which takes value 1 if the trading day *t* is from the first to the fiftheen calendar days of the month, and 0 otherwise. The coefficient α_0 indicates the mean daily return for the trading days in the second half of the month (control category), while α_0 represents the difference between the mean daily return for the first half of the month and control category. The coefficient δ indicates the half month effect in volatility. If there is no half month effect in volatility, the parameter δ is zero.

Estimation of the Turn of the Month Effect

We use a model originally proposed by Ariel (1987), Lakonishok and Smidt (1988), and Agrawal (1994) for estimation of the turn of the month effect. The mean and variance equations are:

$$R_t = \alpha_0 + \alpha_1 T(-3)_t + \alpha_2 T(-2)_t + \alpha_3 T(-1)_t + \alpha_4 T(+1)_t + \alpha_5 T(+2)_t + \alpha_6 T(+3)_t + u_t \tag{7}$$

$$h_t^2 = \alpha + \beta u_{t-1}^2 + \gamma h_{t-1}^2 + \delta_1 T(-3)_t + \delta_2 T(-2)_t + \delta_3 T(-1)_t + \delta_4 T(+1)_t + \delta_5 T(+2)_t + \delta_6 T(+3)_t \tag{8}$$

where dummy variables are used as indication of the turn of the month. Specifically, $T(-3)$, $T(-2)$ and $T(-1)$ are dummy variables that represent the third last, the second last and the last trading day in the month, respectively, while $T(+1)$, $T(+2)$, $T(+3)$ are dummy variables that represent the first, the second and the third trading day in the month, respectively. The coefficients α_1 to α_6 indicate the differences between the mean return of the specific day from the turn of the month and the mean return of the rest of the days in the month. The null hypothesis of the relevant Wald test is $\mathrm{H}_0 : \alpha_i = 0$ for $i = 1,\ldots,6$. If the null hypothesis is rejected, then stock returns should exhibit some form of the turn of the month effect in mean. The coefficients δ_1 to δ_6 indicate the differences in the volatility between the specific day from the turn of the month and the rest of the days in the month. The null hypothesis of the relevant Wald test is $\mathrm{H}_0 : \delta_i = 0$ for $i = 1,\ldots,6$. If the null hypothesis is rejected, then stock returns should exhibit some form of the turn of the month effect in volatility.

DATA

We apply the relevant stock markets indices of all ten SEE countries: BELEX15 (Serbia), SASX10 (Bosnia and Herzegovina), SOFIX (Bulgaria), CROBEX (Croatia), ATHEX Composite (Greece), MBI10 (Macedonia), MONEX20 (Montenegro), BET (Romania), SLOETOP (Slovenia), BIST100 (Turkey). The source of the data is DataStream database. We use daily log returns (in percent) calculated from the price indexes for the stock markets measured in the national currency. Voronkova (2004) argue that usage of the national currencies restricts their changes to movements in the security prices and avoids distorting the analysis with devaluations of the exchange rates. The data covers the period from January 11, 2007 to June 25, 2014. It gives a total of 1945 observations. The main characteristic of the observation period is the Global financial crisis that started to influence the SEE stock markets from the middle of 2007.

Table 1 reports the descriptive statistics of the stock market indices daily returns. Nine of ten SEE stock indices experienced mean negative daily return in the observed period. The exception is BIST100 index (Turkey). The market risk measured with standard deviation is lowest in SLOETOP (Slovenia) and highest in ATHEX (Greece). All indices have positive kurtosis indicating a fatter-tailed distribution than normal.

Table 2 presents the results of the multiple breakpoint tests for the stock market indices daily returns. It is Bai-Perron tests of L+1 vs. L sequentially determined breaks, using methods outlined by Bai (1997) and Bai and Perron (1998). The tests allow for a maximum number of 5 breaks, employ a trimming percentage of 15%, and allow for error heterogeneity. The results suggests that the half of the observed stock market indices daily returns are characterized with structural breaks. So it implies that the analysis considers the whole time period and that there were relevant "crisis" periods in some markets during the time span.

EMPIRICAL FINDINGS

The results of the joint variance-ratio tests for the observed period are presented in the Table 3. The first column of the table reports the maximum variance-ratio test

Table 1. Descriptive statistics of the stock market indices daily returns

	Mean	Std. Deviation	Skewness	Kurtosis
BELEX15	-0.0572	1.4790	0.19	15.56
SASX10	-0.1058	1.4471	-11.93	344.43
SOFIX	-0.0473	1.3608	-1.01	12.70
CROBEX	-0.0309	1.3665	0.02	18.73
ATHEX	-0.0669	2.0728	0.06	5.70
MBI10	-0.0443	1.3791	-0.44	11.92
MONEX20	-0.0317	1.6518	0.80	11.96
BET	-0.0104	1.7485	-0.61	11.07
SLOETOP	-0.0360	1.2416	-0.45	9.82
BIST100	0.0395	1.7836	-0.23	7.05

Source: Authors calculation based on Datastream database data.

Table 2. Bai-Perron tests of L+1 vs. L sequentially determined breaks in the stock market indices daily returns

	Break Test	Scaled F-Statistic	Critical Value	Determined Breaks	Break Dates
BELEX15	0 vs. 1 * 1 vs. 2	11.568 7.329	8.58 10.13	1	3/12/2009
SASX10	0 vs. 1	7.658	8.58	0	/
SOFIX	0 vs. 1 * 1 vs. 2	17.201 2.452	8.58 10.13	1	2/24/2009
CROBEX	0 vs. 1	4.861	8.58	0	/
ATHEX	0 vs. 1 * 1 vs. 2	10.723 4.015	8.58 10.13	1	6/06/2012
MBI10	0 vs. 1 * 1 vs. 2 * 2 vs. 3	9.508 14.823 4.333	8.58 10.13 11.14	2	2/22/2008 5/01/2009
MONEX20	0 vs. 1	3.917	8.58	0	/
BET	0 vs. 1 * 1 vs. 2	12.182 9.201	8.58 10.13	1	2/18/2009
SLOETOP	0 vs. 1	8.461	8.58	0	/
BIST100	0 vs. 1	3.380	8.58	0	/

Note: * indicate significance at the 5% level.

statistics (z-statistic) under the homoscedastic random walk, while the second column reports the maximum variance-ratio test statistics (z-statistic) using heteroskedasticity robust standard error estimates. Under the random walk hypothesis (null hypothesis), the value of the variance-ratio test is 1 and the test statistics has a standard normal distribution (asymptotically). In the case of all SEE indices, except SASX10, the test statistics reject the random walk hypothesis both for homoskedastic and heteroscedastic possibility. For SASX10, the rejection of the null hypothesis of the homoscedastic, but not heteroskedastic random walk, indicate that the rejection of the null hypothesis of the random walk may be due to heteroskedasticity and therefore the index meet at least some requirements of a random walk. These results mean that SEE stock markets, except Bosnian, are not efficient over the observed period.

Table 4 reports the estimates of the day of the week effect in stock returns. The Wald test is not rejecting the null hypothesis that the coefficients α_2 to α_5 are zero only in the case of BIST100. On the other hand, the null hypothesis of no day of the week effect in the mean returns is rejected in all other cases: on 10% significance level for SASX10 and SOFIX, and on 1% significance level in all other cases. In the case of CROBEX, the mean daily return of every trading day in the week is higher than the mean daily return in Monday. In the case of BET and SLOETOP, the mean daily return in Wednesday, Thursday and Friday are higher than the mean daily return in Monday. In the case of BELEX15 and MBI10, the mean daily return

Table 3. Joint variance ratio tests

	Homoskedastic Random Walk Hypothesis	Heteroskedasticity Random Walk Hypothesis
BELEX15	Max lzl (at period 2)	Max lzl (at period 4)
	15.9411***	6.0882***
	(0.0000)	(0.0000)
SASX10	Max lzl (at period 2)	Max lzl (at period 8)
	18.4417***	2.0268
	(0.0000)	(0.1601)
SOFIX	Max lzl (at period 2)	Max lzl (at period 2)
	21.3718***	7.5261***
	(0.0000)	(0.0000)
CROBEX	Max lzl (at period 2)	Max lzl (at period 2)
	18.1843***	6.9553***
	(0.0000)	(0.0000)
ATHEX	Max lzl (at period 2)	Max lzl (at period 2)
	19.7122***	12.5283***
	(0.0000)	(0.0000)
MBI10	Max lzl (at period 4)	Max lzl (at period 4)
	14.6455***	6.3674***
	(0.0000)	(0.0000)
MONEX20	Max lzl (at period 4)	Max lzl (at period 4)
	16.6811***	7.0134***
	(0.0000)	(0.0000)
BET	Max lzl (at period 2)	Max lzl (at period 2)
	20.8048***	9.0154***
	(0.0000)	(0.0000)
SLOETOP	Max lzl (at period 2)	Max lzl (at period 2)
	17.0374***	7.261777***
	(0.0000)	(0.0000)
BIST100	Max lzl (at period 2)	Max lzl (at period 2)
	22.0539***	13.1121***
	(0.0000)	(0.0000)

Note: */**/*** indicate that the parameter is significantly different from zero at 10%/5%/1% level; p values are reported in brackets.

in Thursday and Friday are higher than the mean daily return in Monday. In the case of SASX10 and ATHEX, the mean daily return in Wednesday and Friday are higher than the mean daily return in Monday. In case of SOFIX, the mean daily return in Wednesday and Thursday are higher than the mean daily return in Monday. In the case of MONEX20, the mean daily return for Friday is higher than the mean daily return in Monday.

Table 5 reports the estimates of the day of the week effect in volatility. The Wald test is not rejecting the null hypothesis that the coefficients δ_2 to δ_5 are zero only in the case of SLOETOP. On the other hand, the null hypothesis of no day of the week effect in returns volatility is rejected in all other cases: on 5% significance level for MBI10 (Macedonia) and BET (Romania), and on 1% significance level in

Table 4. The day of the week effect in the mean

					α_5	**Wald Test F-Statistic**
BELEX15	-0.0622	-0.0107	0.0578	0.1164**	0.1617***	3.4831***
	(0.1153)	(0.8434)	(0.2530)	(0.0276)	(0.0040)	(0.0077)
SASX10	-0.1522***	-0.0515	0.1215**	0.0800	0.1291**	2.0328*
	(0.0002)	(0.6498)	(0.0315)	(0.1859)	(0.0262)	(0.0873)
SOFIX	-0.0496	-0.0090	0.1212**	0.1135*	0.0751	2.3331*
	(0.2144)	(0.8691)	(0.0284)	(0.0549)	(0.1807)	(0.0537)
CROBEX	-0.1818***	0.1461**	0.2282***	0.2431***	0.2454***	5.9780***
	(0.0001)	(0.0122)	(0.0001)	(0.0000)	(0.0000)	(0.0001)
ATHEX	-0.1705*	0.0553	0.4002***	0.1956	0.3566***	4.4121***
	(0.0513)	(0.6672)	(0.0009)	(0.1137)	(0.0025)	(0.0015)
MBI10	-0.1002***	-0.0711	0.0439	0.1652***	0.1219**	6.8093***
	(0.0073)	(0.1659)	(0.4155)	(0.0009)	(0.0184)	(0.0000)
MONEX20	-0.0599	-0.0609	-0.0107	0.0486	0.1710**	3.5192***
	(0.2359)	(0.3774)	(0.8725)	(0.4716)	(0.0168)	(0.0072)
BET	-0.0916*	0.0948	0.1606**	0.2482***	0.2215***	3.6901***
	(0.0748)	(0.1692)	(0.0194)	(0.0005)	(0.0021)	(0.0053)
SLOETOP	-0.0997**	-0.0081	0.1306**	0.1332**	0.2160***	4.4238***
	(0.0330)	(0.8972)	(0.0470)	(0.0407)	(0.0005)	(0.0015)
BIST100	0.1699**	-0.0785	-0.0148	0.0173	-0.0987	0.5005
	(0.0383)	(0.4703)	(0.8936)	(0.8745)	(0.3484)	(0.7354)

Note: */**/*** indicate that the parameter is significantly different from zero at 10%/5%/1% level; p values are reported in brackets.

all other cases. In the case of CROBEX, every trading day in the week appears to have lower variances than Monday. In the case of MONEX20 and BET, Tuesday, Wednesday and Friday appears to have lower variances than Monday. In the case of BIST100, Tuesday, Thursday and Friday appears to have lower variances than Monday. In the case of ATHEX, Wednesday and Thursday appears to have lower variances than Monday. In the case of SOFIX, only Friday appears to have lower variance than Monday. In the case of SASX10, Wednesday appears to have lower variances than Monday, while Tuesday and Thursday appears to have higher variances. In the case of BELEX only Friday appears to have higher variance than Monday. In the case of MBI10 only Tuesday appears to have higher variance than Monday.

Table 7 reports the estimates of the half month effect in stock returns. The coefficient α_1 is not significant in the cases of all SEE stock market indices, except in the case of SLOETOP. In the case of SLOETOP, the coefficient is significant at 5% level and it imply that the mean daily return for the trading days in the first half of the month is lower than the mean daily return for the trading days in the second half of the month.

Table 8 reports the estimates of the half month effect in volatility. The coefficient δ is not significant in the cases of BELEX, SOFIX, ATHEX, MONEX20 and BET. In the cases of SASX, CROBEX, MBI10 and SLOETOP, the significant coefficient imply that the volatility of the returns for the for the trading days in the first half of the month is higher than the volatility of the returns for the trading days in the second half of the month. In contrary, in the case of BIST100, the trading days in the first half of the month have lower volatility than the trading days in the second half of the month.

Table 9 reports the estimates of the turn of the month effect in stock returns. The Wald test is not rejecting the null hypothesis that the coefficients α_1 to α_6 are zero in the cases of SASX, CROBEX, MBI10 and MONEX20. The null hypothesis of no turn of the month effect in the mean returns is rejected on 1% significance level for BELEX, ATHEX and BET and on 10% significance level for SOFIX, SLOETOP and BIST100. In the case of BELEX the days $T\left(-2\right)$, $T\left(-1\right)$ and $T\left(+3\right)$ appears to have higher mean daily returns than the mean of the rest of the month trading days, while the days $T\left(+1\right)$ and $T\left(+2\right)$ appears to have lower mean daily returns than the mean of the rest of the month trading days. Similarly, in the case of SLOETOP the day $T\left(-1\right)$ have higher and the day $T\left(-1\right)$ have lower daily returns than the mean daily returns in the rest of the month trading days. In the case of ATHEX significant is only day $T\left(-1\right)$ with lower mean daily returns than the rest of the month days. Contrary, in the case of BET, the days $T\left(-2\right)$, $T\left(-1\right)$ and $T\left(+1\right)$ appears to have higher mean daily returns than the rest of the month days. It is same

Table 5. The day of the week effect in volatility

	α	β	γ	δ_2	δ_3	δ_4	δ_5	Wald Test F-Statistic
BELEX15	0.0291	0.3189***	0.6973***	-0.0053	-0.0021	-0.0544	0.1909***	7.9886***
	(0.4739)	(0.0000)	(0.0000)	(0.9405)	(0.9698)	(0.2867)	(0.0012)	(0.0000)
SASX10	-0.0055	0.1269***	0.7996***	5.7122***	-4.3811***	0.1317***	-0.0124	228.612***
	(0.8520)	(0.0000)	(0.0000)	(0.0000)	(0.0000)	(0.0087)	(0.8147)	(0.0000)
SOFIX	0.1367***	0.2484***	0.7284***	-0.0733	-0.0346	-0.0450	-0.1998***	3.4979***
	(0.0034)	(0.0000)	(0.0000)	(0.3663)	(0.5899)	(0.4668)	(0.0029)	(0.0075)
CROBEX	0.1888***	0.1043***	0.8967***	-0.3006***	-0.2351***	-0.1967***	-0.1644***	12.0108***
	(0.0000)	(0.0000)	(0.0000)	(0.0000)	(0.0000)	(0.0000)	(0.0010)	(0.0000)
ATHEX	0.5297***	0.0903***	0.9011***	-0.1800	-1.1528***	-0.5054*	-0.5192	4.3651***
	(0.0050)	(0.0000)	(0.0000)	(0.6013)	(0.0001)	(0.0802)	(0.1336)	(0.0016)
MBI10	0.0367	0.2422***	0.7576***	0.1079*	-0.0701	0.0019	-0.0198	3.0056**
	(0.3023)	(0.0000)	(0.0000)	(0.0760)	(0.1532)	(0.9674)	(0.7300)	(0.0174)
MONEX20	0.2765***	0.2132***	0.7755***	-0.3586***	-0.1720**	-0.1116	-0.3481***	4.2530***
	(0.0000)	(0.0000)	(0.0000)	(0.0004)	(0.0302)	(0.1620)	(0.0002)	(0.0020)
BET	0.1925***	0.2032***	0.7952***	-0.2068*	-0.2260**	0.0245	-0.2793***	2.6399**
	(0.0018)	(0.0000)	(0.0000)	(0.0640)	(0.0123)	(0.7915)	(0.0080)	(0.0323)
SLOETOP	0.1425***	0.2114***	0.7201***	-0.0877	-0.0471	-0.0306	-0.0251	0.3670
	(0.0110)	(0.0000)	(0.0000)	(0.3591)	(0.5615)	(0.6941)	(0.8061)	(0.8322)
BIST100	0.6236***	0.1206***	0.8496***	-1.0017***	-0.1389	-0.4010*	-1.0438***	6.3718***
	(0.0000)	(0.0000)	(0.0000)	(0.0000)	(0.5125)	(0.0827)	(0.0000)	(0.0000)

Note: */**/*** indicate that the parameter is significantly different from zero at 10%/5%/1% level; p values are reported in brackets.

in the case of SOFIX where only $T(-2)$ and $T(-1)$ are significant, while in the case of BIST100 only $T(+1)$ is significant.

Table 10 reports the estimates of the turn of the month effect in volatility. The Wald test is rejecting the null hypothesis that the coefficients δ_1 to δ_6 are zero for all SEE stock indices. The null hypothesis of no turn of the month effect in volatility is rejected on 5% significance level for SOFIX and MBI10 and on 1% significance level for all other cases. SASX appears to have lower variances in the all turn of the month days in comparison to the variance of the rest of the month trading days. The rest of the stock indices have some combination of the turn of the month days with higher and lower variances in comparison with the variance of the rest of the month days.

CONCLUSION

This paper investigates the random walk hypothesis as well as the three calendar effects (day of the week effect, half month effect and the turn of the month effect) in all ten SEE stock markets for the most recent period (from January 11, 2007 to June 25, 2014) whose immanent characteristic is that it includes the Global financial crisis 2007-2008. Using the variance-ratio test, we found that random walk hypothesis is rejected for all SEE stock markets, except the Bosnian stock market.

Table 6 summarizes the results of the calendar effects. The day of the week effects are present in the mean returns of SEE stock markets. The exemption is the Turkish stock market. Similarly, the day of the week effect in volatility is present in all SEE stock markets, except in Slovenian one. Half month effect in mean returns is present only in the Slovenian stock market, while half month effect in volatility is present in five out of ten SEE stock markets. The turn of the month effect in mean returns is present in six out of ten SEE stock markets. The exemptions are Bosnian, Croatian, Macedonian and Montenegro stock markets. The turn of the month effect in volatility is present in all SEE stock markets.

Table 6. Summary of the selected calendar effects in mean and volatility

	Day of the Week		Half Month Effect		The Turn of the Month Effect	
	Mean	**Volatility**	**Mean**	**Volatility**	**Mean**	**Volatility**
BELEX15	Strong	Strong	None	None	Strong	Strong
SASX10	Weak	Strong	None	Strong	None	Strong
SOFIX	Weak	Strong	None	None	Weak	Moderate
CROBEX	Strong	Strong	None	Moderate	None	Strong
ATHEX	Strong	Strong	None	None	Strong	Strong
MBI10	Strong	Moderate	None	Strong	None	Moderate
MONEX20	Strong	Strong	None	None	None	Strong
BET	Strong	Moderate	None	None	Strong	Strong
SLOETOP	Strong	None	Moderate	Moderate	Weak	Strong
BIST100	None	Strong	None	Strong	Weak	Strong

Note: Weak/Moderate/Strong present the significance */**/*** of the respective Wald test.

REFERENCES

Abraham, A., & Ikenberry, D. L. (1994). The Individual Investor and the Weekend Effect. *Journal of Financial and Quantitative Analysis*, *29*(2), 263–277. doi:10.2307/2331225

Agrawal, A., & Tandon, K. (1994). Anomalies or Illusions? Evidence from Stock Markets in Eighteen Countries. *Journal of International Money and Finance*, *13*(1), 83–106. doi:10.1016/0261-5606(94)90026-4

Alagidede, P., & Panagiotidis, T. (2009). Calendar anomalies in the Ghana Stock Exchange. *Journal of Emerging Market Finance*, *8*(1), 1–23. doi:10.1177/097265270900800101

Bai, J. (1997). Estimation of a Change Point in Multiple Regression Models. *The Review of Economics and Statistics*, *79*(4), 551–563. doi:10.1162/003465397557132

Bai, J., & Perron, P. (1998). Estimating and Testing Linear Models with Multiple Structural Changes. *Econometrica*, *66*(1), 47–78. doi:10.2307/2998540

Bogdanova, B., & Ivanov, I. (2014). Adaptive and relative efficiency of stock markets from Southeastern Europe: A wavelet approach. *Applied Financial Economics*, *24*(10), 705–722. doi:10.1080/09603107.2014.899669

Brooks, C., & Persand, G. (2001). Seasonality in Southeast Asian stock markets: Some new evidence on day-of-the-week effects. *Applied Economics Letters*, *8*(3), 155–158. doi:10.1080/13504850150504504

Chen, H., & Singal, V. (2003). Role of speculative short sales in price formation: The case of the weekend effect. *The Journal of Finance*, *58*(2), 685–705. doi:10.1111/1540-6261.00541

Chow, V., & Denning, K. (1993). A simple multiple variance ratio test. *Journal of Econometrics*, *58*(3), 385–401. doi:10.1016/0304-4076(93)90051-6

Dragota, V., & Tilica, E. V. (2014). Market efficiency of the Post Communist East European stock markets. *Central European Journal of Operations Research*, *22*(2), 307–337. doi:10.100710100-013-0315-6

Dyakova, A., & Smith, G. (2013). Bulgarian stock market relative predictability: BSE-Sofia stocks and South East European markets. *Applied Financial Economics*, *23*(15), 1257–1271. doi:10.1080/09603107.2013.802089

Dyl, E., & Maberly, E. (1988). A Possible Explanation of the Weekend Effect. *Financial Analysts Journal*, *44*(3), 83–84. doi:10.2469/faj.v44.n3.83

Fama, E. F. (1965). The Behavior of Stock-Market Prices. *The Journal of Business*, *38*(1), 34–105. doi:10.1086/294743

Fama, E. F. (1970). Efficient Capital Markets: A Review of Theory and Empirical Work. *The Journal of Finance*, *25*(2), 383–417. doi:10.2307/2325486

Fama, E. F. (1991). Efficient Capital Markets II. *The Journal of Finance*, *46*(5), 1575–1596. doi:10.1111/j.1540-6261.1991.tb04636.x

Fountas, S., & Segredakis, K. N. (2002). Emerging Stock Market Return Seasonality: The January and Tax-Loss Selling Hypothesis. *Applied Financial Economics*, *12*(4), 291–299. doi:10.1080/09603100010000839

French, K. (1980). Stock Returns and the Weekend Effect. *Journal of Financial Economics*, *8*(1), 55–69. doi:10.1016/0304-405X(80)90021-5

Georgantopoulos, A., Kenourgios, D., & Tsamis, A. (2011). Calendar Anomalies in Emerging Balkan Equity Markets. *International Economics and Finance Journal*, *6*(1), 67–82.

Georgantopoulos, A., & Tsamis, A. (2011). Investigating Seasonal Patterns in Developing Countries: The Case of FYROM Stock Market. *International Journal of Economics and Financial Issues*, *1*(4), 211–219.

Georgantopoulos, A. & Tsamis, A. (2012). A Comparative Study on Calendar Effects: Greece vs Bulgaria. *International Journal of Economic Research*.

Gibbons, M., & Hess, P. (1981). Day of the Week Effects and Asset Returns. *The Journal of Business*, *54*(4), 579–596. doi:10.1086/296147

Granger, C. W. J., & Morgenstern, O. (1970). *Predictability of Stock Market Prices*. Lexington, MA: Heath.

Guidi, F., Gupta, R., & Maheshwari, R. (2011). Weak-form Market Efficiency and Calendar Anomalies for Eastern Europe Equity Markets. *Journal of Emerging Market Finance*, *10*(3), 337–389. doi:10.1177/097265271101000304

Gujarai, D. (2004). *Basic Econometrics*. McGraw Hill.

Jensen, M. (1978). Some Anomalous Evidence Regarding Market Efficiency. *Journal of Financial Economics*, *6*(2-3), 95–102. doi:10.1016/0304-405X(78)90025-9

Karadzic, V., & Backovic Vulic, T. (2011). The Montenegrin Capital Market: Calendar Anomalies. *Economic Annals*, *56*(191), 107–121. doi:10.2298/EKA1191107K

Kim, J. H. (2006). Wild bootstrapping variance ratio tests. *Economics Letters*, *92*(1), 38–43. doi:10.1016/j.econlet.2006.01.007

Lo, A. W., & MacKinlay, A. C. (1988). Stock market prices do not follow random walks: Evidence from simple specification test. *Review of Financial Studies*, *1*(1), 41–66. doi:10.1093/rfs/1.1.41

Mills, T. C., & Coutts, J. A. (1995). Calendar Effects in the London Stock Exchange FTSE Indices. *European Journal of Finance*, *1*(1), 79–93. doi:10.1080/13518479500000010

Ogden, J. P. (1990). Turn-of-month evaluations of liquid profits and stock returns: A common explanation for the monthly and January effects. *The Journal of Finance*, *45*(4), 1259–1272. doi:10.1111/j.1540-6261.1990.tb02435.x

Oprea, D. Ş., & Tilica, E. V. (2014). Day-of-the-week Effect in the Post-Communist East European Stock Markets. *International Journal of Academic Research and Accounting. Finance and Management Sciences*, *4*(3), 117–127.

Penman, S. H. (1987). The Distribution of Earnings News Over Time and Seasonalities in Aggregate Stock Returns. *Journal of Financial Economics*, *18*(2), 199–228. doi:10.1016/0304-405X(87)90039-0

Roberts, H. (1967). *Statistical versus clinical prediction of the stock market* (Unpublished manuscript). Center for Research in Security Prices, University of Chicago.

Rogalski, R. J. (1984). New findings regarding day of the week returns over trading and nontrading periods: A note. *The Journal of Finance*, *39*(5), 603–614. doi:10.1111/j.1540-6261.1984.tb04927.x

Rojas, E. & Kristjanpoller, W. (2014). Calendar anomalies in the Latin American stock markets: A Bonferroni testing approach. *Lecturas de Economía, 81*.

Rubinstein, M. (2001). Rational markets: Yes or no? The affirmative case. *Financial Analysts Journal*, *57*(3), 15–29. doi:10.2469/faj.v57.n3.2447

Schwert, G. (2003). Anomalies and Market Efficiency. In Handbook of the Economics of Finance (pp. 939-974). North Holland.

Smith, G. (2012). The changing and relative efficiency of European emerging stock markets. *European Journal of Finance*, *18*(8), 689–708. doi:10.1080/1351847X.2011.628682

Steely, J. (2001). A Note on Information Seasonality and the Disappearance of the weekend Effect in UK Stock Market. *Journal of Banking & Finance*, *25*(10), 1941–1956. doi:10.1016/S0378-4266(00)00167-9

Sullivan, R., Timmermann, A., & White, H. (2001). Dangers of Data mining: The Case of Calendar Effects in Stock Returns. *Journal of Econometrics*, *105*(1), 249–286. doi:10.1016/S0304-4076(01)00077-X

Taylor, S. (2005). *Asset Price Dynamics, Volatility, and Prediction*. Princeton University Press.

Taylor, S. (2008). *Modeling Financial Times Series*. World Scientific.

Tevdovski, D., Mihajlov, M., & Sazdovski, I. (2012). The Day of the Week Effects in South Eastern Europe Stock Markets, Annals of the “Constantin Brâncuşi” University of Târgu Jiu. *Economy Series*, *3*, 20–24.

KEY TERMS AND DEFINITIONS

Calendar Effects: Stock market anomalies in a sense of deviation of actual returns from what would be expected under the efficient market hypothesis, whereby such anomalies are directly related to specific points or periods in time and are cyclical in their nature.

Day-of-the-Week Effect: Presents an anomaly in that the stock returns on Mondays are systematically lower than returns on other days in the week.

Efficient Stock Market Hypothesis: A theoretical hypothesis that asserts that current stock prices embody all information relevant for determining the stock fair values.

GARCH Models: Models for analyzing and forecasting volatility in financial time series, in which current volatility is dependent on past volatility and on past residuals.

Half-of-the-Month Effect: Presents an anomaly in that the stock returns during the first half of the month are on average higher than the returns for the rest of the month.

Random Walk: A statistical model of stock market price behavior that posits that subsequent stock price changes are unpredictable (i.e., random) based on the belief that information on past prices does not provide patterns that could help make future price changes predictable.

Turn-of-the-Month Effect: Presents an anomaly in that the stock returns tend to increase during the last few days and the first few days of each month.

Variance Ratio: A ratio of the n-period stock return to n times the one-period stock return, whose deviation from unity indicates the deviation of actual stock price series from a random walk model time series.

APPENDIX

Table 7. The half month effect in the mean

	α_0	α_1
BELEX15	-0.0102	0.0251
	(0.6666)	(0.4615)
SASX10	-0.0946***	-0.0816
	(0.0016)	(0.4285)
SOFIX	0.0356	-0.0446
	(0.2080)	(0.2484)
CROBEX	-0.0038	-0.0130
	(0.8642)	(0.6745)
ATHEX	0.0351	-0.0001
	(0.4780)	(0.9988)
MBI10	-0.0401	-0.0015
	(0.1034)	(0.9651)
MONEX20	0.0056	-0.0668
	(0.8592)	(0.1196)
BET	0.0430	0.0156
	(0.2228)	(0.7431)
SLOETOP	0.0383	-0.0876**
	(0.1984)	(0.0456)
BIST100	0.1104**	0.0296
	(0.0181)	(0.6367)

Note: */**/*** indicate that the parameter is significantly different from zero at 10%/5%/1% level; p values are reported in brackets.

Table 8. The half month effect in volatility

	α	β	γ	δ
BELEX15	0.0512***	0.3233***	0.6956***	0.0070
	(0.0000)	(0.0000)	(0.0000)	(0.4853)
SASX10	0.3707***	0.2064***	0.3986***	1.2803***
	(0.0000)	(0.0000)	(0.0000)	(0.0000)
SOFIX	0.0671***	0.2481***	0.7311***	-0.0054
	(0.0000)	(0.0000)	(0.0000)	(0.6630)
CROBEX	0.0018	0.1054***	0.8977***	0.0132**
	(0.5743)	(0.0000)	(0.0000)	(0.0268)
ATHEX	0.0243	0.0842***	0.9092***	0.0510
	(0.2442)	(0.0000)	(0.0000)	(0.2164)
MBI10	0.0174***	0.2328***	0.7690***	0.0402***
	(0.0024)	(0.0000)	(0.0000)	(0.0001)
MONEX20	0.0737***	0.2099***	0.7766***	0.0132
	(0.0000)	(0.0000)	(0.0000)	(0.3268)
BET	0.0555***	0.1951***	0.8049***	-0.0104
	(0.0000)	(0.0000)	(0.0000)	(0.5498)
SLOETOP	0.0913***	0.2131***	0.7138***	0.0388**
	(0.0000)	(0.0000)	(0.0000)	(0.0189)
BIST100	0.1557***	0.1106***	0.8610***	-0.1168***
	(0.0000)	(0.0000)	(0.0000)	(0.0006)

Note: */**/*** indicate that the parameter is significantly different from zero at 10%/5%/1% level; p values are reported in brackets.

Table 9. The turn of the month effect in the mean

	α_0	α_1	α_2	α_3	α_4	α_5	α_6	Wald Test F-Statistic
BELEX15	-0.0130	-0.0373	0.2128**	0.2887***	-0.1618***	-0.1616**	0.1528**	9.0433***
	(0.5346)	(0.6246)	(0.0279)	(0.0002)	(0.0001)	(0.0227)	(0.0458)	(0.0000)
SASX10	-0.1492**	0.0954	0.1064	0.0815	0.0237	-0.0343	0.0832	0.3099
	(0.0200)	(0.4399)	(0.4060)	(0.5505)	(0.8177)	(0.8074)	(0.4508)	(0.9321)
SOFIX	0.0063***	0.0566	0.2006**	0.1912**	-0.0967	-0.0360	-0.0895	1.9989*
	(0.7898)	(0.6309)	(0.0342)	(0.0338)	(0.2489)	(0.7130)	(0.3076)	(0.0627)
CROBEX	-0.0307	-0.0156	0.0653	0.2009**	-0.0482	-0.0038	0.0871	1.0547
	(0.1250)	(0.7873)	(0.3551)	(0.0297)	(0.5898)	(0.9638)	(0.2683)	(0.3878)
ATHEX	-0.0325	0.2146	-0.0070	0.7313***	0.0954	0.2412	0.0985	4.0632***
	(0.4684)	(0.3517)	(0.9737)	(0.0000)	(0.5457)	(0.1603)	(0.6480)	(0.0005)
MBI10	-0.0701***	0.0842	0.1231**	0.1036	0.0835	0.0660	-0.0480	1.1729
	(0.0018)	(0.2254)	(0.0388)	(0.1560)	(0.3476)	(0.4302)	(0.6016)	(0.3179)
MONEX20	-0.0382	0.1668	0.1281	0.0323	0.0145	-0.0755	-0.0352	0.8574
	(0.1787)	(0.1044)	(0.2064)	(0.7732)	(0.8651)	(0.4445)	(0.7077)	(0.5256)
BET	0.0123	-0.0660	0.3334***	0.1942*	0.2501**	0.0090	0.1166	3.1220***
	(0.6663)	(0.5873)	(0.0010)	(0.0798)	(0.0456)	(0.9353)	(0.3149)	(0.0048)
SLOETOP	-0.0055	-0.0126	0.2152**	0.1425	-0.0530	-0.2027*	0.0067	1.9713*
	(0.8321)	(0.9102)	(0.0294)	(0.1170)	(0.4809)	(0.0760)	(0.9494)	(0.0665)
BIST100	0.0795**	-0.1061	0.1338	0.2345	0.1143	0.5278***	0.0471	2.0908*
	(0.0354)	(0.5598)	(0.4279)	(0.1378)	(0.6422)	(0.0019)	(0.7609)	(0.0514)

Note: */**/*** indicate that the parameter is significantly different from zero at 10%/5%/1% level; p values are reported in brackets.

Table 10. The turn of the month effect in volatility

	α	β	γ	δ_1	δ_2	δ_3	δ_4	δ_5	δ_6	**Wald Test F-Statistic**
BELEX15	0.0529***	0.3492***	0.6719***	-0.0754	0.1870	-0.0377	-0.2234***	0.0208	0.2864***	10.1171***
	(0.0000)	(0.0000)	(0.0000)	(0.3061)	(0.1069)	(0.7475)	(0.0012)	(0.6928)	(0.0001)	(0.0000)
SASX10	1.2919***	0.1402***	0.4314***	-1.5141***	-0.9293***	-0.6795***	-1.2867***	-0.6287***	-1.0040***	98.4969***
	(0.0000)	(0.0000)	(0.0000)	(0.0000)	(0.0000)	(0.0000)	(0.0000)	(0.0000)	(0.0000)	(0.0000)
SOFIX	0.0648***	0.2464***	0.7267***	0.0363	0.0620	-0.0379	-0.1420*	0.3676***	-0.1932*	2.2186**
	(0.0000)	(0.0000)	(0.0000)	(0.5257)	(0.4879)	(0.6912)	(0.0609)	(0.0030)	(0.0699)	(0.0388)
CROBEX	0.0062*	0.1094***	0.8985***	-0.1176***	0.0241	0.2394***	-0.1783**	0.0223	0.0007	4.8494***
	(0.0869)	(0.0000)	(0.0000)	(0.0002)	(0.5821)	(0.0045)	(0.0459)	(0.8297)	(0.9933)	(0.0001)
ATHEX	0.0463*	0.0904***	0.9020***	1.3795***	-1.0966**	-0.7447***	0.0921	0.3132	0.2681	4.8237***
	(0.0655)	(0.0000)	(0.0000)	(0.0016)	(0.0133)	(0.0080)	(0.7289)	(0.4580)	(0.4914)	(0.0001)
MBI10	0.0344***	0.2358***	0.7660***	-0.1244***	-0.0897*	0.1314**	-0.0721	0.0528	0.1676***	8.0879**
	(0.0000)	(0.0000)	(0.0000)	(0.0081)	(0.0687)	(0.0406)	(0.2342)	(0.3008)	(0.0035)	(0.0000)
MONEX20	0.0881***	0.2202***	0.7684***	-0.2808***	0.1596	0.0351	-0.3251***	0.0262	0.2575***	8.6501***
	(0.0000)	(0.0000)	(0.0000)	(0.0013)	(0.1857)	(0.8060)	(0.0013)	(0.7617)	(0.0014)	(0.0000)
BET	0.0334***	0.2055***	0.7937***	0.2905*	-0.4079**	0.2284	0.1988	-0.1122	0.2675*	3.4986***
	(0.0002)	(0.0000)	(0.0000)	(0.0788)	(0.0228)	(0.1997)	(0.2173)	(0.5135)	(0.0573)	(0.0019)
SLOETOP	0.1063***	0.2193***	0.7077***	0.0804	-0.0857	0.0012	-0.3201***	0.5930***	-0.1613	6.8866***
	(0.0000)	(0.0000)	(0.0000)	(0.3989)	(0.4332)	(0.9921)	(0.0008)	(0.0001)	(0.2246)	(0.0000)
BIST100	0.0808***	0.1047***	0.8692***	0.1006	0.2815	-0.2903	1.5683***	-0.9361*	-0.5170	4.7248***
	(0.0000)	(0.0000)	(0.0000)	(0.7595)	(0.4815)	(0.5068)	(0.0004)	(0.0561)	(0.1808)	(0.0001)

Note: */**/*** indicate that the parameter is significantly different from zero at 10%/5%/1% level; p values are reported in brackets.

Chapter 12
Shocks in Global Economy:
Impulse Model of Macroeconomic Cycle

Andrey Pilipenko
Peoples' Friendship University of Russia, Russia

Zoya Pilipenko
Bank of Russia, Russia

ABSTRACT

This chapter represents an attempt to analyze the role of shocks (impulses) in business cycles in the world economy in connection with the global financial crises of the late 2000s. The theoretical explanation of the origin of any economic shock (external impulse), of economic systems' reaction to it, as well as of the way the global shocks spread its influence all over the world suggests that the analytical predictions of E. Slutsky and R. Frish can be correct. The results provide some evidence for the hypothesis that the cyclical model of development of any economic system means its adjustment to new conditions caused by external impulses (shocks). To reinforce the findings, some results associated with other theoretical investigations and analytical researches are presented.

DOI: 10.4018/978-1-5225-4026-7.ch012

INTRODUCTION

The contemporary world economy is more than six times larger than it was half a century ago. After the 1960s, the global economy went through severe interruptions in growth in every decade. The recurrent financial crises became worldwide events because serious national difficulties were transmitted to other countries through global trade and financial linkages. It means that the world economy has gone through great transformation since the 1960s. The breathtaking of international integration has resulted in a real global village, where countries become much closer because of better models of communication and stronger trade and financial markets. Becoming global, any recession interrupts economic growth around the world and exacts deep and long-lasting human and social costs.

Even now, it is still impossible to predict the location and time of the next financial crisis and the following worldwide recession as well as to prevent the huge human and social losses. Some argue that advanced economies will likely enter a period of secular stagnation because of misguided policies. Others claim that the days of robust growth are behind us because today's innovations are less useful than the major inventions of the past. Another view, though, is that the global economy has enormous potential to generate a healthy dose of growth in the coming decades (M. Ayhan Kose and Ezgi O. Ozturk. 2014).

To make the last words true the problem of cyclical development of the global economy should be solved. Hence, the aim of this chapter is to investigate the interconnection of the economic crises and chocks, the origin of economic, financial, debt chocks and the role of chocks as the impulses to the cyclical development of the global economy, following the hypothesis of E. Slutsky (1937) and R. Frish (1933) as well as the approach of Irma And Frank Adelman (1959).

BACKGROUND

The global economy is becoming more and more integrated, facilitating the spread of crises, recession, uncertainty and risks. The worldwide economic system is undergoing a series of transformations that subject the future to considerable uncertainty, economic and financial chocks and unpredictability. The influence of the financial chocks and cyclical adaptation of the global economy like recession and recovery after the financial crises is of great interest. Hence, the turning points connected with shocks and the trajectory of the cyclical dynamics of the global economy are far from clear.

The often mentioned characteristics in the literature on cyclical development of the world economic system are instability (Hyman P. Minsky, 1986), shocks, uncertainty and risks.

Almost a century ago shocks as one of the above mentioned characteristics were investigated by E. Slutsky. From his point of view, the impulse (as a shock) made the economic system adapt to new circumstances within the cycle. The other authors developed Slutsky's hypothesis of impulse model of cyclical economic development, highlighting shocks (impulses) as the main object of investigation.

The researches of Ragnar Frish (1933) were devoted to the business cycle transformed under the influence of impulses (shocks). The authors of this chapter have got some results that prove the possibility to treat shocks as starting point of the cyclical reaction of the global economy to their influence. This attitude is based on the conclusions of E. Slutsky and R. Frish.

Irma and Frank Adelman (1959) conducted an analytical study of impulse model of business cycle with the help of Klein-Goldberger model. Their impulse transmission approach is of great interest for the authors of this chapter.

The results show the evidence that investigation of shocks as key elements of the impulse model of cyclical economic development is very important for understanding of the contemporary world economy's development as well as its future cycle.

The chapter is structured as follows. The methodology section presents a revision of the investigations dealing with characteristics and influence of shocks and the authors' substantiation to reduce these issues to 3 groups of the interrelated problems.

Analytical part of the chapter is devoted to the modeling of structural connections' changes. They regard to dialectical pairs of participants (buyers and sellers, for example) on the world markets of any tradable asset. The authors start with assessment of the impulse' influence to the structural connections' changes in economy and finish researching subsequent reaction to the shock.

It is emphasized that any economic system changes its structural connections under the influence of shocks. As a result the new trajectory is predetermined by cyclic reaction of any economic system to shock influences of external impulses.

Theoretical results' comparison on the base of the statistical data for the period from the last global financial crisis till 2016th let the authors affirm that it is possible to identify the macroeconomic cycle' beginning as the reaction of economic system on shock influences of external impulses. In any case it confirms authenticity of the impulse transmission character of the hypothesis of impulse' model of macroeconomic cyclical development.

Finally, the last part of the chapter shows the conclusions.

METHODOLOGY

Scientific Researches Preceding the Evolvement of Impulse Model of Cyclical Development of Economic Systems

At the beginning of the 20th century the distinguished Russian scientists in economics, statistics and mathematics - Kondratiev N.D.,

Slutsky E.E. and other representatives of the famous Kondratiev Conjuncture Institute – raised the problem of the cyclical model of the economic system`s reaction to the random effects of impulses as the issue of great scientific importance. Thus, E.E. Slutsky was among the first to doubt the adequacy of determinist models of economic cycles. He validated a hypothesis pointing out that the random effects (“impulses” or contemporary “shocks”) on economic system launched its cyclical response (reaction) to the external influence.

This point of view was shared by the great Norwegian economist Ragnar Frish from the University of Oslo, who, in his famous work “Problems of Impulse Transmission in Economy”, called that approach “impulse transmission” (Economic Essays in Honour of Gustav Cassel. London: Allen and Unwin, 1933) applied to the model of macroeconomic business cycle.

At the end of the 1950s impulse transmission approach was tested by Irma and Frank Adelman engaged in the empirical research of economic fluctuations. Analyzing the influence of random shocks using the Klein-Goldberger model, they proved, that the amplitude and duration of cycles generated by modeled external impulses showed striking resemblance to the actual observations (1959). The model explored by the scientists as a result of their experiment was exposed to the effects of random shocks: the resulting fluctuations of business activity repeated the US economic dynamics, structured on the base of the data of National Bureau of Economic Researches (NBER).

The Essence of Concept of Shocks as Impulses, Generating the Starting Point of Macroeconomic Cycle

To prove the authenticity of the impulse transmission hypothesis the authors reduce the issue to 3 groups of the interrelated problems: (1) determination of the economic activity’s sphere where shocks could arise to transform sharply the macroeconomic development (long run cycle); (2) description of the origin of the impulse, capable to destroy the structural connections between the national participants of the global markets; (3) allocation of the certain structural connection in economic systems, that could be blocked (or destroyed) under the influence of shocks.

Scientific Justification of the Economic Activity's Sphere, Where External Impulses Are Generated as Shocks

It is necessary to choose the sphere of economic system where the impulse could be generated to destroy the structural connections as well as the macroeconomic trajectory of development. It is clear that only some impulses are capable to generate the process of the structural connections' destruction. The last means the processes of integration or disintegration or their simultaneous actions that could change the essential characteristics of the global economy and its national segments. Below there are figures 1-3, describing the influence of the shock of the last global financial crises on the development of the different groups of national economies (IMF, WEO. March, 2017).

The vexing truth is that output per worker and total factor productivity - which measures the overall productivity of both labor and capital and reflects such elements as technology - have slowed sharply over the past decade, and especially since the 2008–09 global financial crisis. This phenomenon is evident in advanced economies and seems to extend to many developing economies as well (see Figure 1)

Figure 1. Five-year average productivity growth rate in the advanced economies in the period of 1990-2016 years (percent)

Sources: Composed on the materials of Penn World Tables 9.0; IMF. World Economic Outlook; Finance and Development. A quarterly publication of the International Monetary Fund. March 2017. -Vol.54. – No.1. - P. 11.

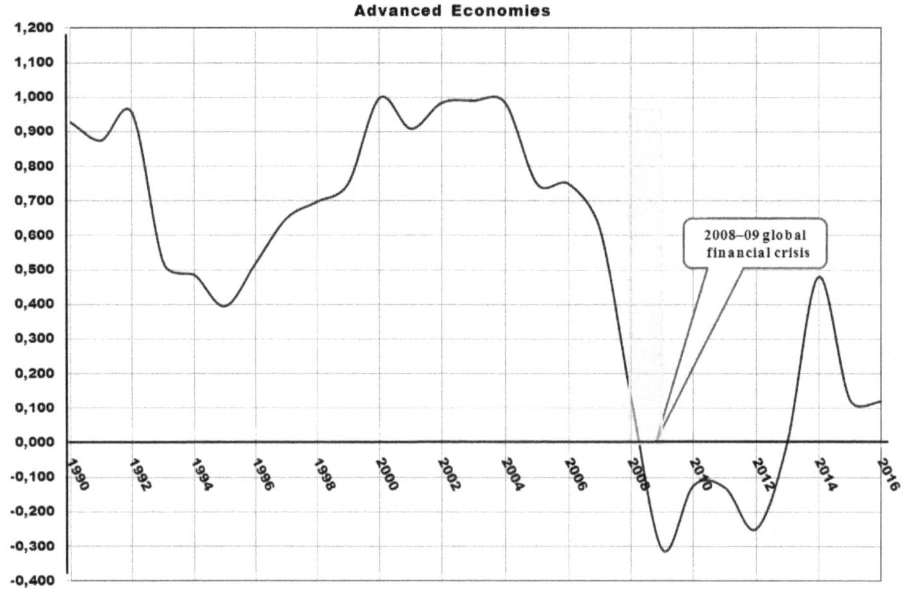

Figure 2. Five-year average productivity growth rate in the emerging market economies in the period of 1990-2016 years (percent)
Sources: Composed on the materials of Penn World Tables 9.0; IMF, World Economic Outlook; Finance and Development. A quarterly publication of the International Monetary Fund. March 2017. – Vol.54. – N°1. – P. 11.

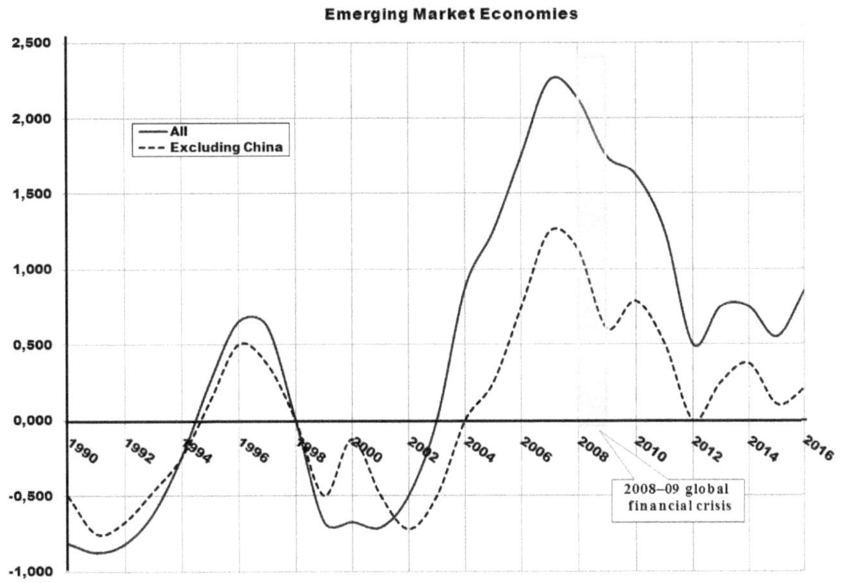

Productivity growth comes from technological innovation and diffusion, and there is no persistent declines in output. Such output losses reflect not only continuing declines in employment and investment but also a permanent drop in productivity (see Figure 2). The dynamics following the global financial crisis were not different. Therefore, a major financial shock could have such large and persistent effects on productivity.

In advanced economies, firms with weaker balance sheets - those with substantial expiring loans or high debt - before the crisis experienced a more abrupt productivity drop than their counterparts with stronger balance sheets (see Figure 3). If these firms had been doing badly before the crisis, their downsizing or outright market exit would have led to higher aggregate productivity - because of the so-called cleansing effect of recessions.

Following the theoretical approach of Karl Marx, the authors share the economic system by phases of GDP formation. It means that on the first stage of GDP formation the producers buy all the factors of production, changing money for goods. In this sphere the external impulse could influence for sure on the national (as well as on the world) economy and finance. The second stage connects especially with the process of production, excluding the external impulse influence. As to the third

Figure 3. Five-year average productivity growth rate in the low-income economies in the period of 1990-2016 years (percent)

Sources: Composed on the materials of Penn World Tables 9.0; IMF, World Economic Outlook; Finance and Development. A quarterly publication of the International Monetary Fund. March 2017. – Vol.54. – N°1. – P. 11.

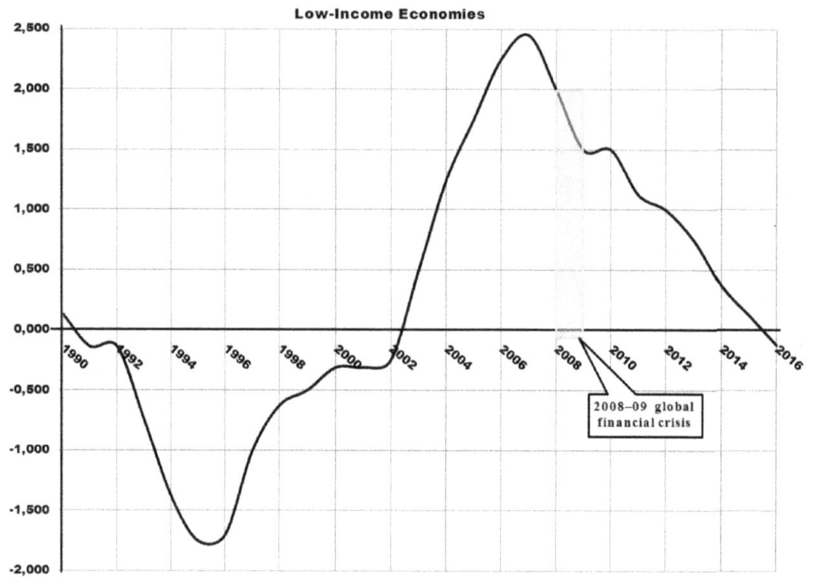

stage of GDP' formation it is connected with the markets, where the produced goods (as well as any tradable assets) are sold. As a result, all the impulses as shocks can exclusively generate on the first and the third stages of the Marx's cycle of GDP reproduction. This is a sphere of circulation of goods, factors of production and other assets. Therefore, the markets as the institutional organization of circulation of goods, services and other assets are responsible for the impulses' generation. Of more importance is the connection of the circulation of goods, services and other assets with the structure of the economic system of any level: regional, national, global, etc. So any impulse realizes as a price shock, influences on the structural (market) relations that means its capability to destroy the structure of the economic system of any level.

The research of the history of well-known economic crises (Kindleberger, Ch., 1996) makes it possible to determine the exceptional sphere of generation of price shocks - on the first and the third stages of GDP reproduction. In this case, the authors suppose the evolution of economic systems from one big wave of Kondratiev "big cycles" to another is realized under the influence of the price shocks on the markets. Therefore, the beginning of macroeconomic cycle is supposed to connect with the reaction of economic systems to the external impulse effects. This conclusion confirms the hypothesis expressed almost a century ago and assumes the impulse transmission character of cyclical development of macroeconomic dynamics.

External Impulses Capable to Cause Shock Effect on Economic Systems of Any Level

Now it is necessary to determine the quality of external impulses to understand their shock effect on the global markets as well as on the economies of any level. This quality connects with the external impulses' potential to change sharply the macroeconomic dynamics (long run cycle). The explanation of this phenomenon is as follows: there are dialectically connected properties of the tradable goods (any asset on the market). From one side the sellers supply them, and at the same time, the buyers demand them. The contradictions and the harmony between supply and demand (as well as between sellers and buyers) relating to the exchange of an asset take the form of market price fluctuations around its base value. The external impulse effect on the structural links between the buyers and sellers as the dialectical pair in the exchange will not be a shock until the price fluctuations do not overcome the marginal level (V.I. Arnold, 2009) for each particular market value. If the market faces the irrationally increasing demand or supply, the market price of an asset can jump smoothly up or fall down compared to its base value ("bifurcation effect"). Therefore any shock's impulse realizes as a price shock, causing the effect of bifurcation in the form of the increasing gap between the market price and the base price of the tradable asset (its actual cost). Hence the external impulse of the price shock is generated by the asset' price overcoming of the price margin of the tradable asset on the particular market. This situation causes shock effect on the structural relations between participants of dialectical pairs - between the buyers and the sellers of the same asset.

Besides exactly the aggressive behavior of one group of participants on the market (either on the demand-side or on the supply-side) determines the assets' price jump over its marginal level (the whole society could not afford to pay for the good at such a speculative price). This phenomenon is confirmed by J. Akerlof and R. Shiller (Shiller R. 2004) introducing "the confidence' multiplier" that works because of the existence of several rounds of the expenditure' circle.

The same situation can be described with the help of mathematical correlations. For example, the increase of the participants' number on the market allows the sellers (principals) of some assets – securities - to increase their supply (issue) in desire to gain the additional profit. In this case, the behavior of the sellers of the securities becomes irrational.

Let the number of market participants grow exponentially with denominator q. Their behavior becomes irrational because they do not analyze the real availability of securities and possible interest payments by issuers without loss of their economic self-sufficiency. Hence, cash inflow to issuers of securities obeys the same geometric progression. This means that during the period n irrational economic agents buy securities for the sum of $q^{n-1}m$. If the behavior of the sellers (principals) was more rational, they could estimate the marginal moment (n - period number τ) when resource' inflow would be completely paid back as interest income. Really, the condition, when the seller has some financial receipts after the interest income has been paid to economic agents, can be written, for example, as follows

$$q^{n-1}m - rm\sum_{i=1}^{n-2} q^i > 0, \qquad (1)$$

where

r = the interest rate for the period τ.

Below there is a formula for the sum of terms of a geometric progression

$$\sum_{i=1}^{n-2} q^i = \frac{q^{n-1} - 1}{q - 1}$$

This inequality (1) can be brought to a form of

$$q^{n-1}m - rm\frac{q^{n-1} - 1}{q - 1} > 0. \qquad (2)$$

As $q^{n-1} > 1$, it is possible to present an inequality (2) as follows

$$\frac{1}{q^{n-1} - 1} > \frac{r}{q - 1} - 1. \qquad (3)$$

The left part of an inequality (3) is always positive. The sign on the right part of an inequality (3) depends on the parity between sizes q and r. It is obviously that two cases are possible.

If $r < (q - 1)$, the inequality (3) will be carried out at any n, i.e. the financial income will increase. If $r > (q - 1)$ at enough big n, the inequality (3) will not be carried out and there will come the moment when the inflow of money is not enough even for interest payment.

The rational sellers (or buyers) of an asset (securities in our case) could easily estimate the moment of price shock connected with the money inflow' reduction. Really, when $r > (q-1)$, the following restriction can be obtained from the inequality (3) that makes sense as below

$$q^{n-1} < \frac{r}{r-q+1}. \tag{4}$$

Taking the logarithm of an inequality (4), we will come to the following estimation of the moment of tendencies' change

$$n_{\lim} = 1 + \frac{\ln\left(\frac{r}{r-q+1}\right)}{\ln q}, \tag{5}$$

where

$n_{\lim}$ = marginal number of the periods of financial operation of irrational economic agents.

Even such simple mathematical correlations of the several following periods throughout let the stock exchange "players" determine the point of default. Hence, if the economic agents on the markets begin increasing purchases or sales of tradable assets regardless of their real cost, it is possible to prove (as done above) mathematically that upon reaching the bifurcation point (marginal divergence of market prices of assets and their real value) any economic system loses its stability because of the breakdown of its structural connections.

As a result change in the confidence will lead to the changes in incomes and confidence in the next round of the expenditure' circle and it will be the same in all the subsequent rounds. This confidence multiplier leads either to increase or to decrease of demand (in direct proportion to the trust) for a particular asset. Finally, the initial increase in demand, pushing the market to a certain margin, finishes causing the massive collapse of all the market operations with tradable goods. In this very process, the bifurcation takes place as the increasing gap between the market price and the base price of the tradable asset (its actual cost).

Multiplying Effect of Shock Transmission All Over the World Markets

The investigation of circulation of goods and services as the exclusive sphere of shocks impulses' generation is the key element to understand the main factors of the global economy' stabilization. The exchange relationships exactly mediate the contacts of dialectically interconnected pairs of participants of buying/selling transactions (households-buyers and companies-sellers, investors and financial recipients, borrowers and creditors and so on in any economic system: regional, national and global). Hence, the shock impact on structural relationships takes place on the markets - in the sphere of circulation. It means that the price shocks destroy the contacts of the dialectically interconnected pairs of market "players" that form the structural relations. Their breakdown leads to the violation of the integrity and sustainability of the market and any market economy as well.

This shock effect is realized because of contradiction, existing inside dialectical unity of the market-defined price of asset and its real price (measured by the manufacturer, issuers, sellers), of the buyer and of the seller. Finally, under the influence of external impulses, the structural links between them overcome their limits and the economic system loses its structural stability.

The same took place in 2007 in the USA on the market of secondary real estate and on the market of unsecured financial derivatives in connection with its default. The price's collapse on the US markets did not stop within the national borders but, all of a sudden, it transmitted the shock effect all over the world markets (see Table 1).

Table 1. Annual growth rate of real GDP per person and GDP per hour worked in the United States or Europe (percent)

Years	United States		EU15	
	Real GDP per Person	Real GDP per Hour Worked	Real GDP per Person	Real GDP per Hour Worked
1950-1973	2.5	2.6	4.0	4.9
1973-1995	1.7	1.3	1.9	2.5
1995-2007	2.2	2.2	2.0	1.5
2014-2023			1.0	0.8
2016-2026	1.0	1.4		

Sources: Conference Board 2016; Havik and others 2014; US Congressional Budget Office, 2016; Finance and Development. A quarterly publication of the International Monetary Fund. March 2017. – Vol.54. – N°1. – P. 4.

Note: The EU15 are the countries that were members of the European Union prior to 2004: Austria, Belgium, Denmark, Finland, France, Germany, Greece, Ireland, Italy, Luxembourg, Netherlands, Portugal, Spain, Sweden, United Kingdom. Periods after 2016 are projections

It becomes clear that contacts between buyers and sellers present dialectical pairs. So difficulties of one partner of dialectically connected pair on the demand or supply-side inevitably generate the breakdown of the whole trade chain. The logical result of this situation is the destruction of transnational trade relations and economic slowdown of the global trade.

Hence, any integration process in the world economy has its "pro" and "contra" and the fundamental goal of any national government is to strengthen its "pro" and diminish its "contra". But today no national government works out effective measures to offset all the negative repercussions of the last global financial crises.

RESULTS AND DISCUSSION

The first result is connected with the determination of the exclusive sphere of shocks impulses' generation - on the first and the third stages of the Marx' cycle of GDP reproduction where goods, factors of production and other assets are traded. So the further scientific researches should be devoted to the price shocks in connection with institutional aspects of markets' regulations, including informal institutions as well as formal ones; on the national and world levels; adopted to specific markets and to different groups of countries. It could be very useful to prevent destructive effects of the similar price shocks in the future.

From the point of view of Camilla Lund Andersen, editor-in-chief of "Finance and Development": "Global trade has been a leading force behind productivity growth, and barriers against it would hurt all economies, large and small. Instead of reaching for easy answers, economists and policymakers must probe their own economies' challenges. As Berkeley economist Bradford DeLong argues: "Only if we do something about it, is it likely that in nine years we will no longer be talking about secular stagnation." (IMF. Finance and Development. March 2017).

As the second result it could be substantiated the price form of any external market shock capable to destroy structural trade relations on the transnational as well as on the national level. If so then the further scientific researches should answer very many questions as follows: what level of the tradable assets' price on the market should be reviewed as marginal; what market should be considered as very important for the shock impulse transition all over the world; what country could be of the great importance for the shock impulse multiplication.

Besides, if financial assets are the preferable assets for the trade speculations it should be of great scientific interest to connect the speculative increase of financial assets' supply on the markets with the definite stages of Kondratiev's big waves. It should be very useful to appeal to the newest publications devoted to these issues, especially that of C. Perez (Perez, Carlota. 2009). It could help to find out some adequate approaches to the solution of the raised problem of the mechanism of the Kondratiev's "big cycles" of economic development.

The third result is the explanation of the multiplying character of shock impulse transmission all over the global economy and financial markets. It is very important to use dialectical method of investigation of the market interconnections in the world economy. The results could help to understand (1) the base factors of the great difference between all the countries all over the world; (2) the reasons of many developing economies' fall behind; (3) the explanation of the unequal influence of the global economy on the national economic development and etc.

It could be very useful to describe mathematically the impulse transmission cyclical fluctuations applied to economic systems (markets, regions, firms) with the help of the theory of oscillatory disturbances transmission of different types and the appropriate models. Hence, it could be possible to review the function of the price shocks as the starting point in the changes of the generated fluctuation process of cyclical economic development.

EMPIRICAL EVIDENCE

If any economic unity is considered as a system then it should keep its stability because of fluctuation' changes of its internal structural connections. These wave oscillations provide system's dynamic equilibrium under the influence of the symmetry law. Hence, all the wave oscillations of the economic systems structural connections correspond with each other. The simplest or monochromatic fluctuations of the economic systems' structural connections could be determined with the help of trigonometric functions "sine" or "cosine" from any argument, linearly dependent on time. In particular, the harmonic oscillatory process is determined with the law of "sine":

$$q(t) = Q_0 \sin\left(\omega_0 t + \varphi_0\right), \tag{6}$$

where

$q(t)$ = deviation of same characteristic of interest to us q (for example, the price of the traded good) of fluctuating system (the market of the given utility as a whole) from the equilibrium position (for example, average value) at the moment of time t;

Q_0 = amplitude of oscillation or maximum deviation of the system (prices for the goods of the same utility) from the equilibrium position;

$(\omega_0 t + \varphi_0)$ = function argument "sine", representing the development phase of the fluctuation process at the current time t;

ω_0 = the so-called circular (or cyclical) frequency of natural fluctuations, connected with the period of natural fluctuations T_0, by the correlation $\omega_0 = \frac{2\pi}{T_0}$;

φ_0 = starting phase of fluctuations or phase value $(\omega_0 t + \varphi_0)$ of sinusoidal oscillation at the time $t = 0$.

Following the accepted designations of the waves' theory it could be possible to determine the square of the circular frequency of natural system's fluctuations $\omega_0^2 = \frac{k}{m}$ as the ratio of system's adaptive properties (structural interrelations on the markets, in the national economy as a whole) k to its inertial properties m. Based on designations of the waves' theory, the authors are going to consider the correlation as economic system internal static rigidity regarding its oscillatory properties.

If the natural fluctuations take place in the system without losses, then the linear oscillator equation is ordinary differential equation of the second order and it can be determined as follows

$$\frac{d^2q}{dt^2} + \omega_0^2 q = 0 \tag{7}$$

Such kind of the oscillator is harmonic, because the function (6) becomes the solution of the given differential equation. The Figure 4 offers the graphical interpretation of the system' natural harmonic oscillations for the case: amplitude of oscillation $Q_0 = 3$, starting phase $\varphi_0 = \pi/12$.

$$q(\omega_0 t) = 3\sin(\omega_0 t + \pi / 12),$$

where the axis of abscissa is graduated with dimensionless units $\omega_0 t$.

Hence, it can be the schedule of any economic integrity' functioning in the case of stable dynamic equilibrium, meaning that no external impulse can destroy the system' structural relations. We can judge about the oscillation' stability of the system' structural relations dealing with the so-called phase portrait of the oscillatory system. It displays the dynamic properties of the model, given, for example, in the form of a linear oscillator (7).

Let the external impulse generate cyclical fluctuations inside the given economic system in accordance with the principals similar to the Huygens-Fresnel principal. It

Figure 4. The schedule of the stable economic system with the model harmonic oscillations according to the low

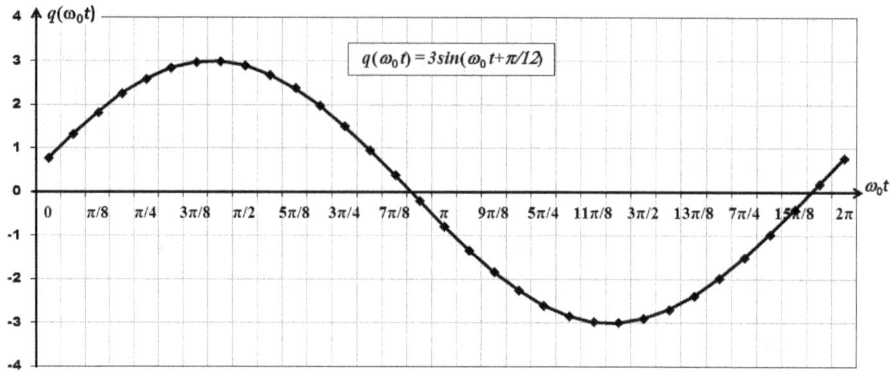

should be noted that some elements (structural relations) of the system can "resist" the influence of the external impulse. Appropriate dynamic model will differ from the linear oscillator (7) as to the term that takes into account the damping of system natural oscillations

$$\frac{d^2q}{dt^2} + 2\beta\frac{dq}{dt} + \omega_0^2 q = 0, \tag{8}$$

This equation describes the damped (non-harmonic) oscillations. Its solution could be determined in the following form

$$q(t) = Q_0 e^{-\beta t} \cos\left(\sqrt{\omega_0^2 - \beta^2}\, t + \varphi_0\right), \tag{9}$$

or in the form

$$q(\omega t) = Q_0 \exp\left(-\frac{\beta}{\omega}\omega t\right)\cos\left(\omega t + \varphi_0\right), \text{ (9´)}$$

where

$\omega \equiv \sqrt{\omega_0^2 - \beta^2}$ = circular frequency of the damped oscillations with the period $T = \frac{2\pi}{\omega}$;

Quantity $Q_0 e^{-\beta t}$ = "amplitude" of the damped oscillations, rapidly diminishing by exponential law.

The Figure 5 offers the graphical interpretation of the system's damped (non-harmonic) oscillations in the form (9) for the case: amplitude of oscillation - $Q_0 = 3.0$, starting phase - $\varphi_0 = 0$, natural harmonic frequency of the system fluctuations – $\omega_0 = 2.094395$; external impulse characteristics of the permanent non-periodic impact to the economic system – $\beta = 0.375$ (or $\beta = 0.750$); frequency of damped oscillations – $\omega = 2.060$ (or $\omega = 1.956$). Note that when $\beta = 0.750$ then significant attenuation of the amplitude of oscillation takes place in the period of fluctuations – T.

Thus, the above demonstrates the graphic interpretation of the economic system's structural connections break, when they become marginal under the influence of the external shock impulse.

Obviously, ordinary differential equation (8) could be applied to any part of the economic system of any level, starting from the national economy and finishing with the global one. Only meaning of parameters of appropriate differential equations can change. In a broad sense, these equations are linear oscillators. This term applies to the systems with small fluctuations around the equilibrium point.

Nevertheless, it is necessary to take into account that under the external impulse influence there could be several different scenarios of the economic system development. If the structural connections' fluctuations (or the elements changes) of the system are coherent (in the case of the same frequency of their oscillations or

Figure 5. The schedule of the attenuation of the system' own fluctuations for the model situations $q(t) = 3\exp(-0.375t)\cos(2.065t)$ *and* $q(t) = 3\exp(-0.750t)\cos(1.956t)$

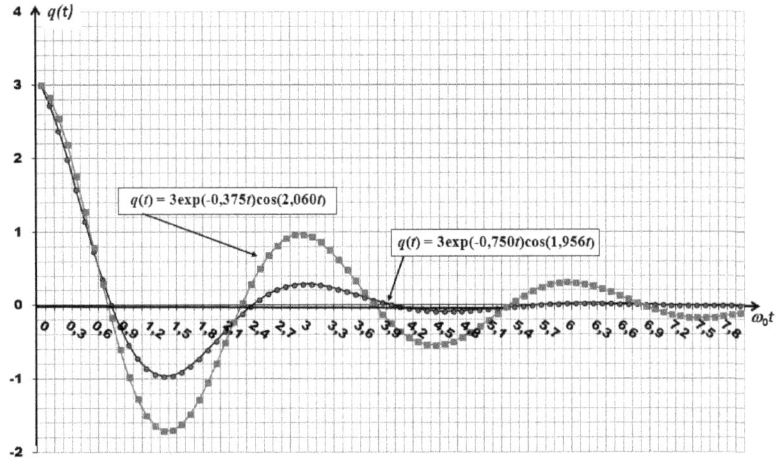

constant phase difference), then system' structural connections (or elements) could change as follows: (1) being in the opposite phases; (2) falling behind or being in advance regarding different waves of fluctuations; (3) coinciding or differing as to amplitude of their fluctuations.

In each of these cases, effects of the shock influence could be different: the system could change in the part; the shock impulse' influence could be neutralized; the system could be pushed to the bifurcation point and its trajectory of further development will change crucially. The last case is predetermined by the effect of resonance following the theory of oscillations. This very kind of impact was rendered by the price shock causing the last global financial crises. It is called the global structural crises because the price shock has destroyed the dialectical (structural) interrelations of the participants of the global market transactions (Figure 1-3).

CONCLUSION

Logic designs of the hypothesis of the cyclical model of the economic system`s reaction on the random effects of shock impulses are based on the theoretical treatment of the economic systems as integrities with dialectic pairs of participants of market relations, of dialectically interrelated operations of purchase and sale and etc. As a result the integrity of the economic system is predetermined by the structural relations of the dialectically interrelated partners that are very difficult to destroy. But there is a phenomenon of price shock that is connected with the gap between market price and the real value of any tradable asset and that is capable to destroy the structure of any economic system causing the bifurcation process in its development. Very many historically known shocks are concentrated in the sphere of circulation of goods, factors of production, services and other assets. All the price shocks appear in the form of assets market prices volatility around their real (base) cost (value). Marginal jump or drop of the market price is accompanied by the speculative behavior of the participants of the market transactions. It could generate the problem of economic instability.

The external impulse influence on the structural links between the buyers and the sellers as dialectical pairs in the exchange will not be a shock until the price fluctuations do not overcome the marginal level for each particular market value. If the market faces the irrationally increasing demand or supply, the market price of an asset can jump smoothly up or fall down compared to its base value ("bifurcation effect"). Hence, any shock's impulse is connected with the price shock, causing the effect of bifurcation of the market price around the asset actual cost (base price). Such an impulse causes shock effect on the structural relations between participants of dialectical pairs of buyers and sellers. In the long run the structural links between them under the influence of external impulses go beyond their marginal levels and the economic system loses its structural stability.

Such approach allows to expand mathematical interpretation of behavior of dialectic pairs to the economic events, processes, systems and agents for the comparison of the main characteristics of their fluctuations. This approach allows to come nearer to answer the question, connected with the problem of the economic dependability: what is the macroeconomic effect for participants of dialectic interaction at coincidence (discrepancy, backlog, an advancing, reflection) of amplitudes of their changes, development stages, etc.

Hence, there appears a problem for the government that must be solved by the control for the parameters that could reach their margins and generate the multiplying process of increasing economic and financial imbalances under the influence of the price shocks. This means the problem of national economic dependability and calls for the monitoring of the basic economic and financial parameters in the country as well as for the development of the government measures aimed at the prevention of the threats to national economic stability.

Theoretical results' comparison with the statistical data for the period from the last global financial crisis up to now let the authors affirm that it is possible to identify the macroeconomic cycle' beginning as the economic integrities' reaction on shock influences of external impulses. In any case, it confirms authenticity of the impulse transmission character of the macroeconomic cyclical development hypothesis.

REFERENCES

Adelman, Irma, & Frank. (1959, October). The dynamic properties of the Klein-Goldberger model. *Econometrica*.

Adler, G., & Duval, R. (2017). Stuck in a Rut. To revive global productivity, start by addressing the legacies of the financial crisis. Finance & Development, 54(1), 11.

Allen, A. (Ed.). (1933). *Economic Essays in Honour of Gustav Cassel*. London: Allen and Unwin.

Andersen, C. L. (2017). What to do about growth. Finance & Development, 54(1), 1.

Arnold, V. I. (2009). The theory of catastrophe. Moscow: Publishing House "URSS".

Kindleberger, Ch. (1996). *Manias, Panics and Crashes. A History of Financial Crises*. New York: John Wiley & Sons, Inc.

Kose, M. A., & Ozturk, E. O. (2014). A World of Change: Taking stock of the past half century. Finance & Development, 51(3), 11.

Minsky, H. P. (1986). *Stabilizing an Unstable Economy*. McGraw-Hill, Yale University Press.

Perez, C. (2009). The Double Bubble at the Turn of the Century: Technological Roots and Structural Implications. *Cambridge Journal of Economics*, *33*(4), 779–805. doi:10.1093/cje/bep028

Reinhart, C. M., & Rogoff, K. S. (2009). *This Time is Different. Eight Centuries of Financial Folly*. Princeton, NJ: Princeton University Press.

Shiller, R. (2004). *Irrational Exuberance* (2nd ed.). Princeton, NJ: Princeton University Press.

Sluckiy, E.E. (1937, April). The Summation of Random Causes as the Source of Cyclic Process. *Econometrica*.

Chapter 13
Globalisation and the Composition of the Welfare State:
Evidence From OECD Countries

Irina Araújo
University of Coimbra, Portugal

Marta Simões
University of Coimbra, Portugal

ABSTRACT

The aim of this chapter is to examine the relationship between globalisation and the size of the welfare state taking into account the respective composition. The efficiency hypothesis argues that globalisation leads to a reduction in the size of the welfare state since this can harm international competitiveness and drive away capital flows, while the compensation hypothesis poses that globalisation induces an increase in the welfare state in order to provide citizens with wider coverage against the risks of globalisation. This relationship is analysed for 31 OECD countries over the period 1980-2010 using data on social expenditures and the KOF Index of Globalisation and their different components. The results obtained indicate that overall there is a positive association between globalisation and the size of the welfare state, more intense for spending on housing-related benefits, active labour market programs and other social policy areas, and mostly felt through political globalisation. Globalisation loses significance for the explanation of family and unemployment benefits.

DOI: 10.4018/978-1-5225-4026-7.ch013

INTRODUCTION

In an OECD report from 2013, (Huwart & Verdier, 2013) ask whether the 2008 financial crisis that started in the USA but "affected most world financial markets almost simultaneously, then turned into an economic crisis in many countries." (p.128) is a crisis of globalisation. Globalisation is defined by (Soubbotina & Sheram, 2000), pp. 66 as "(…) the growing interdependence of countries resulting from the increasing integration of trade, finance, people, and ideas in one global marketplace." This phenomena is viewed by many as beneficial for the aggregate economy since countries can have access to more capital flows, technology, cheaper imports, and larger export markets. However, it does not usually imply that these benefits are shared by all and is also usually associated with higher economic volatility and makes the global economy more susceptible to economic shocks and crises, as the 2008 events have shown ((OECD, 2011)). An institutional feature that acts as a buffer against the economic and social impacts of crises is the welfare state, for instance by guaranteeing an income to those more vulnerable to labour market instability and also helping to recover from economic crisis by putting into action social spending multipliers through domestic expenditure that would otherwise disappear ((Furceri & Zdzienicka, 2012)). Nevertheless, this buffer has also been considered by many as under threat by globalisation, an influence that might undermine the ability of the welfare state and thus the role of government to contribute to post-crisis recovery[1]. The main aim of this chapter is to empirically investigate whether this negative impact of globalisation on the welfare state is confirmed by the data highlighting the influence of the different aspects of globalisation, economic, social and political, and the effects on different components of the social spending. Since different components of social spending contribute differently to long run macroeconomic performance, in particular to human capital accumulation, the former assessment might also have important implications from an economic growth perspective ((Duarte, Simões, & Andrade, 2016)).

Social protection provided by the state can influence to an important extent the living conditions and standards of living of citizens. Social protection helps citizens face a number of contingencies such as unemployment, sickness or incapacity, also ensuring greater equality of opportunities, in particular in terms of access to education and health. However, an extensive social protection system is usually associated with higher labour costs for firms, e.g. in the form of social contributions/social security payments ((Ark, Stuivenwold, & Ypma, 2005)). The increasing economic openness of many countries has moved competition between firms into international markets, which can in turn encourage firms to relocate to low wage countries where the social security system is more limited and thus face lower labour costs in production, in order to become more competitive. This relocation, along with technological progress (which led to a major replacement of labour by capital), makes globalisation the culprit of higher unemployment in the eyes of public opinion, among other threats (e.g. periodic crisis more difficult to manage, growing income gaps at the aggregate and individual levels) since the gains of globalisation are not in principle equally distributed across the population and the workforce (IMF, 2000).

The previous discussion results in the prediction of two opposite sign effects of globalisation on the dimension of the welfare state (in the form of social protection spending) according to the literature. In order to prevent the loss of competitiveness of its firms in a globalised world and especially so that they can compete with firms from low wage countries, governments from countries with more extensive welfare states might feel the need to reduce social contributions and thus at the same time social protection spending. On the other hand, globalisation introduces greater volatility in domestic labour markets, with the workforce facing greater uncertainty in terms of employment and earnings, which can lead voters to demand for more social protection. These two different relationships are identified in the literature as, in the first case, the efficiency hypothesis, which predicts that globalisation leads to a reduction in the size of the welfare state due to a reduced capacity of governments to finance it; and the countervailing hypothesis which, on the contrary, predicts that globalisation induces a greater demand for social security that results in a more extensive welfare state, known as the compensation hypothesis ((Swank, 2002); (Grauwe & Polan, 2005); (Axel Dreher, Sturm, & Ursprung, 2008); (Meinhard & Potrafke, 2012))

The sign of the relationship between globalisation and the dimension of the welfare state is thus an empirical issue. This chapter investigates the globalisation-welfare state nexus for a sample of OECD countries over the period 1980-2010, highlighting not only the impact on the size of the welfare state but also on its composition. Additionally, the authors investigate the disaggregate effects of globalisation according to its different dimensions, political, social and economic[2]. For this purpose they estimate a regression with social spending as the dependent variable and globalisation as the main explanatory variable taking also into account the influence of other main determinants of social spending previously identified in the literature.

The chapter is organized as follows. After the Introduction, the chapter gives a concise presentation of the theoretical predictions on the sign of the relationship between globalisation and the welfare state as well as a presenting some recent empirical evidence. The following Section 3 sets out the empirical model and discusses the estimation results. Concluding remarks are given at the end of the chapter.

THEORETICAL BACKGROUND AND RECENT FINDINGS ON THE RELATIONSHIP BETWEEN GLOBALISATION AND THE WELFARE STATE

From the perspective of welfare state dimension, the fundamental question that has been asked is whether globalisation constitutes an incentive for the expansion of the welfare state or on the contrary necessarily leads to a shrinking social protection system (Swank, 2002). The impact of globalisation on the size of the welfare state remains an unresolved issue in both the theoretical and the empirical literature ((Axel Dreher, Sturm, et al., 2008); (Koster, 2009); (Kallager, 2014)). Theoretical predictions favouring a positive impact of globalisation on the size of the welfare state are known as the compensation hypothesis that focuses on the interplay between two mechanisms, the economic and the political one. This hypothesis poses that globalisation, while benefitting the aggregate economy since countries can have access to more capital flows, technology, cheaper imports, and larger export markets, does not usually imply that these benefits are shared by all. This could be the case, for instance, of workers that are not able to easily find jobs in the industries in which the different countries specialize as globalisation proceeds and are subject to increased labour market volatility. The welfare state can have an important role aiding in this process and making transition smoother by providing higher unemployment benefits and education and vocational training so that workers have the opportunity to acquire the necessary skills. These economic consequences of globalisation would then, according to the political mechanism, lead voters to demand for a more extensive social protection system to help citizens face the contingencies associated with globalisation, thus resulting in a positive association between the latter and the size of the welfare state[3]. An opposing view is known as the disciplining or efficiency hypothesis that gives two economic justifications for a negative impact of globalisation on the welfare state: competitiveness and capital flows. To promote international competitiveness governments have to take measures that reduce the labour costs of domestic firms, such as lower social contributions. Additionally, one fundamental feature of globalisation is higher capital mobility, with governments competing for the attraction of FDI by reducing capital taxation. Both forces imply a retrenchment of the welfare state since there will be less financing sources. (Swank, 2002), p.4 also associates to the efficiency hypothesis a political mechanism according to which "(...) the credible threat of exit may enhance the conventional political resources of mobile assets and their interest associations." that will demand for less government intervention in the form of welfare spending and associated tax burdens. (Chen et al., 2014) however argue that even in a context of increased international competitiveness it is possible to have large-scale public provision of social insurance and progressive systems of redistributive taxation because "(...) contrary to the conventional view, the efficiency gains stemming from increasing international openness strengthen the positive feed-back effects between redistribution policies and the exploitation of aggregate scale economies." (p. 3) The authors specifically test the impact of social spending on relocation decisions by multinational firms and find that the former may be attractive to inward FDI and may also act to avoid domestic firms from leaving the home country. Finally, some authors challenge both these views arguing that the globalisation-welfare state nexus is non-existent since the dynamics of the welfare state are shaped by other more important factors such as, according to (Koster, 2009), p. 8 "(...) the institutional structure of a country (...), the equilibrium between constitutional structure, institutions, and support for social policies (...), political developments (...), or deindustrialization (...)."

The absence of a theoretical model underpinning empirical studies makes it difficult to derive empirical support to a specific theoretical approach[4]. (Koster, 2009) reviews the empirical literature that investigates the relationship between economic openness and the welfare state applying the vote counting method. This method aims at synthesizing existing evidence from different empirical studies (involving in this case 27 outcomes from 22 selected studies[5]) by comparing the number of studies showing a positive (or non-existent) relationship with the number of studies showing a negative one (or welfare state convergence). Additionally, the author evaluates the quality of the studies selected using the impact factor of the journal provided by Thomson Reuters, and also evaluates the impact on the results of the size of the samples and of economic openness and welfare state measures used. The main conclusion of the author is that the empirical research reviewed does not identify economic openness as a threat to the welfare state. In a more recent state-of-the-art evaluation study, (Kallager, 2014) takes stock of the existing evidence by carrying out a meta-analysis of 33 empirical studies encompassing 417 comparable estimates on the effect of globalisation on the welfare state. The main aim was to extract in a systematic way from the selected publications information on the effect of globalisation on the welfare state and to investigate the reasons for the differences between the results in the different studies. The publications were selected according to clearly defined criteria and the results were quantitatively summarized using statistical methods. The results indicate that globalisation has a small positive effect on the welfare state and, more importantly, the differences in results of the published studies are mainly associated with heterogeneity in terms of the measurement of the welfare state[6], the measurement of globalisation[7], the type of data used (cross-section vs. panel), and the academic background of the researchers (political scientists vs. others).

Recent studies that assess the impact of (different aspects of) globalisation on the composition (or overall size) of the welfare state include (Axel Dreher, Sturm, et al., 2008), (Meinhard & Potrafke, 2012) and (Kauder & Potrafke, 2015)). (Axel Dreher, Sturm, et al., 2008) assessed the relative impact of globalisation, i.e. whether globalisation has influenced the composition of government expenditures adopting two types of classifications of government expenditures: capital, goods and services, interest payments, and subsidies and other current transfers; and public services, defence, public order and safety, economic affairs, protection of the environment, housing and community amenities, health, recreation, culture and religion, education and social expenditures. These two classifications implied studying different samples of countries and time periods (108 countries over the period 1971-2001, in the first case, and 15 OECD countries over the period 1990-2001 in the second case) but the results did not change: globalisation (overall and different dimensions) has not affected the composition of government expenditures. (Meinhard & Potrafke, 2012) emphasize the effects of different dimensions of globalisation, social, political and economic on the size of the government sector, proxied by public consumption as a percentage of GDP, on a sample of 186 countries over the period 1970-2004. Using this crude proxy for the welfare state the authors conclude that globalisation has had a positive influence on government sector size around the world, but that this influence is not explained by the economic dimension of globalisation as captured by the KOF index of Globalisation, instead it is due to social and political globalisation[8]. Taking a new approach, (Kauder & Potrafke, 2015) investigate the impact of globalisation on social justice, a prime goal of the welfare state that can be threatened by welfare state retrenchment. In this cross-section analysis of 31 OECD countries, the authors regress an index of social justice (and its different dimensions) built by the German Bertelsmann Stiftung for the period 2008-10 on averaged globalisation (measured as the KOF index of globalisation) over the 1991–2007 period, among other control variables. The results obtained indicate that globalisation enhances social justice with a more pronounced relationship for poverty prevention, social cohesion and equality, and intergenerational justice. On the other hand, globalisation was not associated with the indicators on equitable access to education and labour market inclusiveness.

According to the reviewed evidence to date the most compelling case that can be made in terms of the globalisation-welfare state nexus is that there is a positive (or at most non-existent) association between the two, a result that survives the consideration of different globalisation and/or welfare state dimensions measures[9]. However, given the theoretical ambiguity of the nexus between globalisation and the welfare state and the lack of a firm modelling base it is difficult to interpret the results as confirmation of a specific theory. To arrive at additional insights into how globalisation influences the welfare state this study considers in a more systematic way the different dimensions of globalisation as well as the different dimensions of social protection spending.

DATA, EMPIRICAL STRATEGY, AND BASELINE RESULTS

Our dataset covers the period 1980–2010 with information for 31 OECD countries: Australia, Austria, Belgium, Canada, Chile, South Korea, Denmark, Slovenia, Finland, France, Greece, Ireland, Iceland, Israel, Italy, Japan, Luxembourg, Mexico, Norway, New Zealand, the Netherlands, Poland, Portugal, Spain, Sweden, Switzerland, Turkey, United Kingdom, Czech Republic and the United States. Some OECD countries have been removed from the analysis due to data unavailability for a significant number of years. The data for the main variables refer to social expenditure as a percentage of GDP and globalisation.

We measure globalisation with the help of the KOF index of globalisation, available from the Swiss Federal Institute of Technology in Zurich (ETHZ), an attempt to measure globalisation in a broader sense than just that of economic globalisation that has been widely used in the recent empirical literature[10]. Since globalisation is a complex phenomenon, with different dimensions, to measure the "level of globalisation" of a country or geographic region we should not focus on one dimension alone. The KOF Index of Globalization, introduced in 2002 but only published in (A. Dreher, 2006) and updated in (Axel Dreher, Gaston, & Martens, 2008) is perhaps the most widely used indicator of globalisation. Available for 207 countries for the period 1970-2012, this composite indicator is based on the assessment of the participation of countries in the world market focusing on three dimensions: political, social and economic. Sub-indexes are used to measure these three dimensions. Economic globalisation incorporates economic flows such as data on trade (imports and exports), foreign direct investment and portfolio investment; economic restrictions on international trade and investment and restrictions on capital movements. Social globalisation is characterized by three categories: data on personal contacts, an index that seeks to capture the direct interaction between citizens of different countries, which includes data on international telephone traffic and data on information flows, that is, about the flow of ideas and images, measuring the number of internet users, television sets and newspapers, and media that contribute to the global dissemination of ideas, and data on cultural proximity, assuming that the United States dictates many of the world trends. The level of political globalisation is calculated based on the number of embassies in a country, the number of international organizations to which the country belongs to and the number of international treaties that it has signed, as well as its participation in the missions of the UN Security Council. In order to construct the overall globalisation index, each variable described above is transformed into an index on a scale from zero to one hundred, where the first value means the smallest level of globalisation, and the second one the highest level. Each of these indexes has different weights in the KOF overall index of globalisation calculations: 38%, 36% and 26% for social, economic and political globalisation, respectively.

As can be seen in table 4 in the Appendix, which presents some summary statistics for the overall globalization index and its different dimensions, in the period 1980-2010 the average for the index was 72.16, the maximum value was recorded in 2007, 81.46, and the minimum value was recorded in 1980. From 1980 until 2010 the economic globalisation index recorded an average of 67.15 reaching its peak in 2007. The index of social globalisation, which for the total period records an average of 68.47, reached a maximum in 2008 (79.31). Finally, the index of political globalisation recorded an average value of 81.63, with a maximum of 90.18 in 2009.

This study uses expenditure on social protection as measured by the OECD Social Expenditures database, available from the OECD statistics website as a proxy for the welfare state, which are divided into pensions, incapacity support, family, health, unemployment, housing, survivors' pensions, active labour market programs and other social policy areas. The amount of these transfers is associated with the number of dependents, which varies from country to country, such as the proportion of elderly people, the proportion of unskilled workers, who are more likely to be unemployed or earn a lower income, among other factors. These transfers depend on demographic and economic factors as well as on the political choices of each country concerning the level of social protection they want to provide their citizens with.

Table 5 in the Appendix presents average total social expenditure as a percentage of GDP for each country in the sample over the whole period under analysis, 1980-2010. Mexico, South Korea and Turkey record the lowest figures about 4.72%, 5.25% and 6.49%, respectively. On the other hand, Sweden, France and Austria present themselves as the most socially interventionist countries, with an average social expenditure of 29.14%, 27.15% and 25.93% of GDP, respectively. Social expenditures record a positive trend in all countries except Chile, the Netherlands and Israel that recorded a total decrease of 1.4%, 1.1% and 1%, respectively. Slovenia, Portugal and Greece recorded the highest social expenditure increases, 23.9, 15.6 and 13.9%, respectively.

Table 6 in the Appendix contains data on average total social expenditure (% GDP) for the 31 countries that constitute our sample over the period 1980-2010 and for the years 1980, 1990, 2000 and 2010. For the whole period, average total social expenditure corresponds to 18.73% of GDP. The highest value, 21.92% of GDP, was recorded in the years 2009, while the lowest, 16.67% of GDP, corresponds to 1980. The standard deviation for the period is 1.23. In 1980, Turkey recorded the lowest value, 3.1% of GDP, while the highest corresponds to Sweden, 26% of

GDP. In 2010, the lowest expenditure was that of Mexico (7.8% of GDP) and the highest was that of France (31.7% of GDP). The standard deviation in 1980 is 5.69 and in 2010 it is 5.84. In a more in-depth analysis of the different components of social expenditure, pensions, health and incapacity related support are the most important, representing in the year 1980, 32.65%, 27.67% and 14.39% of total social expenditure, respectively. The components that recorded negative trends over the period were incapacity, survivors, unemployment and other social policy areas. On the other hand, health, pensions, family support, housing and active labour market programs have recorded a positive trend.

In addition to the main variables, the KOF index of globalization and social expenditures as a percentage of GDP, we have also included other control variables given their influence on the size of the welfare. The panel of data is not balanced, since some variables, in particular those relating to the components of social expenditure, record missing values for some years.

Our baseline empirical model is similar to that of (Meinhard & Potrafke, 2012). We use 5-years averages of the variables to explore variation between countries and time, and the model is given by:

$$\log SocExp_{it} = \alpha + \beta \log GLOB_{it} + \varphi' X_{it} + \nu_{it} \quad (1)$$

where *SocExp* is total social expenditures as a percentage of GDP or one of its components; *GLOB* is the KOF index of globalization or one of its components, economic, social or political globalisation; *X* is a vector of control variables and ν_{it} is the error term. We will test for the properties of ν_{it} by considering static panel scenarios: pooled OLS, fixed effects and random effects. The main variables are in logs.

According to the literature review it is not possible from the outset to predict a sign for β the coefficient for the globalisation proxy, since if, on the one hand, the compensation hypothesis predicts a positive impact of globalization on the welfare state, the efficiency hypothesis argues for a negative effect, and we may even have a null effect if both impacts are exactly offset or factors other than globalisation are more important determinants of welfare state dimension. The decomposition of social spending, on the one hand, and the globalization index, on the other, may help to better understand the different influences from globalisation on the welfare state.

The control variables included in vector *X* were selected considering the importance of other factors besides globalisation for the explanation of the behaviour of social expenditure according to the literature and summarized in (Meinhard & Potrafke, 2012). These control variables are: real GDP per capita, which helps to capture the current economic situation (degree of development) of a country - countries with a higher per capita GDP are considered more developed countries thus more able to finance the welfare state so we expect a positive estimated coefficient; the unemployment rate, which is expected to have a positive impact on social expenditure, since an increase in unemployment implies an increase in social precariousness; the age dependency ratio (the population under the age of 15 and over 65 years old as a percentage of working age population), which is expected to impact social expenditures positively since a younger population depends to a greater extent on family allowances and an older population on retirement pensions, additionally at these ages health expenditures will also be higher; total population (in thousands), as a measure of the size of a country which is expected to have a positive influence; the Gini coefficient of income distribution, a measure of inequality, with an increase in this index expected to lead to an increase in social spending in order to reduce inequality; similar to (Meinhard & Potrafke, 2012) we also include a time dummy for the period 1990-2004, a period of some economic slowdown in the OECD and is thus expected to have a positive impact on social spending.

The empirical model is a static panel data model that can behave according to three possible hypothesis, pooled OLS, fixed effects, or random effects. Pooled OLS is appropriate in the presence of samples of countries that present some similarities in their structural characteristics and therefore the constant and slopes in the model will be the same. Fixed effects is more adequate when, although there are common variables that affect the behaviour of the countries under analysis, there are also characteristics intrinsic to each country that affect the respective behaviour and that are different across countries while remaining constant over time. Random effects is used when random variation is expected around a representative mean intercept for the sample of countries. To determine the appropriate estimation method we apply the usual diagnostic tests, the F test, the Breusch-Pagan test and Hausman test. The F test assumes as null hypothesis that there is homogeneity in the constant and, in this case, the most appropriate estimation method will be pooled OLS, against the alternative hypothesis that fixed effects is the most appropriate. The Breusch-Pagan test considers as the null hypothesis that the variance of the error term is zero, favouring in this way the use of pooled OLS, against the alternative hypothesis that random effects should be used. If the null hypothesis of both tests are rejected we should also perform the Hausman test that considers as the null hypothesis that random effects is valid against the alternative that fixed effects should be used. If we reject the null hypothesis for this test then the most appropriate estimation method is fixed effects.

Table 1 presents the results of the three diagnostic tests for the estimation of equation (1) considering as dependent variable total social expenditures as a percentage of GDP and the global KOF index of globalisation as the main explanatory variable. According to Table 1, the results from the F test and the Breusch-Pagan test indicate

Table 1. Selection of the estimation methodology for the baseline model

Test	Test Statistic	p-Value
F	F(30. 117) = 25.2283	3.79068e-038
Breusch-Pagan	Qui-square(1) = 160.884	7.25389e-037
Hausman	Qui-square(4) = 21.3827	0.0003

Source: Authors based on output from GRETL.

that the most appropriate method is fixed effects, in the first case, and random effects in the second case, since the respective p-values are lower than 0.05. We thus have to apply the Hausman test to choose between the two. Since the p-value associated with the Hausman test is also lower than 0.05, fixed effects is the most appropriate estimation methodology for our model.

Before analysing the results of the estimation of equation (1) considering as dependent variable total social expenditures as a percentage of GDP and the global KOF index of globalisation as the main explanatory variable we removed from our empirical model the variables real GDP per capita, total population, the Gini coefficient and the time dummy, since these were not statistically significant. Table 2 contains the results of this regression using the fixed effects method and Table A.4 in the Appendix presents the results of the estimation before the variables that were not statistically significant were removed from the model.

According to the results presented in Table 2, the estimated coefficient for the overall KOF index of globalisation is positive and statistically significant at the 1% level. A 1% increase in the globalisation index leads to a 0.72% increase in total social expenditures as a percentage of GDP. These results are in line with those obtained by for instance by (Meinhard & Potrafke, 2012) and support the compensation hypothesis according to which an increase in globalisation leads to a more extensive welfare state. Recall however that some authors, such as (Chen et al., 2014), argue that even in a context of increased international competitiveness it is possible to have extensive welfare state systems since these are favoured by multinational firms when deciding location. In any case, the threat of globalisation in terms of welfare state retrenchment is not confirmed by the data.

As for the influence of the remaining control variables (vector X in equation (1)), the estimated coefficients for the unemployment rate and population are statistically significant at the 1% level while the estimated coefficient for the age dependency ratio is statistically significant at the 10% level. The impact of the unemployment rate is positive as expected since an increase in unemployment will, ceteris paribus, increase the demand for unemployment benefits and some other components of social expenditure such as family allowances. The estimated sign for the influence of the age dependency ratio is negative in contrast with theoretical predictions since an increase in this ratio would in principle lead to a higher demand for family allowances and/or pensions. However, this estimated coefficient is only significant at the 10% level. For instance, (Meinhard & Potrafke, 2012) find a positive sign for the influence of this variable but not statistically significant. Finally, the estimated coefficient for total population has a positive impact, which is also quantitatively more important.

Table 2 also presents the results of the estimation of equation (1) considering different types of globalisation using the fixed effects method since the diagnostic tests showed that this is the most adequate (see table 8 in the Appendix). According to the results presented in the last three columns of Table 2, it can be seen that the estimated coefficients for all types of globalisation, economic, social and political, present a positive sign and are statistically significant. These results are in line with the results of the estimation of equation (1) considering the overall KOF index of globalisation. Regardless of the type of globalization, an increase in any of these components will be accompanied by an increase in social spending, and the highest estimated coefficient is associated with the index of political globalisation. Contrary to the results obtained by (Meinhard & Potrafke, 2012), the economic globalisation index is statistically significant at a 5% confidence level, which supports the hypothesis

Table 2. Fixed effects results for the estimation of equation (1) with different dimensions of globalisation

Variables	Dimension of Globalisation			
	Global	Economic	Social	Political
Globalisation index	0.7229***	0.3604**	0.4548***	0.7537***
	(0.1400)	(0.1384)	(0.0909)	(0.1418)
Unemployment rate	0.0206***	0.2094***	0.2121)***	0.2282***
	(0.0439)	(0.0480)	(0.0437)	(0.0430)
Age dependency ratio	-0.4627*			-0.7227***
	(0.2534)			(0.2588)
Total population	0.7590***	1.3181***	1.0601****	0.9209***
	(0.2577)	(0.2594)	0.2271	(0.2340)
R^2	0.9446	0.9346	0.9429	0.9452
No. Observations	152	152	152	152

Source: Own calculations.

Notes: *, ** and *** indicate that the coefficients are statistically significant at 10%, 5% and 1% levels, respectively. Standard errors in parenthesis.

that economic globalisation has led to an increase in demand for social security so that governments reward the "losers" from globalisation. On the other hand, the social globalisation index is statistically significant at the 1% level, similar to (Meinhard & Potrafke, 2012), which suggests the presence of the following effect: the greater the connection between citizens from different countries and the size of the welfare state in other countries, more spending will be demanded from the government in each country. The index of political globalisation, which in (Meinhard & Potrafke, 2012) is statistically significant at a 10% confidence level, is in this case statistically significant at the 1% level. The respective estimated coefficient is 0.7537, the highest coefficient associated with any of the globalisation indices, which makes it the index with the greatest impact on social expenditure. A 1% increase in the political globalisation index leads to a 0.75% increase in social spending (% GDP). In other words, the increase in social expenditure as a function of GDP over the years under analysis is explained by globalisation and mainly by political globalisation. These results differ from those of (Meinhard & Potrafke, 2012) since their results suggest that the increase in social spending in recent years was driven mainly by the increase in the index of social globalisation. The concern of (Koster, 2009) referring to the work of (Simmons et al., 2006) that political globalisation is responsible for the spread of neo-liberalism, which in turn might constitute a threat to the welfare state is thus not confirmed. On the contrary, political globalisation seems to be responsible for the spread of ideologies associated with leftist parties that support the expansion of social protection or it might be acting as an indicator of the spreading of a certain type of political regime, in particular democracy, confirming the results from previous studies that democracies are more generous with respect to social spending relative to authoritarian regimes (Rudra & Haggard, 2005).

The sign of the estimated coefficients for the control variables remains the same relative to the ones obtained when using the overall KOF index of globalisation. However, in the case of political globalisation the estimated coefficient for the age dependency ratio is statistically significant at the 1% level. Finally, again some explanatory variables were excluded from the models since they were not statistically significant: the Gini coefficient, the time dummy variable, GDP per capita and the age dependency ratio, except for the latter in the case of the political globalisation index.

The model was also estimated considering as dependent variable each of the components of social expenditure, with, respectively, pensions, other social policy areas, housing, unemployment benefits, active labour market programmes, family, health, incapacity and survivors. A summary of the results is presented in Table 3. In all the regressions we used the overall KOF index of globalisation. The estimations use the fixed effects method, according to the results of the diagnostics tests presented in Table 9 in the Appendix.

Table 3. Fixed effects results of the estimation of equation (1) with different components of social spending as dependent variable

	Dependent Social Expenditure Variable								
	Pensions	Other Social Policy Areas	Housing	Unemployment	Active Labour Market Programs	Family	Health	Incapacity	Survivors
Globalisation index	1.0135***	1.2929***	2.7174***	0.4361	1.3057***	0.5060	0.6943***	-0.5687***	0.7380**
	(0.1580)	(0.4262)	(0.5821)	(0.4029)	(0.3971)	(0.3517)	(0.1926)	(0.1882)	(0.3090)
Unemployment rate	0.2435***	0.3645**		0.6954***		0.3353***		0.2064***	0.3320**
	(0.0662)	(0.1604)		-0.0675		(0.1156)		(0.0626)	(0.1267)
Age dependency ratio	−0.8663**	−3.7863***				-1.3054*		0.8530**	
	(0.3703)	(0.9261)				(0.6744)		(0.3550)	
Total population			-2.3105***	-2.2595***	-2.3853***	3.1020***	1.5356***	1.7175***	
			(0.8263)	(0.7543)	(0.6542)	(0.6762)	(0.3252)***	(0.3681)	
Gini									-1.1110*
									(0.5682)
Time dummy				0.1497**					
				(0.0675)					
R^2	0.9252	0.7763	0.7797	0.8773	0.8766	0.8788	0.8257	0.9647	0.8496
No. Obs.	152	138	132	143	139	151	168	150	139

Source: Own calculations.

Notes: *, ** and *** indicate that the coefficients are statistically significant at 10%, 5% and 1% levels, respectively. Standard errors in parenthesis.

According to the results presented in Table 3, globalisation has a positive influence on the different components of social spending, except for incapacity spending. The quantitatively most important influence is on housing expenditure (2.7174), followed by expenditure on active labour market programmes and spending on other social policy areas. The results obtained are in accordance with the evidence from the analysis using total social expenditures as dependent variable and, therefore, with the hypothesis that for a greater level of openness of countries to the world market citizens demand more of their welfare state, increasing social spending. From a long run macroeconomic performance perspective this effects of globalisation on social spending components are important to sustain economic growth. For economic growth, an important dimension of the welfare state is public expenditure on health, to the extent that it leads to the accumulation of human capital. Better health helps to increase labour productivity, the capacity to learn at school and to grow intellectually and physically. Simultaneously, the decrease in mortality and morbidity allows for an increase in the proportion of the working age population, therefore contributing to raise per capita income. Higher longevity also creates a greater need for people to save for their retirement (Bloom & Canning, 2000). Investment in health can thus generate substantial returns over time, not just at the individual level, but especially for the economy as a whole, and the welfare state can play a crucial role in this dynamic process. Globalisation does not seem to threaten this role, on the contrary it strengthens it. Spending on active labour market programs and policies which enable combining work and family, such as parental leave and day care, can also improve human capital and have a growth enhancing effect. The fact that the index of globalisation has an important influence on active labour market programs spending helps to enhance this role, but the same does not apply to family support since the respective estimated coefficient is not statistically significant.

Other types of social protection expenditures are often regarded as having negative growth effects due to the reduced incentives associated. Unemployment benefits provide an illustration, with many economic models assuming that they discourage labour supply, since they guarantee an income for the unemployed workers (that discourages returning to work) and also serve as a protection to active workers, which are thus discouraged from higher working effort. But it is also possible to argue for positive behavioural effects of unemployment benefits by affecting the incentives of workers to undertake long-term investments in skills (Estevez-Abe, Versen, & Soskice, 2001). When the unemployment benefits are earnings-related they provide to high-skilled workers, with higher wages, some guarantees that their investments in education will not be lost during periods when they are temporarily out of work. However, the globalisation index is not statistically significant in explaining the evolution of unemployment benefits. This might be explained by the fact that governments do not immediately increase their spending on social support in the face of a higher level of globalisation, but rather try to fight higher unemployment by stabilising the labour market through spending more in active labour market programmes. Another possible explanation for this loss of significance is the fact that the unemployment rate, which is closely linked to unemployment benefits, is used as explanatory variable. This explanatory variable, as expected, exerts a greater influence on unemployment expenditure, presenting a statistical significance of 1% and is not statistically significant in explaining the expenditure related to housing, health and active labour market programs so we removed it from the respective estimated equations. On the other hand, for the other components of social expenditure, the estimated coefficient for unemployment rate is statistically significance at the 1% level and exerts a positive influence, as expected. Higher unemployment potentially creates income inequality, financial instability and insecurity, so citizens will need more support from their governments, which will translate into an increase in social spending when it is disaggregated in some its components.

Population aging and the associated increase in the share of elderly render old age pensions an important role in the analysis of the relationship between the welfare state and economic growth. Maintaining the current schemes available in most developed countries would necessarily imply a rise in taxes with its negative growth consequences. Additionally, the positive behavioural and inequality reduction (particularly higher human capital investment) effects are less likely to apply in these situations unless a case similar to that for unemployment benefits can be made: by providing benefits that are proportional to wages, pension schemes provide some guarantees to high-skilled workers that their investments in human capital will not be undermined when they retire. Given the positive estimated coefficient for the effect of globalisation on pensions, the latter argument indicates that globalisation might enhance this growth effect.

Additionally, globalisation also does not seem to threaten the short-term effects of social expenditures on economic activity with the former remaining an area of state intervention in a globalised world and thus keeping their role as spending multipliers that can help alleviate the impact of adverse shocks such as the ones that originated the Great Recession. Although it is not the aim of this study to investigate which components of public spending have the highest impact on output, recent literature indicates that Keynesian multipliers are not the same for different components of public spending. Using a panel of OECD countries from 1980 to 2005, (Furceri & Zdzienicka, 2012) show that social spending has a significant short-term effect on output, especially during downturns. Furthermore, among spending subcategories, social spending on health, on survivors and on unemployment benefits have the greatest effects. The first two categories are positively influenced by globalisation, according to our results, and so do not support the concern with the fact that globalisation, by leading to a retrenchment of the welfare state, might hamper the ability of governments to contribute to a faster economic recovery.

Regarding the control variables, the age dependency ratio, in contrast to the analysis using total social expenditure, has a statistically significant influence on various components of social expenditure. However, except for incapacity, the influence on spending on family, other social policy areas and pensions is negative, contrary to what expected. Total population maintained its level of significance of 1% in the explanation of pensions, other social policy areas and survivors. However, it presents a negative influence on social expenditure on housing, unemployment and active labour market programs. Since the Gini Coefficient is an indicator of inequality in income distribution, an increase in this coefficient would be expected to increase social spending in order to reduce inequality. However, the results go against this prediction since the respective estimated coefficient is negative. Nevertheless, the influence of the Gini coefficient on social expenditure does not seem to be relevant. This variable is only statistically significant in the analysis of the evolution of expenditure on survivors and only at a significance level of 10%. Finally, the time dummy variable is statistically significant at the 5% level in the explanation of unemployment benefits, the only category of social expenditure for which it is significant. This time dummy refers to the period 1990-2004, a period of some economic slowdown in Europe, with workers losing their jobs. Faced with this loss of employment, which leads to an increase in the unemployment rate, it is expected to observe an increase in social spending on unemployment benefits.

CONCLUSION

The main objective of this chapter was to investigate the influence of the level of globalisation on the size of the welfare state, proxied by social spending as a percentage of GDP. The literature points to three possible effects: a positive effect due to the higher economic uncertainty induced by globalisation leading to greater demand for social support from the state; a negative effect, by reducing the financing of social expenditure, with the aim of maintaining international competitiveness, which leads to an inability of the government to provide their citizens with greater support; and a non-existent effect if other more important factors influence the size of the welfare state.

The sample used consists of 31 OECD countries with data for the period 1980-2010. Over the period under analysis there was a impressive increase in the average globalisation index of 20.88 percentage points. All the dimensions of globalisation followed this trend with a special emphasis for the social globalisation index that grew by 26.76 percentage points. In 2010, total social spending accounted for an average of 21.68% of GDP and also recorded a positive trend during the period, increasing by 5 percentage points. With the exception of Chile, Israel and the Netherlands, all remaining countries followed this trend. Despite this overall trend, some of the components of social spending decreased their GDP share, as is the case of incapacity and survivors-related expenditures.

In the econometric analysis of the relationship between the level of globalisation of countries and their social expenditure, regressions were estimated using the fixed effects method to estimate the influence of the globalisation index on social expenditure as well as the influence of the different sub-indices (economic, social and political globalisation). The empirical results show that the globalisation index is statistically significant in explaining the evolution of social spending in the countries that constitute the sample and that it has a positive influence. The effects exerted by each sub-index individually confirm those for the overall index, with a greater influence of the index of political globalisation. The next step in the analysis consisted in examining the effects of globalisation on the different components of social expenditure. The overall globalisation index loses statistical significance in explaining social expenditure for the unemployed and family-related benefits and presenting a small statistical significance in explaining support for survivors. Nevertheless, the globalisation index has a positive influence on social spending in all cases, except incapacity-related.

Overall the evidence does not support the efficiency hypothesis, in a narrow sense, since all components of the globalization index, including the economic one, present a positive sign. The results seem to support the compensation hypothesis according to which the degree of openness of countries to the world market positively affects the size of the welfare state. This positive correlation between globalisation and the welfare state is important from an economic growth perspective since it seems to act through components of social spending that might positively influence human capital accumulation, essential to sustain growth in modern knowledge based economies. Additionally, globalisation also does not seem to threat the short-term effects of social expenditures on economic activity with the former remaining an area of state intervention in a globalised world and thus keeping their role as spending multipliers that can help alleviate the impact of adverse shocks such as the ones that originated the Great Recession.

The analysis provided in this study remains a preliminary and illustrative one. Only a more structural analysis (for instance with simultaneous equations or panel VAR models) with more extensive data, including emerging markets, would allow us to disentangle systematically the individual effects of these related processes, globalisation, welfare state composition and economic activity in the short and the long run. Future research should also involve country-specific analysis given the variety of welfare state models adopted by different countries, along with the consideration of other proxies for the welfare state. Even though this analysis has been conducted for thirty one OECD countries considered to be mostly developed markets (with the exception of Chile, Mexico, South Korea and Turkey - https://www.msci.com/market-classification), their responses to globalisation may also have implications for other emerging markets countries. A natural extension of this research involves its replication for wider samples of emerging markets countries as data becomes available.

REFERENCES

Ark, B. V., Stuivenwold, E., & Ypma, G. (2005). *Unit labour costs, productivity and international competitiveness*. Groningen Growth and Development Centre Research Memorandum No. GD-80.

Baker, A. (2008). *Public Opinion and the Compensation Hypothesis* Paper presented at the International Political Economy Society, University of Pennsylvania, Philadelphia, PA.

Bergh, A., & Nilsson, T. (2014). Is globalization reducing absolute poverty? *World Development*, *62*, 42–61. doi:10.1016/j.worlddev.2014.04.007

Bloom, D. E., & Canning, D. (2000). The Health and Wealth of Nations. *Science*, *287*(5456), 1207–1209. doi:10.1126cience.287.5456.1207 PMID:10712155

Chen, Y.-F., Görg, H., Görlich, D., Molana, H., Montagna, C., & Temouri, Y. (2014). *Globalisation and the Future of the Welfare State*. IZA Policy Paper No. 81.

Dreher, A. (2006). The influence of globalization on taxes and social policy – An empirical analysis for OECD countries. *European Journal of Political Economy*, *22*(1), 179–201. doi:10.1016/j.ejpoleco.2005.04.006

Dreher, A., Gaston, N., & Martens, P. (2008). *Measuring Globalisation*. New York: Springer. doi:10.1007/978-0-387-74069-0

Dreher, A., Sturm, J.-E., & Ursprung, H. W. (2008). The impact of globalization on the composition of government expenditures: Evidence from panel data. *Public Choice*, *134*(3-4), 263–292. doi:10.100711127-007-9223-4

Duarte, A., Simões, M., & Andrade, J. S. (2016). The Welfare State and Economic Performance: Quantiles and Nonlinearities. *Applied Economics Quarterly*, *62*(4), 267–294. doi:10.3790/aeq.62.4.269

Estevez-Abe, M., Versen, T., & Soskice, D. (2001). Social Protection and the Formation of Skills: A Reinterpretation of the Welfare State. In P. Hall & D. Soskice (Eds.), *Varieties of Capitalism: The Institutional Foundation of Comparative Advantage*. New York: Oxford University Press. doi:10.1093/0199247757.003.0004

Furceri, D., & Zdzienicka, A. (2012). The Effects of Social Spending on Economic Activity: Empirical Evidence from a Panel of OECD Countries. *Fiscal Studies*, *33*(1), 129–152. doi:10.1111/j.1475-5890.2012.00155.x

Gaston, N., & Rajaguru, G. (2013). International migration and the welfare state revisited. *European Journal of Political Economy*, *29*, 90–101. doi:10.1016/j.ejpoleco.2012.08.004

Grauwe, P., & Polan, M. (2005). Globalization and Social Spending. *Pacific Economic Review*, *10*(1), 105–123. doi:10.1111/j.1468-0106.2005.00263.x

Huwart, J.-Y., & Verdier, L. (2013). *The 2008 financial crisis – A crisis of globalisation? In Economic Globalisation: Origins and consequences* (pp. 126–143). Paris: OECD Publishing.

IMF. (2000). *Globalization: Threat or Opportunity?* Retrieved from https://www.imf.org/external/np/exr/ib/2000/041200to.htm

Kallager, P. K. R. (2014). *Globalisation and the Welfare State – A Meta-Regression Analysis* (Master's thesis). Department of Comparative Politics, University of Bergen.

Kauder, B., & Potrafke, N. (2015). Globalization and social justice in OECD countries. *Review of World Economics*, *151*(2), 353–376. doi:10.100710290-015-0213-1

Koster, F. (2009). The welfare state and globalisation: Down and out or too tough to die? *International Journal of Social Welfare*, *18*(2), 153–162. doi:10.1111/j.1468-2397.2008.00571.x

Meinhard, S., & Potrafke, N. (2012). The Globalization-Welfare State Nexus Reconsidered. *Review of International Economics*, *20*(2), 271–287. doi:10.1111/j.1467-9396.2012.01021.x

OECD. (2011). *Future Global Shocks: Improving risk governance*. Paris: OECD Publishing.

Potrafke, N. (2013). Globalization and labor market institutions: International empirical evidence. *Journal of Comparative Economics*, *41*(3), 829–842. doi:10.1016/j.jce.2013.02.002

Rudra, N., & Haggard, S. (2005). Globalisation, democracy, and effective welfare state spending in the developing world. *Comparative Political Studies*, *38*(9), 1015–1049. doi:10.1177/0010414005279258

Schulze, G. G., & Ursprung, H. W. (1999). Globalisation of the Economy and the Nation State. *World Economy*, *22*(3), 295–352. doi:10.1111/1467-9701.00205

Simmons, B. A., Dobbin, F., & Garrett, G. (2006). Introduction: The international diffusion of liberalism. *International Organization*, *60*(4), 781–810. doi:10.1017/S0020818306060267

Soubbotina, T. P., & Sheram, K. A. (2000). *Beyond Economic Growth: Meeting the Challenges of Global Development*. Washington, DC: World Bank.

Swank, D. (2002). *Global Capital, Political Institutions, and Policy Change in Developed Welfare States*. Cambridge, UK: Cambridge University Press. doi:10.1017/CBO9780511613371

Vadlamannati, K. C. (2015). Rewards of (dis)integration: Economic, social, and political globalization and freedom of association and collective bargaining rights of workers in developing countries. *Industrial & Labor Relations Review*, *68*(1), 3–27. doi:10.1177/0019793914555851

KEY TERMS AND DEFINITIONS

Compensation Hypothesis: Prediction of a positive association between globalisation and the size of the welfare state since the former induces a greater demand for social security due to the associated risks.

Economic Growth: Long-run behaviour of aggregate output corresponding to a sustained increase in the quantity of goods and services produced by an economy.

Efficiency Hypothesis: Prediction of a negative association between globalisation and the size of the welfare state due to a reduced capacity of governments to finance the latter in order to promote international competitiveness and attract capital flows.

Fixed Effects: Econometric model that assumes that, besides the common variables that explain the behaviour of the individuals under analysis, there are also characteristics intrinsic to each individual that influence their behaviour and that are different across individuals while remaining constant over time.

Globalisation: Global process of integration of different countries by sharing information, ideas, cultures, and markets.

Public Social Expenditure: Provision by public institutions of benefits to households and individuals to help them face a number of contingencies such as unemployment, sickness, or incapacity, also ensuring greater equality of opportunities.

Spending Multiplier: Measure of the effect of a change in spending on aggregate output computed as the ratio of a change in output to the change in spending that caused it.

Welfare State: Intervention through which the state plays a role in protecting and promoting the economic and social wellbeing of its citizens.

ENDNOTES

1 Additionally, public fiscal sustainability problems exacerbated by the crisis have led to austerity programs in some countries that reduced even further government spending for social protection.

2 For instance, (Koster, 2009) refers to the work of (Simmons, Dobbin, & Garrett, 2006) as a possible explanation for the influence of political globalisation on the welfare state. According to the view of these authors, political globalisation is responsible for the spread of neo-liberalism, which in turn might constitute a threat to the welfare state.

3 For instance, (Baker, 2008) tests whether citizens demand more extensive welfare states in response to globalisation and its effects but the results found are inconclusive. In any case, the author finds some support for the hypothesis that citizens in open economies exert greater demand for government spending.

4 For an earlier and more extensive review of the theoretical arguments and empirical evidence on the globalisation-welfare state nexus see (Schulze & Ursprung, 1999).

5 The author selected these studies based on four criteria: (i) being and empirical study, (ii) including an indicator of the economic openness, (iii) including an indicator of the welfare state; and (iv) being international comparisons.

6 For instance, most studies using total social expenditures as a percentage of GDP as the proxy for the welfare state arrive at a negative effect, while studies using components of social expenditure conclude for a positive effect.

7 For instance, studies that use the KOF index of globalisation conclude for a negative effect.

8 In his survey of the literature using meta-analysis, (Kallager, 2014) emphasizes the measurement of the welfare state as one of the factors explaining the lack of consensus of the empirical literature on the effects of globalisation on the welfare state.

9 Other related strands of the empirical literature that are not included in our review investigate the impact on the welfare state of more narrow dimensions of globalisation, such as (Gaston & Rajaguru, 2013) that investigate the impact of international migration, or consider outcomes of the welfare state (not inputs, social spending) potentially affected by globalisation such as labour market regulations and poverty (see e. g. (Potrafke, 2013), (Vadlamannati, 2015) and (Bergh & Nilsson, 2014)). Also in the case of this literature the majority of the results does not endorse the view that globalisation is a threat to the welfare state.

10 Examples can be found at http://globalization.kof.ethz.ch/papers/

APPENDIX

Table 4. Summary statistics for the KOF index of globalisation, 31 OECD countries

Globalisation Index	Period	Mean	Standard Deviation	Minimum	Maximum
Global	1980-2010	72.16	7.43	60.00	81.46
	1980	60.00	12.65	35.49	79.49
	1990	65.25	12.45	60.00	81.67
	2000	79.00	9.98	57.23	91.98
	2010	80.88	8.03	60.32	92.22
Economic	1980-2010	69.15	7.13	56.54	78.57
	1980	56.54	15.30	28.4	92.31
	1990	64.78	13.81	56.54	94
	2000	77.1	13.39	47.41	97.76
	2010	76.29	11.32	46.95	94.69
Social	1980-2010	68.47	9.12	52.27	79.31
	1980	52.27	16.69	23.32	82.08
	1990	61.76	15.69	52.27	83.18
	2000	75.86	12.38	49.61	91.74
	2010	79.03	11.09	51.75	91.61
Political	1980-2010	81.63	5.87	70.90	90.18
	1980	75.96	16.18	43.57	96.77
	1990	70.90	15.17	70.90	90.37
	2000	86.17	10.36	57.46	97.02
	2010	89.89	6.61	71.99	97.74

Source: own calculations with data from the KOF index of globalisation.

Table 5. Average and total growth of total social spending as a percentage of GDP by country, 31 OECD countries, 1980-2010

Country	Average Total Social Spending (% GDP)	Total Growth (%)
Australia	14.66	7
Austria	25.93	6.5
Belgium	25.60	5.3
Canada	16.86	4.7
Chile	10.55	-1.4
Check Republic	17.81	5.3
Denmark	26.2	5.5
Finland	24.87	10.7
France	27.15	11.1
Germany	24.64	5
Greece	17.89	13.9
Iceland	15.54	4.4
Ireland	17.41	7.3
Israel	16.66	-1
Italy	22.69	9.8
Japan	14.54	11.8
South Korea	5.26	6.2
Luxemburg	20.73	2.7
Mexico	4.72	6.1
Netherlands	23.44	-1.1
New Zealand	18.87	4.1
Norway	21.68	6.1
Poland	21.24	5.8
Portugal	16.12	15.6
Slovenia	16.15	23.9
Spain	20.02	11.3
Sweden	29.14	1.9
Switzerland	16.45	6
Turkey	6.5	9.5
United Kingdom	19.10	6.5
United States	14.6	6.5

Source: Own calculations with data from the *OCDE Social Expenditure Database*.

Table 6. Summary statistics for social spending (%GDP), 31 OECD countries

Type of Spending	Period	Mean	Standard Deviation	Minimum	Maximum
Total	1980-2010	18.73	1.23	16.67	21.92
	1980	16.67	5.69	3.10	26.00
	1990	16.51	7.21	0.00	28.50
	2000	18.89	5.46	4.80	28.40
	2010	21.68	5.84	7.80	31.70
Pensions	1980-2010	6.20	0.48	5.44	7.27
	1980	5.44	2.13	1.00	10.00
	1990	5.68	2.45	0.40	9.50
	2000	6.27	2.83	0.00	11.30
	2010	7.27	2.76	1.50	13.30
Health	1980-2010	5.12	0.51	4.56	6.48
	1980	4.61	1.31	0.60	7.50
	1990	4.41	1.56	0.00	6.40
	2000	5.1	1.3	2.10	7.80
	2010	6.34	1.59	2.80	8.70
Family	1980-2010	1.82	0.24	1.46	2.36
	1980	1.64	0.99	0.30	3.80
	1990	1.63	1.08	0.00	4.30
	2000	1.90	0.96	0.10	3.50
	2010	2.25	1.1	0.00	4.10
Incapacity	1980-2010	2.37	0.09	2.14	2.59
	1980	2.4	1.51	0.30	6.50
	1990	2.25	1.48	0.00	6.30
	2000	2.32	1.19	0.10	5.10
	2010	2.25	1.37	0.10	4.80
Unemployment	1980-2010	1.34	0.26	0.76	1.90
	1980	0.98	1.03	0.10	4.80
	1990	1.27	1.19	0.00	4.20
	2000	1.08	1.21	0.00	6.50
	2010	1.13	1.23	0.10	3.60

continued on following page

Table 6. Continued

Type of Spending	Period	Mean	Standard Deviation	Minimum	Maximum
Survivors	1980-2010	1.00	0.08	0.89	1.18
	1980	1.06	0.82	0.10	3.40
	1990	0.92	0.77	0.00	2.90
	2000	0.89	0.77	0.00	2.60
	2010	1.04	0.79	0.00	2.60
Active labour market programmes	1980-2010	0.63	0.07	0.47	0.77
	1980	0.47	0.21	0.20	0.80
	1990	0.51	0.42	0.00	1.60
	2000	0.58	0.48	0.00	1.90
	2010	0.58	0.48	0.00	2.00
Other social policy areas	1980-2010	0.54	0.04	0.43	0.62
	1980	0.37	0.46	0.00	1.90
	1990	0.38	0.46	0.00	2.40
	2000	0.42	0.46	0.00	2.40
	2010	0.56	0.52	0.00	2.70
Housing	1980-2010	0.3	0.04	0.23	0.42
	1980	0.24	0.28	0.00	1.10
	1990	0.28	0.29	0.00	1.20
	2000	0.32	0.34	0.00	1.40
	2010	0.42	0.35	0.00	1.50

Source: Own calculations with data from the *OCDE Social Expenditure Database*.

Table 7. Fixed effects results of the estimation of equation (1) with all control variables

Variables	Fixed Effects
Globalisation index	0.8723***
	(0.2031)
Unemployment rate	0.1869***
	(0.4369)
Age dependency ratio	-0.4724*
	(0.2484)
Total population	1.0551***
	(0.2701)
Gini	-0.0686
	(0.1648)
GDP *per capita*	-0.0790
	(0.0517)
Time dummy	0.0092
	(0.0225)
R^2	0.9451
No. Obs.	145

Source: Own calculations.

Table 8. Selection of the estimation method with the components of globalisation

Globalisation Index	Test	Test Statistic	p Value
Economic	F	F(30. 118) = 34.4641	p =3.46385e-045
	Breusch-Pagan	Qui-square(1) = 206.074	p = 9.87052e-047
	Hausman	Qui- square(3) = 31.2151	p =7.6585e-007
Social	F	F(30. 118) = 27.5283	p =3.10677e-040
	Breusch-Pagan	Qui- square(1) = 185.154	p = 3.63149e-042
	Hausman	Qui- square(3) = 35.5512	p =9.31645e-008
Political	F	F(30. 117) = 30.5214	p =2.9973e-042
	Breusch-Pagan	Qui- square(1) = 154.075	p =2.2304e-035
	Hausman	Qui- square(4) =23.5143	p =9.99302e-005

Source: Own calculations.

Table 9. Selection of the estimation method with the components of social spending

Type of Social Spending	Test	Test Statistic	p Value
Pensions	F	F(30. 118) = 28.3497	p =7.1381e-041
	Breusch-Pagan	Qui-square(1) = 203.313	p = 3.95238e-046
	Hausman	Qui- square (3) = 6.1986	p =1.0233e-10
Other social policy areas	F	F(29.105) = 27.5283	p =2.57653e-017
	Breusch-Pagan	Qui- square (1) = 90.6625	p =1.70392e-021
	Hausman	Qui- square (3) = 13.3622	p=0.0039
Housing	F	F(26.103)=13.0629	p =3.24967e-022
	Breusch-Pagan	Qui- square (1) = 113.353	p =1.80587e-026
	Hausman	Qui- square (2) =8.4962	p =0.0143
Unemployment	F	F(29.109) =19.0908	p =1.11256e-030
	Breusch-Pagan	Qui- square (1) = 68.3633	p = 1.35984e-016
	Hausman	Qui- square (4) =24.3931	p =6.66127e-005
Active labour market programmes	F	F(29.107) =21.3394	p =2.01001e-032
	Breusch-Pagan	Qui- square (1) = 120.388	p = 5.20195e-028
	Hausman	Qui- square (2) =25.0704	p =3.59771e-006
Family	F	F(30. 116) = 11.0249	p =5.24669e-022
	Breusch-Pagan	Qui- square (1) = 87.7598	p =7.3904e-021
	Hausman	Qui- square (4) =38.1282	p =1.05435e-007
Health	F	F(30. 135) = 12.5454	p =2.68646e-026
	Breusch-Pagan	Qui- square (1) = 147.976	p = 4.8016e-034
	Hausman	Qui- square (3) = 22.8905	p =1.07001e-005
Incapacity	F	F(30. 115) = 56.2094	p = 2.13235e-055
	Breusch-Pagan	Qui- square (1) = 129	p = 6.78146e-030
	Hausman	Qui- square (4) = 58.5478	p = 5.85568e-012
Survivors	F	F(26. 109) = 18.7037	p =3.30797e-029
	Breusch-Pagan	Qui- square (1) = 119.848	p =6.82992e-028
	Hausman	Qui- square (4) =38.89141	p =1.04566e-026

Source: Own calculations.

Chapter 14
Land, Debt, and Socialist Market Economy of China

Waiching Li
University of Economics, Czech Republic

ABSTRACT

Is China's development model an alternative to the Western model? The public ownership of land is the major character of the market economy of China. China's local governments take the land under their regional control as the startup asset, playing an active role in promoting China's industrialization and urbanization. One cannot understand China's model without understanding its development logic, involving land, debt, and local government. This chapter makes an in-depth observation the role of land and the financing based on land played in the cycle of capital flow that feeds China's development. Land financing is responsible for debt accumulation on the local government level, especially the period after the financial crisis of 2008. This chapter points out the paradoxical nature of China's dual-track system of land ownership and analyzes its inherent problems in the context of China's contemporary political-economic arrangement.

DOI: 10.4018/978-1-5225-4026-7.ch014

INTRODUCTION[1]

What is China's Model of economic development? Yes, the People's Republic of China has been ruled by the only party, namely Communists, since 1949. However, what kind of communist country would accumulate 20 trillion-dollar worth of debt, which is 268% of its 2016 GDP (IMF, 2017), plus a speculative real estate market? After all, during the time of China under Mao was a nation proud of having neither foreign nor domestic debt, and real estate market didn't even exist.

So is China capitalistic enough after 30 years of market-based economic transformation? Of course not, this matter could not be so simple, some market experts probably will consciously apply the term "authoritarian/state capitalism" (interchangeable) after a moment of name searching, comparing it with the democratic capitalism system in the west, with hesitation. After all, from Brussel to Washington D.C., a savvy trade negotiator will refuse to label China a "market economy'. In November 2017, the U.S. trade representative to WTO formally issued a statement denying China market economy status (Lawder, 2017).

BACKGROUND

How does China see its system? Few months ago, Xi, as the chairman of the communist party of China (CCP), delivered a report which ran for 205 minutes, at the opening session of the 19th CCP Congress on Oct 18, 2017. The report is a call for a "*new era of the great modern socialist country with Chinese characteristics*" (China Daily, 2017).

The report also confirmed a supposition, that China today no longer shies away from displaying confidence in its political system. Many in China, including Ning Jizhe, [2] a Chinese economist, and senior official, believes that China's model not only works for China, but also is inspirational for other nationals seeking for effective development.

So what exactly is the China's model? The objective of this paper is to explore its development logic, by taking an in-depth look at a critical piece of puzzle that had led to China's economic expansion of the past decades, involving the public ownership of land, debt, and the role of local government (LG) in the context of socialist market economy. And at the end, this paper points out the inherent problem lying in China's model despite its economic accomplishment, and explains the new development strategy evolved since the installment of 13th five-year plan, under the stipulation of the supply side reform.

SOCIALISM WITH CHINESE CHARACTERISTICS

"Socialism with Chinese characteristics" is not a new concept. At the 12th National Congress in 1982, the supreme party leader of that time Deng Xiao Ping put forward the phrase to signal that China was disassociating itself from Mao's repressive communism and entering the stage of economic reform and opening-up. Since the establishment of People's Republic of China, China followed the Soviet Model of command economy, but after 30 years experiment of plan and control, that model had left the majority of Chinese living in abject poverty. China ended up in the rank of the poorest nations on the earth, a rare state to China through its history.

In 1982, Deng proclaimed that China must combine the basic principles of Marxism with the concrete reality of the nation at the time, "*take our road, build socialism with Chinese characteristics*" in search of a path to modernity (Tang, 2017). Since then, even though that government report never failed to mention "socialism market economy" at the following sessions of congressional meetings, however, the central topic was always about reform and opening-up, "market economy", and GDP growth.

What Is Socialism in China?

Under the Mao's era, China was a society preoccupied with the idea of "egalitarian social order", where achieving "*social equality was a primary goal*" (Whyte, 2010). Since the economic reform in the early 80s, under Deng's slogan of "to get rich is glorious", the state no longer guaranteed "*iron rice bowl*" employment of life time[3], and today China is country with a serious social polarization between the rich and the poor. The income Gini coefficience has risen from about 0.3 in the early 1980s to more than 0.45 now. (Wildau and Mitchell, 2016)

In Xi's speech, the word "socialist" was not only restated, but he emphasized it as an essential concept to frame his governing ideology, but what does still make China today a socialist nation?

According to Marxism theory of political economy, "*Socialism is an economic system characterized by state or collective ownership of the means of production, land, and capital*" (Rosser, Mariana and Barkley Jr, 2003).

The Dual System of Land Ownership in China

Land ownership is a particularly intriguing issue in China's contemporary political economy arrangement. Based on its constitution, what fundamental to China's economic system is the public ownership of the means of production.[4] The issue of land ownership is vital not only because it is a factor endowment deciding to economic output; but also it is an issue establishing the political characteristics of the Chinese nation. Unlike the former communist countries of Eastern Europe and Russia, where land privatization has been achieved during the time of economic marketization and political liberalization, China never made the same move. Even the Communist party-led neighbor, Vietnam, also endorses land privatization.

Mr. Ba, the Deputy Director of Finance Institute at the State Council of Development Research Center, once commented that *"China has the world's most complex and unique system regarding land right."* (Ba, 2013)

In China, the urban land ownership belongs to the state and the rural land ownership goes to the village collectives. This is so-called dual system of land ownership in China.

Urban Land vs. Rural Land

After the establishment of the PRC, the rural land reform of 1950 confiscated the privately owned land and redistribution it to appeal supports from the peasants. However, *"in the same year, the 'Regulation on Urban and Urban Fringe Land Reform' stipulated that urban land was to become state's and to under the management city governments, but the rural land is in the ownership of village collective"* (Hu, 2013).

In the urban area, the Land Administrative Department of a local government (LG) holds the monopoly right to manage the use right of the land within its regional borderline. In 1988, an amendment was made to the constitution, deleting the code that had prohibited leasing of land, stipulating that *"land-use right may be transferred in accordance with the law"*.[5] Since then, the LG can release land-use right to the primary market through auction, leasing, or based on an agreement.

In the rural area, the issue is more complicated. While the village collective owns the land, the household of the village holds the use right of the plots. Each household has the residential and agricultural plots, assigned to them during the reform of rural household responsibility system in the early 1980s. Although the law proclaims that rural land belongs to the village, but the law also gives an LG the right to incorporate the rural land into a city's urban zoning plan through expropriation.

Today, the LG holds the monopoly right of superintending the land within its borderline. The farmer household makes a living through agricultural production in the plots assigned to them. The state and the rural collective are the owners of land in the legal sense. Such arrangement of separating ownership from use right, differentiating operating right from ownership right, to different entities over a same piece of land, is uniquely China.

The Socialist Market Economy with Chinese Characteristics

In 1982, Deng Xiaoping once pointed out: "*compared with the free market capitalism, the superiority of socialism is that it allows the state to concentrate resource and being focused on achieving its goal*" (Wei, 2014). Deng believed that socialism and the free market economy could coexist in one system, and wanted to harness the advantages of both to fostering growth in China. After 30 years of economic reform and growth, China's economic system has evolved. Today, China is a country that retains the major socialist characteristic - public ownership of land, but it allows the market economy to determine the essential supply and demand of goods and service. China gives its system a special label: "the Socialist Market Economy with Chinese Characteristics".

THE ROLE OF LOCAL GOVERNMENT

The Misalignment of the Resource With Development Burden on LGs

The organization Figure 1[6] shows the main organization body of China's governing system, with the central government in Beijing at the top, subordinating the administrations of the province, followed by the municipality (DiQu), and township(Xian). The administrative unit at the village level is the basic governing organ in rural China. However, since the village heads are elected, not appointed by the officials of higher-ranking, so a village office is only considered a quasi-governmental agency.

Local Government Bears Heavy Responsibilities but Shares Limited Tax Base

In 1994, China carried out the tax-sharing reform. The reform made a significant adjustment to the tax structure. After that, the revenue sharing that goes to the local governments became limited, but development burden put on LGs grew heavier under the pressing central government which set high growth target.

Since then, the central government has the exclusive right to the taxes revenue in consumption and tariffs, including custom duties, value added taxes in trade, luxury taxes, and export rebates etc. The LGs collect income tax and a portion of the sales tax from the service industry (Lam and Wingender,2015). The value-added tax, which is biggest category in China, is shared at 75% to 25% between central and local. According to a government affiliated think-tank, LiaoWang Institution,

Figure 1.
Source: The Ministry of Finance

the tax revenue collected by the central government reduced from 75% to 50% in 2015, however its spending only accounted for 14.5% of the national expenditure. The aggregated spending by LGs was up to 85.5% of the national expenditure (LiaoWang, 2016).

While constrained by the limited fiscal resource, the LGs have to fulfill many obligations and bear many responsibilities, including:

(a) urban and rural infrastructure development and maintenance, including utility facilities and community services, etc., (b) social and public services, including education, public safety, health care, social security, etc., (c) the day-to-day government operating costs, (d) local economic growth targets. (Qiao and Shah, 2006).

The misalignment of the resource to development responsibility put the enormous pressure on LG officials, since their job performance is evaluated based on regional economic performance, mainly by the GDP indicator (Li and Zhou 2005). To meet challenges, the LGs were propelled to find other means to cover the shortage of financial resource. This problem is especially real for the economically more developed coastal provinces, which export net earnings instead of receiving tax transfers from the central government.

THE DEVELOPMENT OF CHINA MODEL

China Model Is More Than the East Asia Model

As an economic late-comer of East Asia, China followed the flying geese model of East Asia to catch up. Since reforming and opening-up in the 1980s, China followed the steps that were walked by its prosperous neighboring countries. It gradually liberalized the financial sector and opened itself to the inflow of foreign capital. Taking advantage of its abundant supply of labor, China grew with labor-intensive manufacturing based on industrial relocation from the advanced economies. Along with the influx of FDI, foreign manufacturing brought technology and knowledge, created massive employment, and connected China with the overseas markets.

Although China learned many useful lessons from the East Asia Model, unlike its smaller scale neighboring countries, China has 1.3 billion people, with a geographical size as large as the United States. Over the past 35 years, China is known for its heavy reliance on investment input to drive its growth. It is true that the foreign capital was crucial for coastal area manufacturing boom, but relying on that alone was far from sufficient to meet the development needs of China.

Fix-asset investment, especially in infrastructure, has consistently been at the center of China's government-led spending spree. The Figure 2 is the trending line that shows China's fix-asset investment as the share to GDP since the early day of economic reform. Investment had contributed around one-half of China's GDP growth in the 2000s (Ahuja and Nabar, 2012). Other than the contribution from the inflow of foreign currency, the fixed-asset investment is the most prominent engine that fuels the supply of broad money base.

At the peak in June 2014, China had over 4 trillion U.S. dollars in reserve, accumulated from FDI inflow and earning from export.[7] In the meantime, the M0 supply of 2014 was 34 trillion Yuan($4.5 trillion)[8], while it was almost on par with that of the U.S., but China's M2 quantity of the same year had reached to 120 trillion Yuan ($20 trillion) when M2 of U.S. was 12 trillion. China's M2 was twice as much as the US GDP, even though China's economy size is only a half of the U.S. (Figure 3.) How was the broad money supply created in China? While the international capital has made a significant contribution, it is land played the essential role in the domestically generated capital expansion. Selling land, and a substantial amount of land as asset stocked on government-affiliated financing platform as collateral, released an enormous amount of credits through the financial system into the economy. Selling land-use right alone has contributed 30 trillion yuan ($4.54 trillion) in the past 18 years (Ye, 2016). Other land-based financing and transaction activities are especially extensive during the following years after 2008 financial crisis.

Figure 2. China's total investment, % of GDP

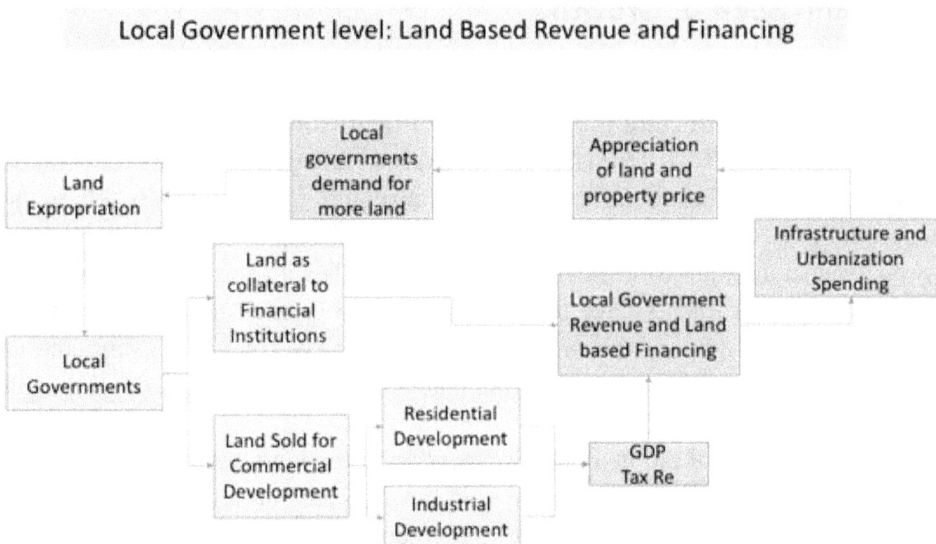

Figure 3.

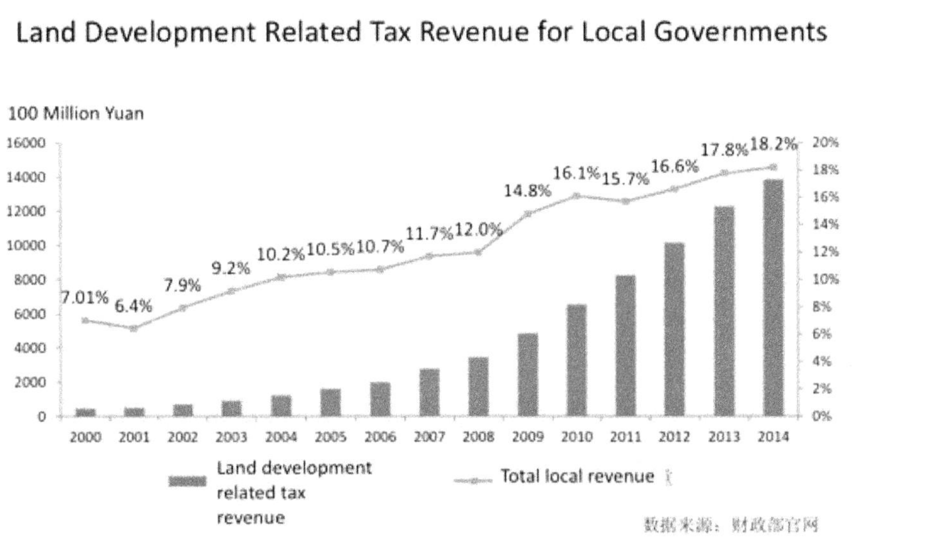

Local Governments Rely on the Land to Sow the Seed of Growth

For years, China puts great emphasis on infrastructure building, annual fixed asset investment on infrastructure in China is more than North America and Western Europe combined (Coy, 2016). They know infrastructure readiness is directly linked to productivity lift. However, funding for infrastructure is a task mainly fell on the shoulder of LGs. On the local level, the land is the most important factor which LGs rely on to generate funds to sow the seed of growth and to cover local fiscal expense.

The local governments have three approaches to gain cash flows from land: 1. selling the use-right of land to developers; 2. creative financing using land as collaterals; 3. collecting tax revenue from land and real estate related development and transactions. (Figure 2).

Due to the nature of public or state ownership of the land, the LGs not only can finance infrastructure project with the land but also has the legal convenience to relocate the people from the land. The implementation of the "Urban Real Estate Management Law" in 1995 made it clear that the revenue from selling land-use right should only be spent on urban infrastructure project and cover the cost associated with land acquisition. Later, the coverage expanded to the categories of improvement of arable land, development of agricultural, expense on land acquisition, living subsidy for land-expropriated farmers, etc.

Figure 4.
Image redrawn[9]

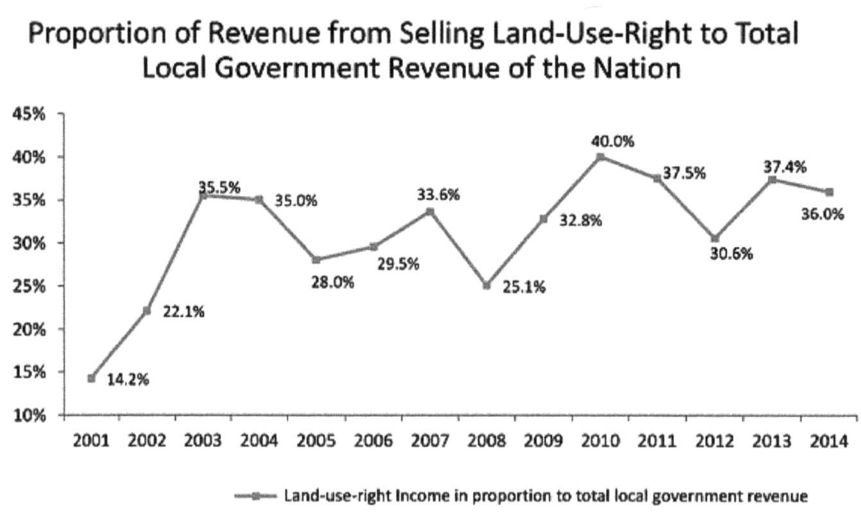

Revenue From Land is Indispensable to Local Governments

The commercialization of the land-use right was a logical step forward on the path of economic liberalization in China. In September 1987, the Municipal of Shenzhen government, for the first time since the establishment of PRC, sold the use right of a piece of state-owned urban land to an enterprise through public bidding. Since then, the LGs in China have started the mode of raising funds through land leasing. Before 1994 tax reform, 40% of such revenue must be submitted to the central government, but after that, central government allowed the LGs to retain the entire proceeding, consequentially encouraging the LGs to enjoy revenue from land leasehold.

Today, revenue from selling land-use right is indispensable to many LGs. According to the Ministry of Finance, the allotted revenue of the entire nation for the first half year of 2017 is 11.07 trillion yuan (1.8 trillion USD) (Ye, 2016). In the meantime, the revenue from selling land-use right amounted to 2.3 trillion yuan (0.35 trillion USD), equivalent to 20% of the budgeted revenue of the nation. According to data gathered by "First Financial Daily," in 18 years from 1999 to 2016, the accumulated revenue from selling land-use right had reached to 30 trillion yuan ($4.54 trillion) (Ye, 2016). Figure 5, created by E-House Real Estate Research Institute, shows that in 2014, the LGs revenue from land-use right sales accounted for 36.08% of LGs total revenue earning.

In addition to the revenue from land use-right transfer, tax collected from developing land is also significant on LGs balance sheet. Figure 6 shows that land development related tax accounted for 18.2% of the total LG revenue in 2014.[10]

Add up numbers listed in Figure 5 and 6, for the year of 2014, revenue from land accounted for 54% of total LGs revenue in 2014. Other real estate related taxes, which also is a meaningful amount, not even included. The revenue from land gradually become a crucial to local fiscal funding, even though the price of land-use right fluctuates in relating to market demand. It is reported that in 2016, proceeds from selling land-use right counted more than 50% of public spending of 169 prefecture-level cities, among them, 44 cities fiscal funding 100% depended on such revenue (21st Century Economic Report, 2017).

Debt and Local Government Financing Vehicles

In the US, the federal government is responsible for the majority of the government debt creation, which makes the government balance sheet relatively transparent to fiscal and monetary policy development body. In China, the opposite is the case, borrowing mainly happens on the local level.

Figure 5.

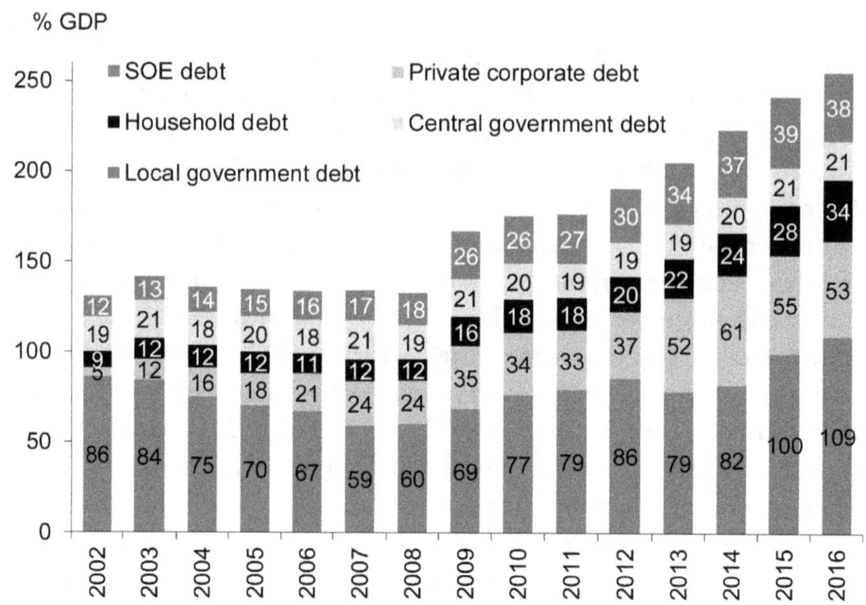

Source: CEIC, Macquarie Research, November 2017

Figure 6.

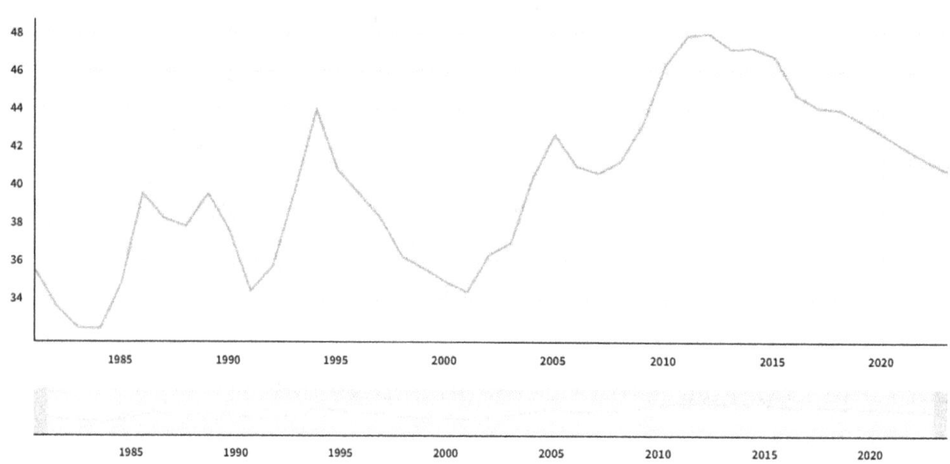

A study released by Macquarie Research in November 2017 revealed that China's debt reached to 260% of its GDP in 2016. The government debt is 59% of the GDP, of which, the LGs responsible for 38% of government debt creation, see Figure 7.

The fast piling up of the local government is a concern to many China market observers. Ironically, the Budget Act of 1995 prohibits the LGs to borrow directly from financial institution. Issuing municipal bond to the public is only a recent happening, tested the water in Shanghai in 2016.[11]

To circumvent the borrowing restriction, the LGs came up a scheme of getting the loan through the government-affiliated business entity, namely Local Government Financing Vehicles(LGFV), registered as a corporate. Land-use right is assigned to LGFV's balance sheet as an asset. Then, under the cover of corporation, the LGs get loans from the banks using land-use right as collaterals. Land financing becomes one of most popular tactics of the LGs to get credit, even from the shadow banking, creating a transparency problem for the central government to know the exact scale of local government debt.

The scale of land financing exploded after the 2008 financial crisis. In 2009, as an attempt to minimize the impact of the fall of trade volume and capital inflow, the state council of China announced a 4 trillion RMB ($586 billion) stimulus plan. The plan intended to opened the door to the biggest credit expansion in China's financial history. However, what less known is that China's central government only contributed 1 trillion yuan ($146 billion)[12] as initiation to the entire plan. After that, Beijing gave the green light to commercial banks and other financial vehicles to provide loans to LGFVs created for infrastructure projects. By the end of 2010, there are more than 10,000 LGFVs existing, an increase of over 25% over 2008, and the local debt balance expanded to more than 1.07 trillion yuan ($148 billion), the LGFVs accounted for 46.38% of that amount (liu, 2014).

Figure 7. China's debt breakdown

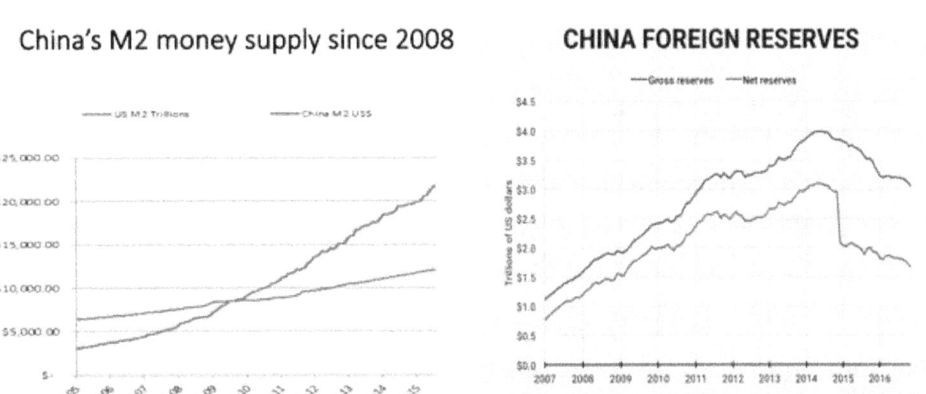

Local Government Expropriates Land at Low Cost

Over the past 30 years, more than 100 million mu (14.61 million hectares) of farmland was expropriated in China (Cao, 2015). Pressed by the expansion of urbanization, village land sitting on the edge of a city is the primary target. The compensation to farmers usually is around 10% of the revenue from selling the land-use right. While the village collective probably fetches 25%-30% of the same revenue, the majority of the 65% goes to the accounts of LGs (Hua, 2014).

To acquire the land, the LGs will strike a deal with the village head, unilaterally prescribe a one-time only compensation, leaving the farmers without much bargaining power.

Although, the local government usually has its own compensation plan to the farmer household, Beijing has set the direction to ensure minimum compensation. The payment includes the amount for the land-use right, resettlement fees, and the crops and other attachments in the field. The minimum payment usually is 6-10 times of the average output value of the land for three years. The resettlement amount calculation is based on the number of residents in a household who demanded relocation.

After the acquisition, the LG will prepare the land with basic infrastructure installment, then sell it to the highest bidder in an auction, or allocated it as an asset to LGFVs.

The Dual Track System of Pricing Land-Use Right

To push for urbanization and industrialization, the LGs intentionally set discriminative pricing policy to differentia the usage of land. The four different purposes are: land for infrastructure construction, roads, airports, etc.; land for public facilities, government buildings, parks, schools, hospitals, etc.; land for industrial base, and land for commercial and residential real estates.

Due to the state ownership attribute, the use right sold does not give a buyer the permanent tenure right of that piece of land. Under regulation, the maximum duration of the land use-right is

(i) 70 years for residence, (ii) 50 years for industrial land, (iii) 50 years for education, science and technology, culture, health and sports land; (iv) 40 years for business, tourism, entertainment (v) 50 years for integrated or other land (Li, 2007)

The use-right of industrial land usually is sold at a meager price, accompanied with varies perks and the tax breaks. It is very common that local government transfers a piece of infrastructure ready land to an enterprise at prices at or below its acquiring cost, for 50 years (Ran, 2012).

The residential and commercial land, on the opposite, only will be released to the highest bidder. The supply of such plots to the market is always under the carefully management of local officials. Study[13] has shown that the number of plots available to the market has a significant impact on China's urban housing prices, and this is especially true to the 1st and 2nd tier cities. The rise of housing prices will lead to the increase in residential land-use right prices, and vice versa the use right prices also contributed to the rise in housing prices. Today, the housing real estate of the major cities in China are on the seller side, with prices on par with that of London and New York.

The dual track system of pricing land-use right has a purpose: let housing sector to subsidize the development of industrial sector. Based on the numbers released by the Ministry of Land and Resources, for many years, the actual price charged to industrial land-use right is less than the one-tenth of the price charged to the residential land in many regions (Sun and Wang, 2017). Cheap industrial land attracts the settlement of businesses, which will not only create employment, but also eventually generate corporate income taxes and value added taxes to local governments along with the growth of GDP.

In the past 20 years, the cheap supply of industrial land and abundant supply of labor were the main driving factors to attract the inflow of FDI, combined with domestic capital and enterprises, private and SOEs alike, gradually grew China to become "the factory of the world". The cheap industrial land had helped Made-in-China products to maintain competitive price on international markets.

The Government Benefits From Value Appreciation of Land

Fostered by economic diversification and expansion, employment opportunity attracts the population moving from rural to cities, consequentially building more demand on the urban housing market. The growth of manufacturing sector also creates multiplier effect, fostering the development of other sectors, such as service in banking, restaurants, entertainment, etc. propagating further urbanization and lift up the value of city properties.

In an economy, when the land is in the private hand, the property value appreciation usually goes to the landowners, that leaves the government in a situation of acquiring land for next infrastructure project becomes more expensive. Funding for infrastructure and public service also is an issue. Investment on infrastructure either based on deficit spending, or on the funds accumulated on the past production surplus of the entire society, collected through taxation. However, tax collection could be a slow and possible costly bargain process with the taxpayers.

In China, value appreciation of land will be reflected in the price of the land use right sold to the next developer, the premium directly shared by the LGs. The local government can often recover the cost of the early infrastructure spending from the value of land appreciation, instead of collecting that from the taxation system. In China, such practice is call land based fiscal operation.

In Figure 8. We see the flow of money from selling land and land-based finance to infrastructure investment. The improved infrastructure attracts inflow of FDI and generates domestic business development, resulting in economic growth and diversification, which pushes the expansion of urbanization. Urbanization will push up the value of city properties, which allows the local government recover the spending on the previous infrastructure from another round of land-based financing, and consequentially another round of investment led economic expansion.

THE INHERENT PROBLEMS OF CHINA MODEL

The major factor differentiates the "China model" from the rest of "East Asia Model" is that China, as a socialist state, land is in public ownership. Local governments are able to employ land to finance fixed asset investment that successfully pushed forward China's industrialization and urbanization.

Figure 8. The route of capital flow in the dynamic of China's economy

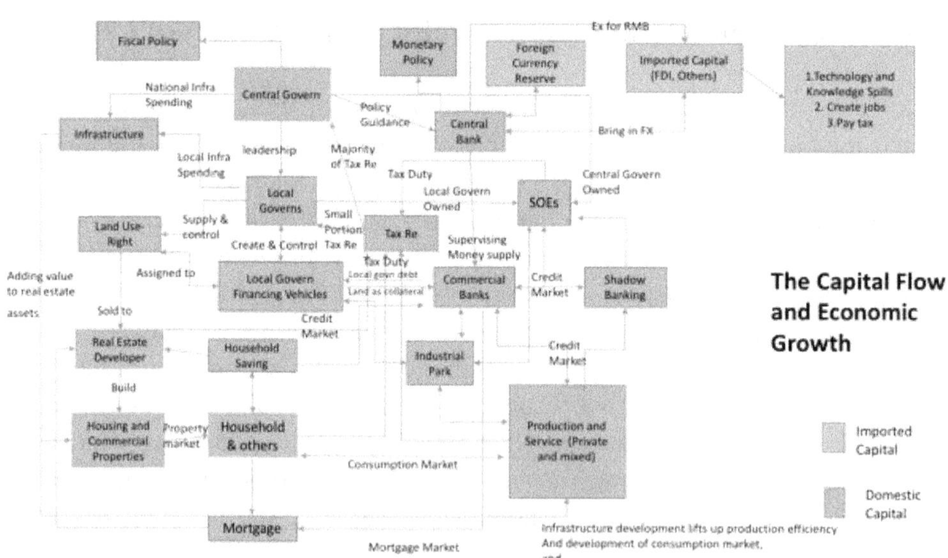

However, is the "China model" a triumph story and a profound paradigm shift? Is it ready to offer inspiration for development beyond China's borders? The development in China is a complex story full of internal contradictions and flaws.

Collective Ownership of Rural Land Deprives Farmer's Right

The expropriation of arable land does give some farming households, residing on the peripheral of an economically dynamic top-tier city, an opportunity to become well-off overnight. For many other farmers, the compensation is far from satisfying. Without a proper settlement, landless farmers end up in unemployment or become part of labor supply to manufacturing. A study conducted by the Chinese Academy of Social Sciences released in 2011, "China Urban Development Report," revealed that among the 40 million landless farmers in China, 60% of them living in difficult situation without a stable income (Caijing Report, 2011).

Sitting on the current system of collective ownership of the rural land, the village heads have the de-facto final say to the sale of a plot of commonly owned village land. The developers often use bribery to obtain the loyalty from them, causing rampage of grass root corruption. In the past two decades, the primary cause of rural conflicts was land grabbing, often resulted in a violent confrontation between farmers and polices. Collective ownership also deprives individual right. The farmer has no right to lease, transfer or mortgage their land. Their residential property is not allowed to enter the property market.

On the government level, the revenue from selling land-use right is also an issue often subject to fueled controversy. Lack of openness and effective audit from the higher-up make land related transaction a breeding ground for corruption, especially at the village level.

Cheap Industrial Land Supply Led to Wasteful Industrial Overcapacity

The low price of industrial land has created excessive supply and wasteful usage of land, encouraging enterprises to casually expand their output.

According to a report created by the Ministry of Land, in the urban areas of China, the proportion of land for industrial use is far higher when compared to the ratio in developed nations during their industrialization time. On average, industrial land in China accounted for 28.0% of a city and the east coast region reached 31.98%. For comparison, Tokyo in 1982 was 2.5%, Osaka in 1985 was 14.5%, and New York in 1988 was 7.5% (Wang, 2016).

The problem of industrial overcapacity intensified after the stimulus policy of 2009. The readily available supply of credit led to a flood of investment in the industrial sector during a short period of time. According to a reported released by the IMF in 2012, China's capacity utilization rate was only 60%. For comparison, the U.S. industrial utilization rate was 66.8%, a ratio recorded during the time of financial crisis. The steel, glass, cement and even the recently emerging photovoltaic cell sectors have idle capacity rates of more than 40% (Sun and Wang, 2017).

Excessive Industrialization Causes Environmental Damage

In retrospect, the wasteful industrial overcapacity is at the expense of China's environment, natural resource, and public health.

Industrial expansion without proper supervision caused tremendous damages. Half of China's rivers are polluted and groundwater in many areas unfit for drinking. In 2014, less than 1% of the 500 largest cities in China had met the air quality standard set by the World Health Organization. High levels of air pollution are linked to serious chronic illnesses, all costly to treat. According to the Asian Development Bank, every year the economic lost resulted from air pollution is equivalent to 1.2% of China's GDP (Lu et al., 2016).

Government Is an Enabler of Housing Bubble

Housing price in many Chinese cities has doubled or tripled in the past ten years, out of reach for many ordinary salary earners.

Liu, the former deputy director of the Development Research Center at the State Council, once said, "*The city government always pushes the house price upwards or unintentionally. There is money in land sales" (Liu, 2017).* In 2014, factoring the cost of the land-use right and the tax related to the land into the price of a property, the portion of revenue for government accounted for more than 80% of a property price. The historical average was 61.7% (Ren, 2016).

The local government has strong incentive to maintain the property price high. As long as the bubble doesn't get busted, the demand and sales price of land-use right will remain high.

In the meantime, the rural homes are prohibited from entering the property market, depriving the urban resident the opportunity to buy, and the country resident the chance to sell. An outcome of this dual track system of land ownership is an obstacle for private capital to enter the countryside, concentrating in the urban area, fostering housing bubbles in the cities.

SUSTAINABILITY OF CHINA'S MODEL?

Today, China is the second largest economy in the world and the term "China model" is often in the media spotlight. "Crossing the river by feeling the stone," Deng once famously used this phrase to describe the uncertainty cowling the nation during the early stage of reform. Probably there never was a China model. China of the past 20 years was in an evolving process based on the legacy of the socialist system, embracing the continuation of reform towards the market economy. China has traveled very far, but it doesn't mean this path is sustainable.

To change the inertia of its growth model, China announced "supply side reform" in its 13th "five years plan." The reform of the rural land ownership system is underway, although Beijing circumvents the sensitive area of land privatization, soon farmers will have both using right and management/control right of their land to their name. In future, the farmer will be allowed to use the "land management right" as collateral to finance, bringing the prospect of allowing city capital to enter the countryside. In 2013, the CCP announced that GDP is no longer the critical to government official job appraisal. Other social well-being and environmental evaluation become part of the matrix. The latest reform is to shift the gear from investment driven to consumption driven. China hopes a structural shift will enforce its growth to become smarter and cleaner, albeit at a slower rate, but innovative and environmentally friendly.

REFERENCES

央地财政事权改革路线图. (2016). [Fiscal Reform Road Map]. Retrieved from http://www.lwinst.com/cjgjzk201621/2424.htm

地方财政收入必须摆脱对房地产业的过度依赖. (2017). [Local Fiscal Revenue Must get Rid of Excessive Dependence on the Real Estate Industry]. *21st Century Economic Report*. Retrieved from http:/epaper.21jingji.com/html/2017-08/14/content_68415.htm

社科院报告指中国失地农民已达4000万-5000万. (2011). [Academy of Social Sciences Reported that the Landless Peasants in China Has Reached to 40 million -50 million]. *Caijing*. Retrieved from http://www.caijing.com.cn/2011-08-09/110804337.html

Ahuja, A., & Nabar, M. (2012). *Investment-Led Growth in China: Global Spillovers.* IMF Working Paper. Retrieved from https://www.imf.org/en/Publications/WP/Issues/2016/12/31/Investment-Led-Growth-in-China-Global-Spillovers-40086

Ba, T. S. (2013). 城乡二元分割是中国现行土地制度的核心症结 [Division of Urban and Rural is a Core Problem of China's Land system]. *China Daily*. Retrieved from http://finance.china.com.cn/roll/20131119/1983317.shtml

Cao, J. Q. (2015). 中国土地制度:农民工与工业化、城市化 [China's Land System, Farmers, and Industrialization]. *Journal of Social Construction*, (3). Retrieved from http://swtt.ecust.edu.cn/show.aspx?info_lb=11&flag=11&info_id=222

Coy, P. (2016). China Spends More on Infrastructure Than the U.S. and Europe Combined. *Bloomberg Business Week*. Retrieved from https://www.bloomberg.com/news/articles/2016-06-15/china-spends-more-on-infrastructure-than-the-u-s-and-europe-combined

Enright, M. (2017). Here's Why Incoming FDI Is Far More Important to China Than Thought. *South China Morning Post*. Retrieved from www.scmp.com/week-asia/opinion/article/2108351/heres-why-incoming-fdi-far-more-important-china-thought

He, ZhiGuo, Chen, Zuo, Liu, Chun, & Liu. (2017). 四万亿"政策背后的地方政府融资困局 [The Dilemma of 4 Trillion]. Retrieved from http://comments.caijing.com.cn/20170919/4333945.shtml

Hu, R. (2013). China's Paradoxical Reforms on Land and Real Estate Property Markets. *Journal of Global Business and Economic Review*, *8*(3), 11–21.

Hua, S. (2014). *An Analysis of the Difficulties in the Reforming Land System under New Agrarian Reforms*. Beijing: Oriental Publishing House.

Lam, W. (2015). *How Can Revenue Reforms Contribute to Inclusive and Sustainable Growth*. Retrieved from https://www.imf.org/external/pubs/ft/wp/2015/wp1566.pdf

Lawder, D. (2017). U.S. Formally Opposes China Market Economy Status at WTO. *Reuters*. Retrieved from https://www.reuters.com/article/us-usa-china-trade-wto/u-s-formally-opposes-china-market-economy-status-at-wto-idUSKBN1DU2VH

Li, H., & Zhou, L. (2005). Political Turnover and Economic Performance: "The Incentive Role of Personnel Control in China. *Journal of Public Economics*, *89*(9-10), 1743–1762. doi:10.1016/j.jpubeco.2004.06.009

Liu, S. J. (2017). 中国房价泡沫收场的N种姿势 [N Possibility of Ending China's Housing Bubble]. *Financial Time (Chinese Edition)*. Retrieved from http://www.ftchinese.com/story/001072362?page=3

Liu, X. Y. (2014, December 1). 地方政府融资平台的风险表现及相关政策变迁. *Journal of China Bond*, 12-17.

Lu, F., Wei, W., Zhang, W., & Cheng, H. (2016). *China Air 2016.* Clean Air Asia Publication. Retrieved from http:// cleanairasia.org/wp-content/uploads/2016/08/China-Air-2016-Report-Full.pdf

Qiao, B., & Shah, A. (2012). *Local government organization and finance in China.* World Bank Paper. Retrieved from http://siteresources.worldbank.org/PSGLP/Resources/1BaoYunAnwarShah.pdf

Ran, T. (2012). 中国增长模式的困境 [The dilemma of China's growth model]. *Brooking Institute*. Retrieved from https://www.brookings.edu/zh-cn/research/中国增长模式的困境

Ren, Z. P. (2016). 土地出让金和税收占房价八成 [Land Transfer Fee and Taxes Together Account for 80% of the Home Price]. *Sina.com*. Retrieved from http://finance.sina.com.cn/zl/china/2016-10-19/zl-ifxwvpar8421254.shtml

Rosser, M. V., & Barkley, J., Jr. (2003). *Comparative Economics in a Transforming World Economy*. MIT Press.

Socialism with Chinese characteristics enters new era: Xi. (2017, October 18). *China Daily.* Retrieved from http://www.chinadaily.com.cn/china/19thcpcnationalcongress/2017-10/18/content_33398070.htm

Staff, I. M. F. (2017, August 15). *China's Economic Outlook in Six Charts.* International Monetary Fund Publication. Retrieved from https://www.imf.org/en/News/Articles/2017/08/09/NA081517-China-Economic-Outlook-in-Six-Charts

Sun, Y., & Wang, X. (2017). 廉价供应的八大弊端. *Journal of Urban China*. Retrieved from http://www.urbanchina.org/n1/2017/0609/c410783-29330273.html

Tang, A. (2017). 在新的历史起点上坚持和发展中国特色社会主义的行动纲领 [To uphold and Develop the Socialist Society with Chinese Characteristics at the New Historical Starting Point]. *China Daily.* Retrieved from http://china.chinadaily.com.cn/2017-07/30/content_30297114.htm

Wang, E.D. (2016, March 30). 国土部巡视员:以土地制度创新促进供给侧结构性改革 [Inspectors of the Ministry of Land: Using Supply System Reform to Innovate Land System]. *21st Century Business Herald.*

Wei, L. (2014). 实行社会主义市场经济是我国经济体制改革的必然选择 [The Socialist Market Economy is an Inevitable Choice for the Reform of Our Economic Structure]. *Journal of China National School of Administration.* Retrieved from http://kyhz.nsa.gov.cn/xzxy_kygl/pf/xzxywz/yksInfoDetail.htm?infoid=2286

Whyte, M. K. (2010). *China's Post Socialist Inequality*. Stanford University Press.

Wildau, G., & Mitchell, T. (2016). China Income Inequality Among World's Worst. *Financial Time*. Retrieved from https://www.ft.com/content/3c521faa-baa6-11e5-a7cc-280dfe875e28

Ye, K. (2016). 18年30万亿卖地收入地方用途不透明 [The Opaque Usage of Total 30 trillion Income from Selling Land in 18 Years]. *the First Financial Daily*. Retrieved from http://finance.sina.com.cn/china/gncj/2016-09-09/doc-ifxvukhx4647035.shtml

ENDNOTES

1 This contribution is processed as an output of the research project at Public Finance in the Czech Republic and the EU registered by the Internal Grant Agency of University of Economics, Prague under the registration number F1/1/2016.

2 Ni Jizhe, currently serves as the vice chairman of the National Development and Reform Commission.

3 In China, "iron rice bowl" means lifetime employment security. Job and benefit were assigned by the state.

4 *Article 6:* The basis of the socialist economic system of the People's Republic of China is socialist public ownership of the means of production, namely, ownership by the whole people and collective ownership by the working people. The system of socialist public ownership supersedes the system of exploitation of man by man; it applies the principle of "from each according to his ability, to each according to his work".

5 It is stated on the website of Ministry of Land and Resource of the People's Republic of China. "The Provisions on Use Right of State Owned land", retrieved from http://f.mlr.gov.cn/201702/t20170206_1437008.html

6 Source: The Ministry of Finance, China

7 Data Source: Trading Economies, http://tradingeconomics.com/china/foreign-exchange-reserves

8 Date Source: Federal Reserve Bank, https://fred.stlouisfed.org/series/MYAGM0CNM189N

9 Figure 4 was redrawn based on the chart the journal article "土地财政该走向何处"? *Journal of Caijing*. Retrieved from http://yuanchuang.caijing.com.cn/2016/1117/4200498.shtml

10 This research institute is affiliated branch to a leading real estate service provider in China. E-House China (R&D Institute), 2015 "我国房地产业对地方财政收入贡献率实证研究"

11 See related announcement on the website of the Ministry of Finance: http://gks.mof.gov.cn/redianzhuanti/guozaiguanli/difangzhengfuzhaiquan/201612/t20161208_2477283.html

12 Data reported by Ifeng (November 21th, 2008). "揭开中国政府4万亿救市的神秘面纱". Retrieved from http://finance.ifeng.com/news/opinion/wylx/20081121/219334.shtml

13 http://www.umac.mo/fba/gcrec2012/83974183/12147-Zhou.pdf

Chapter 15
Effects of Foreign Capital Entry on the Macedonian Banking Industry:
Two-Edged Sword

Filip Fidanoski
University of New South Wales, Australia

Bruno S. Sergi
Harvard University, USA

Kiril Simeonovski
Ministry of Finance, Macedonia

Vladimir Naumovski
University American College Skopje, Macedonia

Igor Sazdovski
Independent Researcher, Macedonia

ABSTRACT

In this paper, the authors investigate the effects of foreign capital entry on bank performance in the Republic of Macedonia for the 2004-2012 period. They develop a theoretical model of foreign bank and foreign capital entry, followed by an empirical model in which they use the return on average assets (ROAA), the net-interest margin (NIM), and the overhead ratio as dependent variables, and the foreign capital factors combined with other control variables on the side of independent variables. The estimation results from the panel regression analysis and indicates to a positive effect the return on average assets (ROAA) and the negative implications of the net-interest margin (NIM) and the overhead ratio.

DOI: 10.4018/978-1-5225-4026-7.ch015

INTRODUCTION

Since the fall of Berlin Wall and fall of the *socialism*, financial globalisation has brought new radical changes to the financial landscape of emerging and transitional markets. The financial markets worldwide are transformed. Deregulation, privatisation and foreign bank entry are main economic movements in a number of emerging banking systems during the last decades as a response to social and economic forces/changes. Foreign banks have increased their presence and share, primarily due to liberalisation of financial marketsin these countries. However, there is still significant debate (*pro et contra*) over cost and benefits caused by financial liberalisation, and especially with increase of foreign bank participation *vis a vis* domestic banks. On the one hand, governments fear that foreign banks will engage in *cherry picking*[1](*cream de la cream*), leaving the domestic banks with bad loans in their portfolio. Moreover, the local banking market can benefit from the better technologies that foreign banks use through learning and spillover effects (Claeys and Hainz, 2006). Importantly, Lensink and Hermes (2004a) argue that at lower levels of economic development, banking markets are generally also less developed, which means that in these cases spillovers of banking techniques and practices may be more important; implementing them, however, raises costs, at least in the short term. Additionally, Hermes and Lensink (2004b) find that foreign bank presence is associated with higher costs and margins of domestic banks at low levels of financial development while it is associated with falling costs and margins of domestic banks at higher levels of financial development. In brief, the effect of foreign bank shows different results according to the different levels of economic development and random exogenous factors (Li and Kim, 2011).

Financial liberalisation around the world is often viewed as *two-edged sword*. Foreign banker once had a nasty ring to it, like *carpetbagger* or *loan shark*. In the harshest terms, foreign banks were seen as parasites that were out to drain financial capital from their hosts (Morgan and Strahan, 2003). But times and traditions (*mores*) have changed. Advocates of financial globalisation believe that foreign banks can meet a wide capital demand and introduce advanced technology[2], new financial products and financial innovations. They emphasise the enhancement of financial competition and improvement of financial performance. However, opponents of financial globalisation consider foreign banks to cause the instability of bank sectors and increase loan losses of domestic banks. In particular, the credit strategy of foreign banks has a likely adverse effect, leading to financial service market segmentation and domestic banks are forced to take risks, which may decrease operational efficiency. Although some consensus is reached, whether foreign banks induce the increase or decrease in financial performance is still under discussion, the most difficult issue on which to reach a consensus (Li and Kim, 2011).

On top of this, Havrylchyk and Jurzyk (2010) find a positive impact of foreign bank ownership on acquired banks' performance, as well as on their market power, in sense that banks become more profitable due to cost minimisation and better risk management, as well as gain market share. Generally, foreign credit to emerging markets is viewed as one means for deepening emerging capital markets and potentially reducing the severity of crises when they occur (Goldberg, 2001). Conversely, Adams-Kane, Caballero and Lim (2013) suggest that domestic monetary authorities should be aware of the potential for greater credit contraction by foreign banks, and support domestic liquidity formation during crises accordingly.

Hence, many emerging countries have witnessed significant and important changes in the structure of their financial systems. Banking sectors in transition economies of Eastern Europe and Former Soviet Union have experienced major transformations throughout the 1990s (Bonin, 2004). In the pre- and early-transition periods, state policies generally distorted resource allocation, as credit was directed toward sustaining existing industries and maintaining living standards through explicit and implicit subsidies to enterprises and households. Since the primary role of the banking system was to channel funds to the real sector, efficiency and profitability were not among the top priorities (Grigorian and Manole, 2002). However, some countries have been successful in eliminating underlying distortions and restructuring their banking sectors. In the post-communist transition, East European banking systems have undergone fundamental transformations (Fries and Taci, 2005).

Foreign bank participation has risen remarkably and strongly in Eastern Europe and especially in Macedonia. In several countries from Central and Eastern European (CEE) countries, the share of foreign capital is close to 90% (Uiboupin, 2004). Its presence in Macedonia has begun shortly after the country's independence in the early 1990s during the time when the monetary system and the banking sector were created, but followed a trend of significant increase in the past decade. A report from National Bank of the Republic of Macedonia (NBRM, 2013a) revealed that the foreign capital accounts up to 75.2% in the ownership structure of the Macedonian banks, while barely half of them are affiliated to foreign banks.

While in previous studies primarily and heavily focus was on developed countries, this study is focused on the development of banking sector in Macedonia. We suppose that foreign banks play the dominant role in the Macedonian financial system because Macedonia is one of the countries with a high foreign participation in banking sector. The objective of this single-country study is to provide an empirical evidence of foreign entry's influence on domestic and foreign bank results on the basis of the example of the Macedonian financial market. In addition, we present literature review about relationship between the presence and entry of foreign banks and bank performance in both developed and emerging markets.

The rest of this paper proceeds as follows. Section 2 briefly describes the empirical evidence and theoretical predictions over foreign bank participation. More precisely, in the Section 2 we present previous researches on the influence of foreign bank entry and the domestic economy. In Section 3 and 4 we present current state and legal framework for foreign bank penetration in Macedonian banking sector. Readers who are interested in our empirical results only, can directly go to Section 5 where we define the dependent and independent variables and present the empirical findings from our exploration. Section 6 contains concluding remarks, limitations of study and agenda for further researches. Generally speaking, this part as well as whole paper, articulate important policy implications and guidelines in light of the post-crisis period.

LITERATURE REVIEW

The opening of financial services and the structural reforms of domestic financial sector are two interwoven processes, both aimed at developing an efficient and competitive financial system to facilitate economic growth (Bayraktar and Wang, 2004). At this place, it is very important to define foreign bank entry in host countries. Therefore, we can define foreign bank entry, from an eclectic point of view, *as the process by which foreign banks execute financial activities in a domestic economy mainly by establishing a branch or a subsidiary.*

Empirically, many studies suggest that foreign bank entry could force domestic banks to reduce costs, increase efficiency, introduce advanced technology and information systems, improve financial service characteristics, improve corporate management structure and skills, accelerate entrepreneurial activity, increase the quality of human capital and know-how, and change capital and risk management to maintain the market share. Most importantly, foreign bank presence contribute to a reduced impact of the government on the domestic financial sector, which may reduce the importance of financial repression policies, such as interest rate controls, directed credit policies, etc (Hermes and Lensink, 2004a). Generally, foreign banks has been shown to exert a positive effects on whole domestic banking sector, efficiency and competition. Although these essential points, in the literature have been document mixed results. In that sense, talking about financial stability of the host country (Van Horen, 2014), foreign banks' increase of supply of loans in foreign currency may harm the financial stability if the borrowers do not hedge this currency risk (Sorsa et al., 2007). A growing body of empirical studies has primarily focused on foreign entry's impact on the profitability and efficiency of domestic banks as well as implications on net interest margin, asset productivity, overheads, non-interest income, loan losses etc. An important note is that a large foreign participation in banking has a positive impact on the development of banking in the transition economies but in certain cases also a market with a very small foreign participation can develop equally well (Uiboupin, 2004).

Foreign banking tended to be more prevalent in countries that were more open to foreign ownership of their banks, more open to banks' engaging in a wider range of financial activities and more open to international trade (Dopico and Wilcox, 2002). By entering a new local market, foreign banks are faced with different environment. Legal, geographical, cultural and institutional differences across countries increase entry costs and reduce the participation of banks in foreign countries. The entry of foreign banks depends on many factors. Location decision of foreign banks include geographical proximity, advantages derived from specific know-how, and more generally, profitability and risk diversification opportunities (Claessens et al., 2008). Group of authors (Grosse and Goldberg, 1991; Brealey and Kaplanis, 1996; Williams, 1998; Yamori, 1998) explain the bank internationalisation as way to provide financial services and expand business, that arises from the bilateral trade and FDI.

Foreign banking activity is significantly reduced between countries that have different legal origins, differences in banking regulation, and in general where the institutional setup (corruption, law enforcement, the burden regulations and the efficiency of the judiciary system) differs (Galindo, Micco, and Serra, 2003). Additionally, Van Horen and Claessens (2009) argue that foreign banks from source countries, geographical or cultural close to the host country, perform better than distant foreign banks. Also, Zhu (2012) suggests that foreign banks are more likely to be in countries where entry restrictions into the banking sector are lower and private monitoring of banks is encouraged. In addition, foreign banks are more likely to be present in countries where overall restriction on banking activities is highe. Mero and Valentinyi (2003) argue the motives for foreign bank entry, saying that whereas in developed countries banks' primarily motive is to keep existing clients, in developing countries the need for effective monitoring becomes more important, as well as good profit and growth prospects. On the other hand, developing countries open up home markets driven by the need for capital as well as expertise during privatisation or following a banking crisis. It is regarded as an important way of importing knowledge, enhancing competition and creating an efficient banking system providing services that could meet international standards.

Further, Dopico and Wilcox (2002) note that restrictions on foreign ownership of domestic banks that were in place in the late 1970s reduced the current extent of foreign banking. Foreign banking was negatively correlated with current restrictions on banks' securities, insurance and real estate activities. Also, foreign banking was found more pervasive in countries where banking was more profitable and where the domestically-owned banking sector was smaller relative to gross domestic product (GDP). More precise explanation and conclusions for the impact of domestic country environment on foreign banks' performance is presented in Bertus, Jahera and Yost (2008). They suggest that countries with greater market discipline have a lower presence of foreign banks operating in their economy. Moreover, their research indicates that capital regulatory oversight and supervisory oversight are not significantly related to foreign bank ownership. Additionally, they suggest that levels of wealth creation and inflation do not significantly explain the percentage of foreign bank ownership. In other words, average GDP growth and inflation remain insignificant even in the absence of controls for monitoring, rule of law, and government ownership of banks. In contrast, Chen and Liao (2011) show that GDP growth rate, country risk, regulatory quality and government effectiveness in host country significantly and negatively affect foreign bank profitability. Specifically, their finding indicates that foreign banks profitability is partially and negatively related to inflation rate, development level and regulatory quality in home country. Also, they provide evidence that foreign banks outperform the domestic banks.

In their paper, Bayraktar and Wang (2004) check the important macroeconomic variables, such as inflation rate, GDP growth, GDP per capita and domestic credits by banking sector. They find that as inflation increases, the net interest margin increases as well. On the other hand, as domestic credits increase, the net interest margin falls. Changes in loan loss reserves are related to changes in the macro variables. As inflation and real interest rates increase, loan loss reserves increase. But changes in the GDP growth and GDP per capita are negatively related to loan loss reserves. Thus, when the macroeconomic environment is weak, loan loss reserves increase. Furthermore, Bayraktar and Wang (2004) show that GDP per capita and GDP growth rates are statistically significant determinants of changes in the net interest margin and before tax profits. Yet, these authors do not find statistically significant evidence for positive or negative relationship between specified macroeconomic variables and changes in overhead costs.

On the other side, Zhu (2012) finds that GDP growth is negatively related to the presence of foreign banks. The negative relationship between the presence of foreign banks and inflation and real interest rates might suggest that foreign banks are less likely to be present in countries where the macroeconomic environment is less stable. In his cross country study, Zhu (2012) investigates managerial knowledge transfer from foreign to domestic banks in 12 Central Eastern European (including Macedonia) and 7 Latin American countries over the period from 1995 to 2006 by examining their managerial efficiency scores using both stochastic frontier approach (SFA) and data envelopment analysis (DEA). The main results from this research suggest that domestic banks' managerial performance is positively associated with foreign bank presence. Even during the period when competition is relatively low, domestic banks are catching up with foreign banks. These results suggest the strong possibility of knowledge spillovers in addition to competition effects and call for future direct evidence. In addition, this study shows that banks in Eastern European countries are on average more efficient than banks in Latin America.

Importantly, Althammer and Haselmann (2011) document that the technological advantage of foreign banks combined with the unstable economic environment are the key factors to explain why most CEE markets are dominated by foreign banks. One of the most extensive empirical researches, which include 319 banks from the CEE countries in 1995-2001, displayed that with the foreign entry, the average interest rate level declines as well as that foreign entry to CEE markets has reduced banks' noninterest rate income and profitability but increased overheads (Uiboupin, 2004). Similarly, Claeys and Hainz (2006) investigate foreign bank entry in Eastern European countries and show that the interest rate decreased after foreign bank entry.

Further, Claessens (1996) explains that the role of banks will nevertheless still remain limited in many transition economies, mainly because of the weak legal infrastructures, problems associated with highly leveraged financial intermediaries-such political interference, fraud and implicit guarantees-limited institutional development, much uncertainty and inside information. Likewise, Green, Murinde and Nikolov (2004) investigate the efficiency of foreign and domestic banks in Central and Eastern Europe. Using a panel regression with 273 foreign and domestic banks, they highlight that foreign banks outperform domestic banks in these economies. Also, they find little or no empirical evidence to sustain the argument that bank ownership is an important factor in reducing the banks' total costs. More significantly, these authors find evidence that, in general, banks in Central and Eastern Europe operate at a reasonable level of efficiency in terms of economies of scale and scope.

Also, Stančić, Čupić and Obradović(2014) studied 74 commercial banks from four transition economies of South East Europe in order to explore the impact of bank governance, ownership structure and other bank specific factors on bank profitability. The results presented that the average board is smaller and less independent than the average board of financial and non-financial firms in both emerging and developed economies. In the same paper, the analysis shows that foreign banks have the highest average ownership concentration ratio (largest and least independent boards), while privately held domestic banks have the lowest ownership concentration ratio (smallest boards and the highest proportion of independent directors).

Nevertheless, most studies in developing countries found that foreign-owned banks out-perform an even crowd-out domestic bank. For instance, Demirgüç-Kunt and Huizinga (1999) provide evidence that foreign banks realise higher interest margins and higher profitability than domestic banks in developing countries, while the opposite holds in industrial countries. Further, they suggest that inflation is associated with higher realised interest margins and higher profitability. According to the research conducted by Claessens, Demirgüç-Kunt and Huizinga (2001) which encompasses 7900 bank observations from 80 countries for the 1988-1995 period, we can conclude that foreign banks have higher profits than domestic banks in developing countries, but the opposite is the case for developed countries. Estimation results from this work suggest that an increased presence of foreign banks is associated with a reduction in profitability and margins for domestic banks.

Regarding the presence of foreign banks in domestic markets, Nikiel and Opiela (2002) and Havrylchyk (2006) finds that foreign banks are more cost-efficient and less profit-efficient than other banks in Poland. In addition, Fang, Hasan and Marton (2011), examines the cost and profit efficiency of banking sectors in six transition countries of South-Eastern Europe (SEE) over the period 1998–2008 and claim that foreign banks are associated with higher profit efficiency but moderately lower cost efficiency. Interestingly, Berger, Hasan and Zhou (2009) investigate the profit and cost efficiency using 256 annual observations over 1994-2003 in Chinese banking market and find that minority foreign ownership is related with significantly improved efficiency. Finally, Bonin, Hasan and Wachtel (2005b), indicate that the timing of privatisation affects bank efficiency; early-privatised banks are more efficient than later-privatised banks. Yet, the privatisation by itself is not sufficient to increase bank efficiency as government-owned banks are not appreciably less efficient than domestic private banks (Bonin, Hasan and Wachtel, 2005a).

In a comprehensive study from Turkey, Denizer (2000) investigates how foreign banks' entry affected performance based on net interest margin (NIM), overhead expenses, and return on assets (ROA). He shows that foreign bank ownership is related to all three performance measures. Specifically, foreign bank entry reduced the overhead expenses of domestic commercial banks and strengthening profits. Claessens and van Horen (2012)also agree that performance may differ, but in this case because foreign banks have more conservative portfolios and operate with less ease in some countries than domestic banks do. They engage relatively less in traditional lending businesses, especially when smaller. Moreover, inflation and real interest rates appear to be positively associated with ROA. Despite their small scale of operations, foreign banks entering the sector had a strong effect on competition measured by Herfindahl-Hirschman Index (HHI). This study shows that HHI is significant and positive which suggest that all banks benefit from market concentration. Contrary, using SFA for a sample of 2095 commercial banks in 105 countries for the years 1998-2003, Lensink, Meesters and Naaborg (2008) find that foreign ownership negatively affects bank efficiency, but in environment with good governance this negative effect is less pronounced.

Also, many studies pointed out that the number of foreign banks may not indicate their actual participation in the market. For example, in 2002, in Estonia foreign banks accounted for 57% of total number of banks but for about 99% of the banks` total assets (Uiboupin, 2004). Another aspect, related to the market participation is presented by Claessenset al. (2008). Namely, when foreign banks are less (more) important in terms of numbers, they tend to play a relatively less (more)important part in financial intermediation. This suggests that when less important in terms of numbers, foreign banks are more niche players. And conversely, when dominant in numbers, foreign banks tend to focus on large operations.

Importantly, different market structure of banking sector has different influence of bank performance. The degree of contestable entry in the financial sector, jointly with competition from other forms of financial intermediation, has been an important determinant of the performance and efficiency of financial sectors (Claessens and Klingebiel, 2001).Regarding the competition issues, Jeon, Olivero and Wu (2011) provide robust empirical evidence that an increase in foreign bank penetration enhances competition in developing countries' banking sectors. Also, they find that this positive foreign bank penetration and banking competition link is associated with a spillover effect from foreign banks to their domestic counterparts. In sum, many other studies support or present similar results and even further, highlight that banking sectors have benefited from the increased foreign bank participation, both in terms of higher efficiency and more competition (e.g. Yildirim and Philippatos, 2007[3]; Poghosyan and Poghosyan, 2010; Cho, 1990).

It is also worth mentioning that Yeyati and Micco (2007) provide evidence that increased concentration (measured by CR3 and CR5) did not weaken banking competition within Latin America, but foreign penetration appears to have led to a less competitive sector. Moreover, Beck, Demirgüç-Kunt and Maksimovic (2003) find that the effect of bank concentration on firms depends on the country's institutional and regulatory framework and on ownership nature. Cross-country experience does indicate that systems should not be "super" competitive, but should allow for adequate franchise value as the existence offuture profits will provide incentives for financial institutions to behave in a prudent manner (Claessens and Klingebiel, 2001). They also suggest that a higher level of financial development and a larger presence of foreign banks alleviate the negative impact of bank concentration.

Regarding the global financial crises, Claessens and Van Horen (2014) show that in terms of local foreign bank presence, the global banking system after the crises has not become more fragmented. Rather, the crisis has accelerated a number of structural transformations, leading to a banking system that is globally less, but regionally more integrated. Their conclusions are based on a research involving more than 5,498 banks active in 138 host countries for the period 1995-2013. The data show that after the crisis only about one-fifth as many foreign banks entered compared to the year just before the crisis, thus the overall net entry became negative. The number of domestic banks declined, as the aggregate market share of foreign banks remained at about 35 percent as of end 2013. Regarding the global bank assets, foreign banks still account for some 11 percent, only 2% less than in 2007. While banks from OECD countries reduced their foreign presence for 5% (but still represent 89% of foreign bank assets), those from emerging markets and developing countries expanded abroad, representing close to two-thirds of the new entries.

Banking crises has significant influence on bank performance and macroeconomic stability. A result from the exploration conducted by Mathieson and Roldos (2001) suggests that foreign banks increase their participation in and control of banks that earn relatively high rates of return on equity. Also, they highlight that a banking crisis and improved macroeconomic conditions are likely to lead to greater foreign participation and control. A higher rate of growth of GDP also significantly increased both the foreign participation and control. In addition, authors argue that the entry of foreign banks could have a major impact on banking system efficiency both directly because of their own operations and indirectly because they forced other banks to become more efficient if they wished to survive. Claessens, Hassib and Van Horen (2014) argue that both in tranquil and crises periods foreign banks can have a positive impact on a country's economic growth as foreign bank presence facilitates trade, above and beyond their impact on lowering the cost and increasing the quality of financial intermediation, especially for economically and institutionally underdeveloped countries.

Interestingly, using data on the foreign bank participation in over 100 developing countries during 1995-2002, Cull and Peria (2007) suggest that countries that experienced a banking crisis tended to have higher levels of foreign bank ownership than those that did not. Furthermore, they also find that GDP growth is significantly and positively related to foreign share of banking sector. Moreover, Claessens et al. (2008) document that banks from developing countries (including Macedonia) are becoming more prominent investors, especially in small developing countries and countries where income levels are low. The importance of economic state in host country, also confirm study written by Hryckiewicz and Kowalewski (2010) which assume that a multinational bank's decision to close a subsidiary in another nation is caused by problems in the home country rather than by weak performance of the subsidiary.

In their survey, Dages, Goldberg and Kinney (2000) argue that bank health, and not ownership *per se*, has been the critical element in the growth, volatility, and cyclicality of bank credit. Diversity in ownership has contributed to greater stability of credit in recent periods of crisis and financial system weakness. Fries and Taci (2005) provide evidence that privatised banks with majority foreign ownership are the most cost efficient, followed by newly established private banks, both domestic and foreign owned. Also, they argue that greater macroeconomic stability and competition in banking from foreign entry, as well as development of the supportive institutions promote cost efficiency. Surprisingly and contrary to these findings, Grigorian and Manole (2002) reveal that privatisation of banks, beyond those involving a transfer of controlling share to foreign owners, does not results in statistically significant improvements in efficiency.

Foreign bank entry has important effects on domestic firm behavior and results. Significantly, Degryse et al. (2009) provide an evidences that there is a significant convergence between foreign and domestic banks in terms of groups of borrowers they lend to, while there is no convergence in terms of maturity and currency, possibly stemming from foreign banks' refinancing possibilities. More specifically, Claessens and van Horen (2014) find a negative correlation between the presence of foreign banks and private credit to GDP. Further, using a large dataset of listed and unlisted companies in Eastern European economies, Giannetti and Ongena (2007) reveal that foreign lending stimulates growth in firm sales, assets, and use of financial debt, but that the effect is dampened for small firms. Additionally, Havrylchyk (2011) find consistent evidence that foreign bank penetration in Central and Eastern Europe has led to lower rates of firm entry and a higher rates of firm exit in opaque industries relative to transparent industries. The author contends that mode of foreign bank entry is crucial negative impact and is driven by the disappearance of domestic banks due to their acquisition by foreign investors.

All in all, given the gap in literature and results of various empirical studies, there is no clear answer about impact of foreign bank participation in domestic economy. Therefore, with this paper we contribute to the economic and finance literature for obtaining new findings and results from Macedonian banking sector as well as for clarifying of effects generate by foreign bank entry and presence in the national economy.

Current State of Foreign Capital and Entry Into the Banking System of Macedonia

From political and economic point of view, the last few years are years of challenge in the macroeconomic environment. To the real sector this means to work and survive in stagnant economic situation, to seek ways to overcome liquidity problems and find solutions in absence of the usual dynamic demand. Additionally, the banking sector remained stable due to the careful operations with the banks and well regulated monetary policy of the National Bank of Republic of Macedonia. The whole banking sector shows continuous improvement of banking service quality. Through the time, the Macedonian banking sector improves the offer of banking services and continued to promote the culture of saving. The wide range of loan services are tailored to the needs of business customers and to the environment in which they operate towards support of the current liquidity of companies and credit lines for investment.

The revitalisation of the real sector in 2013 had a positive impact on growth of assets, particularly to the growth of the deposit base of the banks. The assets of the banking system grew with an accelerated pacedue to the rapid growth of deposits, primarily taking into account the deposit demand of enterprises and deposits in denars. The *denarisation* of deposits properly reflected on the currency structure of loans. Consequently, the lending grew but at a slower pace. The slowdown stems from the corporate sector and reflects the reticence of banks to credit, which still has a view on risks in this sector. An influence had the restrained strategies of major banking groups, which are present in the Macedonian banking system through its subsidiaries.

On 30 September 2013, the bank system of Republic of Macedonia is composed by sixteen banks, eleven of them are with dominant foreign ownership. In contrast with previous quarter, the number of banks that are in dominant foreign ownership is unchanged and still have the main part in most important balance positions. The latest data show that the number of affiliations of foreign banks in the same quarter is also unchanged and their participation in the assets is insignificantly decreased, for 0.3 percentage points. The individual market share (by size of the asset) of banks in dominant foreign ownership is in range of 0.5% to 21.4%, while the total market participation in these banks is 68.3%. Market participation in banks which are in dominant ownership of stockholders from EU is 61.4% (NBRM, 2013b). If we observe the market participation (asset) in banks according to country of origin of dominant foreign stockholders it is evident the predomination of Greece and Slovenia.

The Herfindahl-Hirschman Index (HHI)is a commonly accepted measure of market concentration. Concentration in the banking system remains on high level, but mainly with downward trajectory. The level of concentration above the acceptable range according to HHI is typically applied for loans and deposits, but the value of the indicator constantly decreases. The market share of individual banks in the total bank assets also suggests high concentration in the banking system. The largest three banks accounted for two thirds of the total assets, while nine banks constitute less than 4%.

Bank profitability can be measured with multiple indicators. The source of the following indicators is IMF and they regard to the period of 2008-2012. If profitability of the banking system is measured by ROA we notice that there are not high values, which is in range from 0 to 2%. Also, we may measure the profitability using ROE. Return on equity measures a corporation's profitability by revealing how much profit a company generates with the money shareholders have invested. If the ratio is too high, it means that banks might not have enough liquidity to cover any unforseen fund requirements; if the ratio is too low, banks may not be earning as much as they could be. Most of the time, in the Macedonian banking sector, ROE shows the fluctuations in the range of -2% to 6%. LC Loan to Deposit rate speed is stable in all period (about 4%), while FX Loan to Deposit rate speed is in range of 4% to 6%. Based on the previous indicators, the profitability of Macedonian banking system is low.

The main financing source of banks comes from short-term deposits, and smaller value of funding is coming from long-term deposits, equity and reserves and loans, sub-debt and hybrid securities. The financing of banks from deposits collected from financial institutions, deposits from parent organisations and other sources is insignificant in comparison with the other sources. The LTD ratio (rhs) is in range from 0.8 to 1.1, and it is mostly affected by the main sources like short-term deposits, long-term deposits, equity and reserves and loans, debt, sub-debt and hybrid securities.

The liquidity risk of Macedonian banking system shows rising tendency. The highly liquid assets as percentage of total assets, are in range from 20 to 30%, and the highly liquid assets like a percentage of ST liabilities, are in range from 15 to 30%.

Prudential ratios are presented with the capital adequacy ratio (CAR) and non-performing loans (NPL). It is expressed as a percentage of a bank's risk weighted credit exposures. The latest data show that the capital adequacy ratio in the period od 2008-2012 is in range of 15-17%, and NPLs (percentage of total loans) is in range of 100- 120 indicating rising tendency.

Despite the large number of banks, the unfavourable structure of the banking sector reduces the competition and thus negatively affects their performance. Yet the entry of foreign capital also induces advantages such as: transfer of know-how, introduction of modern IT, modern methods of risk management and additional capital.

Legal Framework and Institutional Environment

Foreign entities are allowed to invest in domestic banks and other forms of trade companies in accordance with the corresponding laws. In a line with the Law on trade companies (Article 30, Official Gazette of the Republic of Macedonia, no. 28/04, 84/05, 71/06, 25/07, 87/08, 17/09, 23/09, 42/10, 48/10, 24/11, 166/12, 70/13, 119/13, 120/13 and 187/13), partner or shareholder can be any foreign entity. A foreign entity may acquire shares in the manner and under conditions provided for citizens of the Republic of Macedonia and legal entities registered in the trade register of the Republic of Macedonia, unless determined otherwise by the law. The participation of a foreign entity in a new-founded and established trade company is not restricted, unless otherwise determined by another law.

According to the Law on takeovers of the joint stock companies (Article 9, Official Gazette of the Republic of Macedonia, no. 69/13, 188/13), an entity or an entity together with other entities acting jointly cannot obtain more than 25% ownership with voting rights issued by certain joint stock company, without prior making a takeover bid. Takeover bid is a public offer, mandatory or voluntary, addressed to all holders of securities in the target company with an aim of acquiring control of the target company (Article 3 of the above mentioned Law). The obligation to provide a quota for takeover stops when the entity acquired at least 75% of the shares with voting rights of the targeted company (final takeover threshold).

With regard to financial and banking law, when securities are acquired by a foreign entity that is not a headquartered on the territory of Republic of Macedonia, the National Bank of Republic of Macedonia shall prescribe the manner and conditions under which non-residents operate with the securities in Republic of Macedonia (Article 16, Law on foreign exchange operations, Official Gazette of the Republic of Macedonia, no. 34/01, 49/01, 103/01, 54/02, 51/03, 81/08, 24/11, 135/11 and 188/13).

Moreover, according to the Banking Law (Article 59, Official Gazette of Republic of Macedonia, no. 67/07, 182/07, 228/07, 229/07, 149/08, 90/09, 67/10, 26/13 and 13/14) as a *lex specialis*, any entity that intends, directly or indirectly, gradually or immediately, to acquire shares from a bank and the total cumulative nominal amount equals or exceeds 5%, 10%, 20%, 33%, 50% and 75% of the total number of shares (the total number of issued shares with voting rights), regardless of whether the shares are acquired solely or together with other related parties, directly or indirectly, is obligated to apply to the Governor for obtaining prior consent. The transaction for the acquisition of shares shall be made within 180 days of receiving the approval of the Governor. When this period expires, a procedure for obtaining new consent is required.

A foreign bank can open a branch in the Republic Macedonia after prior permission from the Governor to open and operate with the branch (Article 47 of the above mentioned Law). The branch of the foreign bank operates in accordance with the laws of Republic of Macedonia. The branch of a foreign bank shall place funds in Macedonia in amount of at least 20% of the collected deposits of the residents in the country (Article 46). As well as that, it is mandatory to have at disposal funds in amount of 120 million denars (about 2 million euros) that need to be transferred to an account in the National Bank prior to receiving consent for establishing and operating new branch (Article 48).In order to strengthen the regulation, supervision and risk management of the banking sector, new comprehensive set of reform measures, developed by the Basel Committee on Banking Supervision, Basel III based on Basel I and Basel II, is accepted and kept to.

EMPIRICAL RESEARCH

Description of Variables

In the following two sections we develop an empirical model using panel data for different set of variables in order to investigate the relationship between the foreign capital entry and bank performance. The independent variables in our study can be divided into several groups including: *foreign capital factors*, *macroeconomic factors*, *sector-specific factors* and *bank-specific factors*. On the other hand, as dependent variables we use measures of bank-specific factors as proxies for *bank profitability* and *bank efficiency*. The panel data were collected for 10 banks, representing more than one half of the banking sector in Macedonia, for the period 2004-2012 with total number of 90 observations.

The *foreign capital factors* include variables that directly explain the extent of the foreign capital entry in the country's banking sector. Here we define two common types of foreign capital presence in the banking sector: (1) foreign banks share and (2) foreign capital share. At first, the foreign banks share describes the presence of foreign bank subsidiaries as measured by the share they have in the banking sector. The two mostly used variables to proxy for this type are: the *number of foreign banks ratio* and the *foreign banks share*. In our analysis we opt for the *foreign banks share ratio* as a better measure because it takes into account the size of the foreign banks present in the banking sector that the *number of foreign banks ratio* does not. The *foreign banks share* thus represents the aggregate amount of the total assets held by the foreign banks relative to the aggregate amount of the total assets held by the total number of banks. Second, the foreign capital share shows the proportion of the capital held by foreign shareholders, regardless of the fact the bank is a foreign bank subsidiary or a domestic bank dominantly owned by foreign shareholders. The variable we use for this type of foreign capital presence is the *foreign capital share*, defined as the aggregate amount of the capital owned by the foreign shareholders in all banks relative to the total amount of capital.

The *macroeconomic factors*are usually introduced to indicate country's macroeconomic development. Claessens, Demirgüç-Kunt and Huizinga (2001), Zajc (2003) and Hermes and Lensink (2003) use the *real GDP growth*, *GDP per capita* and the *inflation rate*as such indicators. Following these studies, we use the *real GDP growth* and the *inflation rate* as macroeconomic variables in our model. In addition, we also consider the *private-credit-to-GDP ratio* as a proxy for the financial development of a country (King and Levine, 1993). The group of *sector-specific factors* focuses on the banking sector as whole. Its scope is tighter than the group of *macroeconomic factors* and the variables derived from this group measure some characteristics of the banking sector. As sector-specific factor we include the *Herfindahl-Hirschman index (HHI)*, which measures the size of the banks in relation to the sector and indicates the amount of competition among them. The last group of variables included in our study has the tightest scope and comprises wide range of measures of the *bank-specific factors*. The variables belonging to this group can be typically accounting-based or market-based measures. In our analysis we employ the *loan-to-deposit ratio* which itself is an accounting-based measure. The *equity ratio*can be calculated when the total amount of bank's equity will be divided with the total amount of bank's assets, and it is used as an indicator to the level of leverage used by a bank. The second bank-specific measure is the *loan-to-deposit ratio*, computed as proportion of the total amount of loans allowed to the customers relative to the total amount of deposits collected. It is usually used as measure to assess liquidity and shows how much of the interest-bearing liabilities are transformed into interest-earning assets.

The dependent variables we use in our model are bank-specific factors measuring *bank profitability* and *bank efficiency*. Consequently, we input the *return on average assets (ROAA)* and the *net-interest margin* as proxies for the *bank performance*, and the *overhead ratio* as measure of the bank efficiency. The *return on average assets (ROAA)* can be computed when the net-income will be divided by the average assets for the current and previous year and is widely used as an indicator that implies how well the bank uses its assets to generate profit. Similarly, the *net-interest margin*, calculated as ratio between the net-interest income and the interest-earning assets, measures bank profitability and shows the ability of the bank to generate income in form of interest earned from the total amount of loans allowed to its customers. Finally, the *overhead ratio*is calculated as proportion of bank's overhead costs in relation to its total assets. Unlike the profitability ratios that measure the ability of generating profit, the *overhead ratio* indicates the efficiency of the bank to minimise its non-interest- and non-provision-bearing costs.

Empirical Model

Before developing the empirical model that will be used to examine the relationship of the foreign capital entry into the banking sector in Macedonia, we find it necessary to present a theoretical model of both the foreign capital entry and the bank performance management. First, suppose that the foreign banks share at time t_0 equals to FBS_0, whereby FBS_0 accounts to less than 1 and thus allows the entry of foreign banks to change that ratio. Then, we assume that a foreign bank enters in the banking sector at time t_1 and after this period the share of the foreign banks changes to FBS_1. The same process may continue over other periods, $t_1, t_2, \ldots, t_m$, which exerts changes in the presence of the foreign banks to $FBS_1, FBS_2, \ldots, FBS_m$, respectively, until it hypothetically ends at time t_n when the foreign banks occupy the whole banking sector and FBS_n gets value equal to 1. In one such setting, the value of foreign bank entry over one time period can be computed simply as a difference between the foreign banks share at the end and the beginning of that period or mathematically expressed as:

$$\Delta FBS_i = FBS_i - FBS_{i-1}.$$

Note that $i = 1, 2, \ldots, n$, whereby n denotes the time at which the foreign banks will hypothetically get full control of the banking sector or $FSB_n = 1$ and $\Delta FSB_n = 0$. Alternatively, when the new foreign banks do not enter in the banking sector but changes in the level of foreign capital presence still exist, the same process runs substituting the foreign banks share with the foreign capital share, i.e. FBS_i with FCS_i.

Further we define the bank's net-income at time t_0 to be π_0 and from the bank's income statements we find the following accounting identify:

$$\pi_0 = nii + nni - oc - llp,$$

where nim denotes the net-interest income, nni the net non-interest income, oc the overhead costs and llp are the loan-loss provisions set aside by the bank. The strategy of every bank at time t_0 is to increase its profitability by maximising its profit. From the accounting identify presented above, banks can achieve this goal by maximising the amounts of their net interest and net non-interest income, minimising their overhead costs and optimising the amount of loan-loss provisions kept. However, changes in the absolute amounts of these items may not lead to the right insight of the banks' abilities to increase their performance, so it is necessary to relate these amounts to the banks' size in order to examine the profitability and efficiency. That said, if we divide the both sides of the accounting identify by the total assets, ta, the aforementioned expression will convert into the following one:

$$\frac{\pi_0}{ta} = \frac{nii}{ta} + \frac{nni}{ta} - \frac{oc}{ta} - \frac{llp}{ta}.$$

By carefully analysing the transformed identify, one can easily find that the first, second and the fourth term are very close in meaning to the *return on average assets (ROAA)*, the *net-interest margin* and the *overhead ratio*, respectively. Hereof, we assume that the banks further their strategy by maximising the *return on average assets (ROAA)* and the *net-interest margin*, while minimising the *overhead ratio*. Now, suppose that the values for these three variables at time t_0 are given by $ROAA_0, NIM_0, and\ 0HEAD_0$. If we assume that the time between t_0 and t_1 is long enough, e.g. one year, then the banks that already exist will be able to react on the entry of a foreign bank. The latter may subsequently lead to changes in the performance of the existing banks and thereby the new values of the three variables after one period will be $ROAA_1, NIM_1, and\ 0HEAD_1$. Recall that we have already defined the values of the foreign bank entry and the change in foreign ownership as differences between the foreign banks share at time t_1 and t_0; thus, in order to investigate the relationship that the foreign bank entry may have on the bank performance, we have to focus on the change that the entry exerted to any of the variables compared to the state before the entry. That is, we need to calculate the changes of the performance measures from the period when the foreign bank entered and the one period before, i.e. to obtain $\Delta ROAA_i, \Delta NIM_i, and\ \Delta 0HEAD_i$, assuming that the analysed period extends from t_{i-1} until t_i. The same logic applies for the macroeconomic, sector-specific and bank-specific variables as well, so the inputs used in the model will be changes in these variables from time t_{i-1} to t_i.

Figure 1. Schematic diagram representing the effects of foreign bank entry and the other related factors on changes in performance of existing banks in the industry
Source: Own research.

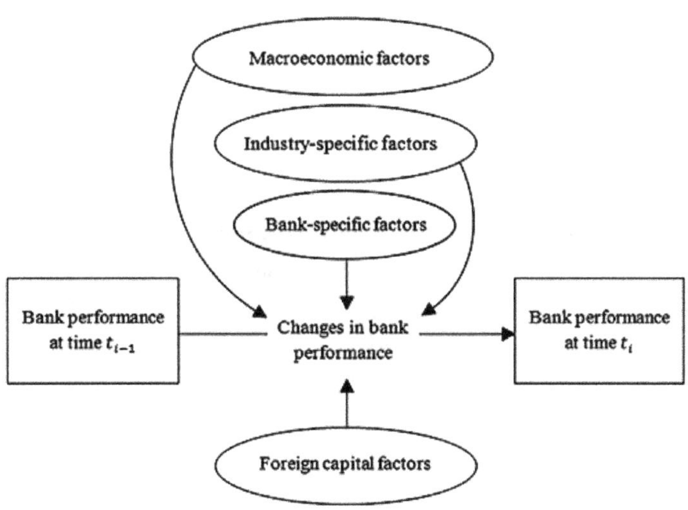

The next step after explaining the theoretical model is to develop the empirical model to study the impact of the foreign capital entry on the bank performance. Since we investigate the relationship of both the foreign bank entry and the change in foreign ownership, we develop two related models to study each of the effects separately. Both models rely on the one used by Claessens, Demirgüç-Kunt and Huizinga (2001). The first one, examining the relationship between the foreign bank entry and the bank performance could be expressed as follows:

$$\Delta BP_{it} = \alpha_0 + \beta \Delta FBS_t + \gamma \Delta FBS_t * PCRED_t + \delta \Delta HHI_t + \theta \Delta LD_{it} + \varepsilon_{it},$$

where i stands for bank, t for time, ΔBP_{it} is an abbreviation for change in a bank performance measure, α_0 is the intercept, ΔFBS_t is a change in *foreign banks share*, the term $\Delta FBS_t * PCRED_t$ represents a variable created as proxy for the financial development similar to the one developed by King and Levine (1993), ΔHHI_t is a change in the *Herfindahl-Hirschman index*, ΔLD_{it} is a change in the loan-to-deposit ratio, β, γ, δ and θ are the coefficients in the regression, and ε_{it} is the error term.Our second empirical model developed to study the relationship between the change in foreign ownership and the bank performance uses the following expression:

$$\Delta BP_{it} = \alpha_0 + \beta \Delta FCS_t + \gamma \Delta FCS_t * PCRED_t + \delta \Delta HHI_t + \theta \Delta LD_{it} + \varepsilon_{it},$$

where ΔFCS_t denotes change in the *foreign capital share*, $\Delta FCS_t * PCRED_t$ represents another definition of the variable created to proxy for the financial development, and the definition of all other terms remains the same.

To solve for the coefficients in these models, we employ a cross-sectional panel regression analysis with both the fixed-effects and the random-effects model. Then, we test the significance of the estimators from the two models using the Hausman test in order to conclude which of the two corresponds better to the analysed data. The null hypothesis of this test states that both the estimators from the fixed-effects and random-effects models are consistent but only the random-effects estimator is efficient so that the random-effects model is preferable choice; under the alternative hypothesis, only the fixed-effects estimator is consistent and thereby its model fits better.

RESULTS

The estimation results from the two models are reported in Table 1 and Table 2. It was indicated with the Hausman test that the null hypothesis cannot be rejected in all regressions, so the coefficients in each of them were estimated using the random-effects model.

From the results reported in Table 1 we find that the foreign bank entry yields different results on the relationship with bank performance using different measures. It has negative effect on the changes in return on average assets (column 1), implying that an entry of a foreign bank in the banking sector increases competiveness and thereby reduces profitability. Column 3 also reports that the foreign bank entry is usually followed with decreasing efficiency due to the increasing tendency on the changes in overhead ratio, meaning that banks pursue activities which bear non-interest and non-provision expenses aiming to strengthen their current positions in the sector. However, we find that a foreign bank entry is associated with positive changes in the net-interest margin (column 2), which indicates to a better management of the interest-earning assets. When examining the impact of financial development factor, the results imply on strong positive effect to the profitability measured by return on average assets and strong negative effect to the net-interest margin and overhead ratio. These results are consistent that banks in countries with highly developed financial systems, generally, exhibit increase in their profitability, reduction in the overhead costs and wide variety of bank services that generate non-interest revenues.

With respect to the control variables that proxy for the macroeconomic, sector-specific and bank-specific factors, we infer positive changes in the return on average assets and negative changes in the net-interest margin and the overhead ratio coming from changes in the GDP growth. We note that these findings are very similar to those implied when using the financial development factor as regressor, indicating that growth in country's economic development positively affects banks' profitability, increases their efficiency by lowering the overhead costs and cuts off the net-interest margins to redirect banks in searching for new ways of generating non-interest profits. Nevertheless, it is worth mentioning that values of the coefficients reflecting the established relationships are significantly lower, which means that changes in economic development do not produce strong influence as in the case with financial development. Changes in the inflation rate cause extremely small negative effect on the return on average assets, albeit statistically insignificant, while it exerts positive changes in the net-interest margin and the overhead costs. Our interpretation of these findings are in accordance with the notion that any growth in the inflation rate increases the nominal interest rates on loans by more percentage points than it does with the nominal interest rates on deposits, i.e. it extends the net-interest spread.

Table 1. Regression results for the effects of foreign banks share on bank performance

	(1) ΔReturn on Average Assets	(2) ΔNet-Interest Margin	(3) ΔOverhead Ratio
ΔForeign banks share	- 0.2239*** (0.0283)	0.2266** (0.0971)	- 0.1177*** (0.0327)
ΔFinancial development (FBS)	3.5778*** (0.4509)	- 6.0226*** (1.5447)	- 1.7037*** (0.5198)
ΔGDP growth	0.0637*** (0.0100)	- 0.5361*** (0.0342)	- 0.2403*** (0.0115)
ΔInflation rate	- 0.0006 (0.0100)	- 0.3667*** (0.0344)	- 0.0433*** (0.0116)
ΔHerfindahl-Hirschman index	- 0.0334 (0.0357)	- 0.6240*** (0.1222)	- 0.1810*** (0.0411)
ΔLoan-to-deposit ratio	- 0.0069** (0.0030)	- 0.0415*** (0.0103)	- 0.0163*** (0.0035)
Adj. R^2 No. of observations	-0.79 86	-0.77 86	-0.94 86

Signs *, ** and *** denote statistical significance at 10%, 5% and 1% level, respectively. Robust standard errors are reported in parentheses.

The results also show statistically insignificant negative effect of the changes in value of the Herfindahl-Hirschman index on the return on average assets, whereas there are significant negative relationship established with the overhead ratio and significant positive one with the net-interest margin. That is the more concentration within the banking sector indicated by the value of this index, the more profitable and efficient banks will be in generating profit from their interest-bearing assets as well as reducing their overhead costs.

Lastly, changes in loan-to-deposit ratio are found to cause small positive effect on the bank profitability measured by the return on average, which is opposite to the negative effect that it was found to cause on the profitability through the net-interest margin. Banks with higher loan-to-deposit ratio exhibit higher level of liquidity, which makes them more prone on generating profits from their activities. Yet, the increased amount of loans allowed logically leads to reduction of the average net-interest income that the bank will earn. The divergence between these two findings can be attributed to the differences in time until the real effect of the changes occurs. Namely, the increased liquidity usually affects the bank performance more quickly compared to the effect coming from changes in the loan structure which emerge after longer period. In addition, our conclusion may not be proper because we do not take into account the movements in the non-interest income. Regarding the effects on the overhead ratio, the estimated result demonstrates a positive relationship, meaning that banks that enlarge the amount of loans allowed bear increased overhead costs.

The results presented in Table 2, using the entry of foreign capital instead, show very similar results to those obtained from the first regression, which is mainly due to the high multicollinearity in the movements of the both variables during the analysed period. All estimated values for the coefficients in these regressions establish relationship in exactly the same direction as previously, whereas differences can be observed only in the strength of the effects or the level of statistical significance. Thus, the results reported in column 3 show positive effect of the foreign capital entry and negative one of the financial development factor, although they are both statistically insignificant. From the same column, we also infer an insignificant positive impact of changes in the loan-to-debt ratio on changes in the overhead ratio. However, the insignificant negative link between the Herfindahl-Hirschman index and the return on average assets demonstrated in the previous regression here appears to be statistically significant, indicating to reduced profitability as result of greater concentration in the sector. As an important difference to the results from the previous regressions, we also indicate on the more-than-two-times greater positive effect of the foreign capital entry on changes in the net-interest income, which implies that the presence of foreign capital in the banking sector causes even better bank management of the interest-bearing assets compared to the case of a foreign bank entry.

Table 2. Regression results for the effects of foreign capital share on bank performance

	(1) **ΔReturn on Average Assets**	(2) **ΔNet-Interest Margin**	(3) **ΔOverhead Ratio**
ΔForeign capital share	- 0.2576*** (0.0444)	-0.5717*** (0.1926)	- 0.0153 (0.0525)
ΔFinancial development (FCS)	-3.9550*** (0.6407)	- 7.8457*** (2.7786)	- 0.1443 (0.7571)
ΔGDP growth	-0.2035*** (0.0316)	- 0.7407*** (0.1369)	- 0.2523*** (0.0373)
ΔInflation rate	- 0.0052 (0.0070)	- 0.1525*** (0.0304)	- 0.0495*** (0.0083)
ΔHerfindahl-Hirschman index	- 0.4215*** (0.0763)	-0.8249** (0.3310)	- 0.1834** (0.0902)
ΔLoan-to-deposit ratio	- 0.0442*** (0.0053)	- 0.0626*** (0.0229)	- 0.0070 (0.0062)
Adj. R^2 No. of observations	-0.79 86	-0.77 86	-0.94 86

Signs *, ** and *** denote statistical significance at 10%, 5% and 1% level, respectively. Robust standard errors are reported in parentheses.

CONCLUSION

The foreign capital entry has become a common practice in developing countries, stemming from the increased financial liberalisation and the other related processes that developed after the fall of socialism. There are two common ways of increasing the foreign capital in the domestic banking sector: (1) through a foreign bank entry, and (2) through a foreign capital entry. Multiple studies have been made to examine the effects that such increases can cause on the banking sector and the macroeconomic environment in general, yielding varying results from one country to another. The authors generally agree that foreign banks entering into emerging economy can easily exploit their advantages of having better management and well-established working practices and thereby outperform the domestic banks, while the opposite holds when investigating the entry of foreign banks into the banking sector of a developed country. The increased presence of foreign bank capital has been also found to cause significant effects on bank profitability and efficiency of both the domestic and foreign banks.

Similarly to the other developing countries, the tendency of foreign capital entry has significantly increased in the banking sector of the Republic of Macedonia. The foreign capital presence in the Macedonian banking industry is subject to legal restrictions, which, however, do not prevent its increased penetration. As result of the capital entry from abroad, the whole banking sector remained stable due to the careful operations with the banks and well-regulated monetary policy of the National Bank of Republic of Macedonia, and in same time it shows continuous improvement of banking service quality. Despite the large number of banks, the unfavorable structure of the banking sector reduces the competition and thus negatively affects their performance.

The results obtained from the panel regression analysis suggest that the foreign capital presence is followed with reduction in profitability due to the more pronounced competiveness in the banking sector, but also an increase in the profit generated from the interest-bearing assets. Overhead costs are found to increase as result of the new bank entry, which mostly relies on the efforts that the existing banks put in their reactions to the foreign capital penetration. Additionally, we find that any increase in financial development will be followed by greater profitability and efficiency, while strong decrease in the revenues coming from the interest-earning assets. The latter implies that banks operating in countries with greater financial development do not rely on the revenues earned from their loans allowed, but also provide other banking services that earn them significant revenues.

Though our analysis yielded convincing results that correspond to multiple other studies, we find that it is still subject to some limitations. *First*, our conclusions are all based on the assumption that the independent variables cause effects on the bank performance after the same period of time, which does not hold in practice since significant changes in, for example, the net-interest margin appear after much longer time than the return on average assets. *Second*, the financial development measure that we use in our study may not represent it at best because there are other significant factors that are not taken into account. *Third*, we also find it disadvantageous that Macedonian banks exhibit lower level of transparency and disclosure.

REFERENCES

Adams-Kane, J., Caballero, J., & Lim, J. (2013). *Foreign bank behavior during financial crises*. Working paper, World Bank.

Althammer, W., & Haselmann, R. (2011). Explaining foreign bank entrance in emerging markets. *Journal of Comparative Economics*, *39*(4), 486–498. doi:10.1016/j.jce.2011.03.002

Annual reports and financial statements of Macedonian banks, 2004-2012.

Banking Law. Official Gazette of Republic of Macedonia, 67/07, 182/07, 228/07, 229/07, 149/08, 90/09, 67/10, 26/13 and 13/14.

Bayraktar, N., & Wang, Y. (2004). *Foreign bank entry, performance of domestic banks, and sequence of financial liberalization.* Working paper, World Bank.

Beck, T., & Brown, M. (2012). *Foreign bank ownership and household credit. Discussion paper*. European Banking Center.

Beck, T., Demirgüç-Kunt, A., & Maksimovic, V. (2003). *Bank competition, financing obstacles and access to credit*. Policy Research Working Paper, World Bank.

Berger, A. N., Hasan, I., & Zhou, M. (2009). Bank ownership and efficiency in China: What will happen in the world's largest nation? *Journal of Banking & Finance*, *33*(1), 113–130. doi:10.1016/j.jbankfin.2007.05.016

Bertus, M., Jahera, J. Jr, & Yost, K. (2008). A note on foreign bank ownership and monitoring: An international comparison. *Journal of Banking & Finance*, *32*(2), 338–345. doi:10.1016/j.jbankfin.2007.04.024

Bonin, J. P. (2004). Banking in the Balkans: The structure of banking sectors in Southeast Europe. *Economic Systems*, *28*(2), 141–153. doi:10.1016/j.ecosys.2004.03.005

Bonin, J. P., Hasan, I., & Wachtel, P. (2005a). Bank performance, efficiency and ownership in transition countries. *Journal of Banking & Finance*, *29*(1), 31–53. doi:10.1016/j.jbankfin.2004.06.015

Bonin, J. P., Hasan, I., & Wachtel, P. (2005b). Privatization matters: Bank efficiency in transition countries. *Journal of Banking & Finance*, *29*(8), 2155–2178. doi:10.1016/j.jbankfin.2005.03.012

Brealey, R. A., & Kaplanis, E. C. (1996). The determination of foreign banking location. *Journal of International Money and Finance*, *15*(4), 577–597. doi:10.1016/0261-5606(96)00022-8

Chen, S., & Liao, C. (2011). Are foreign banks more profitable than domestic banks? Home and host country effects of banking market structure, government and supervision. *Journal of Banking & Finance*, *35*(4), 819–830. doi:10.1016/j.jbankfin.2010.11.006

Cho, K. R. (1990). Foreign banking presence and banking market concentration: The case of Indonesia. *The Journal of Development Studies*, *27*(1), 98–110. doi:10.1080/00220389008422185

Claessens, S. (1996). *Banking reform in transition countries*. Working paper, World Bank.

Claessens, S., Demirgüç-Kunt, A., & Huizinga, A. (2001). How does foreign entry affect domestic banking markets? *Journal of Banking & Finance*, *25*(5), 891–911. doi:10.1016/S0378-4266(00)00102-3

Claessens, S., Hassib, O., & Van Horen, N. (2014). *How foreign banks facilitate trade in tranquil and crisis times: Finance or information?* Working paper, International Monetary Fund.

Claessens, S., & Klingebiel, D. (2001). Competition and scope of activities in financial services. *The World Bank Research Observer*, *16*(1), 19–40. doi:10.1093/wbro/16.1.19

Claessens, S., & Van Horen, N. (2012). Being a foreigner among domestic banks: Asset or liability? *Journal of Banking & Finance*, *36*(5), 1276–1290. doi:10.1016/j.jbankfin.2011.11.020

Claessens, S., & van Horen, N. (2014). Foreign banks: Trends and impact. *Journal of Money, Credit and Banking*, *46*(1), 295–326. doi:10.1111/jmcb.12092

Claessens, S., van Horen, N., Gurcanlar, T., & Mercado, J. (2008). *Foreign bank presence in developing countries 1995-2006: Data and trends*. Unpublished academic paper, World Bank.

Claeys, S., & Hainz, C. (2006). *Foreign banks in Eastern Europe: Mode of entry and effects on bank interest rates*. Discussion Paper, Governance and the Efficiency of Economic Systems, Free University of Berlin, Humboldt University of Berlin, University of Bonn, University of Mannheim and University of Munich.

Cull, R., & Peria, M. S. M. (2007). *Foreign bank participation and crises in developing countries*. Working paper, World Bank.

Dages, G. B., Goldberg, L., & Kinney, D. (2000). Foreign and domestic bank participation in emerging markets: Lessons from Mexico and Argentina. *Economic Policy Review*, *6*(3), 17–36.

Degryse, H., Havrylchyk, O., Jurzyk, E., & Kozak, S. (2009). *Foreign bank entry and credit allocation in emerging markets*. Working paper, International Monetary Fund.

Demirgüç-Kunt, A., & Huizinga, H. (1999). Determinants of commercial bank interest margins and profitability: Some international evidence. *The World Bank Economic Review*, *13*(2), 379–408. doi:10.1093/wber/13.2.379

Denizer, C. (2000). Foreign bank entry in Turkey's banking sector, 1980–1997. In S. Claessens & M. Jansen (Eds.), *The internationalization of financial services: Issues and lessons for developing countries* (pp. 389–405). Dordrecht: Kluwer Academic Press.

Dopico, L. G., & Wilcox, J. A. (2002). Openness, profit opportunities and foreign banking. *Journal of Financial Markets, Institutions, and Money*, *12*(4-5), 299–320. doi:10.1016/S1042-4431(02)00016-1

Fang, Y., Hasan, I., & Marton, K. (2011). *Bank efficiency in transition economies: Recent evidence from South-Eastern Europe*. Discussion paper, Bank of Finland Research.

Fries, S., & Taci, A. (2005). Cost efficiency of banks in transition: Evidence from 289 banks in 15 post-communist countries. *Journal of Banking & Finance*, *29*(1), 55–81. doi:10.1016/j.jbankfin.2004.06.016

Galindo, A., Micco, A., & Serra, C. (2003). *Better the devil that you know: Evidence on entry costs faced by foreign banks*. Working paper, Inter-American Development Bank.

Giannetti, M., & Ongena, S. (2007). Financial integration and firm performance: Evidence from foreign bank entry in emerging markets. *Review of Finance*, *13*(2), 181–223. doi:10.1093/rof/rfm019

Goldberg, L. S. (2001). *When is U.S. bank lending to emerging markets volatile?* Working paper, National Bureau of Economic Research.

Green, C. J., Murinde, V., & Nikolov, I. (2004). The efficiency of foreign and domestic banks in Central and Eastern Europe: Evidence on economies of scale and scope. *Journal of Emerging Market Finance*, *3*(2), 175–205. doi:10.1177/097265270400300205

Grigorian, D. A., & Manole, V. (2002). *Determinants of commercial bank performance in transition: An application of data envelopment analysis*. Working paper, International Monetary Fund.

Grosse, R., & Goldberg, L. G. (1991). Foreign bank activity in the United States: An analysis by country of origin. *Journal of Banking & Finance*, *15*(6), 1093–1112. doi:10.1016/0378-4266(91)90052-N

Havrylchyk, O. (2006). Efficiency of the Polish banking industry: Foreign versus domestic banks. *Journal of Banking & Finance*, *30*(7), 1975–1996. doi:10.1016/j.jbankfin.2005.07.009

Havrylchyk, O. (2011). *The effect of foreign bank presence on firm entry and exit in transition economies. Discussion paper*. Institute for Economies in Transition, Bank of Finland.

Hryckiewicz, A., & Kowalewski, O. (2010). *Predicting foreign bank exits? A logit and probit regression approach*. Available at SSRN: http://papers.ssrn.com/sol3/papers.cfm?abstract_id=1537129

International Monetary Fund. (2013). *Macedonia: Banking sector developments, 2008-2013. Country report*. IMF.

Jeon, B., Olivero, M., & Wu, J. (2011). Do foreign banks increase competition? Evidence from emerging Asian and Latin American banking markets. *Journal of Banking & Finance*, *35*(4), 856–875. doi:10.1016/j.jbankfin.2010.10.012

Law on foreign exchange operations. Official Gazette of the Republic of Macedonia, 34/01, 49/01, 103/01, 54/02, 51/03, 81/08, 24/11, 135/11 and 188/13.

Law on takeovers of the joint stock companies. Official Gazette of the Republic of Macedonia, 69/13, 188/13.

Law on trade companies. Official Gazette of the Republic of Macedonia, 28/04, 84/05, 71/06, 25/07, 87/08, 17/09, 23/09, 42/10, 48/10, 24/11, 166/12, 70/13, 119/13, 120/13 and 187/13.

Lensink, R., & Hermes, N. (2004a). The short-term effects of foreign bank entry on domestic bank behaviour: Does economic development matter? *Journal of Banking & Finance*, *28*(3), 553–568. doi:10.1016/S0378-4266(02)00393-X

Lensink, R., & Hermes, N. (2004b). Foreign bank presence, domestic bank performance and financial development. *Journal of Emerging Market Finance*, *3*(2), 207–229. doi:10.1177/097265270400300206

Lensink, R., Meesters, A., & Naaborg, I. (2008). Bank efficiency and foreign ownership: Do good institutions matter? *Journal of Banking & Finance*, *32*(5), 834–844. doi:10.1016/j.jbankfin.2007.06.001

Levine, R. (1996). Foreign banks, financial development and economic growth. In C. E. Barfield (Ed.), *International Financial Markets: Harmonization versus Competition*. Washington, DC: AEI Press.

Li, T., & Kim, C. (2011). *Foreign bank entry and bank efficiency: Experience for emerging economies and agenda for further research*. Working paper, The Association of Korean Economic Studies.

Mathieson, D. J., & Roldos, J. (2001). *The role of foreign banks in emerging markets*. Paper prepared for the International Monetary Fund-World Bank-Brookings Institution Conference on Financial Markets and Development, New York, NY.

Mérő, K., & Valentinyi, M. E. (2003). *The role of foreign banks in five central and Eastern European countries*. Working paper, Magyar Nemzeti Bank.

Morgan, D., & Strahan, P. (2003). *Foreign bank entry and business volatility: Evidence from U.S. states and other countries*. Working paper, National Bureau of Economic Research.

Nikiel, E. M., & Opiela, T. P. (2002). Customer type and bank efficiency in Poland: Implications for emerging market banking. *Contemporary Economic Policy*, *20*(3), 255–271. doi:10.1093/cep/20.3.255

Poghosyan, T., & Poghosyan, A. (2010). Foreign bank entry, bank efficiency and market power in Central and Eastern European countries. *Economics of Transition, 18*(3), 571–598. doi:10.1111/j.1468-0351.2009.00378.x

Report of the risks in the banking system of Republic of Macedonia. (2012). National Bank of the Republic of Macedonia (NBRM).

Report of the risks in the banking system of Republic of Macedonia. (2013b). National Bank of the Republic of Macedonia (NBRM).

Report on banking system of the Republic of Macedonia. (2013a). National Bank of the Republic of Macedonia (NBRM).

Sorsa, P., Bakker, B. B., Duenwald, C. K., Maechler, A. M., & Tiffin, A. (2007). *Vulnerabilities in emerging Southeastern Europe - How much cause for concern?* Working paper, International Monetary Fund.

Stančić, P., Čupić, M., & Obradović, V. (2014). Influence of board and ownership structure on bank profitability: Evidence from South East Europe. Economic research-. *Ekonomska Istrazivanja, 27*(1), 573–589. doi:10.1080/1331677X.2014.970450

Uiboupin, J. (2004). Implications of foreign bank entry on Central and East European banking market. *Kroon and Economy, 1*, 25–31.

Van Horen, N. (2014). Foreign banks: Access to finance and financial stability. In The social value of the financial sector: Too big to fail or just too big? (pp. 323-343). Singapore: World Scientific.

Van Horen, N., & Claessens, S. (2009). *Being a foreigner among domestic banks: Asset or liability?* Working paper, International Monetary Fund.

Williams, B. (1998). Factors affecting the performance of foreign-owned banks in Australia: A cross-sectional study. *Journal of Banking & Finance, 22*(2), 197–219. doi:10.1016/S0378-4266(97)00054-X

Yamori, N. (1998). A note on the location choice of multinational banks: The case of Japanese financial institutions. *Journal of Banking & Finance, 22*(1), 109–120. doi:10.1016/S0378-4266(97)00040-X

Yeyati, E. L., & Micco, A. (2007). Concentration and foreign penetration in Latin American banking sectors: Impact on competition and risk. *Journal of Banking & Finance, 31*(6), 1633–1647. doi:10.1016/j.jbankfin.2006.11.003

Yildirim, S., & Philippatos, G. (2007). Efficiency of banks: Recent evidence from the transition economies of Europe 1993-2000. *European Journal of Finance*, *13*(2), 123–143. doi:10.1080/13518470600763687

Zajc, P. (2003). *The effect of foreign bank entry on domestic banks in Central and Eastern Europe*. Working paper, University of Ljubljana.

Zhu, M. (2012). *The impact of foreign bank entry in emerging markets: Knowledge spillovers of competitive pressure?* Working paper, Centre for Competition Policy, University of East Anglia.

KEY TERMS AND DEFINITIONS

Banking Crisis: A situation when faith in banking institutions falls and that generates negative shocks for the economy at whole.

Competition: A rivalry between two or more financial (or non-financial) entities in the economy.

Emerging Economy: The country that possess some basic features of the emerged markets, but does not entirely meet criteria to be defined as a developed market.

Financial Liberalization: The full freedom of banks to pursue profits unhindered by strict border directives as well as the removal of restrictions on the foreign ownership of the banks.

Foreign Bank Entry: A process by which foreign banks execute financial activities in a domestic economy mainly by establishing a branch or a subsidiary.

Financial Stability: A state in which the financial system is resistant to various economic disturbances and is fit to smoothly fulfil its basic functions and roles.

Performances: A subjective measure of how well a firm can exploit the resources from its primary operations and generate revenues.

Privatisation: The purchase of outstanding shares of the state-owned company by some private investors.

Takeover: A public offer, mandatory or voluntary, addressed to all shareholders in the acquiring company with an aim of undertaking control of their operations.

ENDNOTES

1 For instance, Beck and Brown (2012) reveal that foreign banks, compared to domestic banks, are more likely to cherry-pick their retail credit customers. In addition, the same study suggests that market share of foreign banks is positively associated with the use of credit cards and mortgage loans among high-income, formally employed and better educated households.

2 Better technology efficiency of foreign banks and spillover effect can be analysed by using Malmquist index which measure efficiency changes with respect to a base year value of 1.

3 This study examines the cost and profit efficiency of banking sectors in 12 transition economies of CEE over the period 1993-2000, using the SFA and the distribution-free approach (DFA). In particular, authors suggest that degree of competition has a positive influence on cost efficiency and a negative one on profit efficiency, while market concentration is negatively linked to efficiency. Further, they show that foreign banks are found to be more cost efficient but less profit efficient relative to domestically owned private banks and state-owned banks.

Compilation of References

Abraham, A., & Ikenberry, D. L. (1994). The Individual Investor and the Weekend Effect. *Journal of Financial and Quantitative Analysis*, *29*(2), 263–277. doi:10.2307/2331225

Acharya, V. V., Drechsler, I., & Schnabl, P. (2014). A Pyrrhic victory? Bank bailouts and sovereign credit risk. *The Journal of Finance*, *69*(6), 2689–2739. doi:10.1111/jofi.12206

Adams-Kane, J., Caballero, J., & Lim, J. (2013). *Foreign bank behavior during financial crises*. Working paper, World Bank.

Adelman, Irma, & Frank. (1959, October). The dynamic properties of the Klein-Goldberger model. *Econometrica*.

Adler, G., & Duval, R. (2017). Stuck in a Rut. To revive global productivity, start by addressing the legacies of the financial crisis. Finance & Development, 54(1), 11.

Afonso, A., Arghyrou, M. G., & Kontonikas, A. (2015). *The determinants of sovereign bond yield spreads in the EMU* (Working paper). Eurosystem: European Central Bank. Retrieved from https://www.ecb.europa.eu/pub/pdf/scpwps/ecbwp1781.en.pdf

Agénor, P. R. (2003). Benefits and costs of international financial integration: Theory and facts. *World Economy*, *26*(8), 1089–1118. doi:10.1111/1467-9701.00564

Agrawal, A., & Tandon, K. (1994). Anomalies or Illusions? Evidence from Stock Markets in Eighteen Countries. *Journal of International Money and Finance*, *13*(1), 83–106. doi:10.1016/0261-5606(94)90026-4

Ahmed, S., & Zlate, A. (2013). Capital Flows to Emerging Market Economies: A Brave New World? *Journal of International Money and Finance*, *48*, 221–248. doi:10.1016/j.jimonfin.2014.05.015

Ahuja, A., & Nabar, M. (2012). *Investment-Led Growth in China: Global Spillovers*. IMF Working Paper. Retrieved from https://www.imf.org/en/Publications/WP/Issues/2016/12/31/Investment-Led-Growth-in-China-Global-Spillovers-40086

Aizenman, J., Jinjarak, Y., & Park, D. (2013). Capital flows and economic growth in the era of financial integration and crisis, 1990–2010. *Open Economies Review*, *24*(3), 371–396. doi:10.100711079-012-9247-3

Alagidede, P., & Panagiotidis, T. (2009). Calendar anomalies in the Ghana Stock Exchange. *Journal of Emerging Market Finance*, *8*(1), 1–23. doi:10.1177/097265270900800101

Albuquerque, R., Loayza, N., & Serven, L. (2005). World Market Integration through the Lens of Foreign Direct Investors. *Journal of International Economics*, *66*(2), 267–295. doi:10.1016/j.jinteco.2004.07.002

Alcidi, C., Giovannini, A., & Piedrafita, S. (2014). *Enhancing the legitimacy of EMU governance (CEPS Special Reports No. 98)*. Brussels, Belgium: Centre for European Policy Studies.

Alcidi, C., & Gros, D. (2015). EMU governance and the limits of fiscal policy coordination. In A. P. Kyriacou (Ed.), *Redesigning European Monetary Union governance in light of the Eurozone crisis* (pp. 47–56). Barcelona, Spain: CIDOB, Barcelona Centre for International Affairs.

Alesina & Perotti. (1997). Fiscal adjustments in OECD countries: Composition and macroeconomic effects. *International Monetary Fund Staff Papers*, *44*, 210–248.

Alexopoulou, I., Bunda, I., & Ferrando, A. (2010). Determinants of Government Bond Spreads in New EU Countries. *Eastern European Economics*, *48*(5), 5–37. doi:10.2753/EEE0012-8775480502

Alfaro, L., Kalemli-Ozcan, S., & Volosovych, V. (2010). *International capital allocation, sovereign borrowing, and growth.* Boston: Harvard Business School Working Paper.

Allen, A. (Ed.). (1933). *Economic Essays in Honour of Gustav Cassel*. London: Allen and Unwin.

Althammer, W., & Haselmann, R. (2011). Explaining foreign bank entrance in emerging markets. *Journal of Comparative Economics*, *39*(4), 486–498. doi:10.1016/j.jce.2011.03.002

Amaro, S. (2017). *Wealth manager warns on bond markets creating the 'biggest financial crisis of our lifetime'*. Retrieved October 12, 2017 from https://www.cnbc.com/2017/10/06/ wealth-manager-warns-on-bond-markets-creating-the-biggest-financial-crisis-of-our-life time.html

Anand, B., (2017). *Economics for Managers*. Harvard Business School, HBX CORe.

Andersen, C. L. (2017). What to do about growth. Finance & Development, 54(1), 1.

Annual reports and financial statements of Macedonian banks, 2004-2012.

APMG International. (2011). *Agile Project Management White Paper*. APMG International.

Ardagna, S. (2004). Fiscal stabilizations: When do they work and why. *European Economic Review*, *48*(5), 1047–1074.

Arellano, M., & Bond, S. (1991). Some tests of specification for panel data: Monte Carlo evidence and an application to employment equations. *The Review of Economic Studies*, *58*(2), 277–297. doi:10.2307/2297968

Ark, B. V., Stuivenwold, E., & Ypma, G. (2005). *Unit labour costs, productivity and international competitiveness*. Groningen Growth and Development Centre Research Memorandum No. GD-80.

Arnold, V. I. (2009). The theory of catastrophe. Moscow: Publishing House "URSS".

Aspachs, O., Goodhart, C., Segoviano, M., Tsomocos, D., & Zicchino, L. (2006). Searching for a Metric for Financial Stability. *LSE Financial Markets Group Special Paper Series.*, *167*, 1–38.

Aßmann, Ch., & Boysen-Hogrefe, J. (2009). *Determinants of government bond spreads in the Euro area – in good times as in bad* (Kiel Working Paper vol. 1548). Retrieved from https://www.files.ethz.ch/isn/108449/kwp-1548.pdf

Atanasijevic, J. & Cupic, V. (2012). *Finansijska integracija, privredni rast I drugi izazovi.* Makroekonomske analize i trendovi - MAT. Br.209

Ayala, D., Nedeljkovic, M., & Saborowski, S. (2015). *What Slice of the Pie? The Corporate Bond Market Boom in Emerging Economies. Working Paper 15/148.* Washington, DC: International Monetary Fund. Retrieved from https://www.imf.org/external/pubs/ft/wp/2015/wp15148.pdf

Ba, T. S. (2013). 城乡二元分割是中国现行土地制度的核心症结 [Division of Urban and Rural is a Core Problem of China's Land system]. *China Daily.* Retrieved from http://finance.china.com.cn/roll/20131119/1983317.shtml

Baek, I. (2006). Portfolio Investment Flows to Asia and Latin America: Pull, Push or Market Sentiment? *Journal of Asian Economics*, *17*(2), 363–373. doi:10.1016/j.asieco.2006.02.007

Bai, J. (1997). Estimation of a Change Point in Multiple Regression Models. *The Review of Economics and Statistics*, *79*(4), 551–563. doi:10.1162/003465397557132

Bai, J., & Perron, P. (1998). Estimating and Testing Linear Models with Multiple Structural Changes. *Econometrica*, *66*(1), 47–78. doi:10.2307/2998540

Baker, A. (2008). *Public Opinion and the Compensation Hypothesis* Paper presented at the International Political Economy Society, University of Pennsylvania, Philadelphia, PA.

Baker, P. (2017). *Trump Abandons Trans-Pacific Partnership, Obama's Signature Trade Deal.* Retrieved June 7, 2017 from https://www.nytimes.com/2017/01/23/us/politics/tpp- trump-trade-nafta.html

Baldwin, R., & Giavazzi, F. (Eds.). (2015). *The Eurozone crisis. A consensus view of the causes and a few possible remedies.* Retrieved from www.VoxEU.org

Balling, M., Lierman, F., & Mullineux, A. (2003). *Technology and Finance: Challenges for Financial Markets, Business Strategies and Policy Makers.* Routledge.

Banking Law. Official Gazette of Republic of Macedonia, 67/07, 182/07, 228/07, 229/07, 149/08, 90/09, 67/10, 26/13 and 13/14.

BankTrack Manual. (n.d.). *The do's and don'ts of sustainable banking.* Academic Press.

Barro, R. J., & Ursúa, J. F. (2012). Rare macroeconomic disasters. *Annual Review of Economics*, *4*(1), 83–109. doi:10.1146/annurev-economics-080511-110932

Barro, R. J., & Ursúa, J. F. (2017). Stock-market crashes and depressions. *Research in Economics*, *71*(3), 384–398. doi:10.1016/j.rie.2017.04.001

Bayoumi, T., & Eichengreen, B. (1993). Shocking aspects of European monetary unification. In F. Torres & F. Giavazzi (Eds.), *Adjustment and growth in the European Monetary Union* (pp. 193–229). New York, NY: Cambridge University Press. doi:10.1017/CBO9780511599231.014

Bayraktar, N., & Wang, Y. (2004). *Foreign bank entry, performance of domestic banks, and sequence of financial liberalization.* Working paper, World Bank.

Beck, T., Demirgüç-Kunt, A., & Maksimovic, V. (2003). *Bank competition, financing obstacles and access to credit.* Policy Research Working Paper, World Bank.

Beck, T., & Brown, M. (2012). *Foreign bank ownership and household credit. Discussion paper.* European Banking Center.

Bekaert, G., Harvey, C. R., Lundblad, C. T., & Siegel, S. (2017). *Economic and Financial Integration in Europe.* Academic Press.

Bekaert, G., Harvey, C. R., & Lundblad, C. (2005). Does financial liberalization spur growth? *Journal of Financial Economics, 77*(1), 3–55. doi:10.1016/j.jfineco.2004.05.007

Bekaert, G., Harvey, C. R., & Lundblad, C. (2011). Financial openness and productivity. *World Development, 39*(1), 1–19. doi:10.1016/j.worlddev.2010.06.016

Berger, A. N., Hasan, I., & Zhou, M. (2009). Bank ownership and efficiency in China: What will happen in the world's largest nation? *Journal of Banking & Finance, 33*(1), 113–130. doi:10.1016/j.jbankfin.2007.05.016

Bergh, A., & Nilsson, T. (2014). Is globalization reducing absolute poverty? *World Development, 62*, 42–61. doi:10.1016/j.worlddev.2014.04.007

Berglöf, E., Korniyenko, Y., Zettelmeyer, J., & Plekhanov, A. (2009). Understanding the crisis in emerging. *Europe.*

Bernoth, K., von Hagen, J., & Schuknecht, L. (2012). Sovereign Risk Premiums in the European Government Bond Market. *Journal of International Money and Finance, 31*(5), 975–995. doi:10.1016/j.jimonfin.2011.12.006

Bertus, M., Jahera, J. Jr, & Yost, K. (2008). A note on foreign bank ownership and monitoring: An international comparison. *Journal of Banking & Finance, 32*(2), 338–345. doi:10.1016/j.jbankfin.2007.04.024

Bhargava, V., & Brooks, R. (2001). Hedging currency risk using futures. In Research in Finance. Emerald Group Publishing Limited.

Bleaney, M. F. (1996). Macroeconomic stability, investment and growth in developing countries. *Journal of Development Economics, 48*(2), 461–477. doi:10.1016/0304-3878(95)00049-6

Bloom, D. E., & Canning, D. (2000). The Health and Wealth of Nations. *Science, 287*(5456), 1207–1209. doi:10.1126cience.287.5456.1207 PMID:10712155

Bogdanova, B., & Ivanov, I. (2014). Adaptive and relative efficiency of stock markets from Southeastern Europe: A wavelet approach. *Applied Financial Economics*, *24*(10), 705–722. doi:10.1080/09603107.2014.899669

Bollerslev, T. (1986). Generalized Autoregressive Conditional Heteroscedasticity. *Journal of Econometrics*, *36*(3), 307–327. doi:10.1016/0304-4076(86)90063-1

Bonetto, F., Redžepagić, S., & Tykhonenko, A. (2009). *Balkan countries: catching up and their integration in the European financial system.* Academic Press.

Bonin, J. P. (2004). Banking in the Balkans: The structure of banking sectors in Southeast Europe. *Economic Systems*, *28*(2), 141–153. doi:10.1016/j.ecosys.2004.03.005

Bonin, J. P., Hasan, I., & Wachtel, P. (2005a). Bank performance, efficiency and ownership in transition countries. *Journal of Banking & Finance*, *29*(1), 31–53. doi:10.1016/j.jbankfin.2004.06.015

Bonin, J. P., Hasan, I., & Wachtel, P. (2005b). Privatization matters: Bank efficiency in transition countries. *Journal of Banking & Finance*, *29*(8), 2155–2178. doi:10.1016/j.jbankfin.2005.03.012

Bordon, I., & Schmitz, B. (2015). *Financial Stability as a Precondition for the Financing of Sustainable Development in Emerging and Developing Countries. Briefing Paper no 23.* German Development Institute.

Boškoska, M. (2007). *Integracija evropskih finansijskih tržišta.* Conference paper.

Brealey, R. A., & Kaplanis, E. C. (1996). The determination of foreign banking location. *Journal of International Money and Finance*, *15*(4), 577–597. doi:10.1016/0261-5606(96)00022-8

Broner, F., Didier, T., Erce, A., & Schmukler, S. L. (2013). Gross capital flows: Dynamics and crises. *Journal of Monetary Economics*, *60*(1), 113–133. doi:10.1016/j.jmoneco.2012.12.004

Broner, F., Erce, A., Martin, A., & Ventura, J. (2014). Sovereign debt markets in turbulent times: Creditor discrimination and crowding-out effects. *Journal of Monetary Economics*, *61*, 114–142. doi:10.1016/j.jmoneco.2013.11.009

Brooks, C., & Persand, G. (2001). Seasonality in Southeast Asian stock markets: Some new evidence on day-of-the-week effects. *Applied Economics Letters*, *8*(3), 155–158. doi:10.1080/13504850150504504

Brown, G. W. (2001). Managing Foreign Exchange Risk with Derivatives. *Journal of Financial Economics*, *60*(2-3), 401–448. doi:10.1016/S0304-405X(01)00049-6

Bruno, V., & Shin, H. S. (2014). *Cross-Border Banking and Global Liquidity. Working Paper 19038.* Cambridge, MA: National Bureau of Economic Research. Retrieved from http://www.nber.org/papers/w19038.pdf

Burnside, C., Eichenbaum, M., & Rebelo, S. (2007). *Currency crisis models.* Retrieved from http://www.kellogg.northwestern.edu/faculty/rebelo/htm/currency%20crisis%20models%20Ed.pdf

Cao, J. Q. (2015). 中国土地制度:农民工与工业化、城市化 [China's Land System, Farmers, and Industrialization]. *Journal of Social Construction*, (3). Retrieved from http://swtt.ecust.edu.cn/show.aspx?info_lb=11&flag=11&info_id=222

Cecchetti, S. G., Cumby, R. E., & Figlewski, S. (1998). Estimation of the optimal future hedge. *The Review of Economics and Statistics*, *7*, 624–635.

Chakraborty, I., Hai, R., Holter, H. A., & Stepanchuk, S. (2016). *The Real Effects of Financial (Dis) integration: A Spatial Equilibrium Analysis of Europe*. Academic Press.

Chang, M. (2016). The (ever) incomplete story of economic and monetary union. *Journal of Contemporary Economic Research*, *12*(1), 487–501.

Chen, Y.-F., Görg, H., Görlich, D., Molana, H., Montagna, C., & Temouri, Y. (2014). *Globalisation and the Future of the Welfare State.* IZA Policy Paper No. 81.

Chen, H., & Singal, V. (2003). Role of speculative short sales in price formation: The case of the weekend effect. *The Journal of Finance*, *58*(2), 685–705. doi:10.1111/1540-6261.00541

Chen, J., & Quang, T. (2014). The impact of international financial integration on economic growth: New evidence on threshold effects. *Economic Modelling*, *42*, 475–489. doi:10.1016/j.econmod.2014.06.011

Chen, S., & Liao, C. (2011). Are foreign banks more profitable than domestic banks? Home and host country effects of banking market structure, government and supervision. *Journal of Banking & Finance*, *35*(4), 819–830. doi:10.1016/j.jbankfin.2010.11.006

Cho, K. R. (1990). Foreign banking presence and banking market concentration: The case of Indonesia. *The Journal of Development Studies*, *27*(1), 98–110. doi:10.1080/00220389008422185

Chow, V., & Denning, K. (1993). A simple multiple variance ratio test. *Journal of Econometrics*, *58*(3), 385–401. doi:10.1016/0304-4076(93)90051-6

Claessens, S. (1996). *Banking reform in transition countries*. Working paper, World Bank.

Claessens, S., & Kose, M. M. A. (2013). Financial crises explanations, types, and implications (No. 13-28). International Monetary Fund.

Claessens, S., Hassib, O., & Van Horen, N. (2014). *How foreign banks facilitate trade in tranquil and crisis times: Finance or information?* Working paper, International Monetary Fund.

Claessens, S., van Horen, N., Gurcanlar, T., & Mercado, J. (2008). *Foreign bank presence in developing countries 1995-2006: Data and trends*. Unpublished academic paper, World Bank.

Claessens, S., Demirgüç-Kunt, A., & Huizinga, A. (2001). How does foreign entry affect domestic banking markets? *Journal of Banking & Finance*, *25*(5), 891–911. doi:10.1016/S0378-4266(00)00102-3

Claessens, S., & Klingebiel, D. (2001). Competition and scope of activities in financial services. *The World Bank Research Observer*, *16*(1), 19–40. doi:10.1093/wbro/16.1.19

Claessens, S., & Van Horen, N. (2012). Being a foreigner among domestic banks: Asset or liability? *Journal of Banking & Finance*, *36*(5), 1276–1290. doi:10.1016/j.jbankfin.2011.11.020

Claessens, S., & van Horen, N. (2014). Foreign banks: Trends and impact. *Journal of Money, Credit and Banking*, *46*(1), 295–326. doi:10.1111/jmcb.12092

Claeys, S., & Hainz, C. (2006). *Foreign banks in Eastern Europe: Mode of entry and effects on bank interest rates.* Discussion Paper, Governance and the Efficiency of Economic Systems, Free University of Berlin, Humboldt University of Berlin, University of Bonn, University of Mannheim and University of Munich.

Codogno, L., Favero, C., & Missale, A. (2003). Yield spreads on EMU government bonds. *Economic Policy*, *18*(37), 503–532. doi:10.1111/1468-0327.00114_1

Collyns, C., Huefner, F., Koepke, R., Bykere, A., Farnham, S., & Shaw, L. (n.d.).*Capital Flows to Emerging Markets.* Institute of International Finance Working Paper. Retrieved from file:///C:/Users/AC4/Downloads/cf_0515.pdf

Commission of the European Communities. (1977, April). *The MacDougall Report — Volume I. Report of the study group on the role of public finance in European integration. General report.* Brussels, Belgium: European Union. Retrieved from https://www.cvce.eu/obj/the_macdougall_report_volume_i_brussels_april_1977-en-c475e949-ed28-490b-81ae-a33ce9860d09.html

Constâncio, V. (2014). The European crisis and the role of the financial system. *Journal of Macroeconomics*, *39*, 250–259. doi:10.1016/j.jmacro.2013.08.009

Coors, C. (2011). *Credit Rating Agencies - Too Big Too Fail?* Thomson Reuters.

Costantini, M., Fragetta, M., & Melina, G. (2014). Determinants of sovereign bond yield spreads in the EMU: An optimal currency area perspective. *European Economic Review*, *70*, 337–349. doi:10.1016/j.euroecorev.2014.06.004

Coy, P. (2016). China Spends More on Infrastructure Than the U.S. and Europe Combined. *Bloomberg Business Week.* Retrieved from https://www.bloomberg.com/news/articles/2016-06-15/china-spends-more-on-infrastructure-than-the-u-s-and-europe-combined

Crockett, A. (1997). *Why is Financial Stability a Goal of Public Policy?* Retrieved from https://www.kansascityfed.org/publicat/sympos/1997/pdf/s97crock.pdf

Cull, R., & Peria, M. S. M. (2007). *Foreign bank participation and crises in developing countries.* Working paper, World Bank.

Cumby, R., Figlewski, S., & Hasbrouk, J. (1993). Forecasting Volatility and Correlations with EGARCH Models. *Journal of Derivatives*, *1*(2), 51–63. doi:10.3905/jod.1993.407877

Cummins, F. (2010). Building the Agile Enterprise-with SOA, business process model and MBM. Morgan Kaufmann Publications.

Daellenbach, H., McNickle, D., & Dye, Sh. (2012). *Management Science. Decision-making through systems thinking* (2nd ed.). Plagrave Macmillian.

Dages, G. B., Goldberg, L., & Kinney, D. (2000). Foreign and domestic bank participation in emerging markets: Lessons from Mexico and Argentina. *Economic Policy Review*, *6*(3), 17–36.

Damijan, J. P., Rojec, M., Majcen, B., & Knell, M. (2013). Impact of firm heterogeneity on direct and spillover effects of FDI: Micro-evidence from ten transition countries. *Journal of Comparative Economics*, *41*(3), 895–922. doi:10.1016/j.jce.2012.12.001

Darıcı, B. (2012). Finansal İstikrar ve Finansal İstikrara Yönelik Kamusal Sorumluluk Çerçevesinde Para Politikası: Türkiye Analizi. *Bankacılar*, 34-66.

Dark, J. (2005). A Critique of Minimum Variance Hedging. *Accounting Research Journal*, *18*(1), 40–49. doi:10.1108/10309610580000674

De Grauwe, P. (2010, May). *Fighting the wrong enemy*. VoxEU.org. Retrieved from http://voxeu.org/article/europe-s-private-versus-public-debt-problem-fighting-wrong-enemy

De Grauwe, P. (1992). *The economics of monetary integration*. Oxford, UK: Oxford University Press.

De Grauwe, P. (2013). The political economy of the euro. *Annual Review of Political Science*, *16*(1), 153–170. doi:10.1146/annurev-polisci-060911-085923

de Guevara Radoselovics, J. F., & Villarroya, J. M. (2010). *Financial Crisis, Financial Integration and Economic Growth*. Fundacion BBVA.

De Haan, J., Eijffinger, S., & Waller, S. (2005). *The European Central Bank: Credibility, transparency, and centralization*. Boston, MA: The MIT Press.

De Vita, G., & Khine, S. K. (2008). Determinants of Capital Flows to Developing Countries: A Structural VAR Analysis. *Journal of Economic Studies (Glasgow, Scotland)*, *35*(4), 304–322. doi:10.1108/01443580810895608

De Witte, B. (2012). Treaty games - Law as instrument and as constraint in the Euro crisis policy. In F. Allen, E. Carletti, & S. Simonelli (Eds.), *Governance for the Eurozone: integration or disintegration?* Philadelphia, PA: FIC Press - Wharton Financial Institutions Center.

Degryse, H., Havrylchyk, O., Jurzyk, E., & Kozak, S. (2009). *Foreign bank entry and credit allocation in emerging markets*. Working paper, International Monetary Fund.

Delice, G. (2007). *Uluslararası Finansal Kuruluşlar ve Finansal İstikrar Sorunu. 1. Basım.* Ankara: Nobel Yayın Dağıtım.

Demircan, E. S. (2003). *Vergilendirmenin Ekonomik Büyüme ve Kalkınmaya Etkisi, Erciyes Üniversitesi İktisadi ve İdari Bilimler Fakültesi Dergisi, Sayı.21*. Temmuz-Aralık.

Demirgüç-Kunt, A., & Huizinga, H. (1999). Determinants of commercial bank interest margins and profitability: Some international evidence. *The World Bank Economic Review*, *13*(2), 379–408. doi:10.1093/wber/13.2.379

Denizer, C. (2000). Foreign bank entry in Turkey's banking sector, 1980–1997. In S. Claessens & M. Jansen (Eds.), *The internationalization of financial services: Issues and lessons for developing countries* (pp. 389–405). Dordrecht: Kluwer Academic Press.

Doğan, S., & Tunalı, Ç. B. (2011). Küreselleşme Sürecinde Finansal İstikrar-Para Politikası İlişkisi: Türkiye için Bir Değerlendirme (2001 Krizi Sonrası). *İktisat Fakültesi Mecmuası*, *61*, 51–81.

Dopico, L. G., & Wilcox, J. A. (2002). Openness, profit opportunities and foreign banking. *Journal of Financial Markets, Institutions, and Money*, *12*(4-5), 299–320. doi:10.1016/S1042-4431(02)00016-1

Dragota, V., & Tilica, E. V. (2014). Market efficiency of the Post Communist East European stock markets. *Central European Journal of Operations Research*, *22*(2), 307–337. doi:10.100710100-013-0315-6

Dreher, A. (2006). The influence of globalization on taxes and social policy – An empirical analysis for OECD countries. *European Journal of Political Economy*, *22*(1), 179–201. doi:10.1016/j.ejpoleco.2005.04.006

Dreher, A., Gaston, N., & Martens, P. (2008). *Measuring Globalisation*. New York: Springer. doi:10.1007/978-0-387-74069-0

Dreher, A., Sturm, J.-E., & Ursprung, H. W. (2008). The impact of globalization on the composition of government expenditures: Evidence from panel data. *Public Choice*, *134*(3-4), 263–292. doi:10.100711127-007-9223-4

Duarte, A., Simões, M., & Andrade, J. S. (2016). The Welfare State and Economic Performance: Quantiles and Nonlinearities. *Applied Economics Quarterly*, *62*(4), 267–294. doi:10.3790/aeq.62.4.269

Dudley, W., & Hubbard, G. (2004). *How Capital Markets Enhance Economic Performance and Facilitate Job Creation*. Global Markets Institute.

Duffie, D. (1989). *Futures Markets*. Upper Saddle River, NJ: Prentice Hall.

Dunne, P. G., Moore, M. J., & Portes, R. (2007). Benchmark Status in Fixed-Income Asset Markets. *Journal of Business Finance & Accounting*, *34*(9-10), 1615–1634.

Dyakova, A., & Smith, G. (2013). Bulgarian stock market relative predictability: BSE-Sofia stocks and South East European markets. *Applied Financial Economics*, *23*(15), 1257–1271. doi:10.1080/09603107.2013.802089

Dyl, E., & Maberly, E. (1988). A Possible Explanation of the Weekend Effect. *Financial Analysts Journal*, *44*(3), 83–84. doi:10.2469/faj.v44.n3.83

Easterly, W. (2001). The lost decades: Developing countries' stagnation in spite of policy reform 1980–1998. *Journal of Economic Growth, 6*(2), 135–157. doi:10.1023/A:1011378507540

Ebner, A. (2009). An Empirical Analysis on the Determinants of CEE Government Bond Spreads. *Emerging Markets Review, 10*(2), 97–121. doi:10.1016/j.ememar.2009.02.001

Ederington, L. H. (1979). The Hedging Performance of the New Future Markets. *The Journal of Finance, 34*(1), 157–170. doi:10.1111/j.1540-6261.1979.tb02077.x

Edison, H. J., Levine, R., Ricci, L., & Sløk, T. (2002). International financial integration and economic growth. *Journal of International Money and Finance, 21*(6), 749–776. doi:10.1016/S0261-5606(02)00021-9

Edwards, S. (2001). *Capital mobility and economic performance: are emerging economies different?* (No. w8076). National Bureau of Economic Research.

Eichengreen, B., & Wyplosz, C. (2016). Minimal conditions for the survival of the euro. *Inter Economics, 51*(1), 24–28. doi:10.100710272-016-0569-z

Ekinci, M. F., Kalemli-Özcan, Ş., & Sørensen, B. E. (2009, January). Financial integration within EU countries: The role of institutions, confidence and trust. In *NBER International Seminar on Macroeconomics 2007* (pp. 325-391). University of Chicago Press.

Enders, J. C., & Remig, M. (2015). Theories of sustainable development: An introduction. In J.C. Enders & M. Remig (Eds.), Theories of sustainable development (pp. 1-5). Routledge.

Engle, R. F. (1982). Autoregressive Conditional Heteroscedasticity with Estimates of the Variance of United Kingdom Inflation. *Econometrica, 50*(4), 987–1008. doi:10.2307/1912773

Engle, R. F., & Mezrich, J. (1995). Grappling with GARCH. Retrieved from https://www.finam.ru/profile/moex–akcii/gazprom/export/

Enright, M. (2017). Here's Why Incoming FDI Is Far More Important to China Than Thought. *South China Morning Post.* Retrieved from www.scmp.com/week-asia/opinion/article/2108351/heres-why-incoming-fdi-far-more-important-china-thought

Epstein, J. (2017). *Trump Threatens Government Shutdown Over Border Wall Funding.* Retrieved October 12, 2017 from https://www.bloomberg.com/news/articles/2017-08-23/trump-threatens-government-shutdown-to-secure-border-wall-funds

Epstein, M. J., & Roy, M.-J. (2001). Sustainability in action: Identifying and measuring the key performance drivers. *Long Range Planning, 34*(5), 585–604. doi:10.1016/S0024-6301(01)00084-X

Estevez-Abe, M., Versen, T., & Soskice, D. (2001). Social Protection and the Formation of Skills: A Reinterpretation of the Welfare State. In P. Hall & D. Soskice (Eds.), *Varieties of Capitalism: The Institutional Foundation of Comparative Advantage.* New York: Oxford University Press. doi:10.1093/0199247757.003.0004

European Central Bank. (2012). Heterogeneity in Euro Area Financial Conditions and Policy Implications. *ECB Monthly Bulletin, 8*, 63–75.

European Central Bank. (2017). *Financial integration in Europe*. Retrieved from https://www.ecb.europa.eu/pub/pdf/other/ecb.financialintegrationineurope201705.en.pdf

European Commission. (2011, December 12). *EU economic governance "six-pack" enters into force* (Press release). Retrieved from http://europa.eu/rapid/press-release_MEMO-11-898_en.htm

European Commission. (2017a). *White paper on the future of Europe*. Brussels, Belgium: European Union. Retrieved from https://ec.europa.eu/commission/sites/beta-political/files/white_paper_on_the_future_of_europe_en.pdf

European Commission. (2017b). *Reflection paper on the deepening of the economic and monetary union*. Brussels, Belgium: European Union. https://ec.europa.eu/commission/sites/beta-political/files/reflection-paper-emu_en.pdf

European Union. (2014). *Regulation (EU) No 910/2014 of the European Par lament and of the Council - on electronic identification and trust services for electronic transactions in the internal market and repealing Directive*. 1999/93/EC The European Parlament and of the Council – Regulation. Retrieved March 2017, from http://eur-lex.europa.eu/legal-content/EN/TXT/?uri=uriserv:OJ.L_.2014.257.01.0073.01.ENG

Eyraud, L., Gaspar, V., & Poghosyan, T. (2017). Fiscal politics in the Euro Area. *International Monetary Fund*. Retrieved from http://www.imf.org/en/Publications/WP/Issues/2017/01/30/Fiscal-Politics-in-the-Euro-Area-44601

Faini, R., Duranton, G., & Hau, H. (2006). Fiscal policy and interest rates in Europe – Discussion. *Economic Policy, 21*(47), 443–489. doi:10.1111/j.1468-0327.2006.00163.x

Fama, E. F. (1965). The Behavior of Stock-Market Prices. *The Journal of Business, 38*(1), 34–105. doi:10.1086/294743

Fama, E. F. (1970). Efficient Capital Markets: A Review of Theory and Empirical Work. *The Journal of Finance, 25*(2), 383–417. doi:10.2307/2325486

Fama, E. F. (1991). Efficient Capital Markets II. *The Journal of Finance, 46*(5), 1575–1596. doi:10.1111/j.1540-6261.1991.tb04636.x

Fang, Y., Hasan, I., & Marton, K. (2011). *Bank efficiency in transition economies: Recent evidence from South-Eastern Europe*. Discussion paper, Bank of Finland Research.

Farhoomand, A., & Lentini, D. (2008). *e-Business Transformation in the Banking Industry: The Case of Citibank*. Retrieved January 2017, from http://www.acrc.hku.hk/case/case_showdetails.asp?ct=newly&c=944&cp=1949&pt=1

Farhoomand, A. (2004). *Managing (e)business transformation*. Palgrave Macmillan. doi:10.1007/978-1-137-08380-7

Favero, C. A., & Missale, A. (2012). Sovereign spreads in the Euro Area: Which Prospects for a Eurobond? *Economic Policy*, *70*(70), 231–273. doi:10.1111/j.1468-0327.2012.00282.x

Federal Reserve Bank of St. Louis. (2017). *Financial Crisis - Full Timeline*. Retrieved April 10, 2017 from https://www.stlouisfed.org/financial-crisis/full-timeline

Ferreira, C. (2010). European Financial Integration and Economic Growth. *JMFS*, 26.

Financial Crisis Inquiry Report Commission. (2011). *The Financial Crisis Inquiry Report*. Author.

Forbes, K. J., & Warnock, F. E. (2012). Capital flow waves: Surges, stops, flight, and retrenchment. *Journal of International Economics*, *88*(2), 235–251. doi:10.1016/j.jinteco.2012.03.006

Fountas, S., & Segredakis, K. N. (2002). Emerging Stock Market Return Seasonality: The January and Tax-Loss Selling Hypothesis. *Applied Financial Economics*, *12*(4), 291–299. doi:10.1080/09603100010000839

Frankel, J. A., & Rose, A. K. (1996). Currency crashes in emerging markets: An empirical treatment. *Journal of International Economics*, *41*(3), 351–366. doi:10.1016/S0022-1996(96)01441-9

French, K. (1980). Stock Returns and the Weekend Effect. *Journal of Financial Economics*, *8*(1), 55–69. doi:10.1016/0304-405X(80)90021-5

Fries, S., & Taci, A. (2005). Cost efficiency of banks in transition: Evidence from 289 banks in 15 post-communist countries. *Journal of Banking & Finance*, *29*(1), 55–81. doi:10.1016/j.jbankfin.2004.06.016

Fu, Z., & Mittnight, E. (2015). *Critical Success Factors for Continually Monitoring, Evaluating and Assessing Management of Enterprise IT*. ISACA. Retrieved August 2016, from http://www.isaca.org/COBIT/focus/Pages/critical-success-factors-for-continually-monitoring-evaluating-and-assessing-management-of-enterprise-it.aspx

Fuller, W. A. (1996). *Introduction to Statistical Time Series*. New York: Wiley.

Fullwiler, S. T. (2015). *Sustainable Finance. Building a More General Theory of Finance*. Working Paper No. 106.

Furceri, D., & Zdzienicka, A. (2012). The Effects of Social Spending on Economic Activity: Empirical Evidence from a Panel of OECD Countries. *Fiscal Studies*, *33*(1), 129–152. doi:10.1111/j.1475-5890.2012.00155.x

Galindo, A., Micco, A., & Serra, C. (2003). *Better the devil that you know: Evidence on entry costs faced by foreign banks*. Working paper, Inter-American Development Bank.

Ganic, M., & Mamuti, A. (2016). Developments, Trends And Features Of Financial Integration In The Western Balkan Region-Crosscountry Comparisons. *International Journal of Management Economics & Business*, *12*, 1.

Gartner. (2013). *Scenario Toolkit: Using EA to Support Business Transformation*. Gartner Inc.

Gaston, N., & Rajaguru, G. (2013). International migration and the welfare state revisited. *European Journal of Political Economy*, *29*, 90–101. doi:10.1016/j.ejpoleco.2012.08.004

Georgantopoulos, A. & Tsamis, A. (2012). A Comparative Study on Calendar Effects: Greece vs Bulgaria. *International Journal of Economic Research.*

Georgantopoulos, A., Kenourgios, D., & Tsamis, A. (2011). Calendar Anomalies in Emerging Balkan Equity Markets. *International Economics and Finance Journal*, *6*(1), 67–82.

Georgantopoulos, A., & Tsamis, A. (2011). Investigating Seasonal Patterns in Developing Countries: The Case of FYROM Stock Market. *International Journal of Economics and Financial Issues*, *1*(4), 211–219.

Gerlach, S., Schulz, A., & Wolff, G. B. (2010). *Banking and Sovereign Risk in the Euro Area* (CEPR Discussion Paper vol. 09). Retrieved from https://www.econstor.eu/bitstream/10419/32799/1/627499228.pdf

Ghosh, A. R., Kim, J., Mahvash, Q., & Zalduendo, J. (2012). *Surges. Working Paper 12/22.* Washington, DC: International Monetary Fund. Retrieved from http://www.imf.org/external/pubs/ft/wp/2012/wp1222.pdf

Ghoul, S., Guedhami, O., Kwok, H., & Mishra, K. (2014). *Corporate Environmental Responsibility and the Cost of Capital—International Evidence*. KAIST College of Business Working Paper Series, No. 2014-008.

Giannetti, M., & Ongena, S. (2007). Financial integration and firm performance: Evidence from foreign bank entry in emerging markets. *Review of Finance*, *13*(2), 181–223. doi:10.1093/rof/rfm019

Gibbons, M., & Hess, P. (1981). Day of the Week Effects and Asset Returns. *The Journal of Business*, *54*(4), 579–596. doi:10.1086/296147

Globerman, S., Shapiro, D., & Tang, Y. (2006). Foreign direct investment in emerging and transition European countries. In *Emerging European financial markets: Independence and integration post-enlargement* (pp. 431–459). Emerald Group Publishing Limited. doi:10.1016/S1569-3767(05)06017-6

Goldberg, L. S. (2001). *When is U.S. bank lending to emerging markets volatile?* Working paper, National Bureau of Economic Research.

Gourinchas, P. O., & Jeanne, O. (2006). The elusive gains from international financial integration. *The Review of Economic Studies*, *73*(3), 715–741. doi:10.1111/j.1467-937X.2006.00393.x

Gourinchas, P. O., & Jeanne, O. (2013). Capital flows to developing countries: The allocation puzzle. *The Review of Economic Studies*.

Granger, C. W. J., & Morgenstern, O. (1970). *Predictability of Stock Market Prices*. Lexington, MA: Heath.

Grauwe, P., & Polan, M. (2005). Globalization and Social Spending. *Pacific Economic Review*, *10*(1), 105–123. doi:10.1111/j.1468-0106.2005.00263.x

Gray, P. (1997). *Artificial legal intelligence*. Dartmouth Publishing Co.

Green, C. J., Murinde, V., & Nikolov, I. (2004). The efficiency of foreign and domestic banks in Central and Eastern Europe: Evidence on economies of scale and scope. *Journal of Emerging Market Finance*, *3*(2), 175–205. doi:10.1177/097265270400300205

Grewal-Carr, V., & Marshall, S. (2016). *Block-chain Enigma*. London, UK: Paradox. Opportunity. Deloitte LLP.

Grewal-Carr, V., & Marshall, S. (2016). *Block-chain Enigma. Paradox. Opportunity*. London, UK: Deloitte LLP.

Grigorian, D. A., & Manole, V. (2002). *Determinants of commercial bank performance in transition: An application of data envelopment analysis*. Working paper, International Monetary Fund.

Grober, U. (2007). *Deep roots: A conceptual history of' "sustainable development" (Nachhaltigkeit)*. WZB Discussion Paper, No. P 2007-002.

Gros, D., & Busse, M. (2013). The macroeconomic imbalance procedure and Germany: When is a current account surplus an 'imbalance'? *CEPS Policy Briefs*. Retrieved from https://papers.ssrn.com/sol3/papers.cfm?abstract_id=2360470

Grosse, R., & Goldberg, L. G. (1991). Foreign bank activity in the United States: An analysis by country of origin. *Journal of Banking & Finance*, *15*(6), 1093–1112. doi:10.1016/0378-4266(91)90052-N

Group, P. R. S. (2015). *International Country Risk Guide*. Retrieved from https://info.worldbank.org/governance/wgi/pdf/prs.xlsx

Guidi, F., Gupta, R., & Maheshwari, R. (2011). Weak-form Market Efficiency and Calendar Anomalies for Eastern Europe Equity Markets. *Journal of Emerging Market Finance*, *10*(3), 337–389. doi:10.1177/097265271101000304

Guiso, L., Jappelli, T., Padula, M., & Pagano, M. (2004). Financial market integration and economic growth in the EU. *Economic Policy*, *19*(40), 524–577. doi:10.1111/j.1468-0327.2004.00131.x

Gujarai, D. (2004). *Basic Econometrics*. McGraw Hill.

Haigh, M. (2012). Publishing and defining sustainable finance and investment. *Journal of Sustainable Finance & Investment*, *2*(2), 88–94.

Hallerberg, M., & Wolff, G. B. (2008). Fiscal institutions, fiscal policy and sovereign risk premia in EMU. *Public Choice*, *136*(3-4), 379–396. doi:10.100711127-008-9301-2

Haustalter, G. D. (2000). Financing Policy, Basis Risk and Corporate Hedging. *The Journal of Finance*, *55*(1), 107–152. doi:10.1111/0022-1082.00202

Havrylchyk, O. (2006). Efficiency of the Polish banking industry: Foreign versus domestic banks. *Journal of Banking & Finance*, *30*(7), 1975–1996. doi:10.1016/j.jbankfin.2005.07.009

Havrylchyk, O. (2011). *The effect of foreign bank presence on firm entry and exit in transition economies. Discussion paper*. Institute for Economies in Transition, Bank of Finland.

He, ZhiGuo, Chen, Zuo, Liu, Chun, & Liu. (2017). 四万亿"政策背后的地方政府融资困局 [The Dilemma of 4 Trillion]. Retrieved from http://comments.caijing.com.cn/20170919/4333945.shtml

Hertie School of Governance. (2015). *The governance report 2015*. Oxford, UK: Oxford University Press.

Hilliard, J., & Jordan, S. (1989). Hedging Interest Rate Risk with Futures Portfolios under Full-Rank Assumptions. *Journal of Financial and Quantitative Analysis*, *24*(2), 217–240. doi:10.2307/2330773

Horvath, R., & Petrovski, D. (2013). International stock market integration: Central and South Eastern Europe compared. *Economic Systems*, *37*(1), 81–91. doi:10.1016/j.ecosys.2012.07.004

Hoxha, I., Kalemli-Ozcan, S., & Vollrath, D. (2013). How big are the gains from international financial integration? *Journal of Development Economics*, *103*, 90–98. doi:10.1016/j.jdeveco.2013.02.003

Hryckiewicz, A., & Kowalewski, O. (2010). *Predicting foreign bank exits? A logit and probit regression approach*. Available at SSRN: http://papers.ssrn.com/sol3/papers.cfm?abstract_id=1537129

Hua, S. (2014). *An Analysis of the Difficulties in the Reforming Land System under New Agrarian Reforms*. Beijing: Oriental Publishing House.

Hull, J. (2017). *Option, Futures and Other Derivatives* (10th ed.). Pearson.

Hu, R. (2013). China's Paradoxical Reforms on Land and Real Estate Property Markets. *Journal of Global Business and Economic Review*, *8*(3), 11–21.

Hüseyin, Saruç, & Keskin. (2011). Kalkınmanın Finansmanı. In Kalkınma Ekonomisi: Seçme Konular. Baskı: Ekin Yayınevi.

Huwart, J.-Y., & Verdier, L. (2013). *The 2008 financial crisis – A crisis of globalisation? In Economic Globalisation: Origins and consequences* (pp. 126–143). Paris: OECD Publishing.

Iara, A., & Wolff, G. (2014). Rules and risk in the Euro area. *European Journal of Political Economy*, *34*, 222–236. doi:10.1016/j.ejpoleco.2014.02.002

IFRS. (2017). *IFRS Standards*. Retrieved April 2017, from http://www.ifrs.org/Pages/default.aspx. IFRS.

IMF. (2000). *Globalization: Threat or Opportunity?* Retrieved from https://www.imf.org/external/np/exr/ib/2000/041200to.htm

International Monetary Fund. (2009). Switzerland: Financial Sector Assessment Program - Detailed Assessment of Observance of Financial Sector Standards and Codes. International Monetary Fund.

International Monetary Fund. (2013). *Macedonia: Banking sector developments, 2008-2013. Country report*. IMF.

Investopedia. (2016). *Business Valuation*. Retrieved April 2017, from http://www.investopedia.com/terms/b/business-valuation.asp. Investopedia.

Investopedia. (2017a). *What is 'Financial Engineering*. Retrieved April 2017, from http://www.investopedia.com/terms/f/financialengineering.asp. Investopedia.

Investopedia. (2017b). *Locked In*. Retrieved April 2017, from http://www.investopedia.com/terms/l/locked_in.asp. Investopedia.

ISACA. (2015). *IT Control Objectives for Sarbanes-Oxley Using COBIT 5* (3rd ed.). ISACA.

ISDA. (2017). *FpML*. Retrieved April 2017, from https://www2.isda.org/functional-areas/technology-infrastructure/fpml/

ITGI. (2007). *COBIT 4.1- Framework Control Objectives Management Guidelines Maturity Models*. IT Governance Institute.

Jednak, D., & Jednak, J. (2013). Operational Risk Management in Financial Institutions. *Management*, (66).

Jednak, S., Kragulj, D., & Bulajic, M. (2017). A comparative analysis of development in Southeast European countries. *Technological and Economic Development of Economy*, 1–18. doi:10.3846/20294913.2016.1212438

Jejunum. (2003). In *Merriam-Webster's dictionary* (11th ed.). Springfield, MA: Merriam-Webster.

Jensen, M. (1978). Some Anomalous Evidence Regarding Market Efficiency. *Journal of Financial Economics*, *6*(2-3), 95–102. doi:10.1016/0304-405X(78)90025-9

Jeon, B., Olivero, M., & Wu, J. (2011). Do foreign banks increase competition? Evidence from emerging Asian and Latin American banking markets. *Journal of Banking & Finance*, *35*(4), 856–875. doi:10.1016/j.jbankfin.2010.10.012

Jeucken, M. (2001). *Sustainable finance and banking: The financial sector and the future of the planet*. London: Earthscan Publications Ltd.

Jin, K., & Zhu, J. (2011). *MET: Multi-party E-Commerce Transaction Model*. IEEE Third International Conference on Social Computing (SocialCom), 2011 IEEE Third International Conference, Boston, MA.

Jin, K., & Zhu, J. (2011). *MET: Multi-party E-Commerce Transaction Model*. Privacy, Security, Risk and Trust (PASSAT). 2011 IEEE Third International Conference on Social Computing (SocialCom), 2011 IEEE Third International Conference, Boston, MA.

Kabzeva, A., Niemann, M., Müller, P., & Steinmetz, P. (2010). Applying TOGAF to Define and Govern a Service-oriented Architecture in a Large-scale "research & development" (R&D). *Proceedings of the Sixteenth Americas Conference on Information Systems.*

Kadiu, F. (2015). Economic Overview and Financial Instability in Balkans. *Procedia Economics and Finance, 26*, 1141–1145. doi:10.1016/S2212-5671(15)00943-0

Kaldor, N. (1978). The dynamic effects of the common market. In N. Kaldor (Ed.), *Further essays on applied economics* (pp. 187–220). London, UK: Duckworth.

Kallager, P. K. R. (2014). *Globalisation and the Welfare State – A Meta-Regression Analysis* (Master's thesis). Department of Comparative Politics, University of Bergen.

Karabıçak, M. (2000). Türkiye'de Ekonomik İstikrarsızlığın Tarihsel Gelişim Süreci. *Süleyman Demirel Üniversitesi İktisadi ve İdari Bilimler Fakültesi, 5*(2), 49-65.

Karadzic, V., & Backovic Vulic, T. (2011). The Montenegrin Capital Market: Calendar Anomalies. *Economic Annals, 56*(191), 107–121. doi:10.2298/EKA1191107K

Karagöz, K., & Ergün, S. (2010). Türkiye'de Ekonomik İstikrarsızlığın Kaynakları: Ekonometrik Bir Değerlendirme. *Süleyman Demirel Üniversitesi İktisadi ve idari Bilimler Fakültesi Dergisi, 15*(2), 169-185.

Kauder, B., & Potrafke, N. (2015). Globalization and social justice in OECD countries. *Review of World Economics, 151*(2), 353–376. doi:10.100710290-015-0213-1

Kaynak, M. (2011). Kalkınma İktisadı. Ankara: Gazi Kitabevi.

Kenourgios, D., & Samitas, A. (2011). Equity market integration in emerging Balkan markets. *Research in International Business and Finance, 25*(3), 296–307. doi:10.1016/j.ribaf.2011.02.004

Kerimov A.K. (2014) Mean-variance future hedging for security portfolio. *Bulletin of Peoples' Friendship University of Russia. Series Economics*, (3), 109–116. (in Russian)

Khoshafian, D. (2014). *Intelligent BPM the next wave for customer-centric business applications.* Pegasystems Inc.

Kılınç, D., Seven, Ü., & Yetkiner, H. (2017). *Financial development convergence: New evidence for the EU.* Central Bank Review.

Kim, J. H. (2006). Wild bootstrapping variance ratio tests. *Economics Letters, 92*(1), 38–43. doi:10.1016/j.econlet.2006.01.007

Kindleberger, Ch. (1996). *Manias, Panics and Crashes. A History of Financial Crises.* New York: John Wiley & Sons, Inc.

Klepsch, C., & Wollmershäuser, T. (2011). Yield Spreads on EMU Government Bonds – How the Financial Crisis Has Helped Investors to Rediscover Risk. *Inter Economics, 46*(3), 169–176. doi:10.100710272-011-0379-2

Koepke, R. (2014). *Fed Policy Expectations and Portfolio Flows to Emerging Markets*. Institute of International Finance Working Paper. Retrieved from https://mpra.ub.uni-muenchen.de/63519/1/MPRA_paper_63519.pdf

Kose, M. A., & Ozturk, E. O. (2014). A World of Change: Taking stock of the past half century. Finance & Development, 51(3), 11.

Kose, M. A., Prasad, E., Rogoff, K., & Wei, S. J. (2009). Financial globalisation: A reappraisal. *IMF Staff Papers*, *56*(1), 8–62. doi:10.1057/imfsp.2008.36

Kose, M. A., Prasad, E., Rogoff, K., & Wei, S. J. (2009a). Finansijska globalizacija: Ponovna procena. *Panoeconomicus*, *56*(2), 143–197. doi:10.2298/PAN0902143K

Koster, F. (2009). The welfare state and globalisation: Down and out or too tough to die? *International Journal of Social Welfare*, *18*(2), 153–162. doi:10.1111/j.1468-2397.2008.00571.x

Kostyunina, G. M. (2005). International capital flow. In International economic relations (pp. 248-295). TK Velbi, Prospect.

Kowall, J., & Fletcher, C. (2013). Modernize Your Monitoring Strategy by Combining Unified Monitoring and Log Analytics Tools. Gartner.

Kroner, K., & Sultan, J. (1993). Time-Varying Distributions and Dynamic Hedging with Foreign Currency Futures. *Journal of Financial and Quantitative Analysis*, *28*(4), 535–551. doi:10.2307/2331164

Kyte, A. (2010). Nine Critical Success Factors for Business Value Through Application Overhaul. Gartner Inc.

Kyte, A. (2010). Nine Critical Success Factors for Business Value -Through Application Overhaul. Gartner Inc.

Lam, W. (2015). *How Can Revenue Reforms Contribute to Inclusive and Sustainable Growth*. Retrieved from https://www.imf.org/external/pubs/ft/wp/2015/wp1566.pdf

Lane, P. R., & Milesi-Ferretti, G. M. M. (2017). *International financial integration in the aftermath of the global financial crisis*. IMF Working Paper No. 17/115.

Lane, P. R. (2013). Financial globalisation and the crisis. *Open Economies Review*, *24*(3), 555–580. doi:10.100711079-012-9266-0

Larch, M. (2010). Fiscal performance and income inequality: Are unequal societies more deficit – prone? Some cross country evidence. *Economic Papers, 414*. http://ec.europa.eu/economy_finance/publications/economic_paper/2010/pdf/ecp414_en.pdf

Laskowski, N. (2017). *Five analytics priorities for 2017*. Retrieved March 2017, from http://searchcio.techtarget.com/news/450410871/Five-analytics-priorities-for-2017

Law on foreign exchange operations. Official Gazette of the Republic of Macedonia, 34/01, 49/01, 103/01, 54/02, 51/03, 81/08, 24/11, 135/11 and 188/13.

Law on takeovers of the joint stock companies. Official Gazette of the Republic of Macedonia, 69/13, 188/13.

Law on trade companies. Official Gazette of the Republic of Macedonia, 28/04, 84/05, 71/06, 25/07, 87/08, 17/09, 23/09, 42/10, 48/10, 24/11, 166/12, 70/13, 119/13, 120/13 and 187/13.

Lawder, D. (2017). U.S. Formally Opposes China Market Economy Status at WTO. *Reuters*. Retrieved from https://www.reuters.com/article/us-usa-china-trade-wto/u-s-formally-opposes-china-market-economy-status-at-wto-idUSKBN1DU2VH

Lemmen, J., & Goodhart, C. (1999). Credit Risks and European Government Bond Markets: A Panel Data Econometric Analysis. *Eastern Economic Journal*, *25*(1), 77–107.

Lensink, R., & Hermes, N. (2004a). The short-term effects of foreign bank entry on domestic bank behaviour: Does economic development matter? *Journal of Banking & Finance*, *28*(3), 553–568. doi:10.1016/S0378-4266(02)00393-X

Lensink, R., & Hermes, N. (2004b). Foreign bank presence, domestic bank performance and financial development. *Journal of Emerging Market Finance*, *3*(2), 207–229. doi:10.1177/097265270400300206

Lensink, R., Meesters, A., & Naaborg, I. (2008). Bank efficiency and foreign ownership: Do good institutions matter? *Journal of Banking & Finance*, *32*(5), 834–844. doi:10.1016/j.jbankfin.2007.06.001

Levin, A., Lin, C. F., & Chu, C. S. J. (2002). Unit root tests in panel data: Asymptotic and finite-sample properties. *Journal of Econometrics*, *108*(1), 1–24. doi:10.1016/S0304-4076(01)00098-7

Levine, R. (1996). Foreign banks, financial development and economic growth. In C. E. Barfield (Ed.), *International Financial Markets: Harmonization versus Competition*. Washington, DC: AEI Press.

Li, T., & Kim, C. (2011). *Foreign bank entry and bank efficiency: Experience for emerging economies and agenda for further research*. Working paper, The Association of Korean Economic Studies.

Li, H., & Zhou, L. (2005). Political Turnover and Economic Performance: "The Incentive Role of Personnel Control in China. *Journal of Public Economics*, *89*(9-10), 1743–1762. doi:10.1016/j.jpubeco.2004.06.009

Liu, S. J. (2017). 中国房价泡沫收场的N种姿势 [N Possibility of Ending China's Housing Bubble]. *Financial Time (Chinese Edition)*. Retrieved from http://www.ftchinese.com/story/001072362?page=3

Liu, X. Y. (2014, December 1). 地方政府融资平台的风险表现及相关政策变迁. *Journal of China Bond,* 12-17.

Lledó, V., Yoon, S., Fang, X., Mbaye, S., & Kim, Y. (2017). *Fiscal Rules at a Glance*. Washington, DC: International Monetary Fund.

Lo Conte, R. (2009). Government Bond Yield Spreads: A Survey. *Giornale degli Economisti e Annali di Economia*, *68*(3), 341–370.

Lo, A. W., & MacKinlay, A. C. (1988). Stock market prices do not follow random walks: Evidence from simple specification test. *Review of Financial Studies*, *1*(1), 41–66. doi:10.1093/rfs/1.1.41

Loayza, N. V., Ranciere, R., Servén, L., & Ventura, J. (2007). Macroeconomic volatility and welfare in developing countries: An introduction. *The World Bank Economic Review*, *21*(3), 343–357. doi:10.1093/wber/lhm017

Lu, F., Wei, W., Zhang, W., & Cheng, H. (2016). *China Air 2016*. Clean Air Asia Publication. Retrieved from http:// cleanairasia.org/wp-content/uploads/2016/08/China-Air-2016-Report-Full.pdf

Lukic, V. (2014). *Financial Integration- Theoretical and Empirical Analysis*. Doctoral Dissertation.

Maltritz, D. (2012). Determinants of Sovereign Yield Spreads in the Eurozone: A Bayesian approach. *Journal of International Money and Finance*, *31*(3), 657–672. doi:10.1016/j.jimonfin.2011.10.010

Manganelli, S., & Wolswijk, G. (2007). *Market Discipline, Financial Integration and Fiscal Rules* (ECB Working Paper vol. 745). Retrieved from https://www.ecb.europa.eu/pub/pdf/scpwps/ecbwp745.pdf?39c651ca2ffcb63b24e84c6cbd68f7ff

Mathieson, D. J., & Roldos, J. (2001). *The role of foreign banks in emerging markets*. Paper prepared for the International Monetary Fund-World Bank-Brookings Institution Conference on Financial Markets and Development, New York, NY.

McKernan, S. M., Ratcliffe, C., Steuerle, E., Quakenbush, C., & Kalish, E. (2017). *Nine Charts about Wealth Inequality in America*. Urban Institute. Retrieved October 12, 2017 from http://apps.urban.org/features/wealth-inequality-charts/

Mehra, R., & Prescott, E. C. (1985). The equity premium: A puzzle. *Journal of Monetary Economics*, *15*(2), 145–161. doi:10.1016/0304-3932(85)90061-3

Meinhard, S., & Potrafke, N. (2012). The Globalization-Welfare State Nexus Reconsidered. *Review of International Economics*, *20*(2), 271–287. doi:10.1111/j.1467-9396.2012.01021.x

Mérő, K., & Valentinyi, M. E. (2003). *The role of foreign banks in five central and Eastern European countries*. Working paper, Magyar Nemzeti Bank.

Mills, T. C., & Coutts, J. A. (1995). Calendar Effects in the London Stock Exchange FTSE Indices. *European Journal of Finance*, *1*(1), 79–93. doi:10.1080/13518479500000010

Minsky, H. P. (1986). *Stabilizing an Unstable Economy*. McGraw-Hill, Yale University Press.

Missio, S. (2012). *Government bond market integration and the EMU: Correlation based evidence* (BGPE Discussion Paper vol. 125). Retrieved from http://www.bgpe.de/texte/DP/125_Missio.pdf

Morck, R., Shleifer, S., Vishny, R. W., Shapiro, M., & Poterba, J. M. (1990). The stock market and investment: Is the market a sideshow? *Brookings Papers on Economic Activity*, *2*(2), 157–202. doi:10.2307/2534506

Morgan, D., & Strahan, P. (2003). *Foreign bank entry and business volatility: Evidence from U.S. states and other countries.* Working paper, National Bureau of Economic Research.

Nagois log server. (2015). *Unified logging system. Nag*ios. Retrieved April 2017, from https://exchange.nagios.org/directory/Addons/Log-File-Management/Nagios-Log-Server/details

Nakamoto, S. (2008). *Bitcoin: A Peer-to-Peer Electronic Cash System.* Retrieved from www.bitcoin.org

National Bureau of Economic Research. (2012). *US Business Cycles Expansions and Contractions*, Retrieved August 12, 2107 from http://www.nber.org/cycles/US_Business_Cy cle_Expansions_and_Contractions_20120423.pdf

Nelson, D. (1990). Conditional Heteroscedasticity and Assert Return. A New Approach. *Econometrica*, *59*(2), 347–370. doi:10.2307/2938260

Nikiel, E. M., & Opiela, T. P. (2002). Customer type and bank efficiency in Poland: Implications for emerging market banking. *Contemporary Economic Policy*, *20*(3), 255–271. doi:10.1093/cep/20.3.255

OASIS. (2009). *OASIS Web Services Reliable Messaging (WS-ReliableMessaging) Version 1.2. OASIS Standard.* Retrieved January 2017, from http://docs.oasis-open.org/ws-rx/wsrm/200702/wsrm-1.2-spec-os.html

Obstfeld, M. (1998). The Global Capital Market: Benefactor or Menace? *The Journal of Economic Perspectives*, *12*(4), 9–30. doi:10.1257/jep.12.4.9

Obstfeld, M. (2009). International finance and growth in developing countries: What have we learned? *IMF Staff Papers*, *56*(1), 63–111. doi:10.1057/imfsp.2008.32

Obstfeld, M. (2009). *International finance and growth in developing countries: what have we learned? Working Paper 14691*. Cambridge, MA: National Bureau of Economic Research. doi:10.3386/w14691

Obstfeld, M. (2013). *Finance at a centre stage: Some lessons of the Euro crisis (European Economy, Economic Papers 493)*. Brussels, Belgium: European Commission. Retrieved from http://ec.europa.eu/economy_finance/publications/economic_paper/2013/pdf/ecp493_en.pdf

OECD. (2002). *Overview of Sustainable Development Indicators Used by National and International Agencies*. Paris: OECD.

OECD. (2011). *Future Global Shocks: Improving risk governance*. Paris: OECD Publishing.

OECD. (2014). *OECD Sovereign Borrowing Outlook 2014*. Paris, France: OECD Publishing.

Ogden, J. P. (1990). Turn-of-month evaluations of liquid profits and stock returns: A common explanation for the monthly and January effects. *The Journal of Finance*, *45*(4), 1259–1272. doi:10.1111/j.1540-6261.1990.tb02435.x

Olson, L. (2008). *Synchronize UDDI registries with WebSphere Service Registry and Repository for better SOA governance*. IBM.

Oprea, D. Ş., & Tilica, E. V. (2014). Day-of-the-week Effect in the Post-Communist East European Stock Markets. *International Journal of Academic Research and Accounting. Finance and Management Sciences*, *4*(3), 117–127.

Oprea, O. R. (2016). European Financial Integration and Economic Growth. *Journal of Public Administration. Finance and Law.*, *10*, 173–181.

Oracle. (2015a). *Using WS-Policy in ALSB Proxy and Business Services*. Oracle. Retrieved March 2017, from http://docs.oracle.com/cd/E11036_01/alsb30/security/ws_policy.html

Oracle. (2015b). *About Web Services Policy*. Oracle. Retrieved August 2016, from http://docs.oracle.com/cd/E11036_01/alsb30/security/ws_policy.html

Osada, M., & Saito, M. (2010). *Financial integration and economic growth: An empirical analysis using international panel data from 1974-2007*. Research and Statistics Department, Bank of Japan.

Padoa-Schioppa, T. (2004). *The euro and its central bank: Getting united after the union*. Cambridge, MA: MIT Press.

Pagano, M., & von Thadden, E. L. (2004). The European bond markets under EMU. *Oxford Review of Economic Policy*, *20*(4), 531–554. doi:10.1093/oxrep/grh031

Panetta, K. (2016). *3 Trends Appear in the Gartner Hype Cycle for Emerging Technologies, 2016. Are block-chain, smart machines, IoT and other emerging technologies on their way up or down the Hype Cycle?* Retrieved March 2017, from http://www.gartner.com/smarterwithgartner/3-trends-appear-in-the-gartner-hype-cycle-for-emerging-technologies-2016/

Paniagua, J., Sapena, J., & Tamari, C. (2015). *Sovereign debt spreads in EMU: Disentangling the role of fundamentals and market perceptions*. Retrieved from: http://www.uv.es/inteco/jornadas/jornadas11/paniagua_sapena_tamarit.pdf

Parežanin, M., Jednak, S., & Kragulj, D. (2016). The Impact of FDI on the Economic Growth of Serbia. *Management: Journal of Sustainable Business and Management Solutions in Emerging Economies*, *21*(78), 25–32.

Pâris, P., & Wyplosz, C. (2014). *PADRE: Politically acceptable debt restructuring in the Eurozone (Geneva Reports on the World Economy Special Report 3)*. Geneva, Switzerland: International Center for Monetary and Banking Studies.

Partant, F. (2002). Kalkınmanın Sonu “Bir Alternatif mi Doğuyor?”. *Türkiye ve Orta-Doğu Forumu Vakfı, Özgür Üniversite Kitaplığı*, *35*, 2.

Penman, S. H. (1987). The Distribution of Earnings News Over Time and Seasonalities in Aggregate Stock Returns. *Journal of Financial Economics*, *18*(2), 199–228. doi:10.1016/0304-405X(87)90039-0

Pentecost, E. J., & Van Poek, A. (Eds.). (2001). *European monetary integration. Past, present and future*. Cheltenham, UK: Edward Elgar Publishing.

Perez, C. (2009). The Double Bubble at the Turn of the Century: Technological Roots and Structural Implications. *Cambridge Journal of Economics*, *33*(4), 779–805. doi:10.1093/cje/bep028

Petersen, M. F., & Thiagarajan, S. R. (2000). Risk Management and Hedging: With and Without Derivatives. *Financial Management*, *29*(4), 5–30. doi:10.2307/3666367

Peterson, P. (2010). *Saving Schools: From Horace Mann to Virtual Learning*. Harvard University Press.

Peterson, S. (2011). *Why it Worked: Critical Success Factors of a Financial Reform Project in Africa*. Faculty Research Working Paper Series. Harvard Kennedy School.

Phillips, P. C. B., & Perron, P. (1988). Testing for a unit root in time series regression. *Biometrika*, *75*(2), 335–346. doi:10.1093/biomet/75.2.335

Piketty, T. (2015). The economics of inequality. Cambridge, MA: The Belknap Press of Harvard University Press. doi:10.4159/9780674915565

Pisani-Ferry, J. (2012). *The euro crisis and the new impossible trinity (Bruegel Policy Contribution, 2012/01)*. Brussels, Belgium: Bruegel.

Pisano, U., Martinuzzi, A., & Bruckner, B. (2012). *The financial sector and sustainable development: Logics, principles and actors*. European Sustainable Development Network, Quarterly Report No. 27.

Poghosyan, T., & Poghosyan, A. (2010). Foreign bank entry, bank efficiency and market power in Central and Eastern European countries. *Economics of Transition*, *18*(3), 571–598. doi:10.1111/j.1468-0351.2009.00378.x

Posen, A. S., Chopra, A., Ubide, A., Mauro, P., Kirkegaard, J. F., & Veron, N. (Eds.). (2014). *Rebuilding Europe's common future: Combining growth and reform in the Euro area (PIIE Briefing No. 14-5)*. Washington, DC: PIEE.

Potrafke, N. (2013). Globalization and labor market institutions: International empirical evidence. *Journal of Comparative Economics*, *41*(3), 829–842. doi:10.1016/j.jce.2013.02.002

Prasad, E. S., Rajan, R. G., & Subramanian, A. (2007). *Foreign capital and economic growth (No. w13619)*. National Bureau of Economic Research. doi:10.3386/w13619

Qiao, B., & Shah, A. (2012). *Local government organization and finance in China.* World Bank Paper. Retrieved from http://siteresources.worldbank.org/PSGLP/Resources/1BaoYunAnwarShah.pdf

Quadrio Curzio, A. (2011). On the different types of Eurobonds. *Economics and Politics*, *28*(3), 279–293.

Radosavljevic, R. (2013). *Financial integration of the European Union and its impacts on the financial market of Serbia.* Doctoral Dissertation.

Ran, T. (2012). 中国增长模式的困境 [The dilemma of China's growth model]. *Brooking Institute*. Retrieved from https://www.brookings.edu/zh-cn/research/中国增长模式的困境

Ranciere, R., Tornell, A., & Westermann, F. (2008). Systemic crises and growth. *The Quarterly Journal of Economics*, *123*(1), 359–406. doi:10.1162/qjec.2008.123.1.359

Randelman, R. (1993). A Reconciliation of Potentially Conflicting Approaches to Hedging with Futures. *Advances in Futures and Options Research*, *6*, 81–92.

Reinhart, C. M., & Rogoff, K. S. (2008). *This time is different: A panoramic view of eight centuries of financial crises (No. w13882)*. National Bureau of Economic Research. doi:10.3386/w13882

Reinhart, C. M., & Rogoff, K. S. (2009). *This Time is Different. Eight Centuries of Financial Folly*. Princeton, NJ: Princeton University Press.

Ren, Z. P. (2016). 土地出让金和税收占房价八成 [Land Transfer Fee and Taxes Together Account for 80% of the Home Price]. *Sina.com*. Retrieved from http://finance.sina.com.cn/zl/china/2016-10-19/zl-ifxwvpar8421254.shtml

Report of the risks in the banking system of Republic of Macedonia. (2012). National Bank of the Republic of Macedonia (NBRM).

Report of the risks in the banking system of Republic of Macedonia. (2013b). National Bank of the Republic of Macedonia (NBRM).

Report on banking system of the Republic of Macedonia. (2013a). National Bank of the Republic of Macedonia (NBRM).

Roaf, J., Atoyan, R., Joshi, B., & Krogulski, K. (2014). *25 years of transition: post-communist Europe and the IMF*. Washington, DC: International Monetary Fund.

Roberts, H. (1967). *Statistical versus clinical prediction of the stock market* (Unpublished manuscript). Center for Research in Security Prices, University of Chicago.

Rodrigues, M. J. (2015). The Eurozone crisis and the transformation of EU economic governance. In M. J. Rodrigues & E. Xiarchogiannopoulou (Eds.), *The Eurozone crisis and the transformation of EU Governance. Internal and external implications* (pp. 173–189). London, UK: Routledge.

Rogalski, R. J. (1984). New findings regarding day of the week returns over trading and nontrading periods: A note. *The Journal of Finance*, *39*(5), 603–614. doi:10.1111/j.1540-6261.1984.tb04927.x

Rojas, E. & Kristjanpoller, W. (2014). Calendar anomalies in the Latin American stock markets: A Bonferroni testing approach. *Lecturas de Economía, 81*.

Rosser, M. V., & Barkley, J., Jr. (2003). *Comparative Economics in a Transforming World Economy*. MIT Press.

Rubinstein, M. (2001). Rational markets: Yes or no? The affirmative case. *Financial Analysts Journal*, *57*(3), 15–29. doi:10.2469/faj.v57.n3.2447

Rudra, N., & Haggard, S. (2005). Globalisation, democracy, and effective welfare state spending in the developing world. *Comparative Political Studies*, *38*(9), 1015–1049. doi:10.1177/0010414005279258

Sanchis i Marco, M. (2014). *The economics of the monetary union and the Eurozone crisis*. New York, NY: Springer. doi:10.1007/978-3-319-00020-6

SAP. (2015). *ALM103: Implementation Tools: SAP Business All-in-One and Rapid Deployment Solutions*. SAP.

Sarisoy-Guerin, S. (2003). *The relationship between capital flows and current account: volatility and causality* (Unpublished Manuscript). Dublin: Trinity College.

Schilirò, D. (2017). Rules, imbalances and growth in the Eurozone. In R. Mirdala & R. R. Canale (Eds.), Economic imbalances and institutional changes to the euro and the European Union (pp. 65-89). Bradford, UK: Emerald Publishing Limited. doi:10.1108/S1569-376720170000018005

Schilirò, D. (2013). A new governance for the EMU and the economic policy framework. In M. C. Malaguti, B. Bossone, S. Cafaro, & S. Di Benedetto (Eds.), *Legitimacy and efficiency in global economic governance*. Newcastle upon Tyne, UK: Cambridge Scholar Publishing.

Schilirò, D. (2014). Changes in Eurozone governance after the crisis and the issue of growth. *International Journal of Social Science Studies*, *2*(2), 110–119. doi:10.11114/ijsss.v2i2.317

Schmidt, V. (2015). Changing the policies, politics, and processes of the Eurozone in crisis: will this time be different? In D. Natali & B. Vanhercke (Eds.), Social developments in EU 2015. Brussels, Belgium: European Social Observatory (OSE) and European Trade Union Institute (ETUI).

Schmidt, V. A. (2016). *The new EU governance: New intergovernmentalism, new supranationalism, and new parliamentarism* (IAI Working Papers 16/11). Rome, Italy: IAI.

Schoenmaker, D. (2015). *Firmer foundations for a stronger European banking union* (Bruegel Working Paper 2015/13). Brussels, Belgium: Bruegel.

Schuknecht, L., von Hagen, J., & Wolswijk, G. (2010). *Government risk premiums in the EU revisited: The impact of the financial crisis* (ECB Working Paper vol. 1152). Retrieved from: http://www.ecb.europa.eu/pub/pdf/scpwps/ecbwp1152.pdf

Schulze, G. G., & Ursprung, H. W. (1999). Globalisation of the Economy and the Nation State. *World Economy*, *22*(3), 295–352. doi:10.1111/1467-9701.00205

Schwert, G. (2003). Anomalies and Market Efficiency. In Handbook of the Economics of Finance (pp. 939-974). North Holland.

Serven, L., & Montiel, P. (2004). Macroeconomic stability: The more the better? In R. Zagha & G.T. Nankan (Eds.), Economic growth in the 1990s: Learning from a decade of reforms (pp. 95-120). Washington, DC: World Bank Group.

Servén, L. (2011). *Financial globalisation and financial crisis. Teaching notes*. CEMFI.

Service Architecture. (2017). *Service Architecture*. Retrieved February 2017, from http://www.service-architecture.com/articles/xml/rixml.html

Shahrokhi, M. (2008). E-finance: Status, Innovations, Resources and Future Challenges. *Managerial Finance*, *34*(6), 365–398. doi:10.1108/03074350810872787

Shahrokhi, M. (2008). *E-finance: Status, Innovations, Resources and Future Challenges. Managerial Finance,* 34, 365–398.

Shiller, R. (2004). *Irrational Exuberance* (2nd ed.). Princeton, NJ: Princeton University Press.

Simmons, B. A., Dobbin, F., & Garrett, G. (2006). Introduction: The international diffusion of liberalism. *International Organization*, *60*(4), 781–810. doi:10.1017/S0020818306060267

Simonovska, I., Choudhry, M., Pesakovic, G., Fidanoski, F., & Simeonovski, K. (2015). Financial (in)stability in selected countries: What did we learn from the crises? In *International Conference on Economic recovery in the post-crisis period.* Cyril and Methodius University in Skopje.

Sluckiy, E.E. (1937, April). The Summation of Random Causes as the Source of Cyclic Process. *Econometrica.*

Smith, A. (2008). *The wealth of nations. Radford.* Wilder Publications. (Original work published 1776)

Smith, G. (2012). The changing and relative efficiency of European emerging stock markets. *European Journal of Finance*, *18*(8), 689–708. doi:10.1080/1351847X.2011.628682

Socialism with Chinese characteristics enters new era: Xi. (2017, October 18). *China Daily*. Retrieved from http://www.chinadaily.com.cn/china/19thcpcnationalcongress/2017-10/18/content_33398070.htm

Soppe, A. (2004). Sustainable corporate finance. *Journal of Business Ethics*, *53*(1-2), 213–224. doi:10.1023/B:BUSI.0000039410.18373.12

Sorsa, P., Bakker, B. B., Duenwald, C. K., Maechler, A. M., & Tiffin, A. (2007). *Vulnerabilities in emerging Southeastern Europe - How much cause for concern?* Working paper, International Monetary Fund.

Soubbotina, T. P., & Sheram, K. A. (2000). *Beyond Economic Growth: Meeting the Challenges of Global Development*. Washington, DC: World Bank.

Sourcemaking. (2015). *AntiPatterns: The Survival Guide-Vendor lock in.* Retrieved March 2017, from https://sourcemaking.com/antipatterns/vendor-lock-in

Staff, I. M. F. (2017, August 15). *China's Economic Outlook in Six Charts.* International Monetary Fund Publication. Retrieved from https://www.imf.org/en/News/Articles/2017/08/09/NA081517-China-Economic-Outlook-in-Six-Charts

Stančić, P., Čupić, M., & Obradović, V. (2014). Influence of board and ownership structure on bank profitability: Evidence from South East Europe. Economic research-. *Ekonomska Istrazivanja, 27*(1), 573–589. doi:10.1080/1331677X.2014.970450

Steely, J. (2001). A Note on Information Seasonality and the Disappearance of the weekend Effect in UK Stock Market. *Journal of Banking & Finance, 25*(10), 1941–1956. doi:10.1016/S0378-4266(00)00167-9

Stulz, R. M. (1984). Optimal Hedging Policies. *Journal of Financial and Quantitative Analysis, 19*(2), 127–140. doi:10.2307/2330894

Sudana, I. P. (2015). *Sustainable development and reconceptualization of financial statements. In Procedia – Social and Behavioral Sciences 2011* (pp. 157–162). Elsevier.

Sullivan, R., Timmermann, A., & White, H. (2001). Dangers of Data mining: The Case of Calendar Effects in Stock Returns. *Journal of Econometrics, 105*(1), 249–286. doi:10.1016/S0304-4076(01)00077-X

Summers, L. H. (2000). International financial crises: Causes, prevention, and cures. *The American Economic Review, 90*(2), 1–16. doi:10.1257/aer.90.2.1 PMID:18459243

Sun, Y., & Wang, X. (2017). 廉价供应的八大弊端. *Journal of Urban China*. Retrieved from http://www.urbanchina.org/n1/2017/0609/c410783-29330273.html

Swank, D. (2002). *Global Capital, Political Institutions, and Policy Change in Developed Welfare States*. Cambridge, UK: Cambridge University Press. doi:10.1017/CBO9780511613371

Syriopoulos, T. (2011). Financial integration and portfolio investments to emerging Balkan equity markets. *Journal of Multinational Financial Management, 21*(1), 40–54. doi:10.1016/j.mulfin.2010.12.006

Szarowská, I. (2013). Fiscal Discipline as a Driver of Sovereign Risk Spread in the European Union Countries. In *22nd IBIMA Conference on Creating Global Competitive Economies: 2020 Vision Planning & Implementation* (pp. 793-804). Rome: IBIMA.

Szarowská, I. (2014). Do Fiscal Drivers Matter for Sovereign Risk Spread in EU15? In *11th International Scientific Conference on European Financial Systems 2014* (pp. 629-637). Brno: Masaryk University.

Szarowská, I. (2015). Relationship between government bond yield spread and fiscal fundamentals in selected EU countries. In *12th International Scientific Conference on European Financial Systems 2015* (pp. 596-604). Brno: Masaryk University.

Taleb, N. (2007). *The Black Swan-The Impact of the Highly Improbable*. Random House, Inc.

Taleb, N. (2012). *Antifragile: Things that gain from disorder*. Library of Congress Cataloguing-in-Publication Data.

Tang, A. (2017). 在新的历史起点上坚持和发展中国特色社会主义的行动纲领 [To uphold and Develop the Socialist Society with Chinese Characteristics at the New Historical Starting Point]. *China Daily*. Retrieved from http://china.chinadaily.com.cn/2017-07/30/content_30297114.htm

Tang, D. (2016). Has the Financial Integration affected the European Union (EU) trade with the New Member Countries from Central and Eastern Europe (CEEC) during 1994–2013? *Journal of Economic Asymmetries*, *13*, 8–20. doi:10.1016/j.jeca.2015.10.004

Tan, W., Carter, A., & Toleman, M. (2009). *Implementing information technology services management: A case study focusing on critical success factors*. Toowoomba, Australia: Univ. of Southern Queensland.

Taylor, S. (2008). *Modeling Financial Times Series*. World Scientific.

Taylor, S. (2005). *Asset Price Dynamics, Volatility, and Prediction*. Princeton University Press.

TCMB. (2006). *Finansal İstikrar ve Merkez Bankaları, Bülten, Sayı.3, Eylül, Ankara*. Retrieved from http://www.tcmb.gov.tr/wps/wcm/connect/94348b7d-dc4d-4e99-a7a5-6950b9b4faf9/bulten-turkce3.pdf?MOD=AJPERES&CACHEID=94348b7d-dc4d-4e99-a7a5-6950b9b4faf9

TCMB. (2015). *Finansal İstikrar*. Ankara: Türkiye'de Finansal İstikrar Gelişmeleri, Türkiye Cumhuriyet Merkez Bankası.

Tevdovski, D., Mihajlov, M., & Sazdovski, I. (2012). The Day of the Week Effects in South Eastern Europe Stock Markets, Annals of the "Constantin Brâncuşi" University of Târgu Jiu. *Economy Series*, *3*, 20–24.

The Open Group. (2011a). *Risk and monitoring (2014). Risk Monitoring and Governance (Phase G)*. Retrieved March 2017, from http://pubs.opengroup.org/architecture/togaf9-doc/arch/chap31.html#tag_31_07

The Open Group. (2011b). *Gap Analysis*. Retrieved March 2017, from http://pubs.opengroup.org/architecture/togaf9-doc/arch/chap27.html

The Open Group. (2014a). *The Open Group's Architecture Framework-Building blocks-Module 13*. Retrieved March 2017, from www.open-group.com/togaf

The Open Group. (2014b). *The Open Group's Architecture Framework*. Retrieved March 2017, from www.open-group.com/togaf

The Open Group. (2015a). *Architecture Skills Framework*. The Open Group. Retrieved April 2017, from http://pubs.opengroup.org/architecture/togaf8-doc/arch/chap30.html

Tonveronachi, M. (2014). *The ECB and the single European financial market: A proposal to repair half of the flawed design (Public Policy Brief No. 137)*. Hudson, NY: Levy Economics Institute of Bard College.

Tornjanski, V., Knežević, S., & Delibašić, B. (2017). A CRM Performance Measurement in Banking Using Integrated BSC and Customized ANP-BOCR Approach. *Management: Journal of Sustainable Business and Management Solutions in Emerging Economies*, *22*(1), 71–85.

Trad, A. & Kalpić, D. (2017c). *A Neural Networks Portable and Agnostic Implementation Environment for Business Transformation Projects-The Agnostic Implementation Environment.* Submitted article.

Trad, A., & Kalpić, D. (2014a). The Selection and Training Framework (STF) for Managers in Business Innovation and Transformation Projects - Integrating the restructuring process of the global economy. IMRA.

Trad, A., & Kalpić, D. (2017a). The Business Transformation and Enterprise Architecture Framework-The Financial Engineering (e)Risk Management and (e)Law Integration. IGI-Global. (under review)

Trad, A., & Kalpić, D. (2017a). The Business Transformation and Enterprise Architecture Framework-The Financial Engineering Global Strategy. IGI-Global. (under review)

Trad, A., & Kalpić, D. (2017b). The Business Transformation and Enterprise Architecture Framework- The Financial Engineering Technology Concept. IGI-Global. (under review)

Trad, A., & Kalpić, D. (2017b). The Business Transformation and Enterprise Architecture Framework-The The Financial Engineering (e)Risk Management and (e)Law Integration. IGI-Global. (under review)

Trad, A. (2017). *The Transformation Framework's Resources Library*. IBISTM.

Trad, A. (2017a). *Using Google analytics to determine the leading business transformation framework that are based on enterprise architecture*. IBISTM.

Trad, A., & Kalpić, D. (2014a). *The Selection and Training Framework (STF) for Managers in Business Innovation and Transformation Projects - Integrating the restructuring process of the global economy*. Cambridge, UK: IMRA.

Trad, A., & Kalpić, D. (2015a). *The Business Engineering Transformation Framework for (e) commerce Architecture-Modelling Projects. In Encyclopedia of E-Commerce Development, Implementation, and Management*. IGI-Global.

Trad, A., & Kalpić, D. (2015b). *The Business Engineering Transformation Framework for (e) commerce Control and Monitoring Pattern. In Encyclopedia of E-Commerce Development, Implementation, and Management*. IGI-Global.

Trad, A., & Kalpić, D. (2016a). *The Business Transformation Framework and its Financial engineering Law support for (e)transactions*. IGI-Global.

Tüzün, O., & Kahyaoğlu, H. (2015). Makro İhtiyati Para Politikası Amacı Olarak Finansal İstikrar: Türkiye Üzerine Bir Uygulama. Finans Politik ve Ekonomik Yorumlar Dergisi, *52(603)*, 25–45.

Uiboupin, J. (2004). Implications of foreign bank entry on Central and East European banking market. *Kroon and Economy*, *1*, 25–31.

UNCHE. (1972). *Declaration of United Nations Conference on the Human Environment* (No. A/Conf.48/5). Stockholm: UNCHE.

Universität St. Gallen. (2015). *EMBA in Financial engineering*. Retrieved April 2017, from http://www.es.unisg.ch/de/programme/emba/embe.php

Vadlamannati, K. C. (2015). Rewards of (dis)integration: Economic, social, and political globalization and freedom of association and collective bargaining rights of workers in developing countries. *Industrial & Labor Relations Review*, *68*(1), 3–27. doi:10.1177/0019793914555851

ValuAdder. (2017). *Business Valuation: The Three Approaches*. Retrieved April 2017, from http://www.valuadder.com/valuationguide/business-valuation-three-approaches.html

ValuAdder. (2017). *Business Valuation: The Three Approaches*. Retrieved March 2017, from http://www.valuadder.com/valuationguide/business-valuation-three-approaches.html

Van Horen, N. (2014). Foreign banks: Access to finance and financial stability. In The social value of the financial sector: Too big to fail or just too big? (pp. 323-343). Singapore: World Scientific.

Van Horen, N., & Claessens, S. (2009). *Being a foreigner among domestic banks: Asset or liability?* Working paper, International Monetary Fund.

Van Rompuy, H. (2017). Europe means more than just crisis. *Economics and Politics*, *34*(1), 1–10. doi:10.100740888-017-0055-5

Verbeek, M. (2000). *A guide to modern econometrics*. New York: John Wiley & Sons Inc.

Véron, N. (2015). *Europe's radical banking union (Bruegel Essay and Lecture Series)*. Brussels, Belgium: Bruegel.

Véron, N., & Wolff, G. B. (2015). *Capital markets union: A vision for the long term (Bruegel Policy Contribution, No. 2015/05)*. Brussels, Belgium: Bruegel.

Vithessonthi, C., & Kumarasinghe, S. (2016). Financial development, international trade integration, and stock market integration: Evidence from Asia. *Journal of Multinational Financial Management*, *35*, 79–92. doi:10.1016/j.mulfin.2016.03.001

von Hagen, J., & Eichengreen, B. (1996). Federalism, fiscal restraints, and European Monetary Union. *The American Economic Review*, *86*(2), 134–138.

Von Hagen, J., Schuknecht, L., & Wolswijk, G. (2011). Government bond risk premiums in the EU revisited: The impact of the financial crisis. *European Journal of Political Economy*, *27*(1), 36–43. doi:10.1016/j.ejpoleco.2010.07.002

von Weizsacker, J., & Delpla, J. (2010). *The blue bond proposal (Bruegel Policy Brief, N.2010/03)*. Brussels, Belgium: Bruegel.

Walsh, D. (1995). Risk Management Using Derivative Securities. *Managerial Finance*, *21*(1), 43–65. doi:10.1108/eb018496

Wang, E.D. (2016, March 30). 国土部巡视员:以土地制度创新促进供给侧结构性改革 [Inspectors of the Ministry of Land: Using Supply System Reform to Innovate Land System]. *21st Century Business Herald*.

WCED. (1987). *Report of the World Commision on Environment and Development: "Our common future" (No.A/42/427)*. World Commision on Environment and Development.

Wei, L. (2014). 实行社会主义市场经济是我国经济体制改革的必然选择 [The Socialist Market Economy is an Inevitable Choice for the Reform of Our Economic Structure]. *Journal of China National School of Administration*. Retrieved from http://kyhz.nsa.gov.cn/xzxy_kygl/pf/xzxywz/yksInfoDetail.htm?infoid=2286

Whyte, M. K. (2010). *China's Post Socialist Inequality*. Stanford University Press.

Wikipedia. (2015). *Master of Financial engineering*. Retrieved from https://en.wikipedia.org/wiki/Master_of_Business_Engineering

Wildau, G., & Mitchell, T. (2016). China Income Inequality Among World's Worst. *Financial Time*. Retrieved from https://www.ft.com/content/3c521faa-baa6-11e5-a7cc-280dfe875e28

Wilhelm, K. (2013). *Return on sustainability: How business can increase profitability and address climate change in an uncertain economy*. FT Press.

Williams, B. (1998). Factors affecting the performance of foreign-owned banks in Australia: A cross-sectional study. *Journal of Banking & Finance*, *22*(2), 197–219. doi:10.1016/S0378-4266(97)00054-X

Wilson, C. (2010). Why should sustainable finance be given priority? Lessons from pollution and biodiversity degradation. *Accounting Research Journal*, *23*(3), 267–280. doi:10.1108/10309611011092592

World Bank. (2015). *Global economic prospects: The global economy in transition*. World Bank Group Report. Retrieved from http://documents.worldbank.org/curated/en/264521468179081631/Global-economic-prospects-June-2015-the-global-economy-in-transition

WSSD. (2002). *Report of the Word Summit on Sustainable Development* (No. A/Conf.199/20). New York: United Nations.

XBRL. (2017). *XBRL, the business reporting standard*. Retrieved from https://www.xbrl.org/

XBRL. (2017). *XBRL, the business reporting standard*. Retrieved January 2017, from https://www.xbrl.org

XE. (2017). *Currecy exchange*. Retrieved April 2017, from http://www.xe.com/currencycharts/?from=USD&to=EUR&view=10Y

Xiaohong, Ch. (2011). *Research on E-Commerce Transaction Cost-Benefit Characteristics and Evaluation Approaches*. Management and Service Science (MASS), *2011 International Conference*, Wuhan, China.

XML. (2003). *XML Standards for Financial Services*. Retrieved January 2017, from http://www.xml.com/pub/a/2003/03/26/financial.html

Yamori, N. (1998). A note on the location choice of multinational banks: The case of Japanese financial institutions. *Journal of Banking & Finance*, *22*(1), 109–120. doi:10.1016/S0378-4266(97)00040-X

Ye, K. (2016). 18年30万亿卖地收入地方用途不透明 [The Opaque Usage of Total 30 trillion Income from Selling Land in 18 Years]. *the First Financial Daily*. Retrieved from http://finance.sina.com.cn/china/gncj/2016-09-09/doc-ifxvukhx4647035.shtml

Yeyati, E. L., & Micco, A. (2007). Concentration and foreign penetration in Latin American banking sectors: Impact on competition and risk. *Journal of Banking & Finance*, *31*(6), 1633–1647. doi:10.1016/j.jbankfin.2006.11.003

Yildirim, S., & Philippatos, G. (2007). Efficiency of banks: Recent evidence from the transition economies of Europe 1993-2000. *European Journal of Finance*, *13*(2), 123–143. doi:10.1080/13518470600763687

Zajc, P. (2003). *The effect of foreign bank entry on domestic banks in Central and Eastern Europe*. Working paper, University of Ljubljana.

Zhu, M. (2012). *The impact of foreign bank entry in emerging markets: Knowledge spillovers of competitive pressure?* Working paper, Centre for Competition Policy, University of East Anglia.

Ziolo, M., Fidanoski, F., Simeonovski, K., Filipovski, V., & Jovanovska, K. (2016). *Sustainable Finance Role in Creating Conditions for Sustainable Economic Growth and Development*. Springer International Publishing.

Zuleeg, F. (2015). Can the Eurozone's economic governance combine political accountability, legitimacy and effectiveness? In A. P. Kyriacou (Ed.), *Redesigning European Monetary Union governance in light of the Eurozone crisis* (pp. 57–65). Barcelona, Spain: CIDOB, Barcelona Centre for International Affairs.

Zumbach, G. (2013). *Discrete Time Series, Processes, and Applications in Finance*. Springer. doi:10.1007/978-3-642-31742-2

地方财政收入必须摆脱对房地产业的过度依赖. (2017). [Local Fiscal Revenue Must get Rid of Excessive Dependence on the Real Estate Industry]. *21st Century Economic Report*. Retrieved from http://epaper.21jingji.com/html/2017-08/14/content_68415.htm

央地财政事权改革路线图. (2016). [Fiscal Reform Road Map]. Retrieved from http://www.lwinst.com/cjgjzk201621/2424.htm

社科院报告指中国失地农民已达4000万-5000万. (2011). [Academy of Social Sciences Reported that the Landless Peasants in China Has Reached to 40 million -50 million]. *Caijing*. Retrieved from http://www.caijing.com.cn/2011-08-09/110804337.html

About the Contributors

Bruno S. Sergi is an Instructor at Harvard University, where he is also an Associate of the Davis Center for Russian and Eurasian Studies, and a Faculty Affiliate in the Institute for Quantitative Social Science. He also teaches at the University of Messina and has taught at New York University. He is an Associate Editor of The American Economist and his longstanding research interests center on the economics of emerging markets. Published extensively, Professor Sergi's work has been reviewed in a broad spectrum of scholarly journals such as Comparative Economic Studies; European Journal of Development Research; International Labour Review; International Journal of Production Research; Journal of Economic Issues; Journal of Higher Education Policy and Management; Journal of Management Development; Journal of Post Keynesian Economics; Management Decision; Technology Analysis & Strategic Management; Thunderbird International Business Review. He holds a Ph.D. in economics from the University of Greenwich Business School – London.

Filip Fidanoski is one of the leading Macedonian economists and scholars. He is the first experimental economist from Republic of Macedonia. His alma mater are Ss. Cyril and Methodius University in Skopje and University in Luxembourg. He has worked at the several European research universities. Importantly, he is continuing the career as a Scientia scholar at the University of New South Wales in Sydney and currently is Director of the Institute of Advanced Financial Economics at the International Center for Emerging Markets Research in Moscow, RUDN University and Harvard University. His major subject of career is professionally dedicated to applied microeconomics, asset pricing, banking, behavioral finance, contract theory, experimental finance, financial economics, game theory, institutional economics and governance, organizational economics and risk, through consultancy and scientific research. He is a reviewer, editor, translator, author and coauthor of a many articles, papers and chapters published in distinguished journals. Specifically, he has edited two books, two special issues and organized and chaired several academic conferences, workshops and seminars in Portugal, Poland, UK, Greece, Macedonia, Serbia, Germany and Italy. Further, he serves as a member of the editorial boards of four journals and as a referee for a dozen journals. He completed many projects in cooperation with the best world universities and international organizations, such as Hong Kong Polytechnic University, European Commission, Wharton School of the University of Pennsylvania, Stanford University and so on. He is a member of the Society for Economic Measurement. In addition, his texts and interviews have appeared in influential mediums in Republic of Macedonia. Also, he actively participates in different scientific organizations and professional events from his fields of interest. At last but not at least, he is prominent translator and writer from the Republic of Macedonia.

Magdalena Ziolo is Associate Professor, PhD hab. at University of Szczecin, Poland. She is a head of Institute of Sustainable Financial Systems. Her research and teaching scope of interest are finance and banking, especially sustainable finance and green banking, sustainable development, public finance. She has received scholarships from the Dekaban-Liddle Foundation (University of Glasgow, Scotland, 2013), Impakt Erasmus + (Ulan Bator, Mongolia, 2017) and CEEPUS (University of Prishtina, Kosovo, 2015, 2016, 2017). Her scientific achievements encompass over 100 reviewed papers, including academic books (editor, author or co-author).

Vladimir Naumovski is Associate Professor at the UACS School of Business Administration at the University of American College Skopje. He earned his doctoral degree at the European Center for Peace and Development – University of Peace established by the United Nations, Belgrade, Serbia. He was the Director of the Anti-Money Laundering Office, Founding Manager of the Macedonian Bank for Development Promotion and Minister in the Government of the Republic of Macedonia. Also, he was member of the Securities and Exchange Commission of the Republic of Macedonia. President of the State Commission on Religious Matters, President of the Volleyball Coach Organization of Skopje, Coach of the National Team of the Republic of Macedonia in Volleyball, President of the State Census Commission of the Republic of Macedonia, Founder and President of the Management Board of the Money Market and Short-Term Securities and Head of Delegation to the Washington Conference on Holocaust. In addition, he is the President of the Association of Economists of the City of Skopje, Representative in the Bern Union, Representative of the Association of Development Banks of South-East Europe, Expert inMONEYVAL against money laundering and financing of terrorism within the Council of Europe in Strasbourg, Representative of the Republic of Macedonia in the EgmontGroup of Financial Intelligence Units and the Member of the Business Council at the University American College Skopje. He participated both at the European Economic Forum and World Economic Forum. Finally, he is a reviewer, editor, author and coauthor of a many journal articles, working and professional papers, reports, chapters and books in English, Serbian and Macedonian.

* * *

Irina Araujo, currently living in Lisbon, graduated with a bachelor's degree in economics in 2014 from the Faculty of Economics, University of Coimbra and finished her master's degree at the same faculty in 2016. She is a Market Specialist in Corporate Actions working in Bnp Paribas Securities Services.

Halil İbrahim Aydin is an Assistant Prof. Ph.D. at the Department of Economics, Faculty of Economics and Administrative Sciences at Batman University, Batman, Turkey. His teaching and research fields are international and development economics. His research interests include Economic Development, Regional Development, Regional Development Agency, Social Capital, Poverty, Economic Growth, Economic Crises. He is vice-dean at the Faculty of Economics and Administrative Sciences of Batman University, head of department of economic theory and deputy head of department of economy. He is author of many national and international works in these research areas. In this context, he has seven books, 16 book chapters, 13 articles and 16 conference proceedings. Also, his articles, books, and proceedings cited in above forty studies. There are many books that he edited; "The Economic Crisis and Turkey's Economy," "Articles on Regional Development," "Economics and Politics Articles on Development," "Monetary-Banking and Finance," "Economic Development: Social & Political Interaction." Besides, he has written a book which was named "Social Capital and Development."

Svetlana Balashova is an Associate professor in the department of mathematical modeling in economics at the RUDN University, executive director of the International Center for Emerging Markets Research at RUDN University – Moscow. She has been elected as a visiting professor at the Belgrade Banking Academy in 2013. She teaches econometrics, financial econometrics and related subjects for undergraduate and graduate students. In addition to teaching, Svetlana Balashova is actively engaged in scientific research. Her personal field of research is economic growth and innovation development, applications of econometric modeling. She is the author or co-author of several textbooks and numerous research papers. She has taken part in many international conferences and seminars, including being a speaker at the seminar on "New Reality" and Russian Markets at Harvard's Davis Center for Russian and Eurasian Studies in April 2017. Balashova holds her Ph.D. in theoretical physics at RUDN University. She then widened her sphere of interests and studied economics at High School of Economics in Moscow and High School of Economics and Political Science in London. She is a regular participant in Spring courses on econometrics at Coimbra University, Portugal.

Maroua Ben Ghoul, a Tunisian Ph.D. fellow in Anadolu University, Faculty of Science Department of Statistics, Turkey. She graduated as a Statistician from the School of statistics in Tunisia, and she has a master degree in Econometrics and Economic Modeling from Tunisian Polytechnic School. She worked as a professional statistician and a project leader at data matrix (CRO Company) for almost six years. Her main research interests include econometrics, biostatistics, data analyses and modeling.

Vladimir Filipovski is a full professor at the Ss Cyril and Methodius University, Faculty of Economics in Skopje, Republic of Macedonia. He teaches undergraduate courses in principles of economics and securities analysis/portfolio management, as well as postgraduate courses in international finance. Recent publications in English include co-authored papers/book manuscripts on business cycles synchronization for the small EU-accession country, stock market integration in South Eastern Europe, sustainable finance, financial regulation, corporate governance, microeconomics of entrepreneurship. Professional experience includes membership in Macedonian stock exchange governing board (1996-1998), Macedonian securities market regulatory agency (2003-2010), the supervisory board of a local commercial bank.

Dejan Jednak holds Ph.D. in Finance from the Faculty of Organizational Sciences, University of Belgrade, and M.Sc and B.Sc. degrees from the Faculty of Economics, University of Belgrade. He is employed as CFO at Belgrade City Markets, Serbia. Before, he has worked in the banking sector and as a lecturer in various Finance courses. He has published papers in international and national journals, conferences proceedings and a textbook "Financial markets."

Sandra Jednak is employed at the Faculty of Organizational Sciences, the University of Belgrade as an Associate Professor. She has published scientific research papers in international and national monographs, journals and conferences proceedings. Her teaching areas are Introduction to Economics, Macroeconomics, Microeconomics, Economic Development, and EU. Her research focus is on the economic growth and development of SEE countries. Besides, her research interests are Knowledge (Based) Economy, Energy Economics, International Economics and Higher Education.

Damir Kalpić is retired professor of computer science at the University of Zagreb Faculty of electrical engineering and computing, Croatia. He was teaching Programming, Information systems, Databases and most of the time and recently only Algorithms and data structures and Operational research at the graduate and postgraduate level. He was also advising at student seminars, projects, graduation and Ph.D. theses. He graduated and received his Ph.D. degree in computer science at the same faculty. His main professional interest is in the application of operational research in real-world information systems, and in other applications with humans as direct users. In the period from 2000 to 2002, he was the vice dean of the Faculty. From 2005 to 2010 he was the head of the newly formed Department of applied computing. He served as chairman of the Information Technology Interfaces international conferences from 1993 to 2001. He can communicate, with descending fluency, in English, German, Italian, Spanish, French and Portuguese.

Alexander K. Kerimov is an Associate Professor at Economics Faculty of RUDN University. He holds a Ph.D. in mathematics from Mathematical Institute of Academy of Science in Moscow. His main research interests lie in the areas of computational finance, financial modeling, optimization and actuarial mathematics.

Waiching Li is a Ph.D. student at the University of Economics, Prague. Li has a MBA concentrated in Finance (American University), BA, Accounting (UW-Madison) Supportive Teaching Staff for political, economic study at Harvard University, DCE Center. Li has years of work experience in the field of accounting, banking, and investment service. Li is also a freelance economic journalist for Chinese media. Li has had interviews and commentary articles published by a wide range of prominent Chinese media platforms.

Vladimir Matyushok graduated from Peoples' Friendship University of Russia in 1978. In 1982, he became Ph.D. In 1986, he founded the department of mathematical methods of economic analysis (present department of economic and mathematical modeling), which was a pioneer in informatization educational process and scientific research at the humanities science at Peoples' Friendship University of Russia. Vladimir delivered lectures and research works to several universities in the United States, France, Germany and other countries. In 2003, he defended his Doctor of Economic Sciences thesis and became a full professor. He is Honorary Worker of Higher Professional Education and Vice-Chairman of the dissertation committee. He is the scientific director for "International Economy" program and director of The International Center for Emerging Markets Research. Vladimir mentored dozens of specialists, bachelors and master's students and 14 PhD students. He is a member of the International Academy of Organizational Sciences and the head of undergraduate double-degree program Economics and Management, and graduates program International Business in cooperation with the University of Nice, double-degree program International Project Management in cooperation with CNAM University (Paris). Vladimir is an expert at the Russian Humanitarian Scientific Fund. He is Vice-president of the International Association of Economists "CEMAFI international." Vladimir Matyushok was elected to the International Francophone Academic Network CEDIMES, which was founded in 1972 and includes researchers and scientists from 33 countries participate in CEDIMES. He was the President of the international jury for awarding prizes to young scientists at CEDIMES. Vladimir is the author of more than 160 scientific publications, including textbooks and monographs.

Oleg I. Pavlov received his Ph.D. in mathematics from Moscow State University. He is an Associate Professor at Economics Faculty of RUDN University. His main research interests include general topology, mathematical modeling in economics and optimization.

Inna Petrenko is currently a Ph.D. student in the department of mathematical modeling in economics at the RUDN University in Moscow. She received her Bachelor degree in Economics (2013) and Master degree in Management (2015) at RUDN University in Moscow. Her field of research is capital flows and financial stability in emerging market countries. She has taken part in various local and international conferences and seminars. To widen the scope of interests at the international level, Inna Petrenko was enrolled in the University of Applied Science of Chur (Switzerland) in the Business Administration program in 2017.

Andrey Igorevich Pilipenko received his diploma of Higher Education from Leningrad State University (Faculty of Mathematics and Mechanics) in 1972. In 1984 he received his degree of Candidate of Science in Physics and Mathematics from the Institute of Physical Chemistry of the USSR' Academy of Science. In 1998 he received a degree of Doctor of Science in Pedagogics from Russian Academy of Education. For 40 years he has been a Professor at many Russian Universities: Lomonosov's Moscow State University, Russian Academy of National Economy under the Government of RF, etc. He has been invited as a Professor by Gumilyov' Eurasian National University (Kazakhstan). He is currently a Professor at the Department of Economics and Mathematics Modeling (Peoples' Friendship University of Russia). He has many publications, indexed by RISC (RF), Scopus, SSRN. His scientific interests lie in the areas of psychological and cognitive barriers in education, bifurcation effect' modeling in the shocks theory.

Zoya Andreevna Pilipenko received her Master's Degree in Economics from Lomonosov's Moscow State University in 2003. In 2004 she received her degree of Candidate of Science in World Economy, Finance, and Banking from Lomonosov's Moscow State University. In 2013 she received her degree of Doctor of Science in World Economy, Finance, and Banking from Lomonosov's Moscow State University. For 15 years she has worked as a financial analyst for the Insurance Company "Gefest," the Joint Stock Company "Sberbank of Russia," Central Bank of Russia. She has had teaching and research experience: 50 publications, indexed by RISC, and one - by Scopus. She has got certificates in Banking and Finance from practical seminars in Great Britain, Luxembourg, Austria, Italy, France. She is currently a financial advisor for the Department of the Financial Markets' Development of Bank of Russia. Her scientific interests lie in the area of the shocks theory and the impulse model of cyclical economic development.

Igor Sazdovski is an economist, open knowledge activist, public speaker and master student at the Faculty of Economics in Skopje. He holds undergraduate degree from the Faculty of Economics in Skopje. His fields of interest are diverse and includes asset pricing, financial regulation, banking, macroeconomics and others. He has also been actively involved in numerous domestic and international conferences.

Daniele Schilirò is associate professor of Economics, Department of Economics, University of Messina. Daniele has her B.A. (Laurea) in Economics, Catholic University of Milan, 1979, M-Phil program in Political Economy at the University of Cambridge (UK), 1979/1980, and is a Special Graduate Student at the University of Yale (USA), 1980. She is a winner of the Scholarship "Bonaldo Stringher", Bank of Italy, Rome, 1980. She is a Researcher and Member of the Scientific Committee of the Centre of Research in Economic Analysis (CRANEC) Università Cattolica di Milano. Daniele is a Visiting Professor at University of Twente (NL), University of Dubai (UAE), University of Valencia (ES). She is a member of Editorial Board of *Frontiers in Management Research* (Isaac Scientific Publishing) and *Economics* (Science Publishing Group), *Journal of Mathematical Economics and Finance* (Asers Publishing). She is Co-Editor of the *Journal of Advanced Research in Economics and International Business* (Asers Publishing). Her current research interests are in History of Economic Analysis, Microeconomics and Industrial Organization, Behavioral Economics, Knowledge Economy, Green Economy, European Economy.

Kiril Simeonovski is an economist, open knowledge activist, public speaker and doctoral student at the Faculty of Economics in Skopje. He holds undergraduate and postgraduate degrees from the Faculty of Economics in Skopje. His fields of interest are diverse and include macroeconomics, financial regulation, corporate governance, strategic planning, entrepreneurship, experimental economics, information economics, online marketing and others. He has also been actively involved in project and event management and has participated in numerous international conferences both as attendee and speaker.

Marta Simões is an Assistant Professor at the Faculty of Economics, the University of Coimbra and a researcher affiliated with the Centre for Business and Economics Research (CeBER). Her research interests include economic growth, human capital, innovation and applied econometrics. She is the author, or co-author of over 40 publications in international scientific peer-reviewed journals, book chapters, and conference proceedings. She serves as a reviewer for several national and international publications and regularly attends international scientific conferences in her fields of research. She has 20 years teaching experience mostly in the field of Macroeconomics (BsC, Masters, Ph.D., MBA levels) and has supervised more than forty Master's dissertations. She holds Ph.D., Masters and bachelor degrees in Economics from the Faculty of Economics, University of Coimbra. She is currently vice-director of CeBER.

Irena Szarowská finished her doctoral study in Economics and Management in 2011. She has been employed as a full-time Assistant Professor at the Department of Finance and Accounting, School of Business Administration in Karviná, Silesian University in Opava since 2005. Since September of 2008, she has been the Deputy Head of the Department. She lectures courses focused primarily on public and municipal finances. Her professional and research orientation is focused on public finance, fiscal policy, and fiscal discipline. She is a member of Czech Economic Society and a member of international editorial board of scientific journals.

Dragan Tevdovski is an Associate Professor at the Ss Cyril and Methodius University, Faculty of Economics in Skopje, Republic of Macedonia. He teaches undergraduate and postgraduate courses in Statistics and Quantitative methods in finance. He has published extensively in several journals, including: *Economics of Transition, Economic Systems, Empirical Economics, Empirica, European Journal of International Management.* The areas of interest include quantitative finance, macroeconomic policies, income distribution. He was in the Postdoctoral program in econometrics at the CREATES, Aarhus University in Denmark in 2013-2014. From June 2017 Dragan Tevdovski is the Minister of Finance in the Government of the Republic of Macedonia.

Adam Wood is an expert in international infrastructure, trade, sustainability, and governmental relations. Amassing 15 years of unique time and place experience in India, Kazakhstan, Dubai, Egypt, Germany, France, Spain, Switzerland, UK, and Canada, Adam has managed projects for, or on behalf of, the U.S. government, as well as private and public entities worth over $1B USD. He has been recognized by President George W. Bush (Presidential Nomination 2004), and his socioeconomic and geopolitical advisements have followed former U.S. Secretary of the Treasury,

Hank Paulson in global interviews. Adam has given presentations at Harvard University on the National Debt in the United States, International Trade and the US-Sino Deficit and the Remedies, and the FDIs Brightest Emerging Market (India). He is the author of, The Good Government American. Professionally, Adam currently serves as the Vice President of Infrastructure Development for Veterans Venture, Economic Policy Advisor (United States) for the International Center for Emerging Markets Research, as well as a Global Trade & Quantitative Specialist (Macro) specializing in Relative Risk & Inferential Statistics for Enhanced Investor, the Global Day-trading Hedge Fund which operates out of UC Berkeley. His policy framework has been recognized by Amazon, AWS, and Tata Motors for two, multi-billion-dollar infrastructure projects in Brazil and India. Adam is proud to serve as the president of one of Harvard's veterans organizations on-campus. With his team, he has helped establish two (2) new scholarships for active duty and veteran service-members for veterans at various schools at Harvard University (premedical post-baccs, medical, dental, business school, prerequisites, public service, engineering, and law). Undergoing extensive education and training in aerospace, electrical, and communications engineering while serving in the US Navy and Pennsylvania State University, Adam is now a high honors student at Harvard University (Economics and Government) and has aspirations to attend Tufts Fletcher School of Law and Diplomacy, MIT's Sloan School of Management, and Harvard Law School upon graduation from Harvard. Adam's research interests are in banking, monetary and fiscal policy, and economic development, especially the role finance plays in it.

Index

L

M

O

P

Q

R

S

T

V

W

www.ingramcontent.com/pod-product-compliance
Lightning Source LLC
LaVergne TN
LVHW080342011026
849161LV00009B/2161